Modern Masters Vol

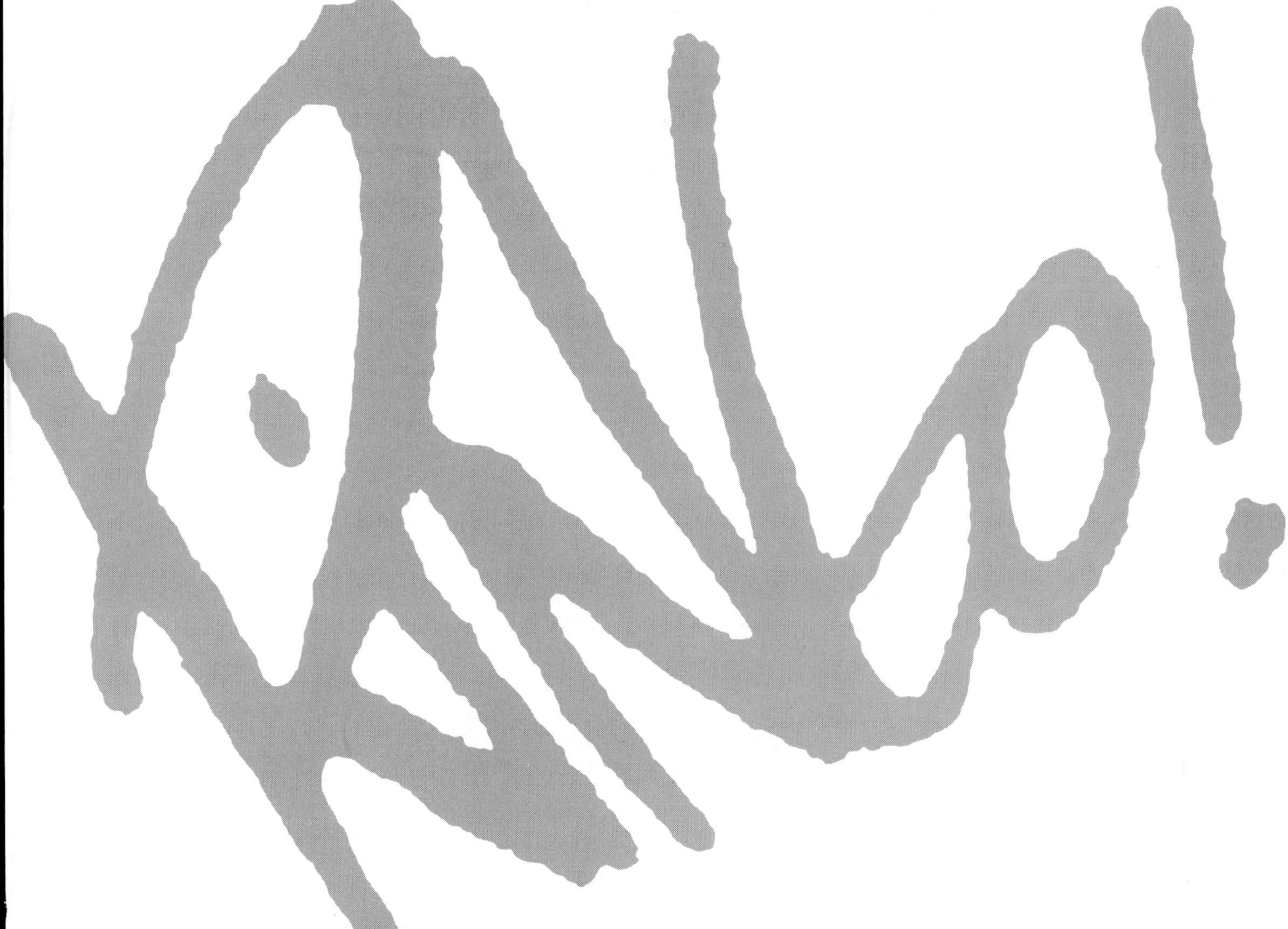

MODERN MASTERS VOLUME NINE:
MIKE WIERINGO

edited and designed by Eric Nolen-Weathington
front cover pencils by Mike Wieringo
front cover inks by Sean Parsons
front cover color by Tom Ziuko
all interviews in this book were conducted by Todd Dezago
proofreading by Christopher Irving

TwoMorrows Publishing
10407 Bedfordtown Drive
Raleigh, North Carolina 27614
www.twomorrows.com • e-mail: twomorrow@aol.com

First Printing • November 2006 • Printed in Canada

Softcover ISBN: 1-893905-65-9

Dedication
To Nick Cardy, a wonderful human being and a true inspiration.
And to my wife, Donna, my son, Iain,
and my daughter, Caper—the best family I could hope for.

Acknowledgements

Mike Wieringo, for all his time and for allowing us to rummage through his art files, and for simply being a great guy.

Terry Austin, for his usual basket of goodies.

Mark Waid, for a nice last-minute punchline.

Special Thanks
Rick McGee and the crew of Foundation's Edge
Russ Garwood and the crew of Capital Comics
John and Pam Morrow

Modern Masters Volume Nine:

MIKE WIERINGO

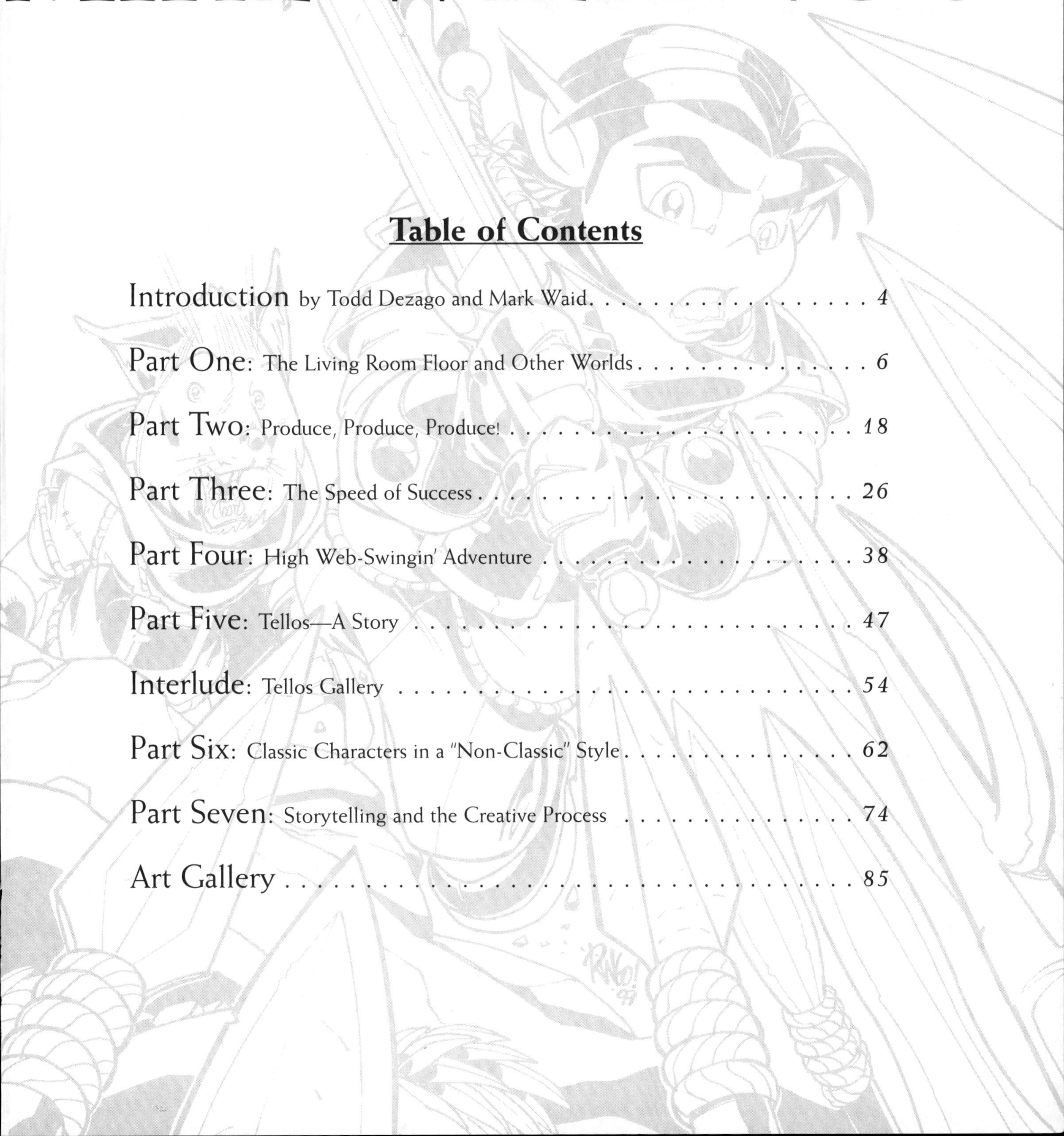

Table of Contents

Introduction

I should have called Mark Waid....

As our pal and Mike's other frequent collaborator, not to mention a much better writer than I, Mark would be the perfect guy to kick off this book and give some unique insight into Mike Wieringo, both the man and the artist. Mark was, after all, there at the beginning, when Mike was given his first monthly gig penciling the adventures of *The Flash*, and the two became fast friends. They made some magic during their run on that book and, in the process, co-created one of my all-time favorite characters! Mark would undoubtedly have had some really nice things to say about Mike and gone on about what a really friendly guy he is and an absolute pleasure to work with.

I should have called Mark....

But I didn't.

I guess it's 'cause I'm kinda selfish and there was one more thing that I wanted to say. See, this introduction is, in reality, more of an afterword. What I mean is, I'm writing it after we've done everything else. We've done the interview and chosen the artwork and edited out all (most of) the goofy stuff that always comes out when Mike and I chat. So I know what happens. I've been privy to everything you're about to read. And while I tried, in this, my first assignment ever as interviewer, to ask questions that would be both informative and provocative, that would hopefully give you a better glimpse into the life and career of this guy, my friend and comrade in storytelling, there was one thing that, in retrospect, I realized I hadn't been able to get around to.

Why?

Why do we like Mike's work so much?

When I was a kid I wanted to draw comic books. I had been drawing for as long as I could remember and when I discovered comics I used to trace and copy all my favorite artists: Nick Cardy, Jim Aparo, Neal Adams. I did okay on my own, too, but was never really satisfied. The head was too small, that arm was too short, perspective, anatomy—it never looked as good as the pros. My mother would watch proudly and patiently as I would work for hours and hours on one picture or another, only to sigh in disbelief and exasperation when

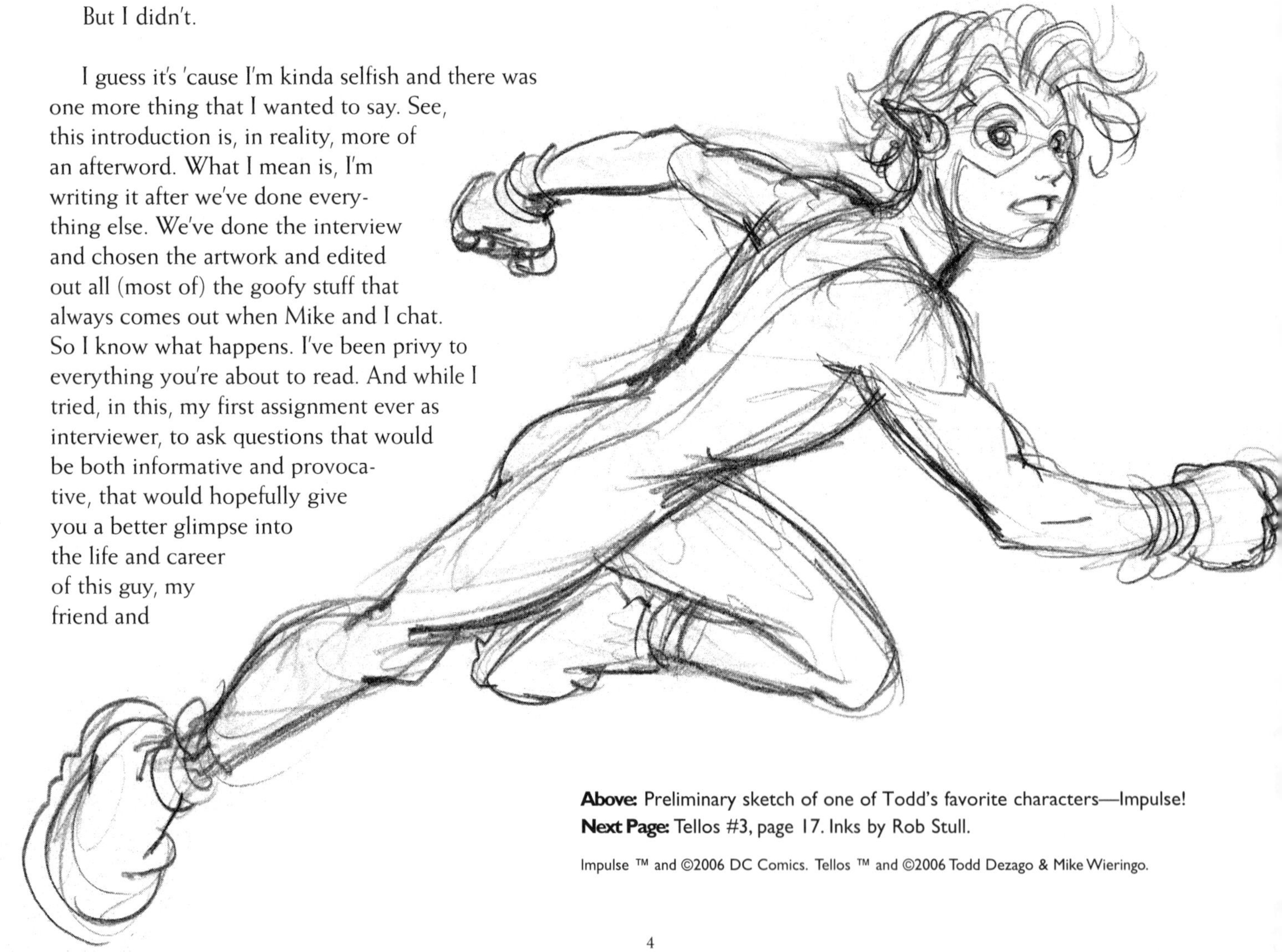

Above: Preliminary sketch of one of Todd's favorite characters—Impulse!

Next Page: Tellos #3, page 17. Inks by Rob Stull.

Not that I just sit there and watch my family read my comics, but I happened to be at my folks house when, about halfway through *Tellos #3*, my Mom looked up and said, "This is wonderful! I know why you and Mike work so well together. He draws the way you always wished you could!"

Of course, some people might read that as some sort of backhanded dis, but I assure you, my Mom and I were always the best of friends and I knew exactly what she meant. In Mike's work she could see what I had always aspired to, had always dreamed of being able to do.

And I think that's it. The reason we love Mike's artwork so much. Why it's so appealing. Why it touches us in such a unique way....

Mike draws the way we would draw. Oh, there are other, wonderful artists, but Mike somehow channels all of our fantasies into his work. He brings these stories—these worlds!—to life through eyes tinted with childhood wonder. His characters are full of an energy that makes them bounce right off the page and draws us in all at the same time! And though I know this because I know him—and maybe you will too by the time you've finished reading this book—there is so much Mike in every panel.

My Mom nailed it.
Mike draws the way we always wished we could.
I can't think of a better compliment.

Todd Dezago
Elizaville, NY
October 2K6

I'd become frustrated with my shortcomings and crumple the picture up and throw it in the garbage. She would try to save it and encourage me, telling me that it was very good, but I wouldn't hear it. I knew how I wanted it to look and it just wasn't getting there.

I continued to draw, and still do; my Christmas cards, the occasional poster for a friend's play or a T-shirt design for some community event. But my journey as a storyteller took a different path and now I write. I've been incredibly fortunate to work in a field that I've loved for so long and have become friends and/or acquaintances with many artists whose work we all admire. Kevin Nowlan, Art Adams, Adam Hughes (just to name a few)—who wouldn't want to be able to draw like them?

Well said, sir. Only Mark Waid could have written more eloquently, more beautifully, more poignantly and with more insight as to how amazing and rewarding it is to collaborate with Mike.

Mark Waid
Los Angeles, CA
Still Waiting For That Call

Part 1: The Living Room Floor and Other Worlds

MODERN MASTERS: So you were born on June 24, 1963, but spent the first 16 years in a backyard air raid shelter because your father thought the New Year's fireworks were the Commies?

MIKE WIERINGO: It's not very well known, but the movie *Blast from the Past* starring Brendan Frazer and Alicia Silverstone was actually an adaptation of my autobiography entitled *Mole Boy: My Life Underground as Part of a True Nuclear Family*. [*laughter*] No... in reality, my father was in the Army, and while he was stationed in Vicenza, Italy, his wife—who coincidentally, is also my mother, if you can grasp that mind-bender—gave birth to little old me. And that was *indeed* on June 24, 1963. From there, we moved several times—to places like New York City... then upstate New York [Geneva], then to Virginia, then *back* to Europe to Germany, where we spent 3 years... and then eventually back to Virginia. I had my eleventh birthday there some several months after we arrived. My father owned some property in a veeeeery rural area, and that's where we lived—and they still live to this day.

MM: How did your folks meet? Where were they from? What did they do?

MIKE: My father tells the story of driving down the road with a friend of his and seeing this young woman walking. They stopped and asked her if she wanted a ride. She agreed, and they sped off. During the ride, Dad ends up relating a story to her about how his youngest brother was eaten by one of their huge hogs. From that point on, in order to keep the spirit of his little brother alive with the family, they let the hog eat dinner with them each night. My dad was then, and is still now, quite the storyteller. I guess it runs in the family. Despite having been told the strangest, most unbelievable yarn she'd ever heard, my mother still agreed to go out with my father. They ended up falling in love and eventually getting married. To give you a sense of the times, their early dates were chaperoned by my grandmother—my mother's mom.

My mother lived in an area called Madison Heights, Virginia. My father lived in Lynchburg, Virginia—which is only a few miles from Madison Heights. They both lived in very rural areas. Their families were both what you could consider poor, financially. My dad has often spoken of waking up on winter mornings and being able to see through the slats of his wall and see snow coming down outside. My mother worked at the local box factory with my grandmother. My father worked in his parents' convenience store. Their situation improved considerably once my father joined the Army and they were married.

MM: So total Army brat. Moving around constantly until... what age?

MIKE: Uhhh... remember that part when I said "had my eleventh birthday there some several months after we arrived. My father owned some property in a veeeeery rural area, and that's where we lived—and they still live to this day"...? So, the answer would be eleven. And except for going off to college in Richmond, Virginia, for four years, I was living with my folks until I was almost 30. God, to say that now just makes me shudder. I can't believe I was there that long. That was one of the huge motivating factors in my making a big push to try to break into the comics industry—specifically with Marvel and/or DC. I was feeling very claustrophobic at home... and I had the feeling, whether real or simply imagined on

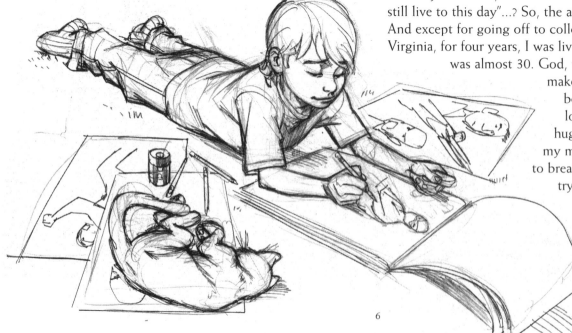

my part, that I was underfoot at my folks' home. I felt like it was past time to get out... and so fortunately, I was able to, within a couple of years after graduating college in 1991—I got a late start in most everything in life, and so I didn't finish college until I was 27—get regular work with DC comics. Once I got invited to join the studio that eventually became Artamus Studios down here in North Carolina, it became time to finally move.

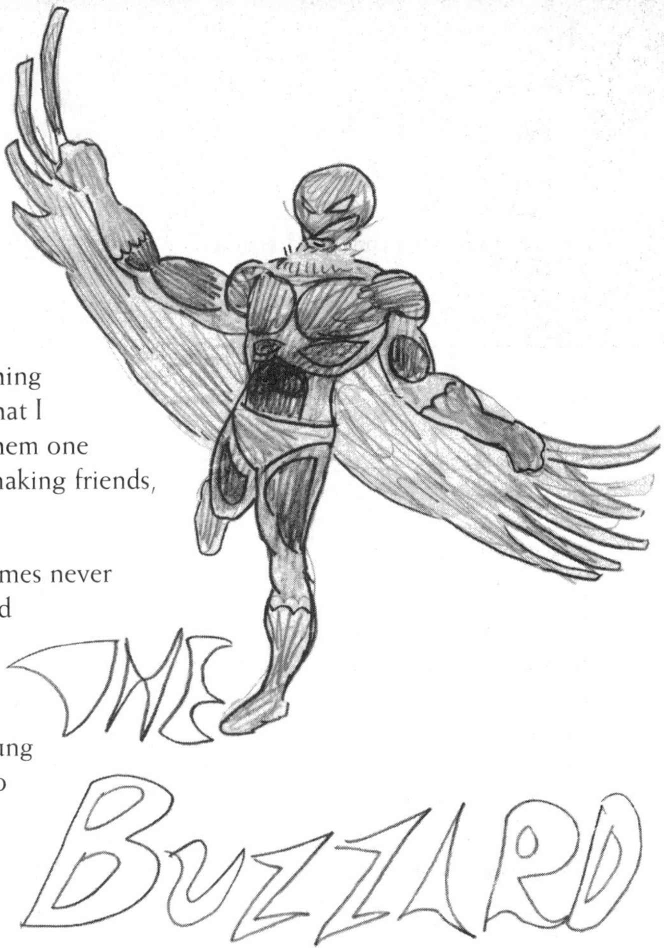
THE
BUZZARD

MM: Do you think that that whole "Army brat, moving around" thing had an effect on you? On your development? Your personality? What I mean, is, many kids who grow up that way say that it galvanized them one way or another, either in becoming very outward, social, good at making friends, or more introverted and able to entertain oneself?

MIKE: I think it *absolutely* had an effect on me. Moving all those times never allowed me to form lasting childhood relationships or feel like I had roots anywhere. We moved twice while my Dad was stationed in Germany in addition to the moves from country to country and state to state before Germany. I think the resulting effect on me was two-fold. On the one hand, I didn't have many friends as a young child, and so mostly kept to myself. And that, in turn, caused me to live within my imagination most of the time. The situation in the camps in Germany was pretty brutal for a young kid who was basically a pacifist like me. I don't really have a violent bone in my body, and I was pretty much fair game for the many bullies that made up a lot of the children that were living in the Army camps—the term "Army brats" was very, very true for a lot of the kids there. I was beat up quite a bit over there. It wasn't a pleasant situation. And so, I spent a lot of time keeping to myself, making up stories and imaginary friends, and I think that was the start of my journey toward becoming obsessed with storytelling that led to the career I have now. I used to make up these elaborate construction paper scenes of gallows and other torture and execution devices—I was also a bit morbid, I suppose—and played with clay a lot. I also had quite a few action figures, like the old Action Jackson sets... and I used to put them through a lot of imagined adventures.

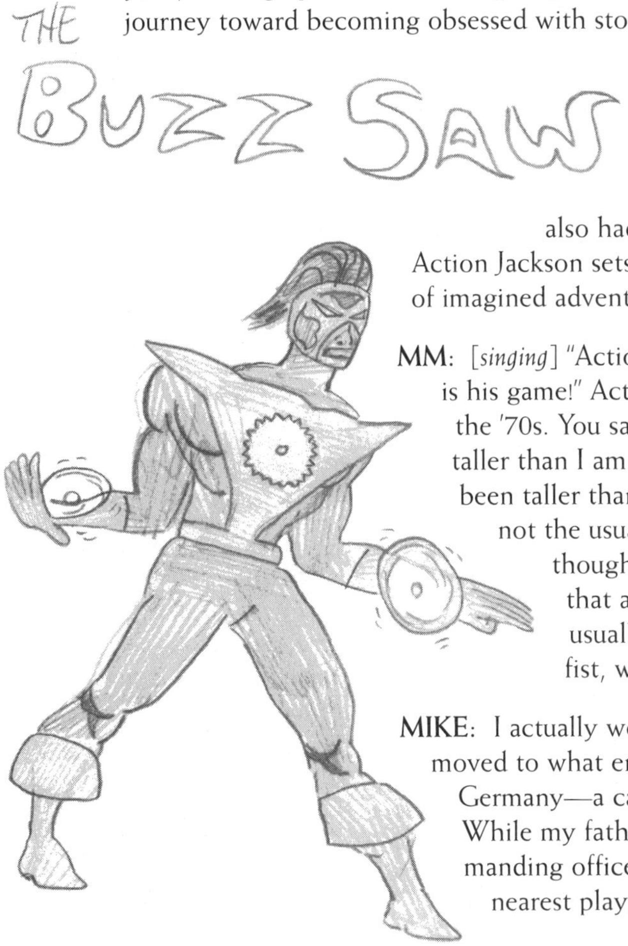
THE
BUZZ SAW

MM: [*singing*] "Action Jackson is his name, bold adventure is his game!" Action Jackson was the Mego G.I. Joe for the '70s. You say that you were beat up a lot—you're taller than I am and so I always imagine you as having been taller than the other kids in school as well, so not the usual target that bullies would pick on—though I guess there are always older kids that are bigger, right? What were the fights usually about? And, being basically a pacifist, would you ever fight back?

MIKE: I actually won the first "fight" I was in when we moved to what ended up being our final destination in Germany—a camp in a town called Göeppingen. While my father and mother met with my dad's commanding officer and his wife, his son took me to the nearest playground and proceeded to try to beat

Previous Page: Like the child in this warm-up sketch, Mike spent much of his childhood drawing on the living room floor. **This Page:** The Buzzard and The Buzzsaw—inspired by The Vulture and Gladiator, respectively—were two of Mike's many childhood creations.

me up in front of all the kids there. I don't know why... maybe to show off that he could dominate the "new kid" or something. But I got the better of him and ended the scuffle holding him down on the ground and yelling at him to stop. After that, he became my friend. But that was about it as far as my luck went. From there on in, I either was beaten up by tougher—and more aggressive—kids, or worse yet, manipulated by still others into being their "henchmen" and doing their dirty work for them—which would end up with me getting my brains beat out. I don't know why I would allow myself to be used like that, since I really had no heart for it, but it happened at least once. I guess I was gullible as well as being somewhat docile. For the most part, I felt like I was in a community of very aggressive, mean-spirited kids—with some exceptions, don't get me wrong... there were some really good kids there—and I was kind of out of my depth.

MM: And were you a comic book reader as a child?

MIKE: I also first became aware of comic books while living in Germany. My father used to take me with him to the Camp PX [Post Exchange] and he'd buy a lot of comics. He had been a fan of comics from back when *he* was a kid, and he collected almost everything he could get his hands on while we were stationed overseas. Most everything Marvel and DC both put out that made it over there, he bought and read. He let me and my brother read his comics, and those are my earliest memories of comic books. I didn't have quite a grasp on just how many comics my dad had until we got back to the States, though. He had *tons* of comics that he'd shipped back with our stuff... and my brother and I tore through them when we found them in all the stuff he had stored in a small building behind the house. Unfortunately, my brother and I weren't too... tender... with my dad's books, and we pretty much ragged them out. Sometimes I feel really heartbroken over that fact, because he had some really wonderful early issues of *Spider-Man*, *The Avengers*, *The Hulk*, *Uncanny X-Men*... almost all that great stuff from Marvel. And then all the great stuff from DC... *Superman*, *Batman*—and all their offshoots—*Justice League*, and all sorts of other wonderful DC comics. All stuff from the early to mid-'70s. It's kind of crappy how we treated those books. My dad still jokingly refers to how we used to walk on them and handle them roughly until they were pretty badly beat up.

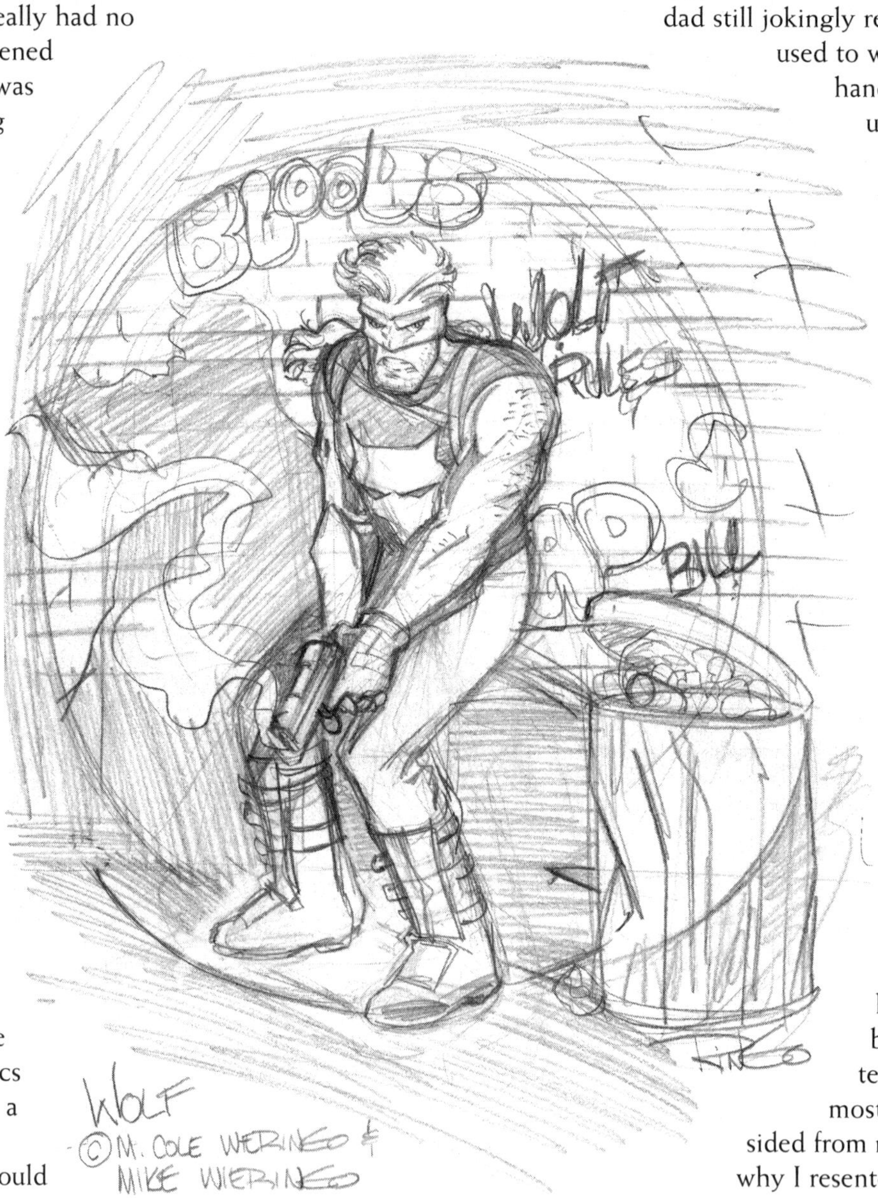
WOLF
©M. COLE WIERINGO &
MIKE WIERINGO

MM: Ah—I was waiting for you to mention Matt. So you have one brother. Older or younger? And were you guys friends growing up? Would you play together? Fight?

MIKE: Matt is five years younger than me. I have to say that I wasn't a very good brother to Matt growing up. There was some of the usual sibling rivalry that happens in most all brothers and sisters... but for the most part, it was one-sided from me. I don't know why I resented Matt... but I didn't want him to do anything *with* me, or to do anything that I did... especially when it came to collecting comics. He was a huge comic book fan—still is—like I was/am, and as kids I came up with this rule—that when I think about it now, seems so utterly idiotic on my part—that Matt couldn't collect any of the comic titles that I did. We could trade complete collections of different titles back and forth, but we couldn't buy the same titles.

And I wasn't very nice to Matt about much else, either. I still harbor a lot of regret about that—but for Matt's part, he never gives it much thought, he tells me. He's got every right to harbor a lot of resentment toward me for my past attitudes and actions towards him, but he's a great guy and has a big heart... he's a real sweetheart. So I guess he's too good a person to let things like that affect him. I wish I had that capacity. I carry stuff around with me like heavy baggage all the time... my whole life seems to be predicated on what came before. As adults, though, Matt and I are great friends as well as being brothers.

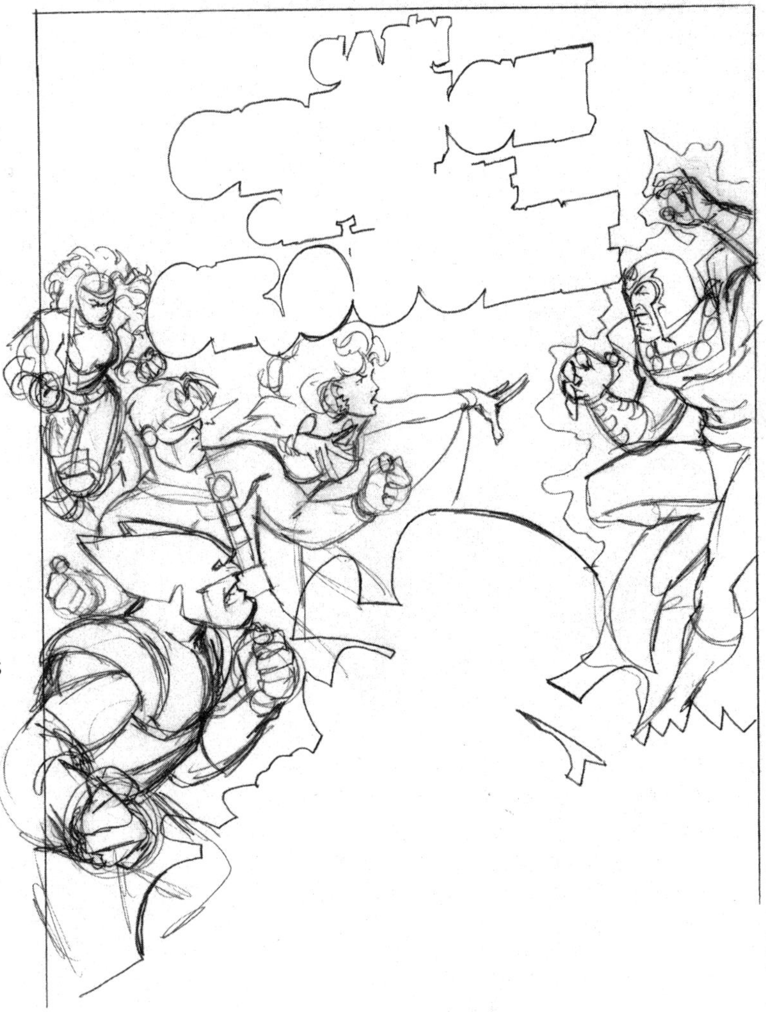

MM: At that time, what were your favorite comic books? Who were your favorite characters?

MIKE: Honestly, I liked everything. As I said, I read all my dad's comics—and he had more DCs than Marvels. I enjoyed the DC stuff a lot, but when I started buying my own comics at around eleven years old, I bought Marvels. There was something about Marvel comics that really connected with me. They seemed more colorful and powerful than the DC stuff, which felt a bit more... whimsical to me. The first two comics I can remember buying were *Uncanny X-Men* #104 and *Captain Marvel* #50, and they blew my mind, especially the *X-Men*. I immediately set out to find all the back issues of that title. There seemed to be something special about it. The characters, the situations... the idea of mutants fighting for their place in the world really connected with the introverted, isolated-feeling kid that I was. I think a lot of other kids of my age group that collected comics also connected with the X-Men. But I started buying so much Marvel stuff... *The Avengers*, *Fantastic Four*, *Spider-Man*... you name it. There weren't nearly as many different titles back then as Marvel has now, so it was easier to keep up with what they published. Of course, as the years went by, the number of titles they published went up... and I tried to keep up with them. I was pretty voracious as far as loving comics goes.

MM: So, though I know you now as this funny, joking guy who can do countless voices and drop into a comedic improv at the drop of a hat, you were the shy, sensitive type as a kid....

MIKE: I remember my first day of school back in the States in, I think, 1975—starting sixth grade. It was evident from the first day that all the kids in my class had spent their early school years all together as classmates and friends... and I was the new kid. I was kind of set apart.... kind of

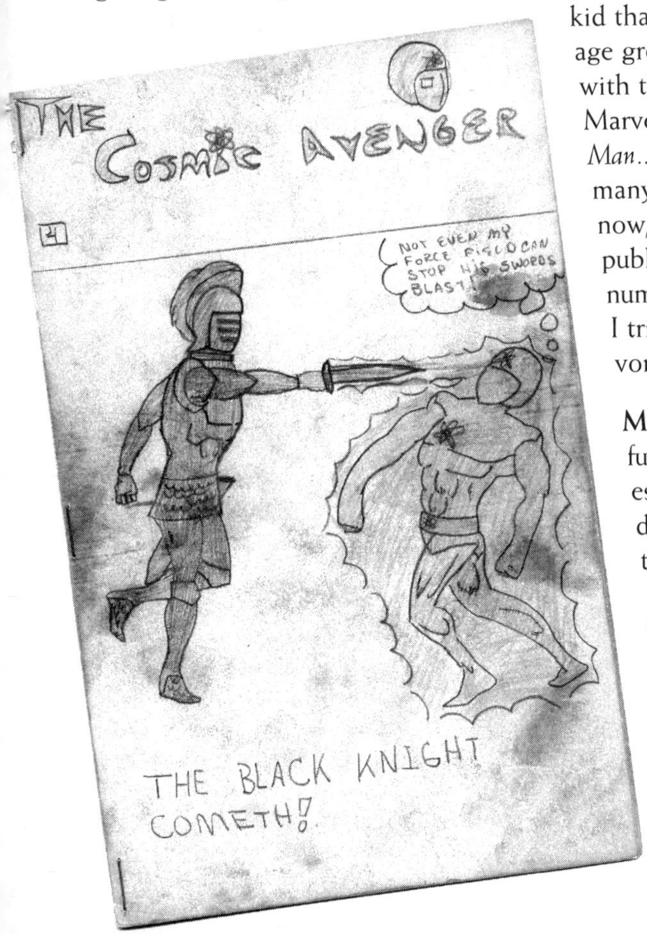
THE COSMIC AVENGER
4
NOT EVEN MY FORCE FIELD CAN STOP HIS SWORDS BLAST!
THE BLACK KNIGHT COMETH!

Previous Page: Just before he finally broke in with DC Comics, Mike and his brother, Matt, co-created Wolf.
Above: What goes better with childhood and Saturday morning cartoons than a good, sugary cereal? Mike's layout for a Cap'n Crunch cereal box featuring the X-Men.
Left: Mike's cover to *The Cosmic Avenger* #4. This 7-page adventure featured none other than The Cosmic Avenger—a stand-in for (Marvel's) Captain Marvel.

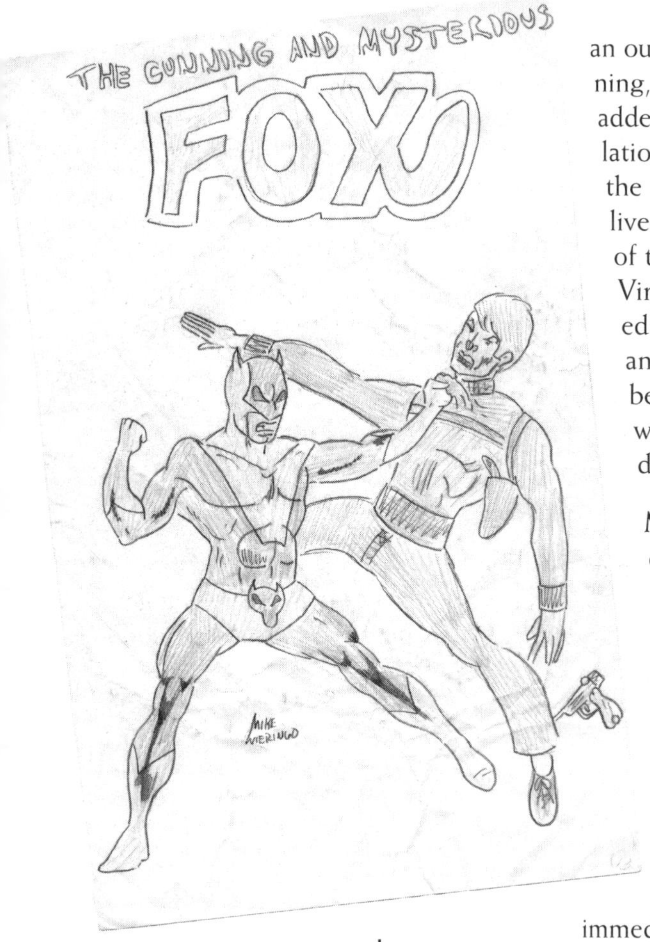
THE CUNNING AND MYSTERIOUS
FOX
MIKE WIERINGO

an outcast from the beginning, really. That just added to my feeling of isolation, and combined with the fact that my family lived in a very rural, out of the way area in Virginia, I really retreated into my imagination, and that's when I became totally obsessed with comics—and drawing.

MM: And were you drawing comics?

MIKE: Oh, yeah. When I started buying and reading lots of comics, the aspect of comic book storytelling in plot and art really just rang a bell in my young mind. I immediately got sucked into whatever I was reading—it's like my brain was hardwired for reading comics, and no matter what the style of the artist was, I'd instantly get plugged into the world that he/she created with their work. I'm still like that to this day—the second I crack open a comic book, I'm right there in that world from the first glance. So since I was already into drawing—even from a very, very young age—I knew I wanted to draw comics as well. I used to create my own adventures for already published characters early on—like Iron Man and Green Lantern—but as time went on, I started creating my own versions of those characters to create stories with.

This Page: The Fox remains one of Mike's favorite childhood creations. He even had his own rogue's gallery, including Buzzsaw and The Bull & The Ram. **Next Page:** Recently, Mike waxed nostalgic on his blog—found at *www.mikewieringo.com*—and reimagined many of his childhood creations. Case in point, this action scene pitting the Fox against his old enemies, The Bull & The Ram.

MM: You've featured on your blog, both your original creations at—what, 12, 13?—and your recently updated renderings of them. I remember that I wanted to draw comics, too, at that age, but I was content with Batman, Superman, Spider-Man—I just wanted to create my own original character who could pal around with them.... What made you feel the urge to recreate the archetypes? To create your own universe?

MIKE: I'm not sure. I think it's something that's always been a part of my character. I was never really satisfied with drawing established Marvel and DC characters. Maybe that's because everything about them was already set on paper by their respective copyright holders... and maybe it's because I really just liked the idea of having my own versions of those characters to build from the ground up, I don't know.

Even as a young kid, I was very interested in the idea of "ownership." I remember when I was 13 or so, I became briefly fascinated by the idea of creating some sort of park or resort on my parents' property. There's a very long and winding creek area, and I—along with a friend of mine—built some makeshift bridges and picnic areas and dams and were really into the idea of having some sort of campground. It never occurred to me that I was wasting my time and that no one would have been interested in any campground that a little kid came up with—not to mention that my parents would never have allowed it even if it *did* become a possibility. To my little fevered imagination, it was a great idea and was going to happen. Then reality set in, and I realized it was a pipe dream. But it was a lot of fun to imagine the possibilities—no matter how unrealistic.

So I've always been like that with everything. I have always

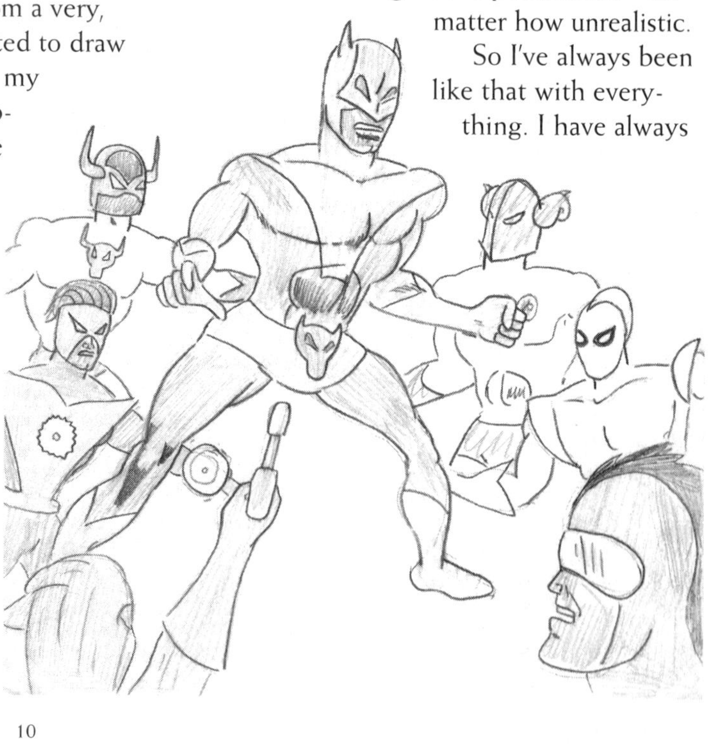

loved the idea of owning my own characters and being wholly responsible for guiding their path through their fictional lives. Even to this day, I'm always creating new characters... or fleshing out things I came up with as a child to perhaps one day work with, should the time ever present itself. I'm just totally enamored with the idea of owning and working with my own characters. I greatly admire creators like Jeff Smith, Terry Moore, Robert Kirkman, Mike Allred, Linda Medley, Carla Speed McNeil and a whole host of other creators who have their own characters they pour the majority of their creative energies into.

MM: And were your parents supportive of your artistic talents? Did they encourage you to draw?

MIKE: Oh, yes. My parents were very, very encouraging of my drawing and my desire to become a comic book artist. I think my mother wanted me to find something that made me happy. She's a very nurturing and caring person—a real sweetheart in every sense of the word. And so when she saw that I was into drawing and sketching, she really encouraged me to keep it up. And my father had drawn a lot when he was a kid himself, so he prompted me to keep it up. There were times, when I was in my early teens, that my dad would bring home these black-and-white magazines... they were knock-offs of the Warren magazines... and he'd drop them on the floor next to me while I was laying there on my stomach drawing—as I could usually be found in the afternoons after school—and say something like, "You draw a lot better than the guys in this magazine—you should work up some samples and submit to them!" Now, even *my* immature mind realized that I wasn't in the same class as the artists in these magazines—even though they *were* pretty awful—but the mere fact that my dad was encouraging me to go for something like that just thrilled me and spurred me on even harder to keep drawing and get better. I still don't know if he really even meant it—about me being ready—but it's still a fond memory I hold. So, yeah, they were both always greatly supportive.

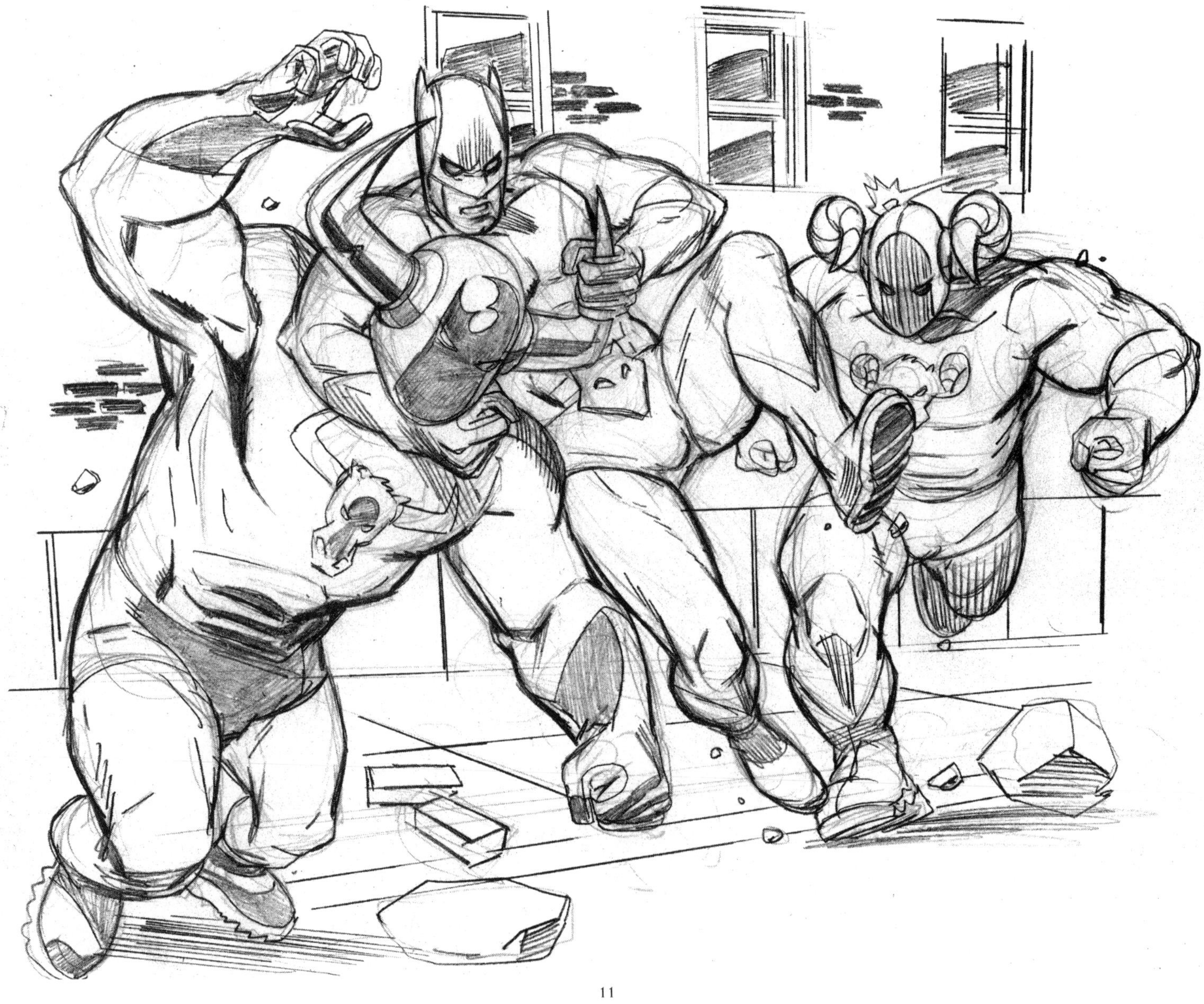

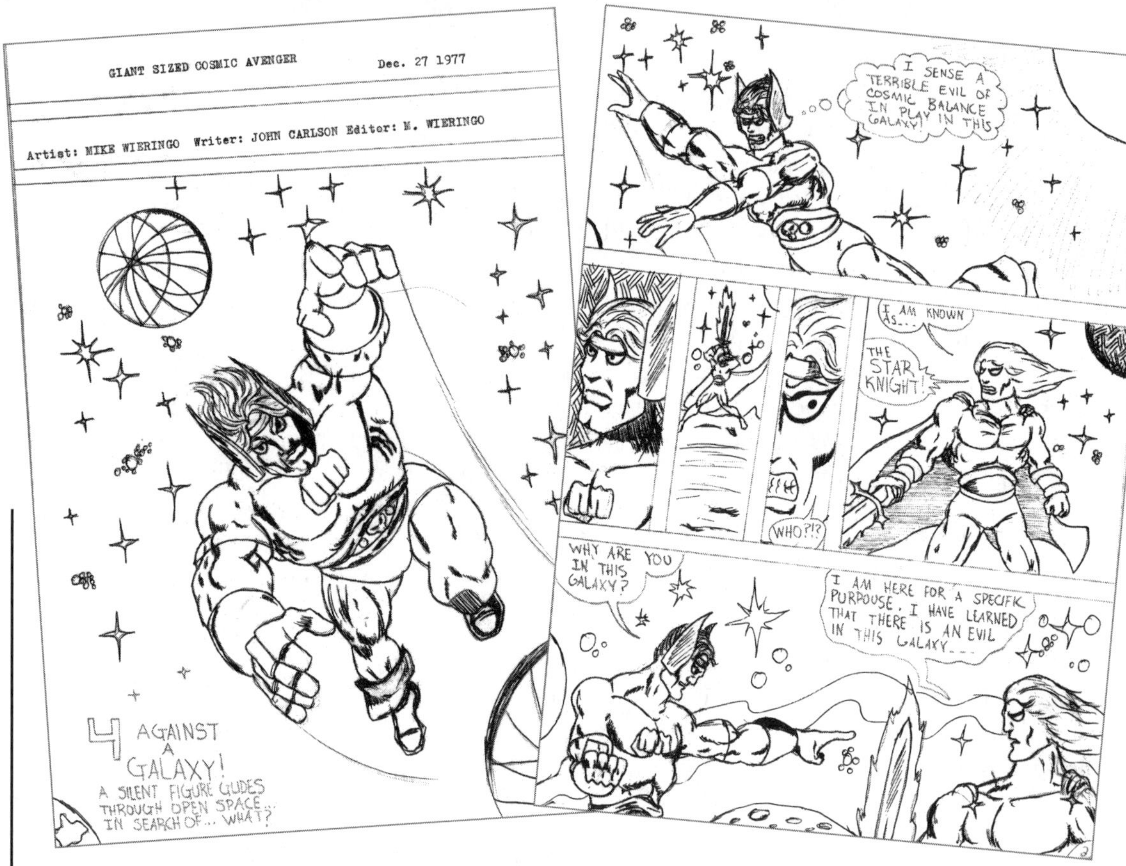
GIANT SIZED COSMIC AVENGER Dec. 27 1977
Artist: MIKE WIERINGO Writer: JOHN CARLSON Editor: M. WIERINGO
4 AGAINST A GALAXY!
A SILENT FIGURE GLIDES THROUGH OPEN SPACE... IN SEARCH OF... WHAT?
I SENSE A TERRIBLE EVIL OF COSMIC BALANCE IN PLAY IN THIS GALAXY!
WHO?!?
I AM KNOWN AS...
THE STAR KNIGHT!
WHY ARE YOU IN THIS GALAXY?
I AM HERE FOR A SPECIFK PURPOUSE. I HAVE LEARNED THAT THERE IS AN EVIL IN THIS GALAXY...

Right: The first two pages of *Giant Sized Cosmic Avenger* #1—penciled by Mike and inked by his frequent childhood partner, Carlton Hill.
Below: Another childhood creation, The Outcasts.
Next Page: And the recent reimagination of The Outcasts.

MM: And aside from being a talented and dynamic artist, you are a storyteller as well! Rather than simply design your stable of new super-heroes, you were eager to use them, to put them into adventures and create entire sagas for them! That is fairly rare, I've found.

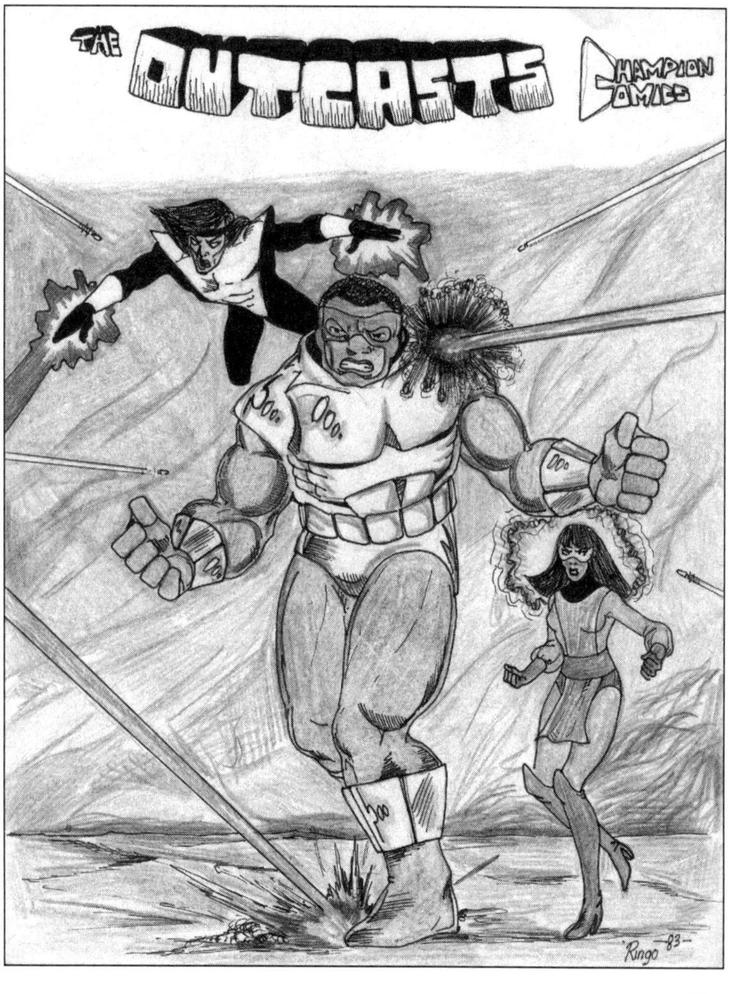
THE OUTCASTS
CHAMPION COMICS
Ringo -83-

MIKE: Oddly enough, it *wasn't* that rare in the area I lived. One of my best friends in middle and high school, Rodman Johnson, had a super-hero character of his own called Super-Fly, who was a sort of knock-off of Yellowjacket, and he would write and draw his adventures just as I did with my own bunch of characters. Rodman got into that, I suspect, because not only did his friend—me—do the same thing, but more importantly, his cousin Carlton Hill, was *huge* into comics and creating his own universe of characters. When I was, I think, a sophomore in high school, Rodman introduced me to Carlton, and it was somewhat of a revelation. Carlton had just graduated from high school, and he was going to be moving with his family to another state. But he had wanted to meet me before he left, and one day we met on the bleachers in the gym in my school. Carlton had a lot of his own work with him, and I brought some of mine to share with him. I was really amazed at how prodigious his imagination and grasp of creating comic books was. His abilities were much more developed than mine—he had a sophistication in his writing ability and character development that I didn't even come close to. But he was kind of impressed with my drawing, I think... and he suggested that we work on some stuff together. We became fast friends, and even after he and his family moved away, we kept in touch, and wrote each other and spoke on the phone all the time.

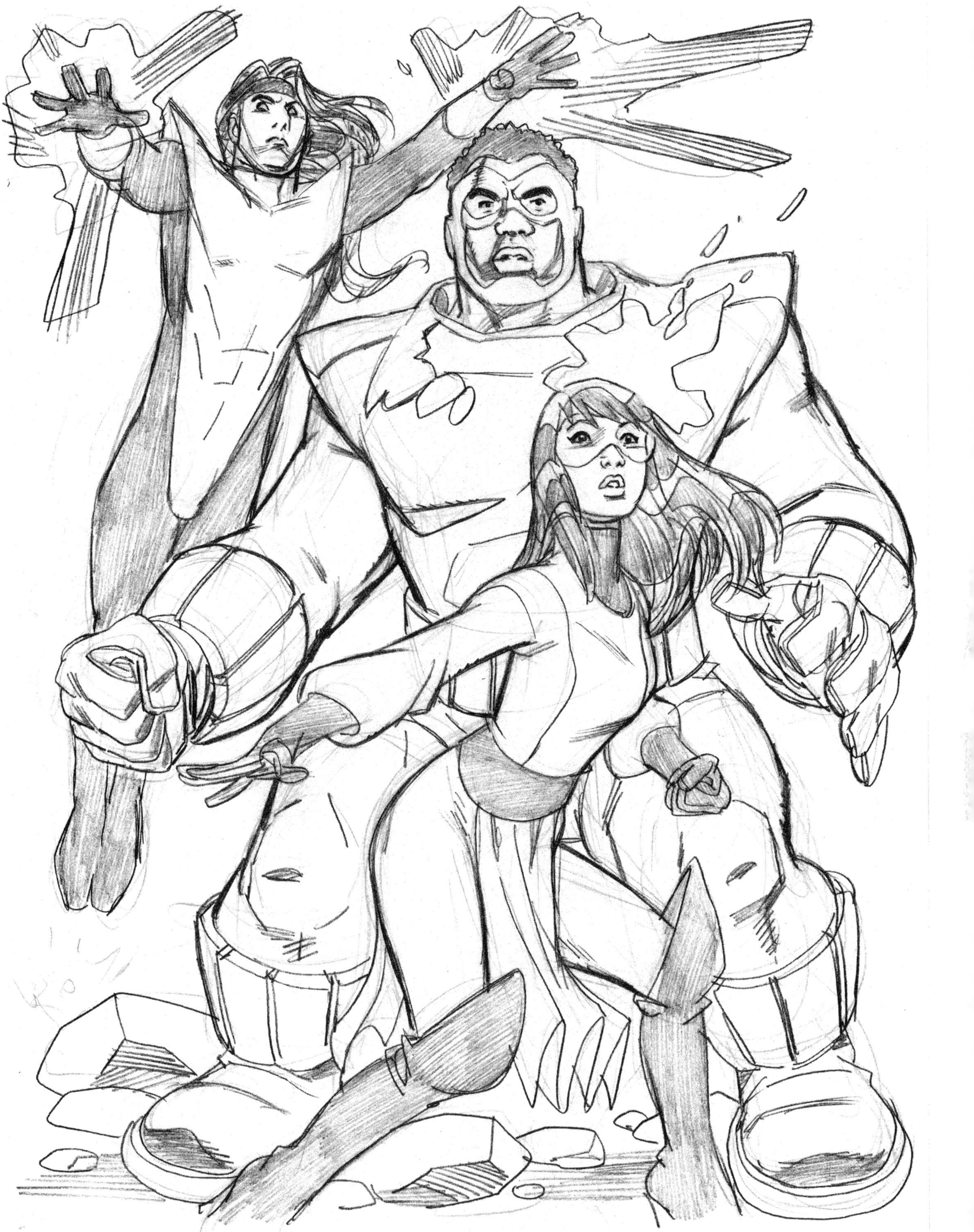

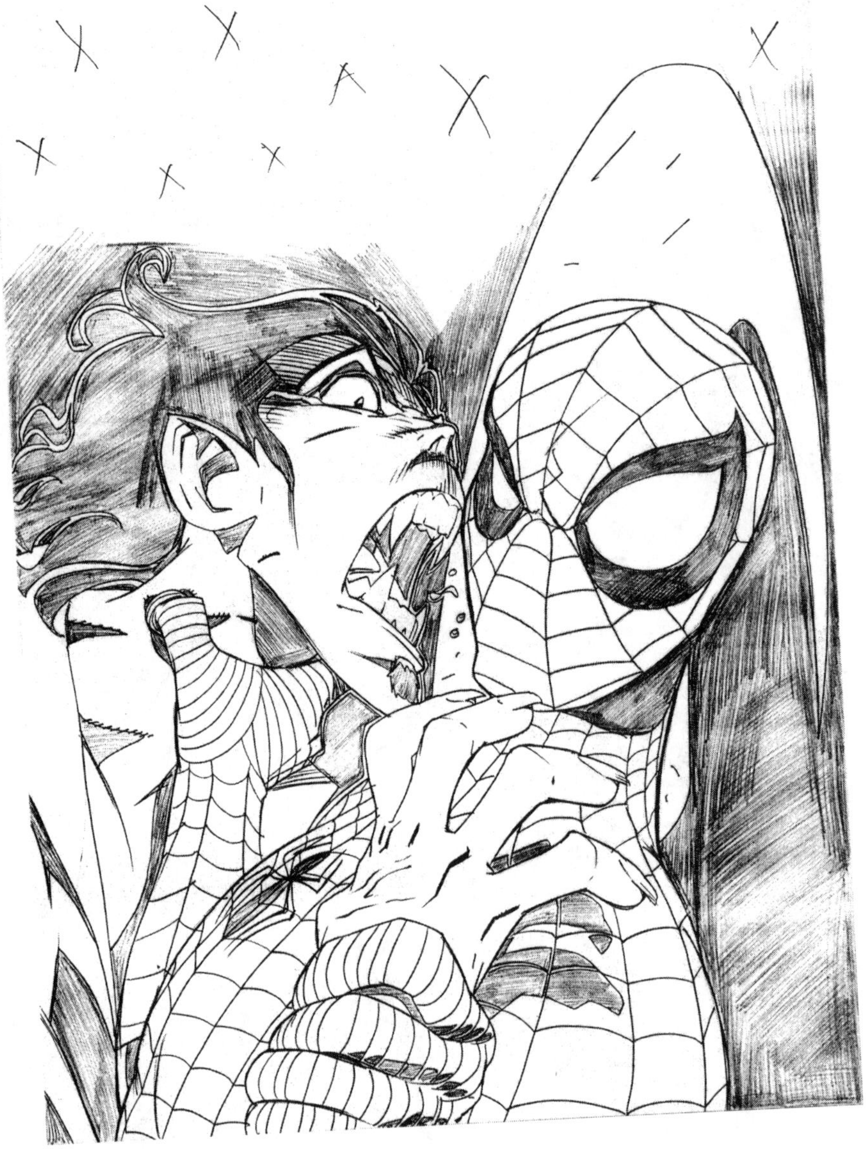

Above: Occasionally, Mike gets to revisit his early fascination with vampires, as in this cover for *Marvel Selects: Spider-Man* #2, featuring Morbius, the Living Vampire.
Next Page: Mike spent many hours of his youth watching the clouds roll by. Perhaps the world would be a better place if we could all take the time to let our imaginations soar among the clouds now and again.

We were really obsessed with making comics together and discussing comics as much as time allowed. It was a really fun time, and I would anxiously wait for every package of letters and copies of drawings and homemade comics I'd get from Carlton. I've still got all that stuff in a big grocery bag in a closet here in my home, including all the correspondence. That was a special time. It seemed like almost anything was possible creatively at that time... like the world was wide open. Eventually, I think, Carlton fell out of the comics thing, and moved on to other interests. I stopped hearing from him after a couple of years.

MM: Where do you think your innate sense of story comes from?

MIKE: I'm not sure about that. My parents have both always been huge readers... they still read voraciously. They go through tons of novels each year... and I think I got that love of reading and story from them. That might have filtered into my love for reading comics, and connected so viscerally and immediately with the combination of the visual as well as the written word that comics employ. It was a confluence of all those things, I think, that led to my having such a strong desire to draw comics and to concentrate on good, solid visual storytelling. Some of that might also come from the fact that I was *also* raised, to a large extent, with the television-as-baby-sitter paradigm. I was a TV addict from early on—and still am. My mother had a lot of work to keep the household under control while my father was at work—and there was a period where he was stationed in Vietnam during the war, and was gone for a couple of years. So early on, I was watching a lot of TV and got into animation. A lot of the early Japanese animated shows like *Astro Boy* and *Speed Racer*, as well as a lot of American cartoons. Anything that looked drawn, I immediately connected with. So I'm sure that also had a big effect on my sense of storytelling... the fact that I was always involved in either reading or watching something on TV.

MM: What were your favorite shows? Favorite cartoons?

MIKE: Early on—I don't have a clear memory of all the shows I watched beyond the *Astro Boy* and *Speed Racer* stuff... lots of cartoons, I guess. *Gigantor*. The old Warner Brother stuff was always a favorite. Of course, when I was a kid, there wasn't all that much on TV the way it is now... this is way before cable was even a thought—I'm guessing... who knows, someone may have been thinking about it. *Later* in life—as a teenager—I watched all kinds of fun stuff that sparked my imagination. I loved *Dark Shadows*... I was a huge nut for the vampire lore, and *Shadows*, though dull in places, had such a sense of creepiness and foreboding that it fascinated me. They had it all: vampires, witches and werewolves. But I also watched tons of sitcoms with my family—y'know, *All in the Family*, *Barney Miller*, *The Andy Griffith Show*, *Alice*, *Three's Company*... stuff like that. I was also crazy for stuff like *The Six Million Dollar Man*, *The Incredible Hulk*, *The Man from Atlantis*, *Battlestar*

Galactica, Buck Rogers in the 25th Century, Star Trek... all that science-fiction stuff. If it was science-fiction, fantasy, or super-hero based, I was into it.

MM: Remember when we saw Erin Gray at the San Diego Con? She was still stunningly beautiful. I'm pretty sure she was lookin' at you.

MIKE: She was beautiful! She must have that natural beauty that women like Jaclyn Smith and Cheryl Tiegs have that keep them beautiful into later life.

MM: What kind of books did you enjoy then?

MIKE: I was a huge reader of science-fiction and fantasy novels then, too—it wasn't just comics. I read stuff by Marion Zimmer Bradley, Robert E. Howard, Edgar Rice Burroughs, John Jakes, C. J. Cherryh, Tanith Lee, J.R.R. Tolkien—I was totally nuts for the *Lord of the Rings* books—really anything I could get my hands on. I can't really remember all the authors I read, there were so many. There was a publishing company called DAW back in the '70s and early '80s that specialized in science-fiction and fantasy novels, so I would actively seek out their logo any time I went to a newsstand or used book store. I could always count on enjoying whatever it was they published. I was rarely disappointed by anything they published. Now, some of it I would probably feel is a bit cheesy—but back then, I was so voracious, I was absorbing just about anything I could find.

MM: What is your happiest memory from childhood?

MIKE: I don't think I have any specific fond memory of a moment in time from my childhood. I think, instead, I have wonderful impressions of happiness during times when I would be laying on my stomach in my folks' living room floor drawing my pictures and comics. There was a time before becoming more self-aware and self-conscious of my work and its mistakes and limitations when that personally created world of my own drawing was everything to me. It didn't occur to me at those times that my work was lacking and crude—immature or uninformed and naïve. It just *was*... it was a part of me, and that's all I needed. I would get as absorbed in what I was doing as I would get in reading the professionally created comics I was so in love with. Those young times in my childhood were special—and it felt like the sky was the limit, and anything in the world was possible. I used to go out in the pastures near my folks' property and lay in the grass on warm days and just cloudwatch. I felt like I could do anything during those times. Not just comics, but anything I put my mind to. So I really loved those times. I

Below: Peter Parker had some scary times, as well, such as in this nightmare sequence from *Sensational Spider-Man* #-1. Inks by Richard Case.
Next Page: At least Robin doesn't seem to have trouble with the ladies. The cover for *Robin* #35, from layout to inks. Inks by Terry Austin.

think there's something about living in the country that sparks the imagination. Being close to nature was something that felt really amazing—and I think it had a lot to do with nurturing my creative energies.

MM: What's your scariest memory from childhood?

MIKE: I think my scariest moment from childhood would have to be a terrible school bus accident my brother and I were in when I was about 13 years old. A long-haul driver of an 18-wheel rig fell asleep at the wheel after being awake much longer than he was supposed to, and he slammed

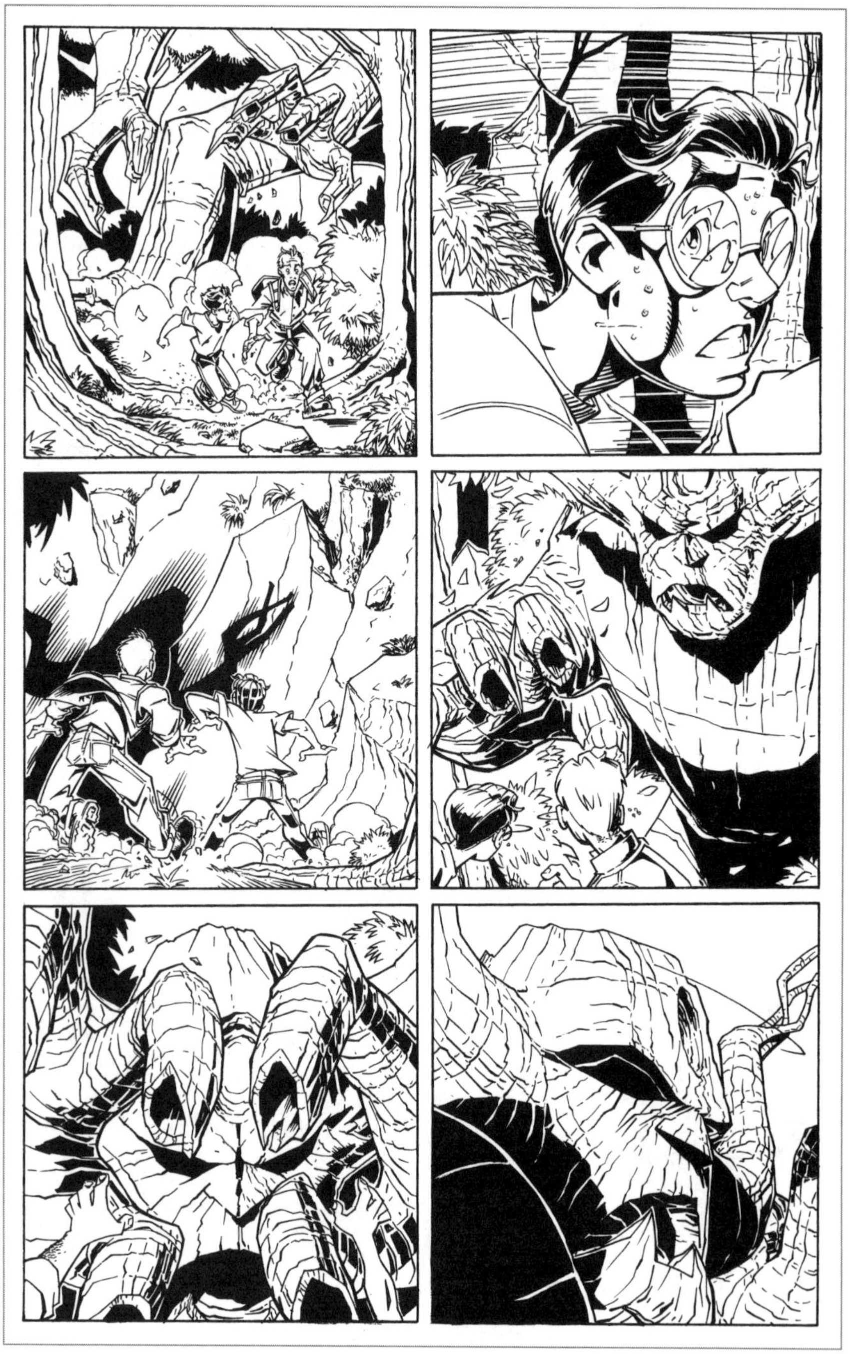

into the back of the school bus I was in when it was stopped to pick up another kid. It was a horrific accident. The big-rig was traveling at more than 60 mph... and when it slammed into the back of the bus, it propelled it forward and over onto the median between the two sections of highway, where it turned over on its side. Two kids in the back were immediately killed—crushed to death. And another little girl was thrown over the rail of the front of the bus where she was sitting, and she was crushed as she fell out the door as the bus fell over on its side. There was dust and pulverized/powdered glass filling the bus in the aftermath of the crash, and papers and shoes and backpacks littering the side of the bus, which was now the floor. Kids were bloody, screaming, and crying. Since the bus had fallen over on the side with the door, we had to wait for rescue teams to show up and free us before we could get out. A couple of kids escaped from the windows on the side/now top of the bus... but my head was too big to fit through, so I had to wait. It was a terrible scene of destruction and carnage. Fortunately, neither my brother nor I were seriously injured. I came out of it with a cut, and my brother had some back pain, but it went away soon after. I still think some times about how fortunate we were to come out of that rather unscathed.

MM: So, going back a little bit, we've established that you were a quiet, comics-drawin' kid with a few friends doing the same thing. Did you have other friends? Did the transition from elementary school into high school bring you out more?

MIKE: Yeah, I had more friends in high school. I started coming out of my shell and interacting with people a bit more. I joined the high school newspaper, I joined the track team—although I sucked at it—I even went out for basketball and football, but I was really not much good physically back then. I was tall and gangly and not at all in tune with my body. I certainly wasn't what you'd call athletic, and yet I really wanted to get into sports in school. I just wasn't gifted enough, physically, to make any teams beyond the track team, and even then, I made that because there was

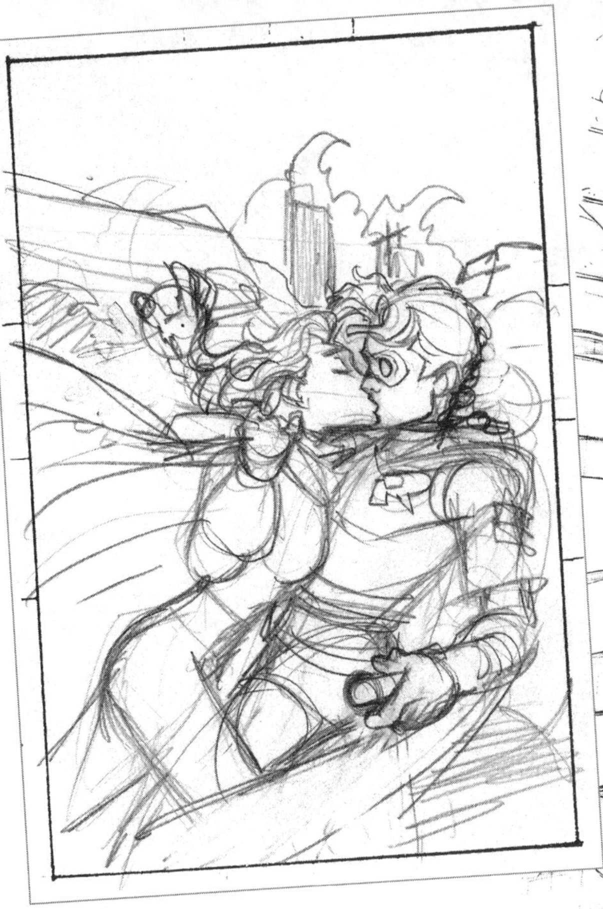

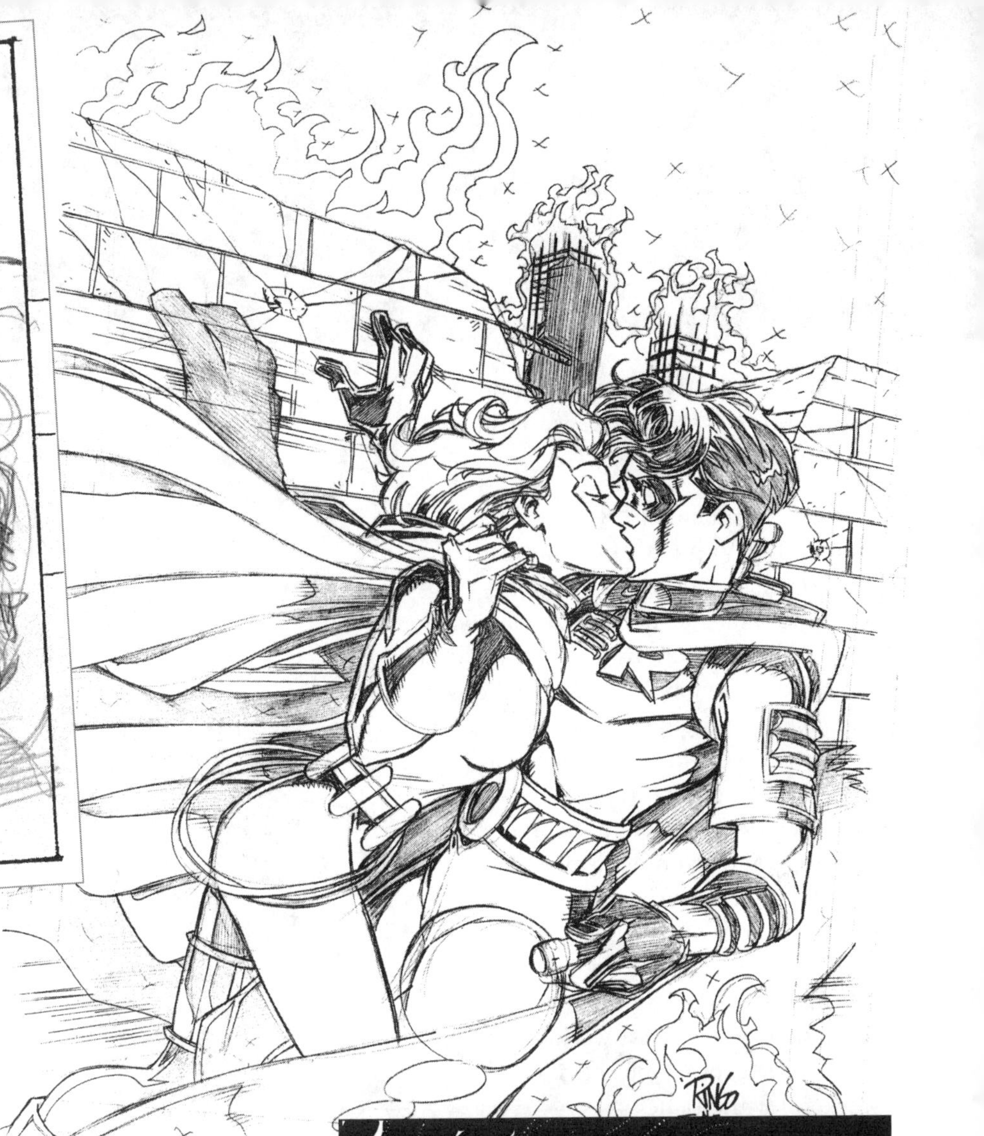

room and the coach had a philosophy of letting everyone participate if there was room for them on the team. So I "made" the team, but I was slow and not very agile. But I made several friends, I think, because I was kind of naïve, soft-spoken, and self-deprecating. I think it was easy for people to talk to me because I listened to them. I was a good sounding board for the other kids, so even a lot of the "real" athletes in school liked me. It didn't hurt that I could draw pretty well. That was always something that helped me connect with people. It was pretty different in high school. I wasn't one of the "cool kid elite" by any means, but I fit in a bit better. By high school, pretty much *everyone* felt new and not in a specific clique—I'm speaking of the class I was in that went from elementary on to Rustburg High—which was my school.

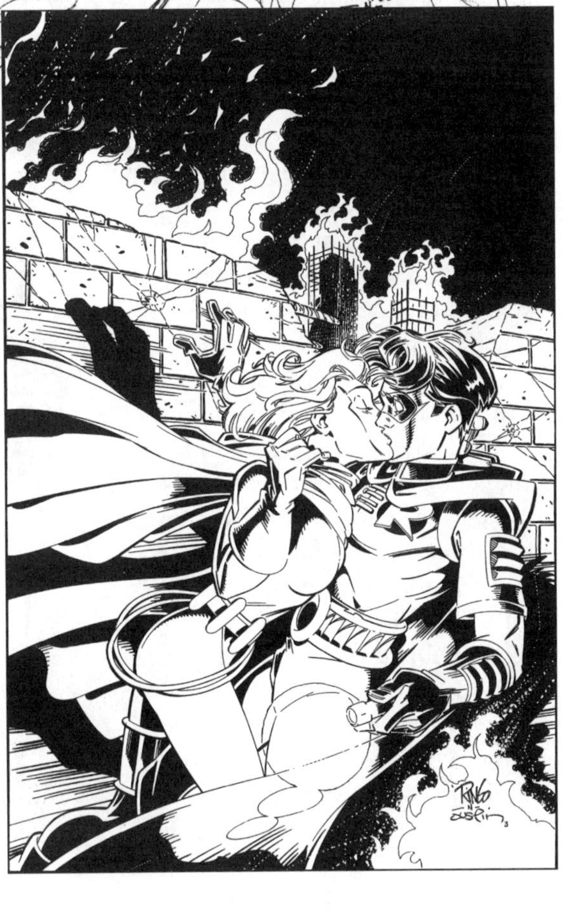

MM: And what about girls? For us shy and retiring types, sometimes that doesn't come up until well into college. Did you have a girlfriend, or girlfriends, in high school?

MIKE: No. No action with the girls for me. As far as the young ladies in high school went, I *was* an outsider. I asked out a couple of girls, but they turned me down. I remember asking a certain classmate of mine to the Ring Dance—a dance and ceremony held for Juniors where they gave out the class rings for next year's Senior year. She turned me down by telling me that she wasn't going. I found out later that she had indeed gone, and it hurt my feelings. I would have rather been turned down flat than to be lied to. But no, I never had any luck with girls in school. Even my prom was a set-up with a friend. It was fun, but certainly not romantic.

Part 2: Produce, Produce, Produce!

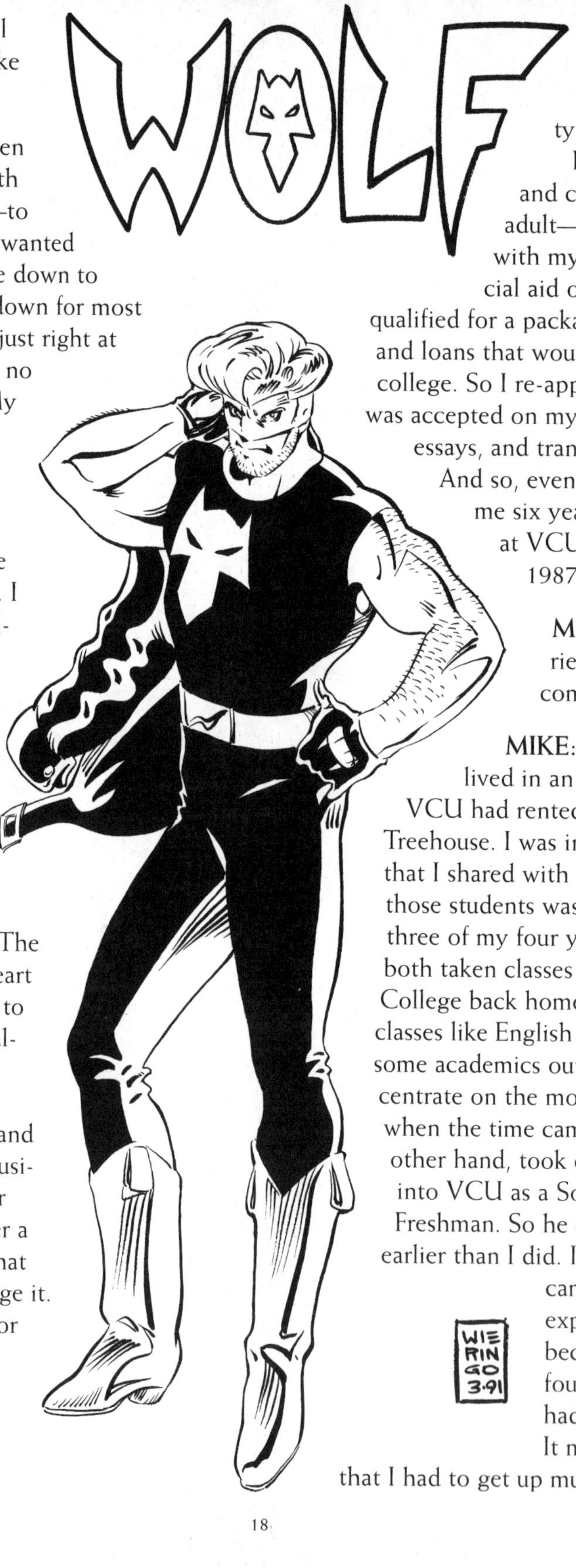
WOLF
WIE
RIN
GO
3·91

MM: So, you graduate high school in, what, '83? What happens to Mike Wieringo next?

MIKE: I graduated in '81. I had been accepted to Virginia Commonwealth University in Richmond, Virginia—to the School of the Arts—and really wanted to attend there. But my folks sat me down to tell me that they had been turned down for most financial aid packages. They made just right at too much to qualify—but they had no money to send me on their own. My dad offered to take out a second mortgage and sell one of their cars to help—but looking into their eyes, I could see that they were scared of the consequences of those actions. So I didn't attend just then. I spent several years just working full-time in the grocery business. I worked for the same grocery chain for close to seven years. The chain changed hands twice while I was there, but I kept my job because I was a hard worker and didn't make trouble. I actually became a Produce Manager at one of the smaller stores before it was closed. The previous Produce Manager had a heart attack and never recovered enough to return. So although I was sent initially to just spell him until he got better, I ended up getting the job full-time. But although I busted my ass and worked very hard, I was never enthusiastic about being a full time "worker drone" in the grocery business. After a while, I felt like I'd get trapped in that life if I didn't do something to change it. I had sort of fallen out of drawing for some time after having to defer going to college—kind of out of bitterness—and I started drawing again around '85 or so. I started to get the drive to draw again, and my mind started turning back to the possibility of college once more.

Fortunately, since I was older and considered an independent adult—even though I still lived with my folks—I applied for financial aid on my own and found that I qualified for a package that was a mix of grants and loans that would allow me to actually go to college. So I re-applied to VCU in '86, and I was accepted on my portfolio, application essays, and transcripts from high school. And so, even though it ended up taking me six years to get there, I ended up at VCU in their art program for the 1987-88 school year.

MM: And how was that experience? Did you live at VCU or commute?

MIKE: Kind of a combination. I lived in an apartment complex that VCU had rented out the majority of called Treehouse. I was in a two-bedroom apartment that I shared with three other students. *One* of those students was my brother for the first three of my four years in school. He and I had both taken classes at Lynchburg Community College back home, but I only took a couple of classes like English Lit and Art History to get some academics out of the way so I could concentrate on the more artistic classes at VCU when the time came. My brother, Matt, on the other hand, took classes full-time, so he came into VCU as a Sophomore, while I was a Freshman. So he ended up graduating a year earlier than I did. I don't know if living in off-campus housing was a better experience for me or not, because I was at Treehouse all four years of school and never had anything to compare it to. It made it a bit more difficult in that I had to get up much earlier and get ready to

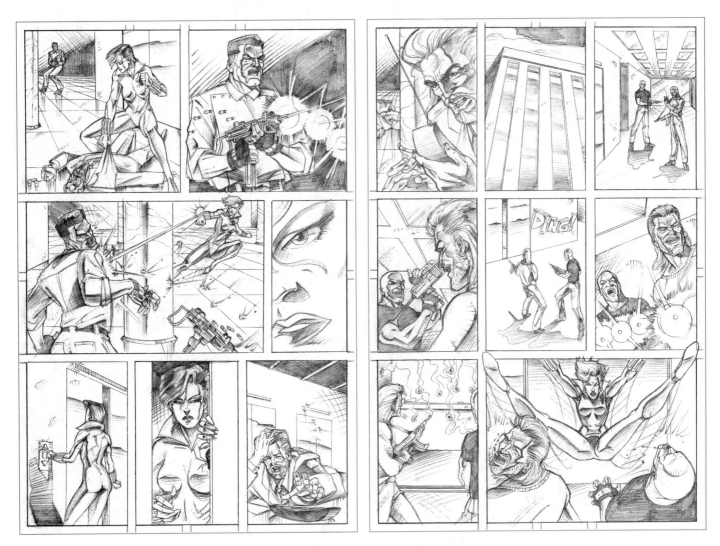

grab a bus onto campus—the apartment complex was about ten miles from school. If I lived on campus, I could have slept in another hour before early classes, but in retrospect, it probably helped to reinforce good habits as far as being on time and getting my work done.

I did enjoy the apartment experience, for the most part, though. I had a couple of roommates that I didn't get along with very well, but that's going to happen when you pack four guys into a small apartment. The apartment itself was pretty shabby and filthy. I don't know how long it had been since they had put in new furniture and carpet... it was all very old and grungy. But my Senior year, I had only one other roommate, so we each had a room to ourselves. Senior year was very cool. We were also in a new apartment, so it was really great. And it was my first experience with independent living... well, as independent as *college* living can get.

MM: And how was the work? Did you feel that it was preparing you for where you wanted to go? Were you a good student?

MIKE: After my first semester, I *was* a good student. I got caught up in partying and hanging out more than I should have in my first semester. Like I said, it was my first time living away from home for any significant period of time, and I kind of lost my priorities for a while. But after getting my grades for that first period and coming up with a bunch of Cs, I was shocked out of that fog of partying and being lazy and really settled down. I ended up making the Dean's List each semester for the rest of my college career. As for the work and whether it prepared me for a career in the art world, I'd have to say that if I hadn't had my experience at VCU, I don't think I would have gotten anywhere near as far as I have in my working life. I had some great classes with some really terrific instructors. In particular, a figure drawing class that I had with a man

Previous Page: Another drawing of Mike and Matt's creation, Wolf. **Above:** Two pages of a Black Widow sample from Mike's 1991 portfolio, which he showed at conventions while looking to break into comics.

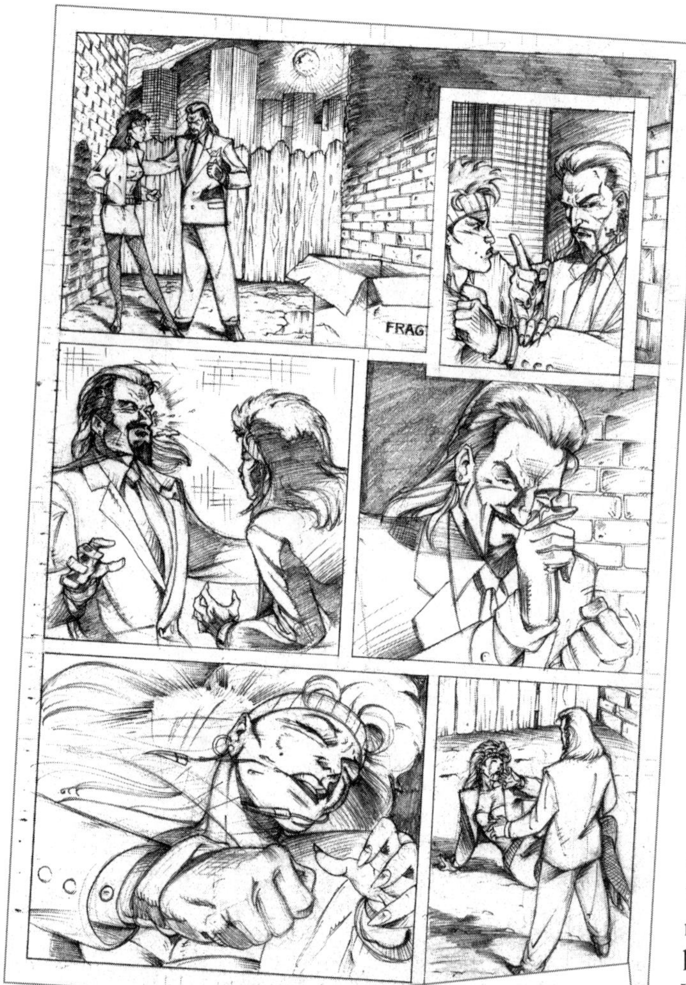

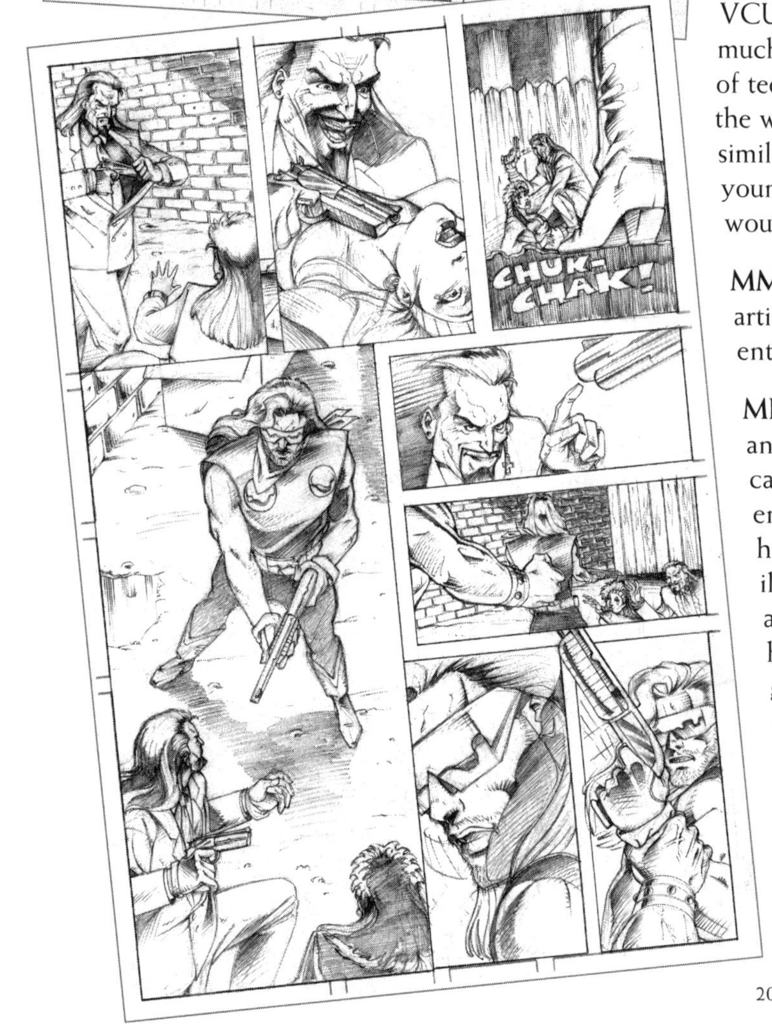
CHUK-
CHAK!

named Donald Early. Mr. Early was the best thing that happened to me at VCU. He was a rough, tough taskmaster, and my first semester with him was a shock to my system, because I'd never met anyone as... hard-nosed... about art as he was/is. He's kind of what you hear about tough football coaches, in that he breaks you down before building you up. He immediately began to forcibly strip away all the preconceived bad habits that every student brought into his class. It was pretty harsh. Most of us responded to this after the initial shock, but some didn't. There were a few students in class who kind of shut down in the face of this kind of approach and one or two actually dropped out. It was like "Figure Drawing Bootcamp," and not everyone is built to handle that kind of stress and atmosphere. For me, Mr. Early's class and teaching ended up being very instrumental, I believe, to my growth as someone who was able to see the figure, understand it, and draw it from life—which then helped to translate into being able to draw from my imagination.

I wouldn't have traded that experience for anything. It was very tough at times, but being totally immersed in the act of figure drawing like that was amazing. I had a full year of it in Art Foundation in Freshman year with other instructors, but meeting Mr. Early in Sophomore year and having a good eight to ten hours each week of that kind of intense figure-drawing work was just amazing. I actually look back on my time at VCU as some of the most wonderful times in my life. The college atmosphere and the School of the Arts at VCU was a place that was very special. I was exposed to so much in the art world... so many kinds of art, so much by way of technique, that it was a very exciting time. It seemed like the world was wide open and anything was possible. It was a similar feeling to the kinds of thoughts I would have as a young kid—that the world was wide open—and that art would be my passport to anywhere I wanted to go.

MM: And your intent all along was to become a comic book artist? Were you ever intrigued or tempted to take your talents into advertising or animation instead?

MIKE: Well, my major in school was Fashion Illustration, and going in, I actually had the intent to pursue that as a career. I loved the work being done in Fashion... and I was enamored with the idea of being involved with it. Mr. Early had been a hugely successful, greatly sought-after fashion illustrator in New York City, and seeing his printed work and his technique really sparked my interest in the field. I had originally applied to the Communication Arts program, which was more editorial/advertising illustration related—lots of design work, computer work, and traditional media for illustration. I didn't make it, though, and it ended up being the best thing that could have happened to me. I've always been more into the more organic side of drawing, and design and computer work didn't really appeal to me once I saw it in action by looking in on some of the CA classes. It's ironic, now that I use a computer almost every day in my work, but back then, I really just wanted to draw.

I think I always had, in the back of my mind, though, the idea that I *really* wanted to do comics. It was a dream since I was about eleven years old, and I still—deep down—wanted to draw comic books. The decision was solidified for me, however, when the head of the Fashion Illustration department called all of us together at the beginning of our Senior year to announce that fashion illustration had taken a huge downturn and was basically dead as a career option. They did some emergency class shifting and added a class in learning the Mac. This was in 1990, so it was one of the early versions of the Mac... I think we were learning on a Mac SE. Very small computer with a black-&-white screen. It took forever to perform a function, and I kind of felt like I was wasting my time learning to use this thing, because I didn't think I'd ever end up using one. Funny, huh...? Now, I use a Mac every day and can't imagine life without it. The idea was to make us all into Art Directors. But we still had our drawing classes as well, and all my classmates and I still wanted careers in art—not art direction. So my mind began to shift seriously back to the idea of pursuing getting into the comic book industry once I finished with school.

MM: To go back a little bit—we talked about the influence that TV and books—and *comics*—had on your life and your developing sense of story. About eleventh or twelfth grade was when I really started getting into movies—or film—not just 'cause it was an excuse—or an alibi—to get out of the house and be with my friends, but I realize now that I was also gleaning storytelling tips from that arena as well. Did you go through the same thing?

MIKE: I'm not sure if I was specifically consciously aware that I was absorbing storytelling tips and techniques. Maybe in an abstract way, in that I was fascinated with storytelling, and television and movies just played into that obsession. With reading novels, my imagination would immediately conjure up the images that the books were describing in words for settings and mood and actions. With comic books, the visuals were there already, but were static. But since I was so attuned to that mode anyway, my mind would immediately fill in the areas *between* the panels—as well as absorb and appreciate the art inside the panels themselves. Even looking at the static images, they would immediately take on a feeling of movement for me. And so moving to television and movies, the actual fluid, moving images of film was like having all the mental work done for me. I suppose this allowed my mind to—if nothing more than subconsciously—concentrate on the more technical aspects of the storytelling in whatever I was watching. I still do it to this day. I was watching *Cinderella Man* on HBO the other day, and

Previous Page and Below: A three-page Nomad sample from Mike's 1991 portfolio.

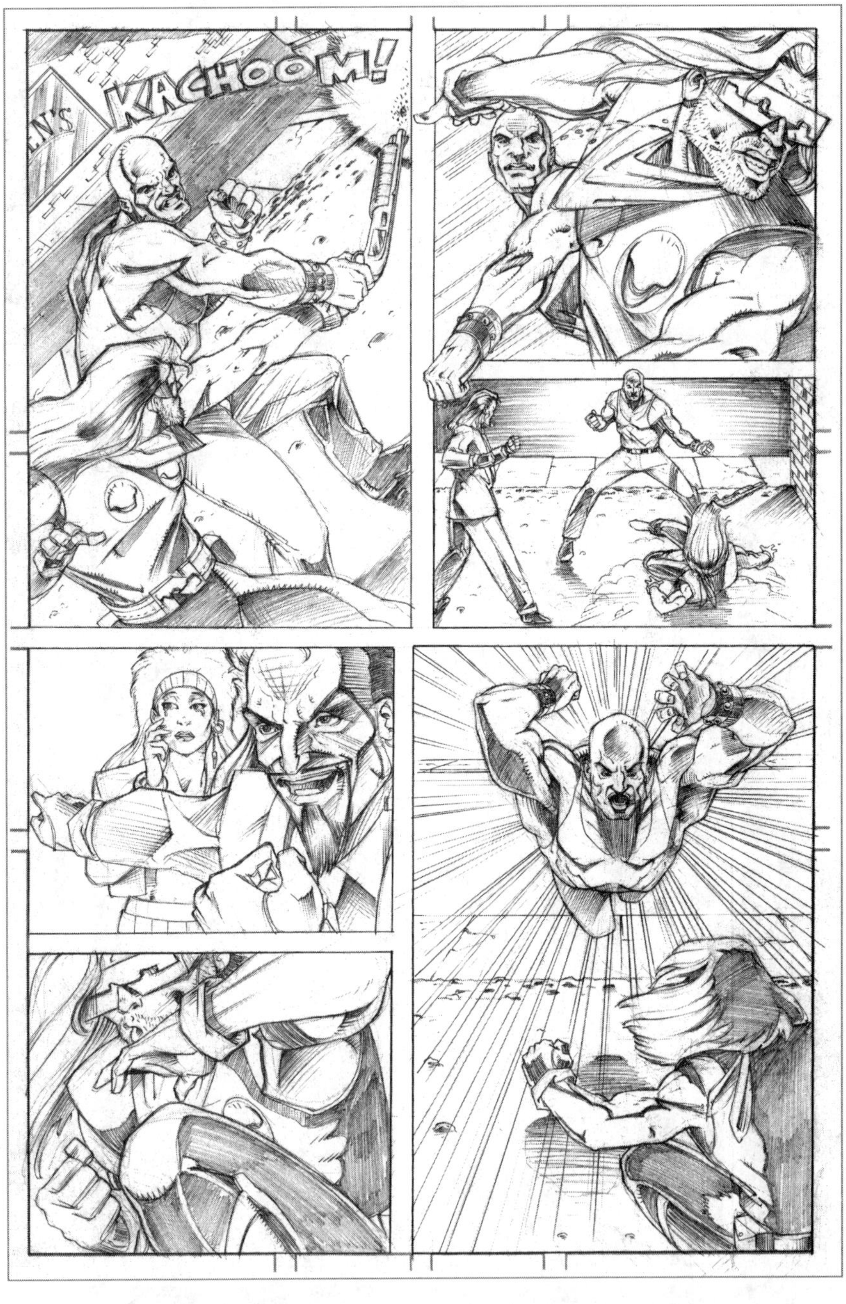
KACHOOM!

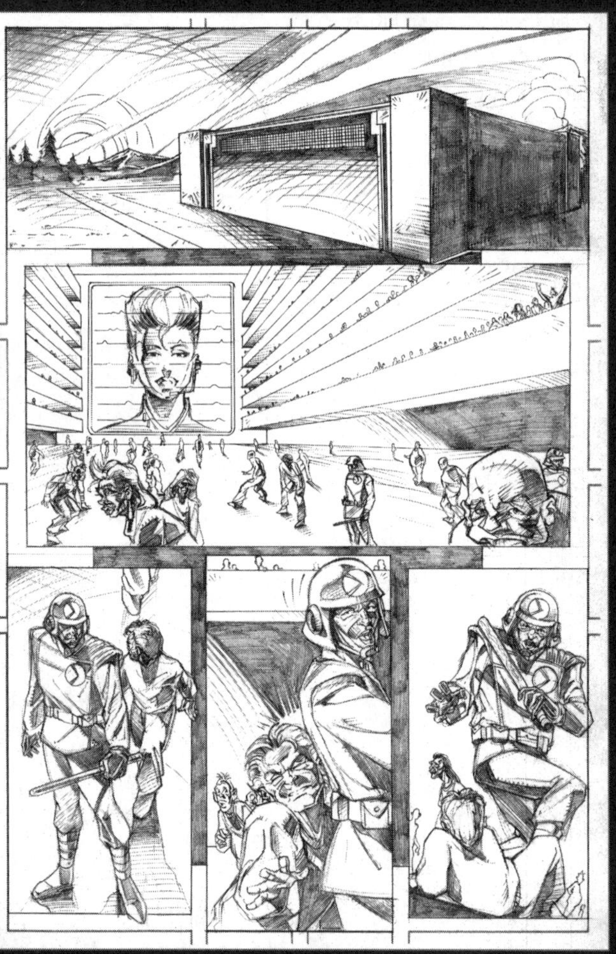

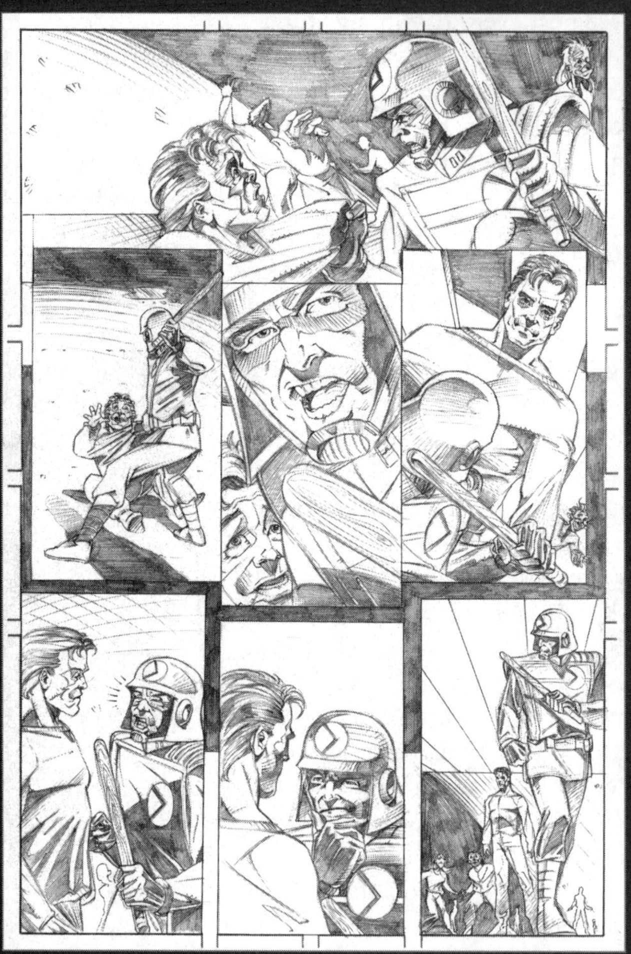

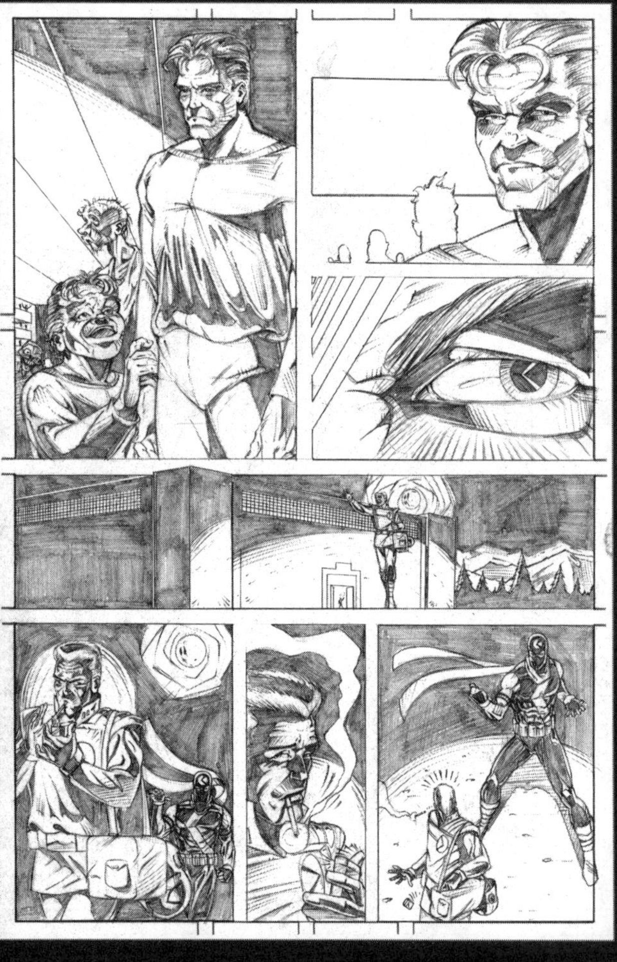

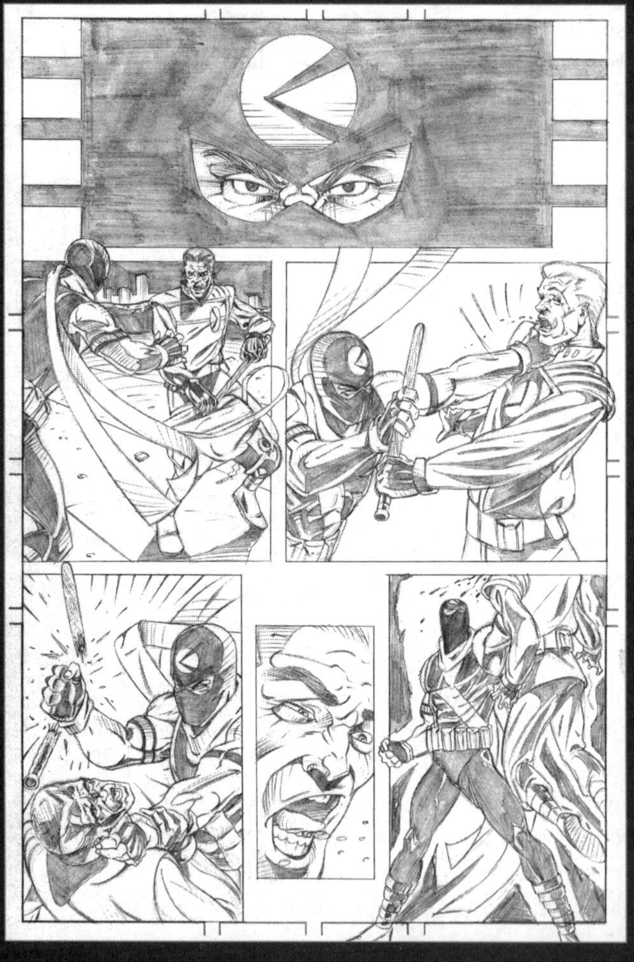

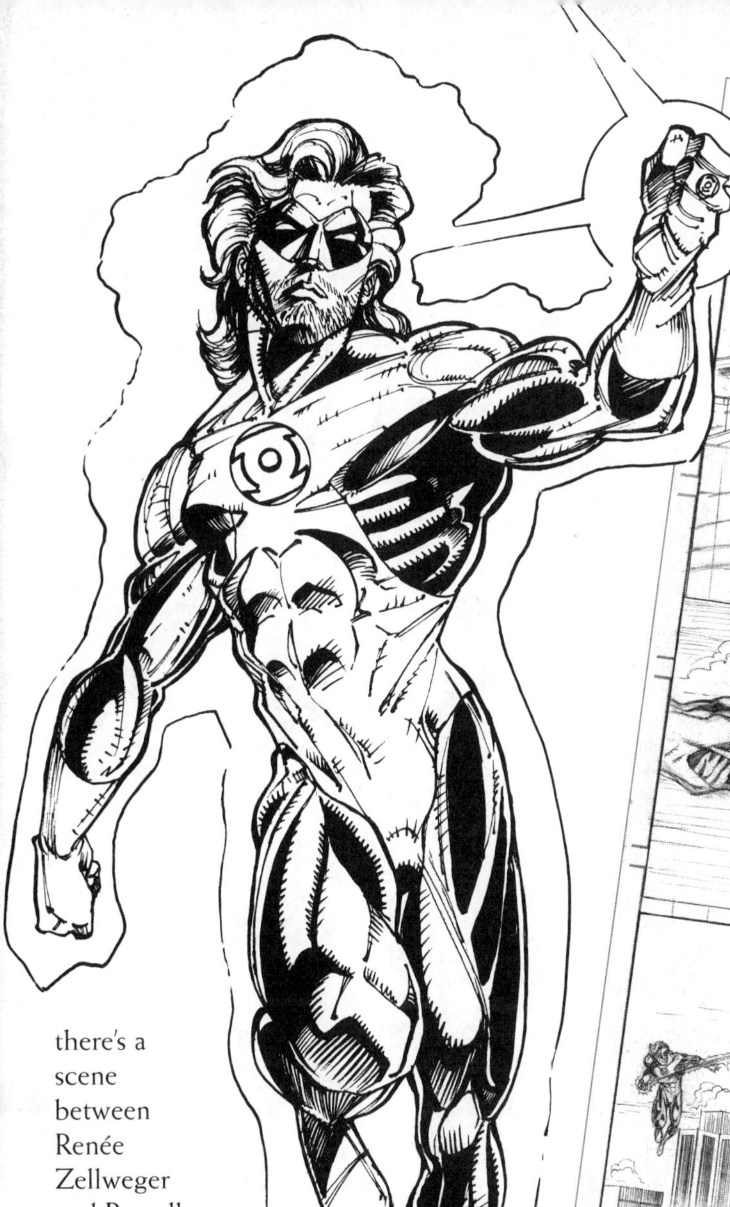

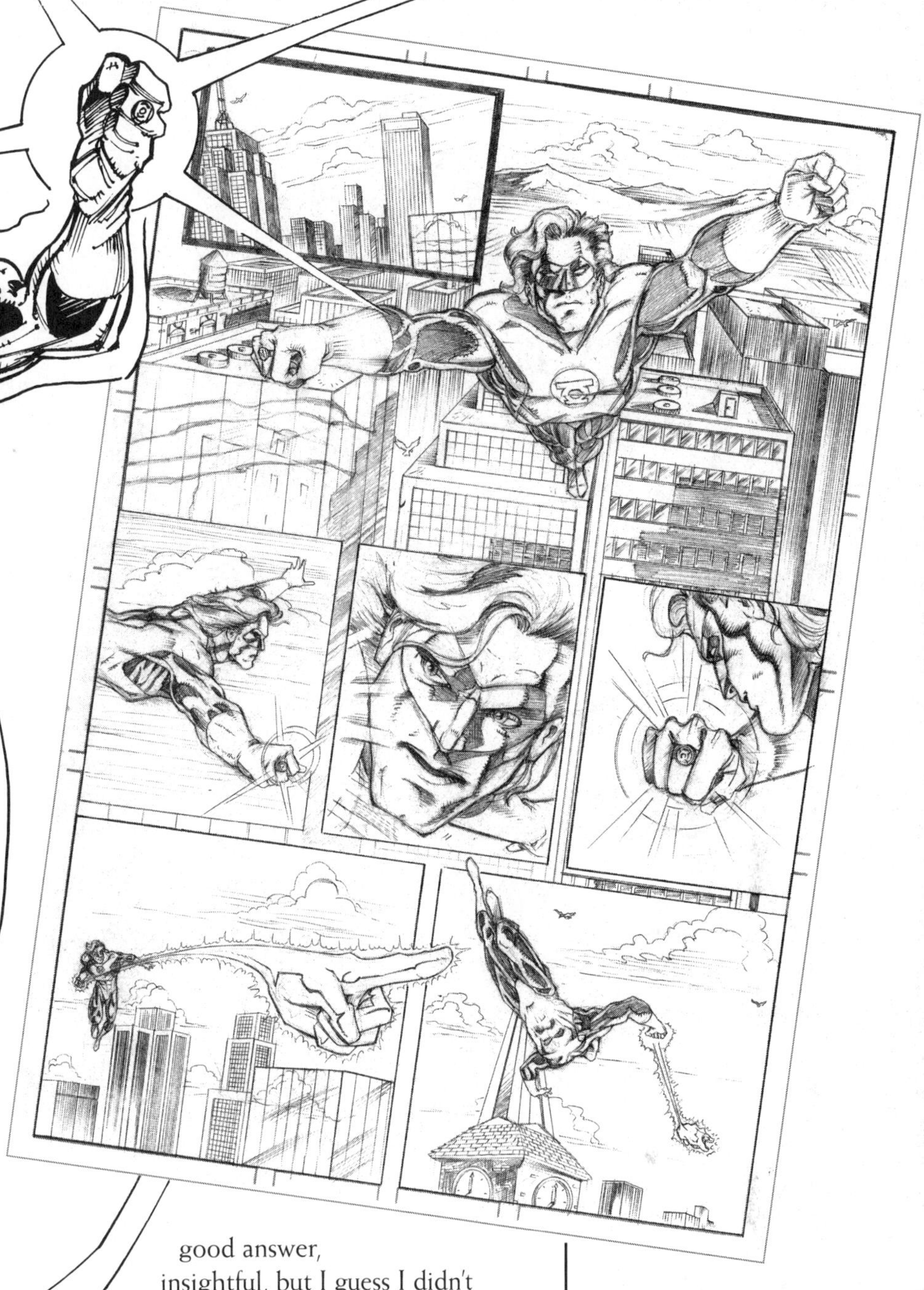

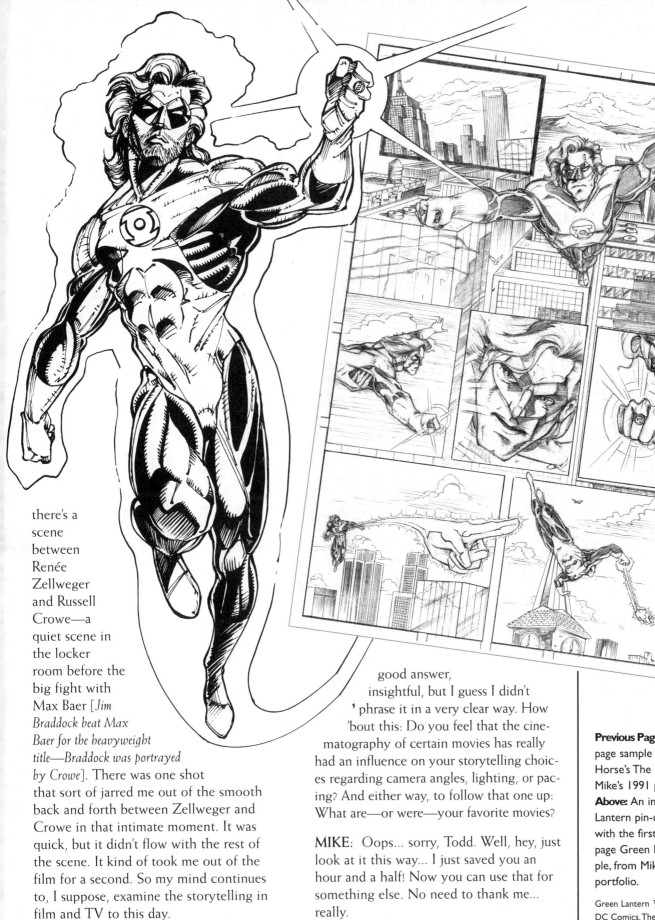

there's a scene between Renée Zellweger and Russell Crowe—a quiet scene in the locker room before the big fight with Max Baer [*Jim Braddock beat Max Baer for the heavyweight title—Braddock was portrayed by Crowe*]. There was one shot that sort of jarred me out of the smooth back and forth between Zellweger and Crowe in that intimate moment. It was quick, but it didn't flow with the rest of the scene. It kind of took me out of the film for a second. So my mind continues to, I suppose, examine the storytelling in film and TV to this day.

MM: Hey. Well, thanks for wrecking *Cinderella Man*. Hadn't seen it yet. Now I don't have to.... Nice. Anyway, that was a good answer, insightful, but I guess I didn't phrase it in a very clear way. How 'bout this: Do you feel that the cinematography of certain movies has really had an influence on your storytelling choices regarding camera angles, lighting, or pacing? And either way, to follow that one up: What are—or were—your favorite movies?

MIKE: Oops... sorry, Todd. Well, hey, just look at it this way... I just saved you an hour and a half! Now you can use that for something else. No need to thank me... really.

As for any specific movies having an influence on me storytelling-wise... I'd have to say that there's not one movie that stands out to my mind. So the short

Previous Page: A four-page sample of Dark Horse's The Mark, from Mike's 1991 portfolio. **Above:** An inked Green Lantern pin-up, along with the first of a three-page Green Lantern sample, from Mike's 1991 portfolio.

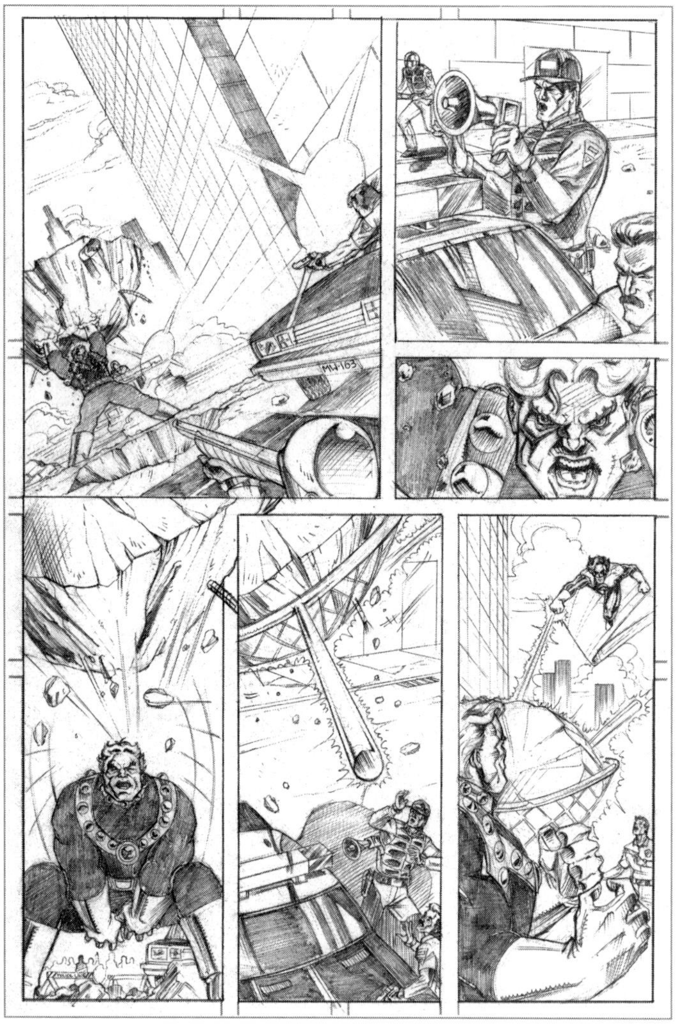

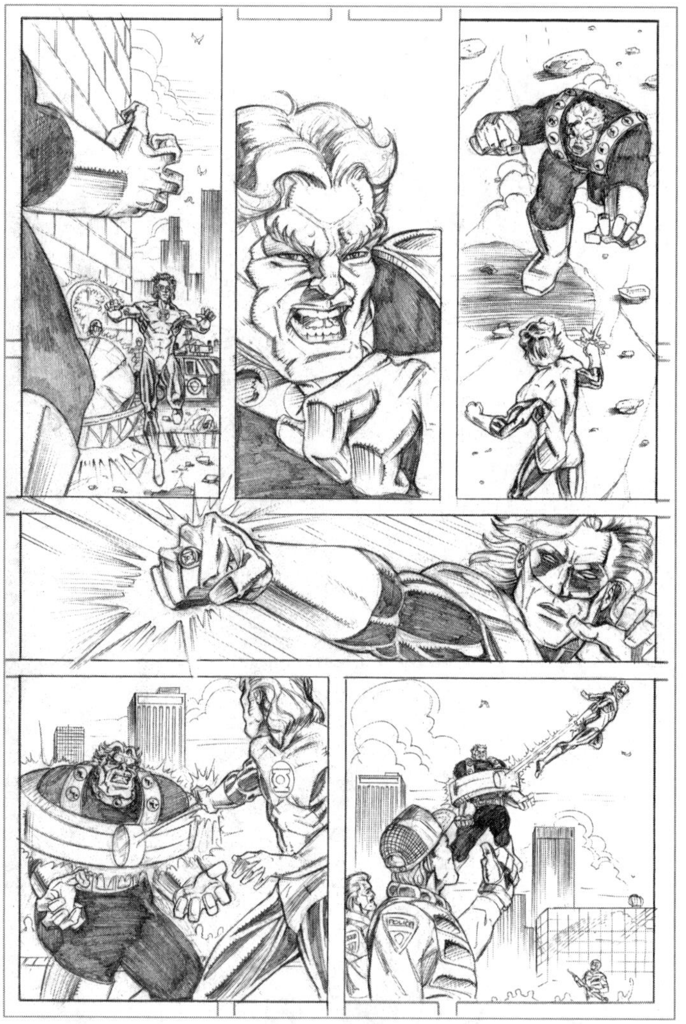

Above: The last two pages of Mike's 1991 Green Lantern sample. **Next Page:** A Wonder Man sample page and a Kent Shakespeare (of the Legion of Super-Heroes) pin-up. The moral here is that a good portfolio should, first and foremost, show off your storytelling skills—both in action scenes and in quieter scenes—and have a few pin-ups mixed in to show you can do that, as well.

answer is no. The longer answer would be that there might have been a cumulative effect on me from movies I saw as a kid—but I think that might be manifested in a more.... conservative sense of storytelling, I guess. Film storytelling has evolved over the years with the influx of some directors that come from the realm of music videos, and they've brought a very energetic, kinetic sense of storytelling that some people may like and others might not. I like the stretching of techniques that these folks have brought to film, but my roots are in the '70s and '80s... so I guess I'm more influenced by that era of storytelling.

As for favorite films—the funny thing is, when I look back at movies I adored as a kid *now*, they just don't hold up. A perfect example is the Ralph Bakshi film, *Wizards*. I was so obsessed with that movie back then that I couldn't get it out of my mind. It was a blend of fantasy and science-fiction done in animation that just blew my mind. But not too many years back, I rented a copy of it to watch out of nostalgia, and I just couldn't make it all the way through. I had to stop it out of boredom. Or maybe just disappointment. But y'know, things *always* seem more special as a childhood memory than they end up being to my adult mind. As far as more recent films go, some of my favorites are films like *The Fifth Element*, *Unforgiven*, *Heat*, *Kung Fu Hustle*, the *Kill Bill* films, *Aliens*, *Terminator 2*... there are a lot of more modern films... stuff done in the last 15-20 years that I'm really fond of. I've also got a lot of animation favorites, like *Iron Giant*, *Mulan*, *The Emperor's New Groove*, *Lilo and Stitch*, *Giant Robo*, *The Incredibles*, *The Road to El Dorado*... and a bunch of other stuff.

MM: Yeah, you gave me some *Giant Robo* for Christmas one year and have gotten me hooked on some other titles as well over the years. You mentioned *Astro Boy* and *Speed Racer* earlier—which I think we all watched as kids, and none of us admit to watching *Kimba*—when did you become aware of anime and what about it has made you such a big fan?

MIKE: I think I was a little kid. I could tell that there was something different about the animation in *Astro Boy* and *Speed Racer*, but I didn't really make any kind of connection or personal diagnosis that it was Japanese. I was just too young to see that, I think. So ultimately, for years afterward, Japanese animation sort of fell below my radar. When I began to *really* become aware of anime was my freshman year in college. I met some guys who were *huge* anime fans and had a little club going. I can't even remember how I met them, but I remember a bunch of them came over to my apartment at Treehouse. If I remember correctly, at least one of them was a Waldron brother. The Waldron twins are a couple of guys who used to do "American Manga"... and I think they got pretty big in it for a while. Maybe they were both there...

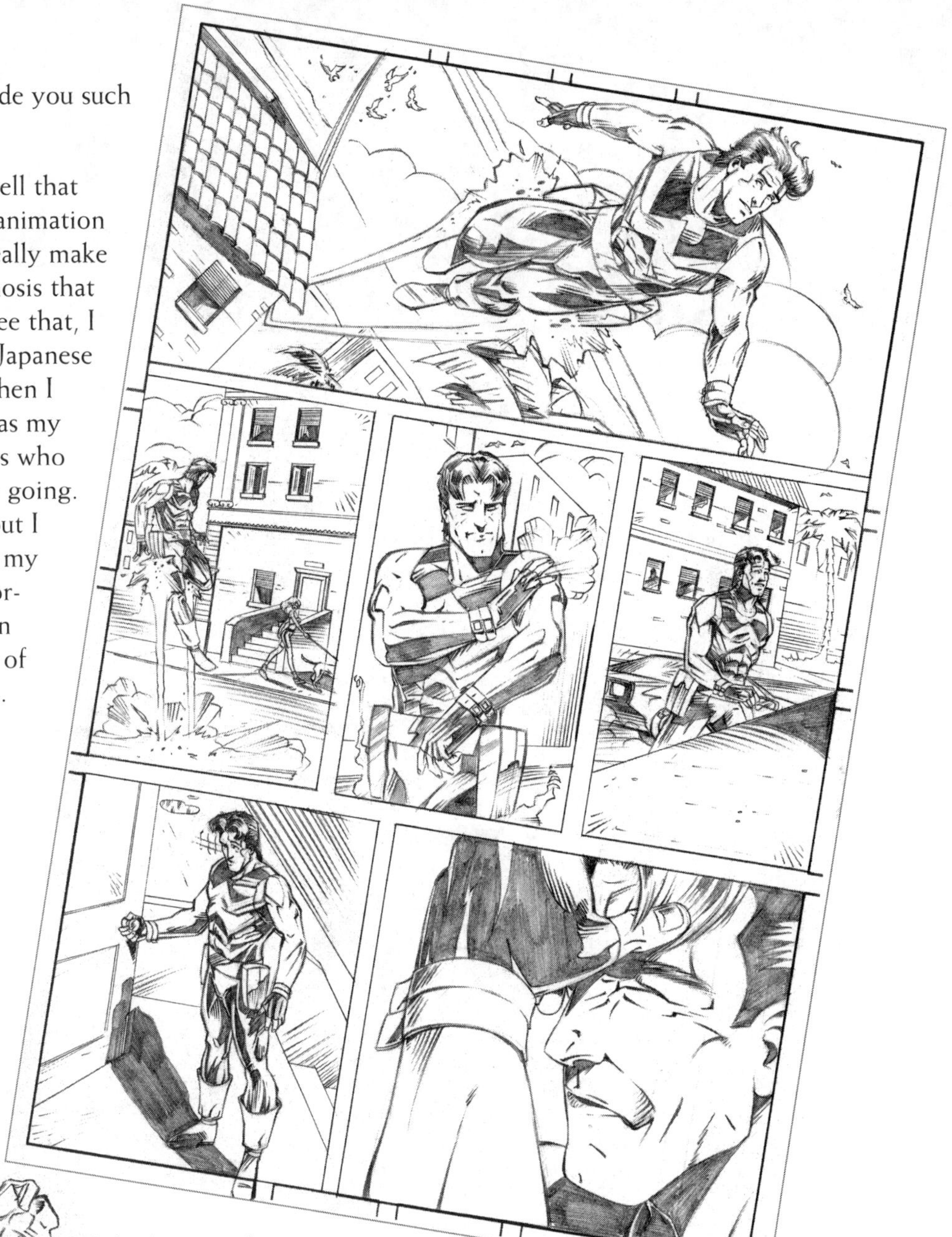

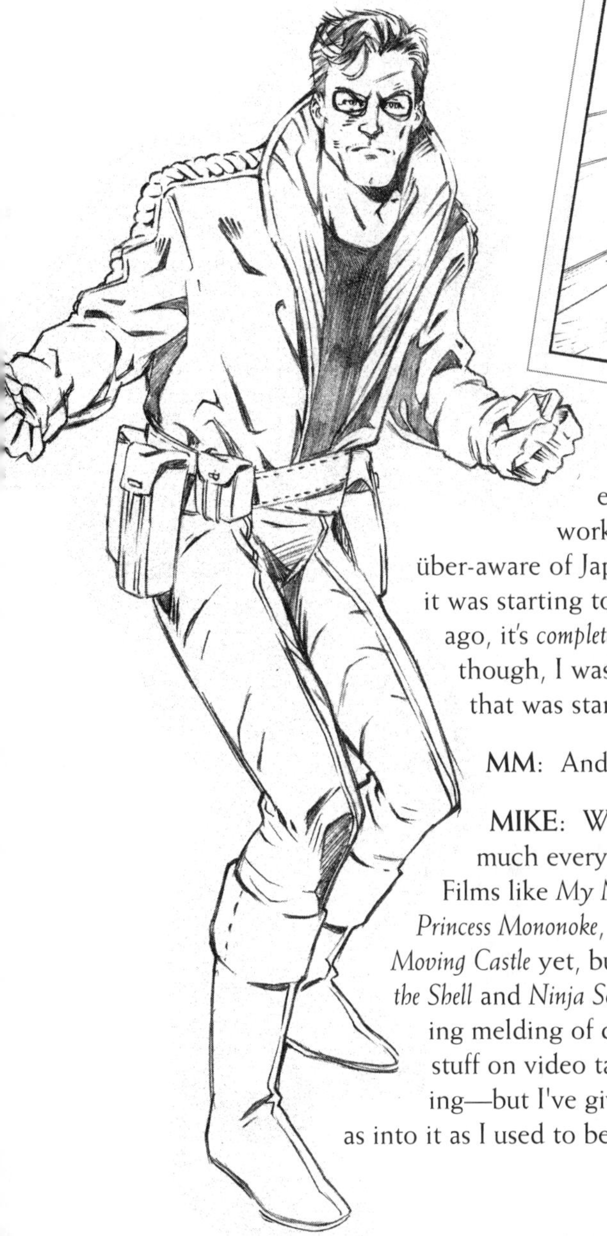

I don't remember exactly. I don't know if they're still working now or not. But that was the first time I became über-aware of Japanese animation and how cool it could be—and just how prevalent it was starting to become in the U.S. Of course, since that time some 17 years or so ago, it's *completely* blown up and is a huge force in our culture now. Back then, though, I was starting to catch some of the *Macross* stuff and some other anime that was starting to become popular here.

MM: And what are some of your favorite titles?

MIKE: Well, beyond the aforementioned *Giant Robo*... I'm a nut for pretty much everything Hayao Miyazaki has done that I've been exposeu to, at least. Films like *My Neighbor Totoro*, *Kiki's Delivery Service*, *Nausicaä and the Valley of the Wind*, *Princess Mononoke*, and *Spirited Away* are absolute favorites of mine. I haven't seen *Howl's Moving Castle* yet, but I'm anxious to. I'm also a huge fan of anime like *Akira* and *Ghost in the Shell* and *Ninja Scroll*. Very recently, I picked up a new *Appleseed* DVD that is an amazing melding of computer and traditional looking animation. I used to have tons of stuff on video tape that I'd buy and watch—anything that looked remotely interesting—but I've given most of that away and haven't replaced it on DVD. I'm not quite as into it as I used to be. But the stuff like the Miyazaki films, I really cherish.

Part 3: The Speed of Success

MM: So let's finally get into your art and how you broke into comics. So... hey, Mike—how'd you break into comics?

MIKE: Man, it's about time... jeez.

After I graduated from VCU, my folks were very generous and gave me enough spending money to get me through the summer of 1991 that would allow me to devote 100% of my time during those months to work on samples that I could then show to try to get work in the comics industry. I had heard of the huge Comic-Con show in San Diego, and I knew that it was the biggest comic book-related show in the country. I also knew that every comic book company, large and small, had a presence at the show—and that included many, many editors. So I knew that San Diego would be the best place to go to get my samples in front of the most number of editors—and to be able to allow them to place a face with those samples. I figured that meeting these folks face-to-face would be much more effective than just sending samples through the mail. So I worked up some samples, and then booked a flight and hotel room in time to attend the show that year of 1991. It was a good trip, and I got a lot of favorable responses to my initial samples. This allowed me to then build the initial relationship with those editors that might show some interest in my work that would allow me to then follow up with more samples through the mail—or FedEx, which is what I used, really—to show them that my work was progressing and getting better.

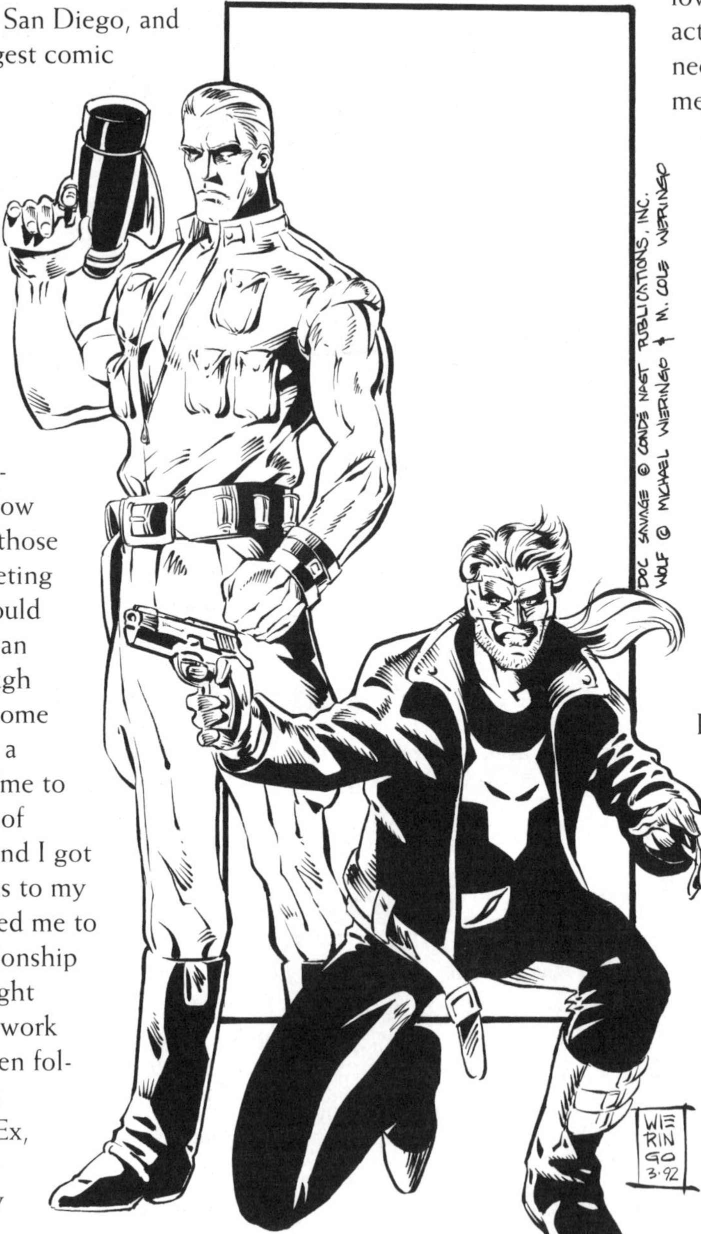

DOC SAVAGE © CONDÉ NAST PUBLICATIONS, INC.
WOLF © MICHAEL WIERINGO + M. COLE WIERINGO
WIERINGO 3·92

Of all the people that I met during this initial visit, the most encouraging—and the most willing to follow up and continue contact after the show—was a fellow named Neal Pozner, who was then the New Talent Director for DC Comics. He was the guy who was charged with looking for new artists—people that showed promise—that he could hopefully help to develop into people that DC could ultimately give pro assignments to. Neal, rather than just respond to my follow-up samples via mail, would actually call me and discuss what I needed to work on, and to give me progress reports about his showing my work around the offices to try to get interest from the editors there in my work. It was very encouraging to actually *hear* from someone in Neal's position. It really kept me going, kept me driven to work up more samples, knowing that there was someone who was an advocate for new talent actually in the offices showing my stuff around. It took a while, but ultimately, having Neal shoving my stuff under the noses of these editors is what finally got me noticed and offered work at DC. I owe a lot to Neal in that regard. Sadly, he's since passed on.

MM: Yeah, I'd heard that Neal was a great guy and very supportive. He was instrumental in helping a lot of new talent at that time hone their work so that editors would want to use them. How did Neal guide you? What were the tips and suggestions that he would give?

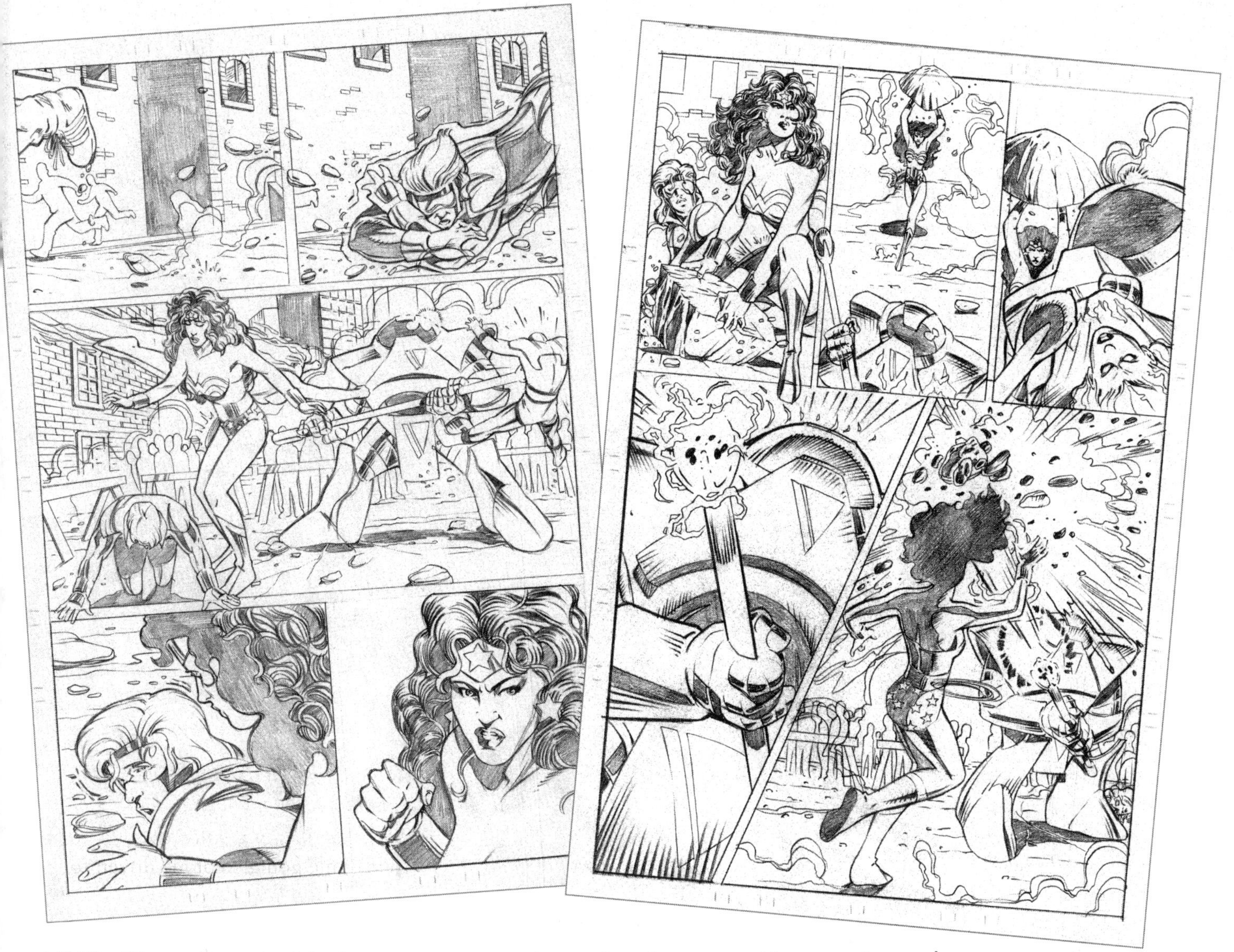

MIKE: Y'know, honestly, I don't remember any of the specific details of the guidance he gave me. I do remember that he was impressed with the quality of my storytelling ability in my sample pages. But beyond that, there was actually a lot of work I needed on everything else. I got my start in the industry at a time when, I think, the "bigs" were more willing to allow someone time to learn and grow on-the-job. In the early '90s, there were still several anthology comics being published by DC—I'm not sure about Marvel—that would be a part of the line of DC's more popular lines of books. This was a place that allowed DC to try out new talent without throwing them into the deep end of the pool right off the bat. This way, they could gauge a prospect's talent and ability to meet a deadline sort of off to the side while still giving them actual paying work. So Neal's efforts to keep putting my samples in front of editors, even at a very early, rough and raw period for me as far as being ready for professional work, resulted in Brian Augustyn and Ruben Diaz giving me a shot at a couple of short stories in a book called *Justice League Quarterly*.

MM: Did he feel that you had any strengths or weaknesses? Did *you* feel that you had any strengths or weaknesses?

MIKE: I think he felt that my weaknesses were in pretty much every realm. And *I* felt that same way. As far as strengths at that time, I suppose there was the storytelling that I mentioned before—and probably the sort of natural quality I brought to my character work. I can remember most editors—Neal included—telling me that my characters didn't seem posed or forced... that they had a natural feel to them beyond the more cartoony aspect of their rendering. I suppose that came from all those years of getting life-model drawing practice in.

Previous Page: Wolf meets the Man of Bronze. Around the time Mike and his brother Matt were developing Wolf, Mike got the gig to draw a *Doc Savage* mini-series.
Above: A two-page JLA sample from Mike's 1991 portfolio. A few months later and Mike was penciling back-up stories for *Justice League Quarterly*.

MM: What were your samples of? Did you include both storytelling and pin-up samples in your portfolio?

MIKE: I'm pretty sure they were just storytelling samples. I had been told many times that editors weren't all that interested in seeing the fact that an artist could do cool, dynamic pin-ups or covers, but were instead much more interested in seeing that the artist could tell a story effectively—as well as be able to draw well. So I kept my samples pretty clear of pin-ups, I think. If I had any, they would have been placed in my portfolio behind the storytelling stuff. As for what the actual samples consisted of, I remember doing samples using Green Lantern, and another set using Nomad, as well as a set featuring the Wonder Man character. I also did some samples featuring The Mark, a Dark Horse character. I was trying to do something that would show each of the major companies how I would handle their characters.

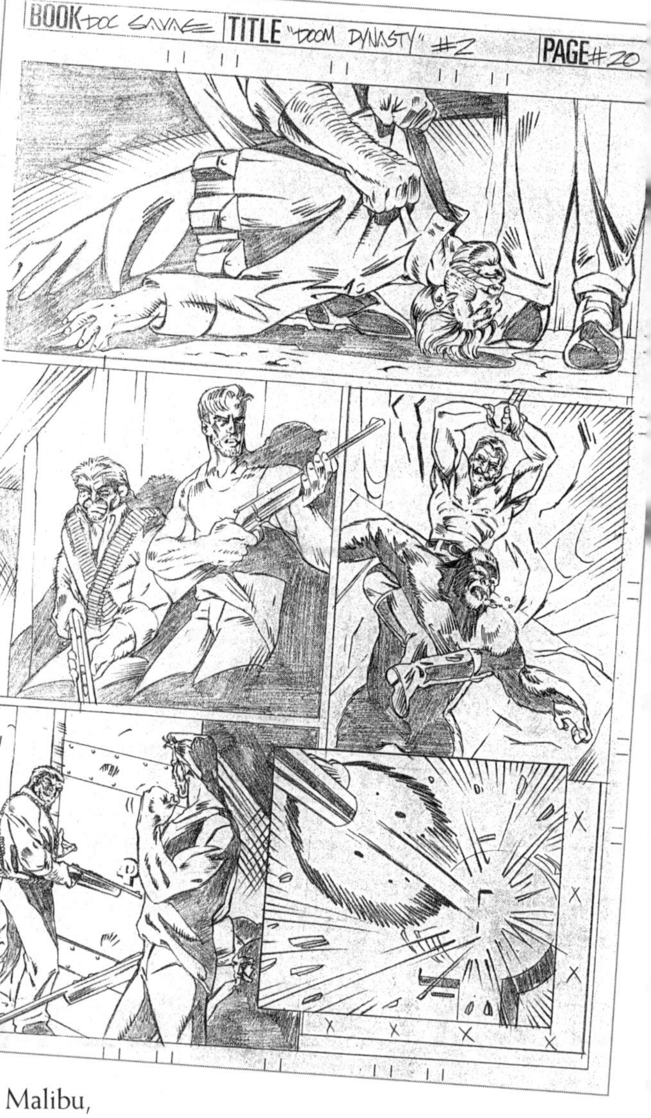

BOOK DOC SAVAGE
TITLE "DOOM DYNASTY" #2
PAGE#20

MM: And so was that, the *Justice League Quarterly*, your first professional gig?

MIKE: Actually, no. My very first professional gig was for a small company called Millennium Publications. They were based in Florida, and run by a guy named Mark Ellis. Millennium had the rights to *The Wild, Wild West* and Doc Savage. They had seen a lot of success with publishing comics based on those properties... this was back when comics were still selling huge numbers, and there were a lot of new smaller publishers like Millennium, Now, and Innovation, as well as the others that were more established already like Comico, Malibu, and the like. Mark Ellis had a good relationship with the guys at Gaijin Studios, and I had established a relationship with them, as well, in my travels to various shows in the quest to show my samples around to as many folks as possible. I would often show my work to artists just as often, if not *more* often than editors, in the hopes of getting some good advice on what I needed to work on. The Gaijin guys ended up being a wonderful, very encouraging group, and I've become great friends with many of them in the years since. They saw promise in my work, I suppose, so when Mark Ellis asked them about recommendations for the penciling gig on Millennium's second *Doc Savage* mini-series, they recommended me.

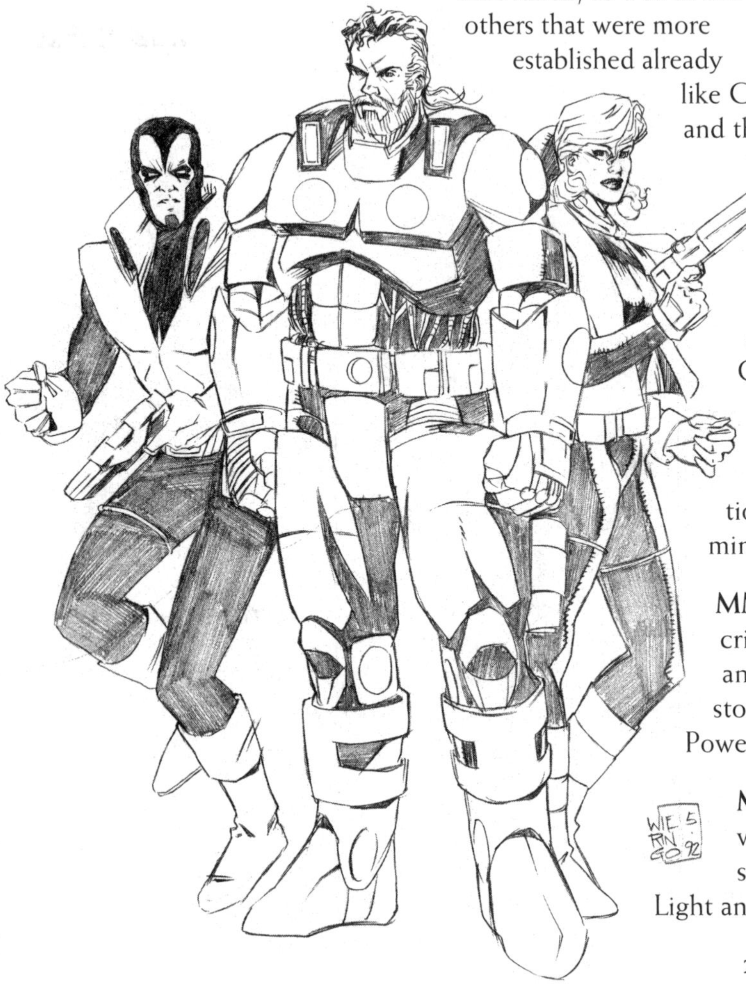

MM: I've seen that book and have heard you say that you cringe when you see it now. So first there was *Doc Savage*, and then the *Justice League Quarterly*—#11, right? That was a story with all the girls: Wonder Woman, Ice, Crimson Fox, Power Girl. Were you nervous?

MIKE: There were two of them that I worked on, and they were both featuring female members of the JLA. The first story I drew was a *Thelma and Louise*-style story featuring Dr. Light and Ice driving across the desert in a convertible. The second was a story featuring all the women of the League having a slumber party. Was I nervous...? You bet I was. I felt completely out of my depth. It was an otherworldly feeling to be working on these DC characters that I had read so much of as a fan—and now here I was actually drawing a story featuring these characters that DC was going to publish. I didn't feel like I was ready for these kinds of assignments, but that was, as I said, the atmosphere at DC during that time in that they were willing to allow an artist to essentially learn on the job. It was a frightening, but special and exciting time.

MM: I know that on both the writing side and the art side there is this initial grace period where a writer or an artist needs to learn a lot of things they think they already know. There are a lot of hidden rules and tricks that, as a fan, we go, "Yeah, I know how to draw—or write—a comic..." but when the time comes and you actually sit down to do it.... Did you find a lot of that going in—

discovering limits to how detailed you could get or shortcuts for storytelling?

MIKE: My work's never been particularly detailed, so I've always worked in a sort of "shorthand" style. So deciding how much detail to leave in or out wasn't the learning curve that I experienced. My particular curve involved the basics of drawing, really. I had a pretty good foundation as far as storytelling—and even anatomy and the ability to draw facial expressions. What I experienced was—and still is, honestly—the wide-open world of shot selection, speaking in terms of how to lay out the page. Doing the layouts for each page has always, from the very beginning, been my Achilles' heel. When sitting down to lay out a page, my imagination literally swims with all the myriad permutations for the entire page, and within that page, each panel. I have a constant struggle with trying to create the most dynamic, yet clear, easy to read page that I can.

Previous Page Top: Pencils from *Doc Savage: Doom Dynasty* #2.
Previous Page Bottom: Mike met and developed friendships with many artists while making the rounds at conventions. Along with the gang from Gaijin Studios, he became friends with Chris Sprouse, who at the time was working on *Hammerlocke* for DC.
Below: Pencils for pages 13 and 15 of *Flash* #83.

Flash, Hammerlocke ™ and ©2006 DC Comics. Doc Savage ™ and ©2006 Conde Nast Publications, Inc.

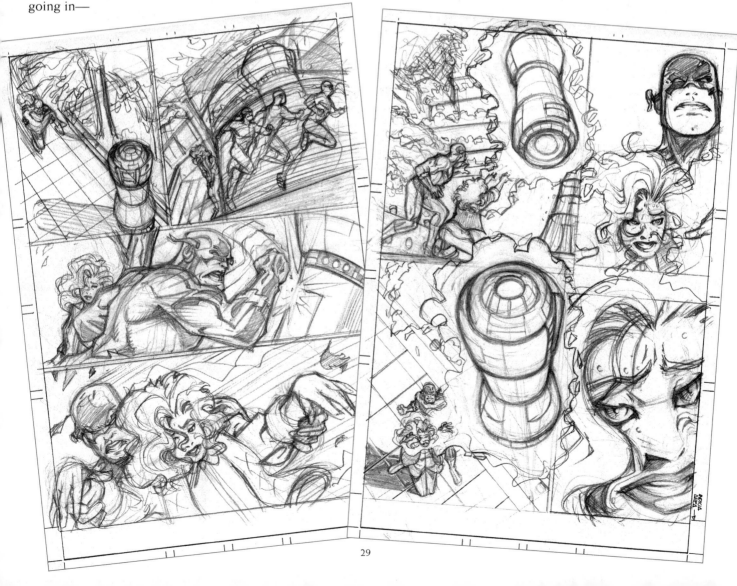

Right: From Flash to Wally in four quick steps.
Below: The splash page from Mike's debut in *Flash* #80.
Next Page: Flash doing Flash-y things. Layout sketches for Flash trading cards.

Flash ™ and ©2006 DC Comics.

That has always been the battle I have with myself every day and on every page. Unfortunately, I haven't gotten more comfortable with it over the years—even after 13 years of working professionally. I'm a bit more confident and comfortable with finding short-cuts for anatomy, facial structure and I think my backgrounds and props have also improved, so there are things that I've been able to come to grips with as far as the details of working a page.

MM: So, it was those two *Justice League Quarterly* jobs and then... is that when you were tapped for *The Flash*? Was there anything in-between?

MIKE: To answer that, I'll have to go back a bit in the time line. Once I'd spent the summer of 1991 post-graduation working up samples and traveling to as many conventions around the country as I could afford to attend to show my work around, the money my parents gave me ran out and I had to go back to work at a "real job." I'd been working in the grocery business, like I said earlier, up until I went to college. And even when I would come home for the summer and holidays, I'd go back and work at my old store. They were always happy to take me back, because as I said, I was a hard worker. So once the money was used up, I got back into working at the grocery store, and working on new samples, and the *Doc Savage* mini-series when that came along, as well. And I was *still* working there when Brian Augustyn and Ruben Diaz contacted me about the *Justice League Quarterly* stories. I would work on pages at night and on weekends... and the DC folks knew this, so they gave me some pretty lax deadlines on the JLQ shorts. Once I'd finished those,

SHOT FOR COLOR ☐   SHOT FOR CODE ☐   DC COMICS STANDARD FORMAT (ONLY)   PROOFREAD ☐
TITLE: FLASH | ISSUE/MONTH | STORY PAGE 2

Instructions for Two Page Spread:
Butt paper at EDGES, TAPE ON BACK. *DO NOT OVERLAP AT CENTER!* Each half should measure 10⅝" wide, Full Spread = 21¼" wide.

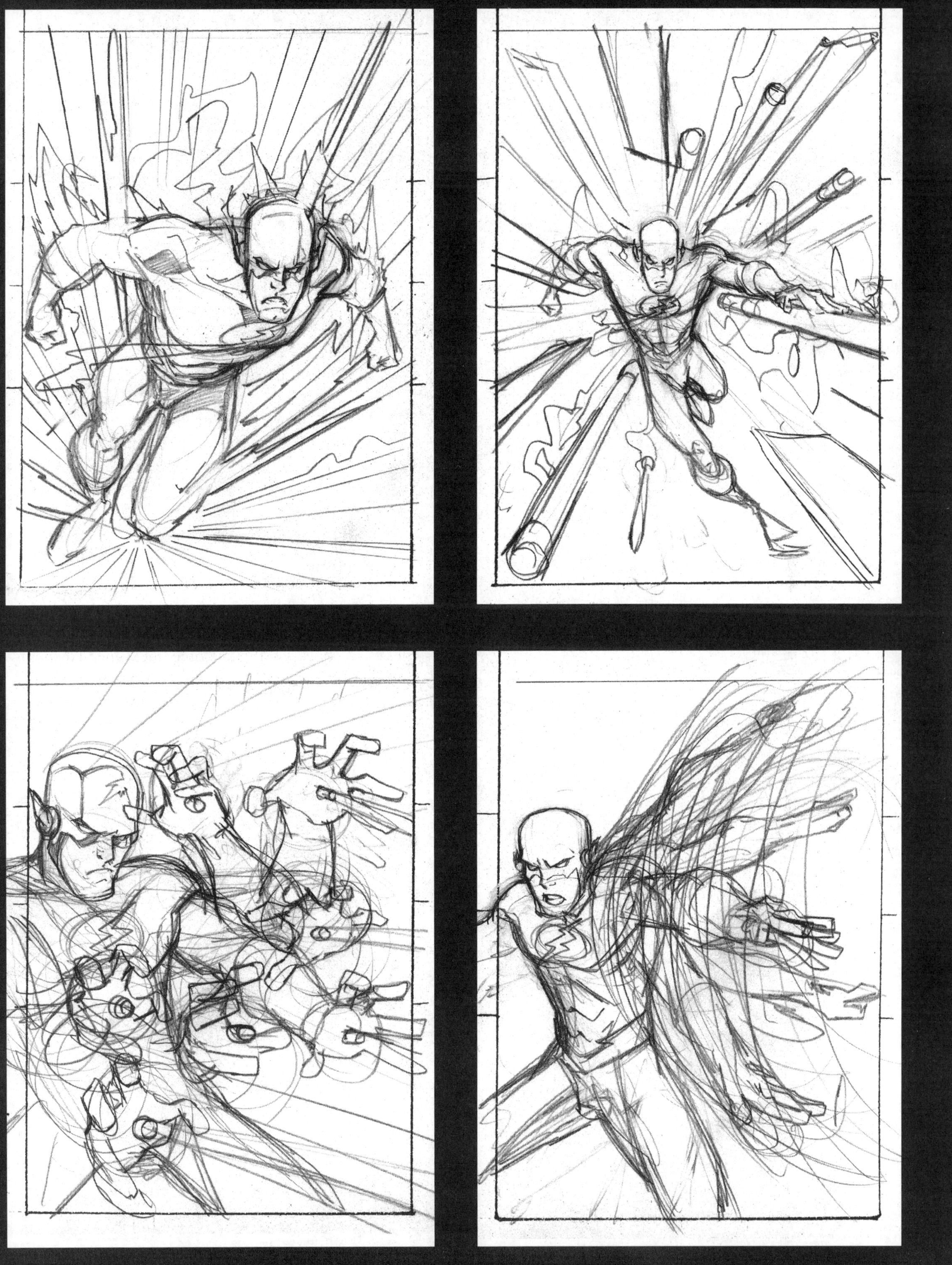

and they seemed to like them very much, Brian told me that there might be an opening on the *Flash* title, and he asked me to work up a couple of pages of "Flash-related" stuff. It didn't necessarily have to be storytelling, but instead, just a bunch of vignettes showing Flash doing Flash-y things... and the supporting cast and Wally in his civilian clothes, just to show them how I'd handle all that stuff in the book if I were to work on it. Once I had done that and sent the pages in—I remember like it was yesterday getting a phone call from Brian. He knew that I'd been working at the store all during our budding working relationship, and so when he called me about *Flash*, he said, "Now... if I offer you *Flash* on a monthly basis, will you be willing to quit your job at the store...?" My answer, was of course, a huge "*Yes!*"

MM: So that's a pretty nice step, from a couple of try-outs and right onto *The Flash*! Were you intimidated?

MIKE: I think "intimidated" would be an understatement. I was terrified... petrified. Y'know that old saying that goes, "Be careful for what you wish for—you just might get it"? Well, I'd been dreaming about getting a gig drawing the monthly adventures of a major comic book icon since I was around eleven years old, and here I was having that dream come true. As it turned out, the dream was much more hectic, difficult, time-consuming, and frustrating than I ever thought it would be. The monthly deadline was entirely intimidating and from the get-go; it felt crushing to me. I feel like I've been living under the gun ever since. The stress associated with a monthly comic book deadline is very high.

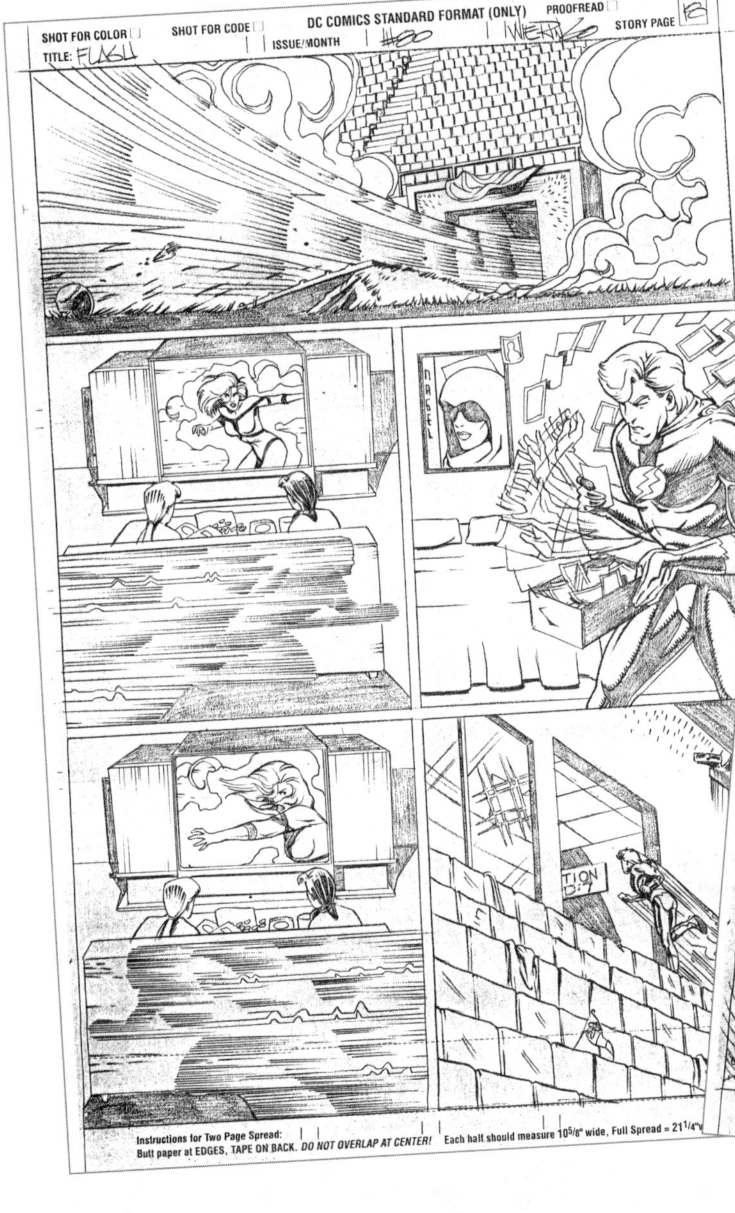
SHOT FOR COLOR
SHOT FOR CODE
DC COMICS STANDARD FORMAT (ONLY)
PROOFREAD
STORY PAGE
ISSUE/MONTH
Instructions for Two Page Spread:
Butt paper at EDGES, TAPE ON BACK. DO NOT OVERLAP AT CENTER!

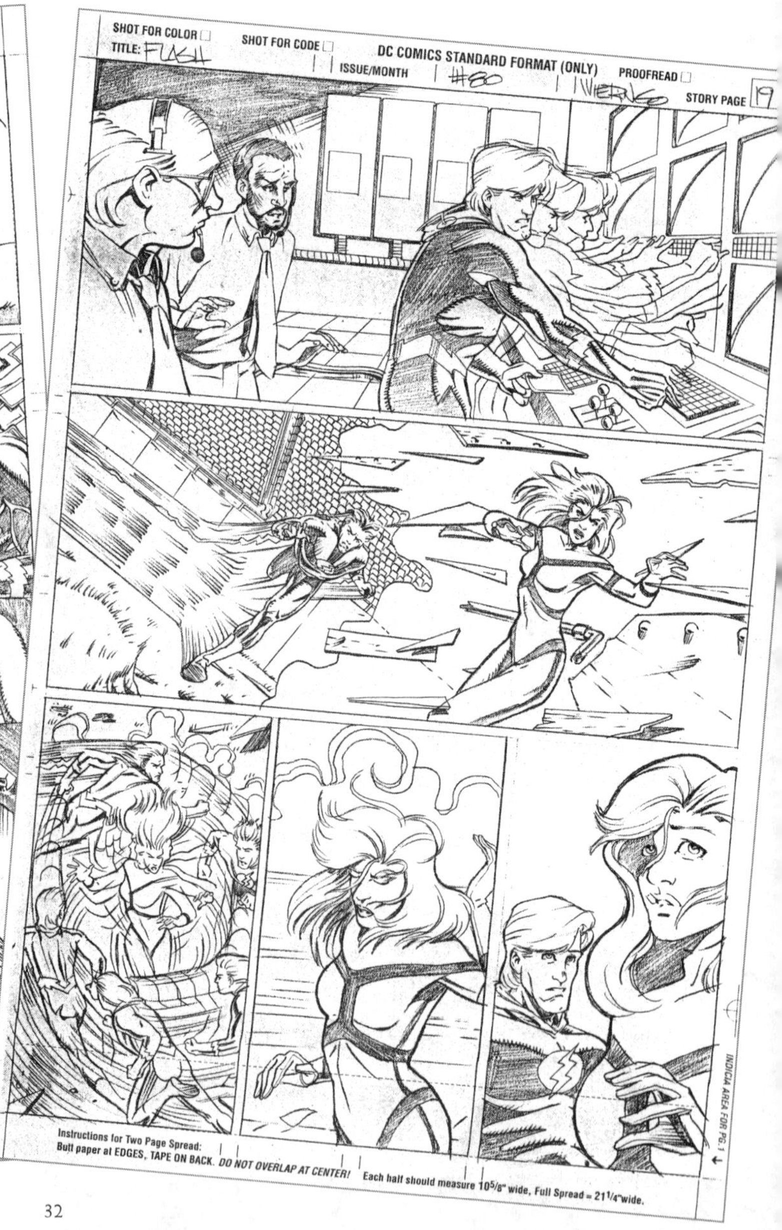
SHOT FOR COLOR
SHOT FOR CODE
DC COMICS STANDARD FORMAT (ONLY)
PROOFREAD
STORY PAGE
ISSUE/MONTH
Instructions for Two Page Spread:
Butt paper at EDGES, TAPE ON BACK. DO NOT OVERLAP AT CENTER!
INDICIA AREA FOR PG. 1

Below: Flash has to do some quick thinking to put a stop to an ex-girlfriend's super-powered rampage. More pencils from *Flash* # 80.
Next Page: Layouts for *Flash* #85, page 21, and *Flash* #86, page 13. The second panel of the latter was basically the same as the first, only with a "Flash blur" in the background, so it wasn't necessary to fill in.

MM: So now you were on a regular book, with a schedule. And Mark Waid was writing it. How was your relationship with him? Did you talk much?

MIKE: I have to give a lot of thanks to Mark Waid. I think that Mark was very indulgent with me—very patient. *Everyone* in the *Flash* editorial office and creative team was very patient and nurturing to me. I really wasn't ready for a monthly assignment at the time Brian and Ruben offered me *Flash*. I was so very raw, but I suppose they were willing to let me grow on the job. I don't think that's the case in comics anymore. I think everyone who breaks into the "bigs" has to be fully formed and at the top of their game. I don't think, with the market the way it is now, that there's room for letting someone grow on the job the way there was back in the early '90s.

As for my early relationship with Mark, he was always very encouraging, as—like I said—all the *Flash* team was. Mark has always, as long as I've known him, been a real "booster" of mine; he's always made me feel like a part of the team when we work together, and he did that right from the beginning of our working relationship on *Flash*. It was funny, though, especially now to think back on it with a bit of distance, how our first conversation went after I had turned in the first part of my first issue of *Flash* pencils. Brian called me when he got them to confirm that they'd arrived and to give me feedback on the work, and Mark happened to be visiting the offices. Brian put me on the phone with Mark, and though he was very kind and, as I said, encouraging, I could tell there was an underlying hesitance... like he was very unsure about whether I'd actually make it on the book. Hell, I wasn't sure as to whether I'd make it *myself*. I felt completely overwhelmed, but I give credit to Brian, Ruben, and Mark for helping me through that rough beginning. And as my work improved issue by issue, Mark was very excited and really pumped me up with his encouragement and kind words. When I started turning in work on my third issue, Mark called me to tell me how much of a big leap in quality he thought I'd made, and how much he really liked what he was seeing. He's a good guy—as well as being one hell of a writer—and we've kept in contact and stayed friends over the years, whether we happen to be working on something together or not.

MM: So, aside from the frantic schedule of cutting your teeth on a monthly book, were there any other moments that stand out, either in the development of your style or just the goings-on of newfound celebrity?

MIKE: I can't really think of anything during that period that stands out, other than the rather odd feeling of finding myself in the world of being a comic book artist as I'd always been fantasizing about from early in my childhood. There was, of course, a lot more involved in the business than I had thought of when I was younger. I had not only a responsibility to the editorial staff of the book, but also to the rest of the creative team to keep work moving through

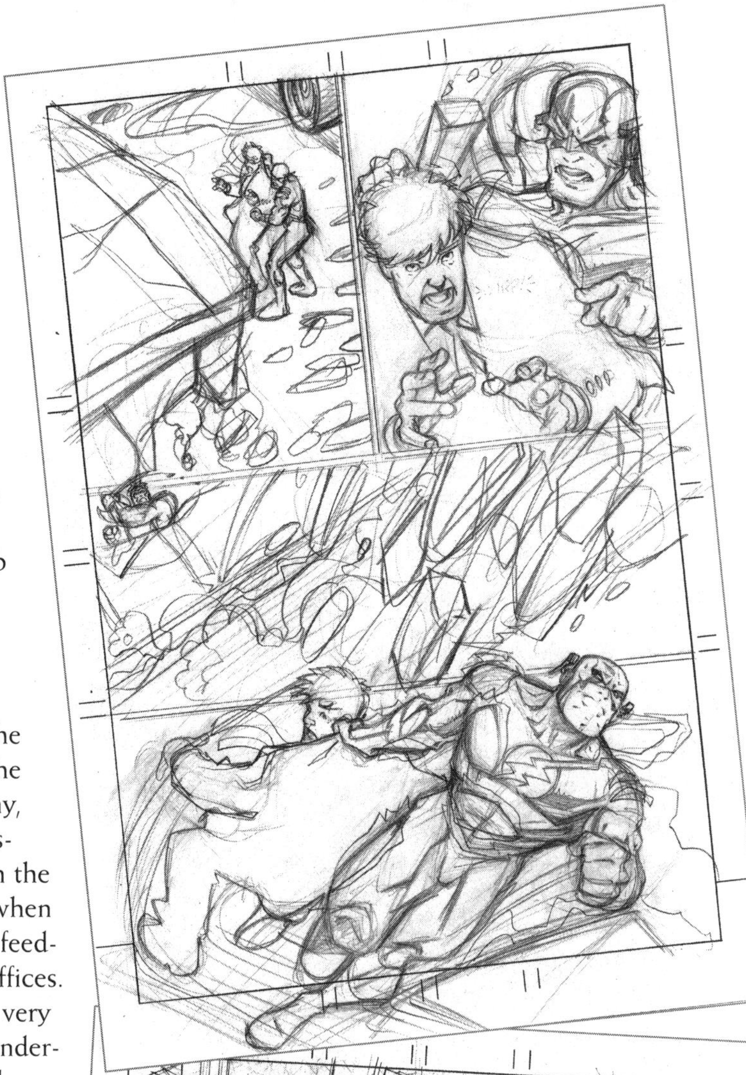

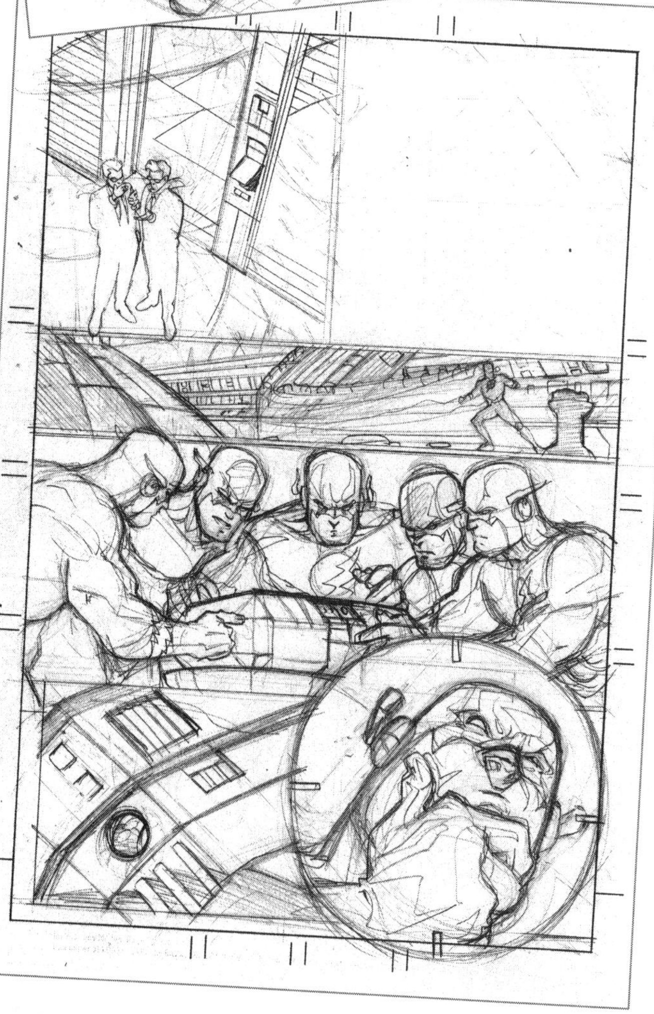

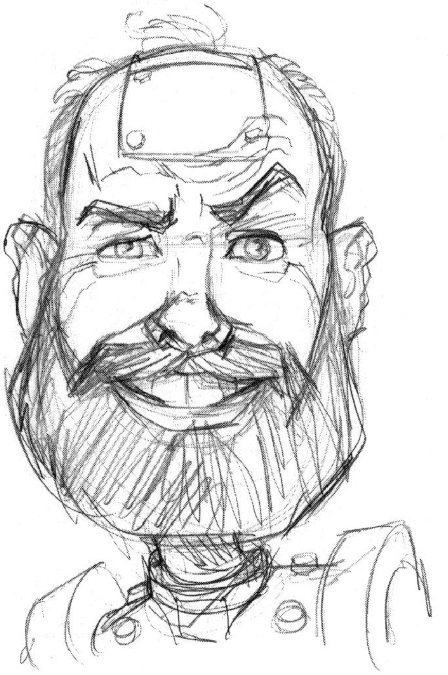

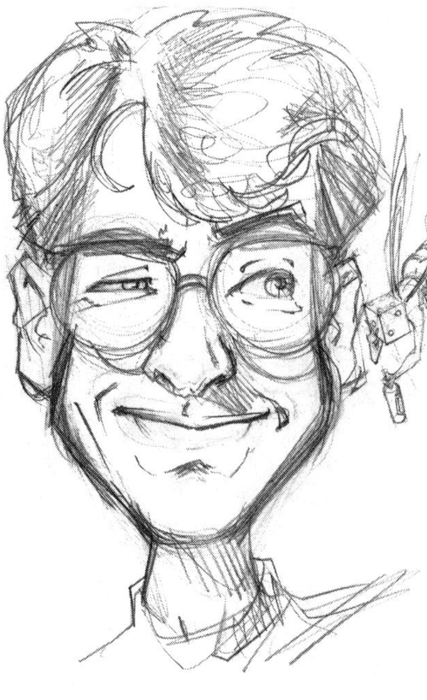

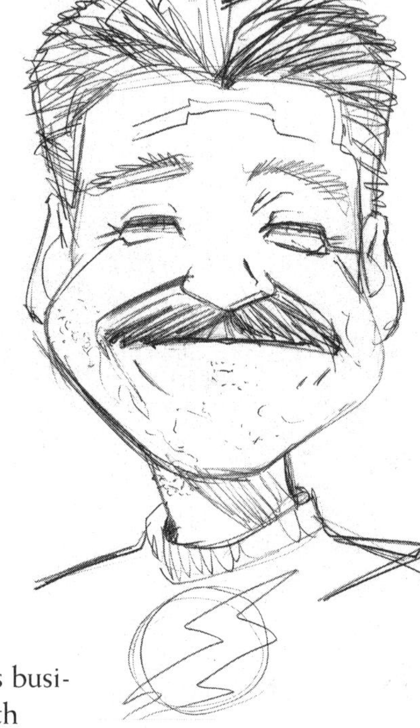

the pipeline so that others could do their jobs and get paid. Everything about this business was very daunting starting out. I was also dealing with moving down to North Carolina to join a studio full of other comic book creators. I had been invited by Chuck Wojtkiewicz and Richard Case to join them and several others in forming a new studio. I thought the idea of working with a bunch of other creative types under one roof—as well as moving out of my parents' house—was a great idea. So I took them up on it, and we formed Artamus Studios. I moved down in 1993 when I was at the half-way point of my third issue of *Flash*. And at that point, I was so new in the business I don't think there *was* much by way of newfound celebrity. I can't really remember if my first issue of *Flash* had even shipped at that point... and this was well before the Internet and online fandom became what it has... so I didn't really have much feedback from anyone beyond my editors and Mark.

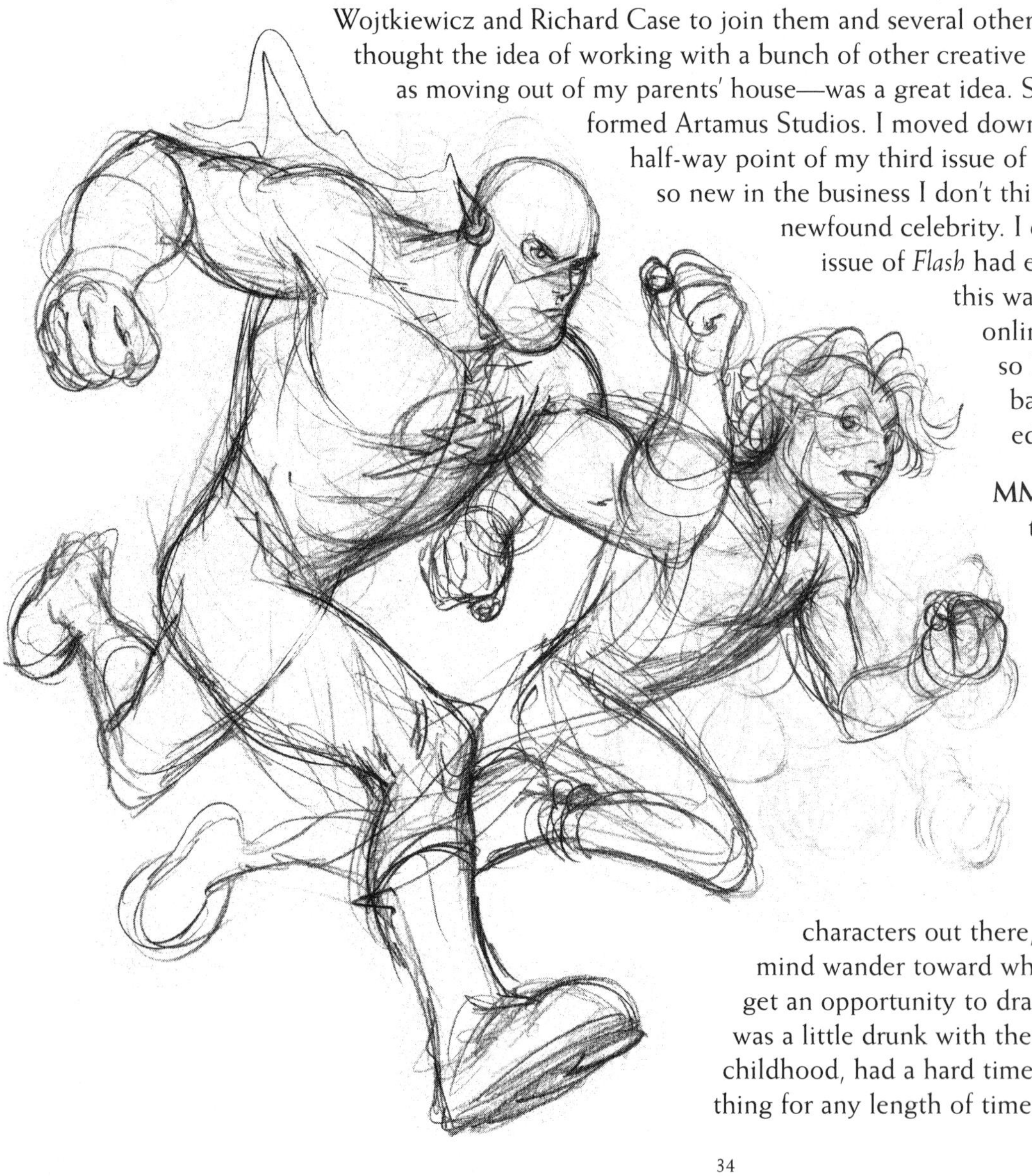

MM: You were on the book for twelve issues, doing some now-classic stories and along the way creating one of my favorite comic book characters of all time: Impulse! What made you leave *The Flash*? How did that go?

MIKE: I left because at that point, I was like a kid in a candy store. I saw all the possibilities of all the different characters out there, and I couldn't help but let my mind wander toward what it might be like to actually get an opportunity to draw all those characters. I guess I was a little drunk with the possibilities. I had also, from childhood, had a hard time holding my attention onto one thing for any length of time. I was always looking toward

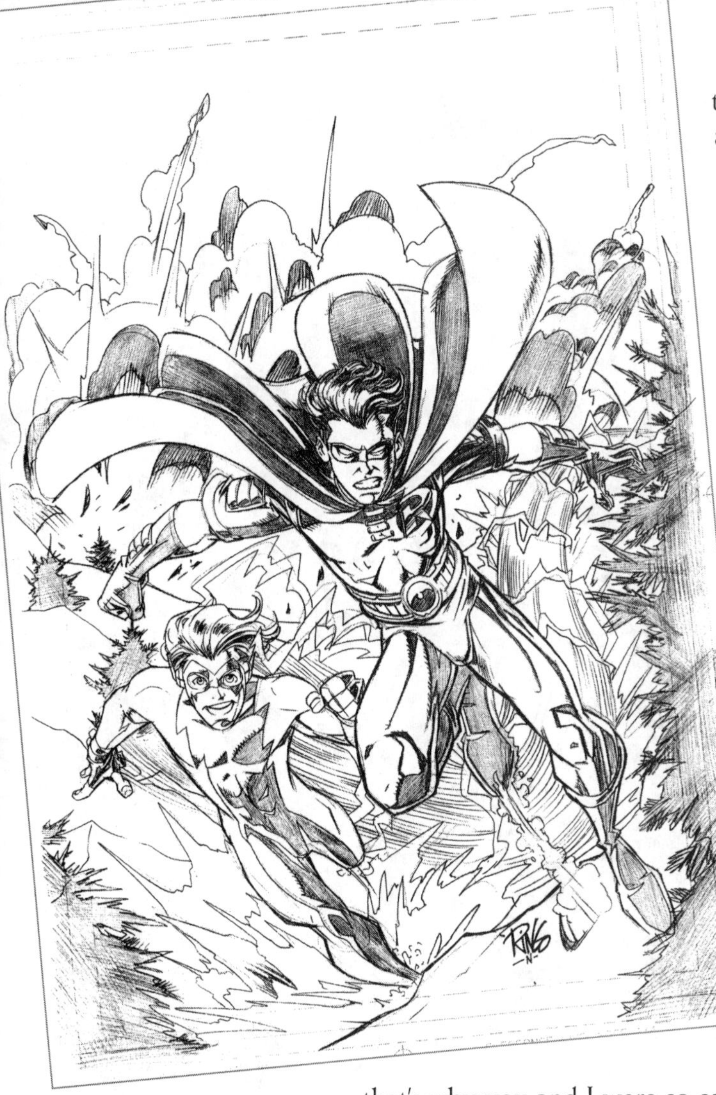

that next shiny thing that might attract my attention. In fact, early on, Mark Waid would call me "The Magpie," because every time we spoke, I would be excited about something different that I'd like to draw, when he, I'm sure, would have preferred that I just concentrate on my *Flash* duties. I had a twelve-issue continuity contract from DC on *Flash*, and when the contract was up, I decided to move on. The folks at DC were very encouraging, and I remember having this wonderful conversation with Brian Augustyn at a big show in Philadelphia near the end of my twelve issues where Brian laid out all the possibilities for me at DC. It seemed very exciting and wide open.

Previous Page Top: Mike's caricatures of some of the Artamus gang—Chuck Wojtkiewicz, Richard Case, and himself.
Previous Page Bottom: During Mike's tenure on *Flash*, he created the look for Impulse.
Left: Cover pencils for *Robin Plus* #1, featuring Impulse.
Below: Layout for a Robin trading card.

MM: Oh, you *are* easily distracted! I think that's why you and I were so eager to make our *Sensational Spider-Man* run into more of a *Marvel Team-Up* and why *Tellos* consists of such shifting landscapes and many colorful characters. Do you think that your "grass is always greener"/Attention Deficit Disorder has gotten you in trouble during the course of your career?

MIKE: Well, I've made it a point to follow through with the projects I take on. Early on, I had that "grass is greener" attitude, but I still tried to do at least a significant number of issues of whatever project I took on. My idea of "significant" is probably different from that of other folks, but I think it was the type of stories that would make me move on rather than an itch to draw something new once I committed to a series. For instance, I left *Robin* after drawing nine issues, but I stayed on the book as cover artist long after that. I have always had a great affinity for Robin... it was just the more urban level of the stories in the book that didn't grab me. At that time, I was really wanting to draw some big, heavy super-hero punch-out action, and *Robin* was very grounded. I think that if the type of stories interest me, I'm more than happy to stay on a book for a longer period of time. My run on *Fantastic Four* with Mark Waid, I think, shows that. I was loving Mark's stories—and I think I would have stayed on the

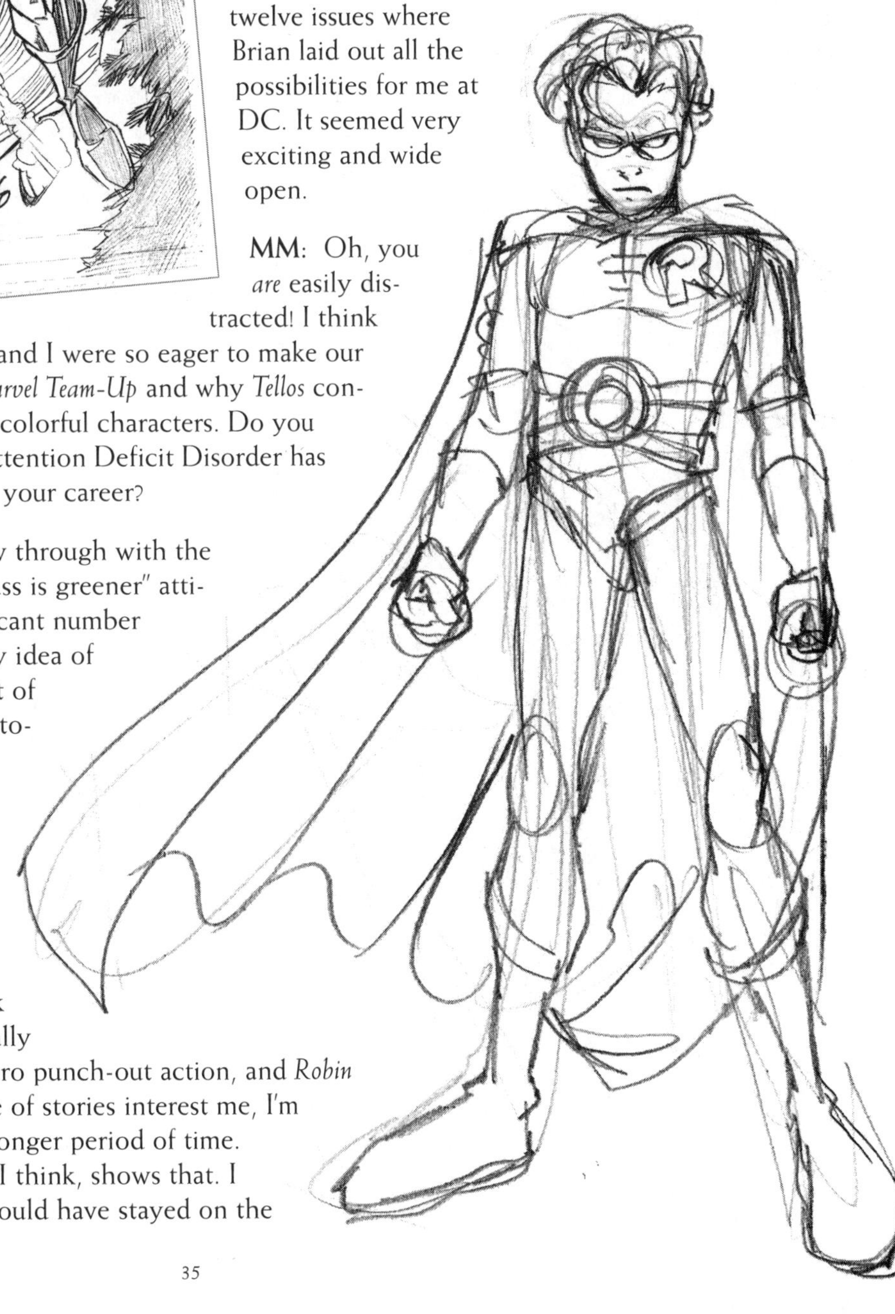

Right: Robin takes on some run-of-the-mill bad guys in *Robin* #19. Inks by Stan Woch.
Below: Preliminary Rogue sketches.
Next Page: Cover art for *Rogue* #1. Inks by Terry Austin.

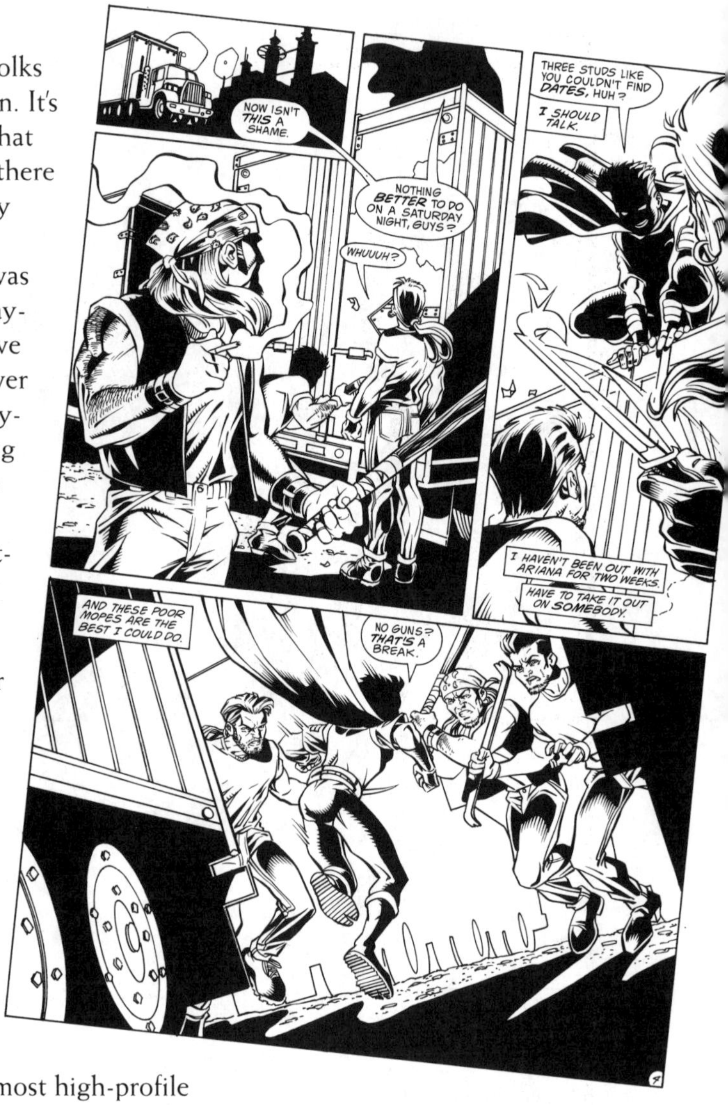
NOW ISN'T THIS A SHAME.
NOTHING BETTER TO DO ON A SATURDAY NIGHT, GUYS?
WHUUUH?
THREE STUDS LIKE YOU COULDN'T FIND DATES, HUH?
I SHOULD TALK.
I HAVEN'T BEEN OUT WITH ARIANA FOR TWO WEEKS.
HAVE TO TAKE IT OUT ON SOMEBODY.
AND THESE POOR MOPES ARE THE BEST I COULD DO.
NO GUNS? THAT'S A BREAK.

book for a while longer had the folks at Marvel not asked us to move on. It's true that I was getting a little of that itch to draw something new, but there was a comfort level and familiarity with the *FF* characters combined with the great stories that Mark was writing that made me feel that staying on for another year would have been just fine. I don't think I've ever really gotten into trouble with anyone over my penchant for jumping around on projects. I think comic book editors are pretty understanding as long as you're straight-up with them about your reasons and motivations for moving on.

MM: From *Flash* you shifted over to Marvel for the *Rogue* mini-series. Was that a fun project?

MIKE: I'll say that I was initially very, *very* excited to be asked to draw the *Rogue* mini-series. I had been a long-time X-Men nut, and it was a thrill and an honor to be asked to draw a mini-series that featured one of the most high-profile of those characters. That excitement and enthusiasm helped to carry me through the completion of the project, but as an overall experience, I would have to say no, the project wasn't fun. My thinking at the time was that if there was going to be a mini of a character—something set apart and supposedly special—that the story should be special and have impact. The *Rogue* mini was not very... special, let me say. At the end of the day, I didn't really see the need or the purpose for it. It could have easily have been used as a sub-plot in one of the ongoing X-Men books, but I didn't think it was something that deserved its own mini. Don't get me wrong, however—by working on the *Rogue* mini, my profile increased greatly... and the royalties were great. So from a career and financial standpoint, it was a good thing. As a story, though, it was pretty lacking. The writer even called me to apologize for his work on the book... so that was the atmosphere.

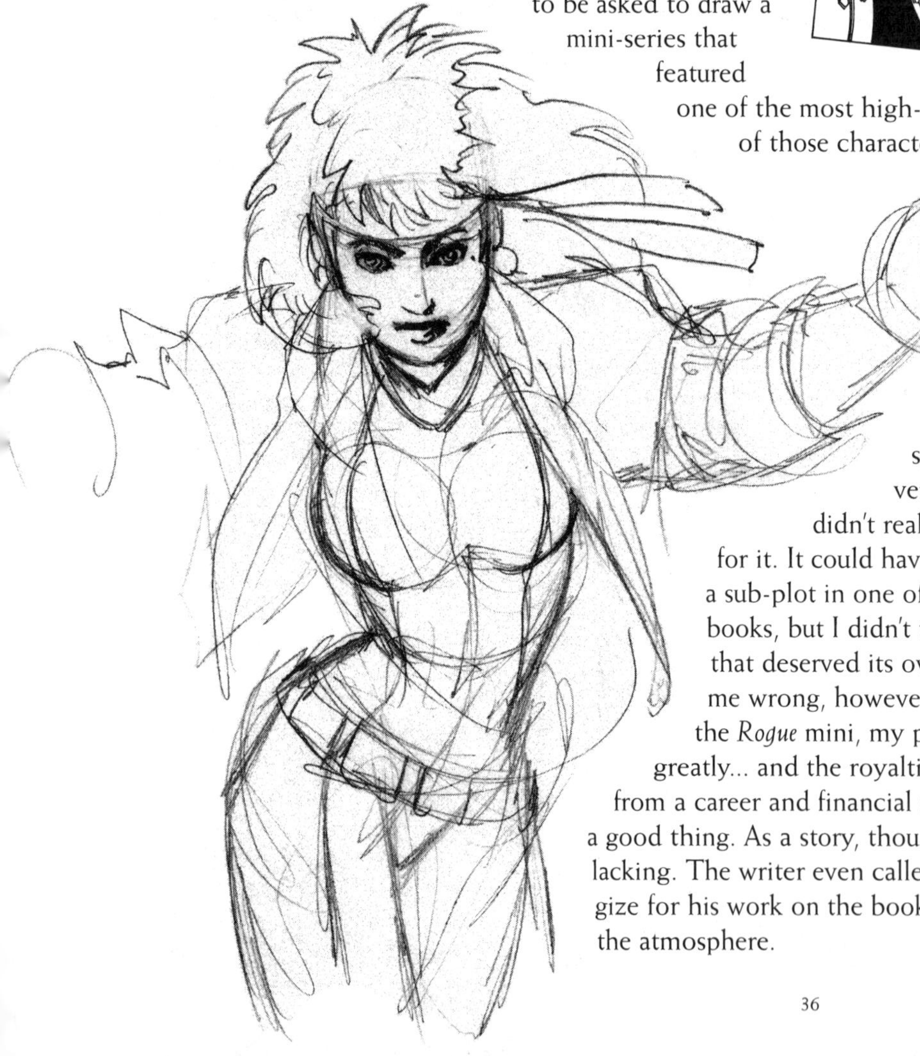

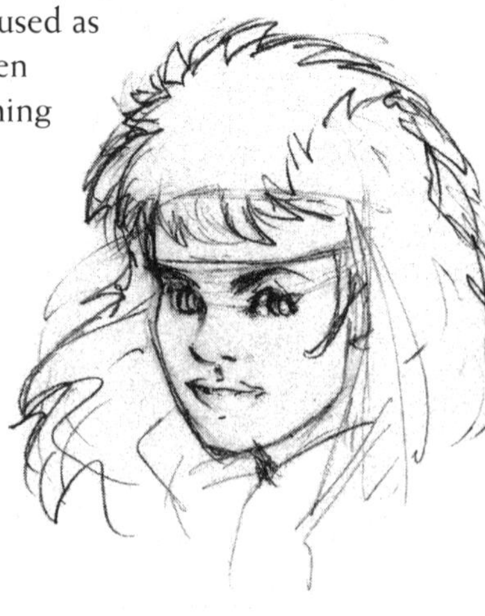

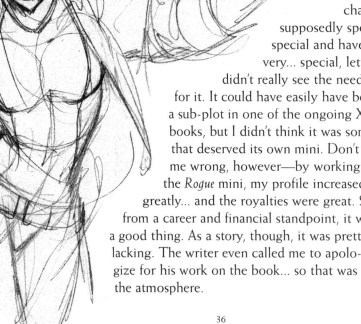

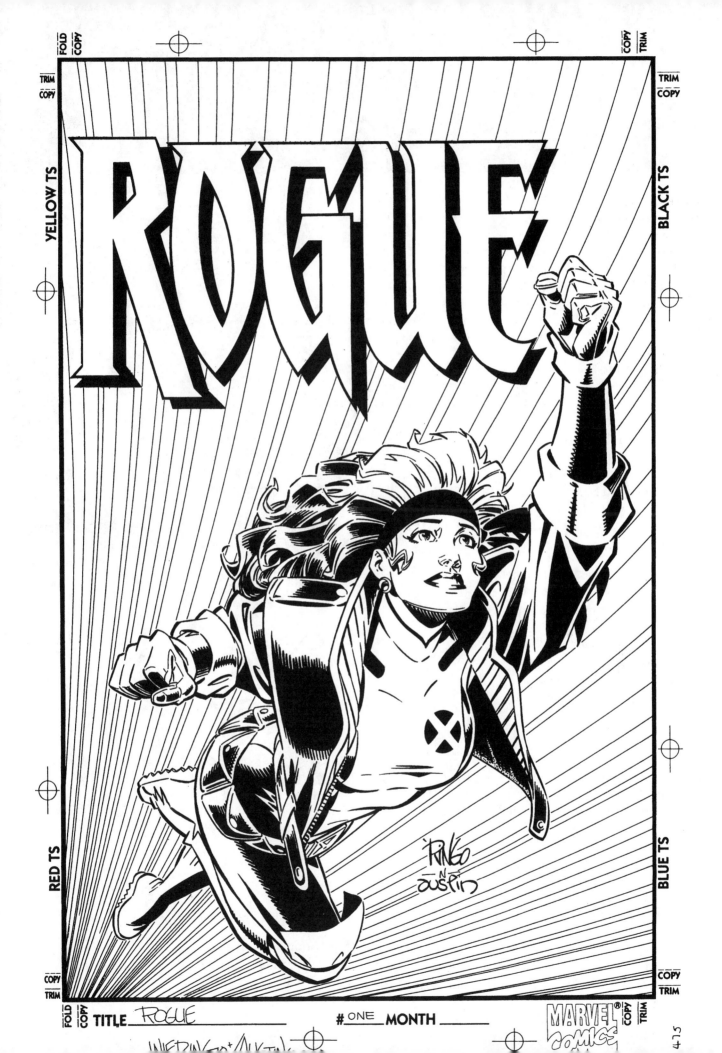

TITLE __ROGUE__   #__ONE__ MONTH _____

MARVEL® COMICS

4-15

Part 4: High Web-Swingin' Adventure

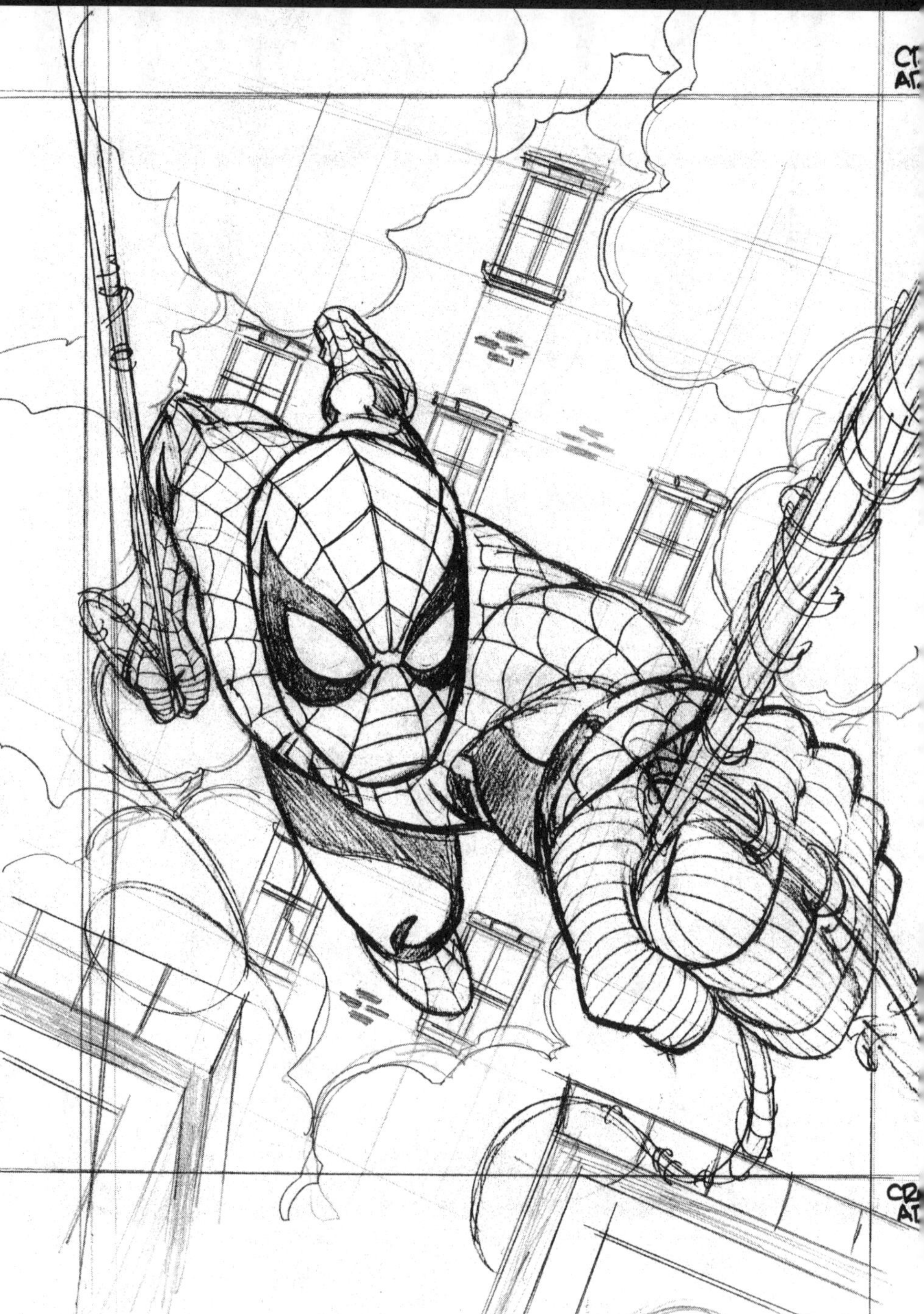

MM: You've mentioned *Robin*, which was your next regular gig. You were there for nine issues and continued doing the covers for a while. What came next? Was it *Spider-Man*? Was it where you met and began working with the greatest writer you ever knew?

MIKE: Yeah... I think *Sensational Spider-Man* was next. I'd just quit *Robin* and I guess word got out that I was off that book, and almost right on the heels of that, I got a call from Ralph Macchio, who asked me if I'd be interested in taking over penciling *Sensational*. And yeah, that is indeed where I met this writer named... Tom—or Todd-something....

MM: He's a hack. Plus, I've heard, not a real person at all. He's a pseudonym for Tom DeFalco. Anyway, before I came along, Ralph had originally been planning to team you up with Mark [Waid] again on that book....

MIKE: You mean I could have worked with Mark on *Sensational*???!?!? I never knew that... my whole life could have taken a different path! Actually, the only other writer I remember being offered as a partner on the book was Dan Jurgens. He was writing and drawing the book and wanted to leave, but apparently he was willing to keep writing the title. I kind of wanted to start with a clean, different writer to go in a whole new direction. As I recall, they'd asked you to write a couple of issues until a permanent writer could be found, and we had such an immediate connection and had such similar backgrounds and tastes that we decided we wanted to keep working together. That's how we became the "team supreme" on *Sensational*.

MM: You had worked on *The Flash*, one of the big guns, and *Robin*.... How did you feel coming on to draw Spider-Man?

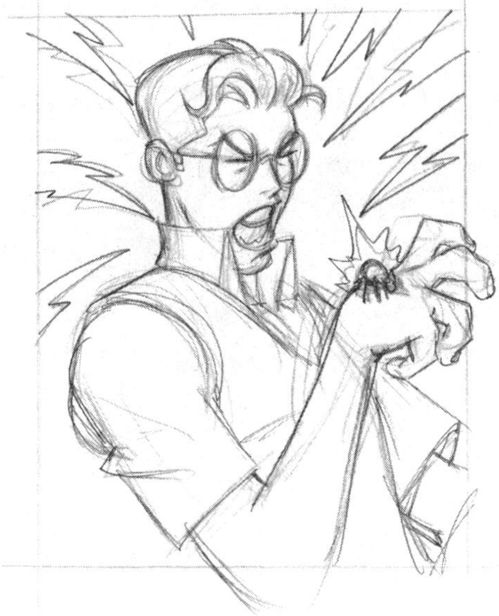

MIKE: At that point in my career, I didn't think I'd ever get to draw a character of the caliber of Spider-Man. Sure, Flash and Robin are great characters and very iconic, but you don't *get* any more iconic than Spider-Man. So I was incredibly intimidated coming on to the book. With the great artists who have made their marks on the web-slinger like Ditko; John Romita, Sr.; Gil Kane; Ross Andru; and even Todd McFarlane... that's a lot to live up to, and although my enthusiasm and sense of honor was sky-high when Ralph Macchio first called me, by the time I actually started on my first issue, I was pretty well ready to pee my pants with the magnitude of the situation. Fortunately, I worked through that pretty quickly and got into the groove on the book. With monthly periodicals, you either rise to the challenge, or freeze up and fall on your face, I guess. Having had a lot of conversations with you, and connecting the way we did from the very beginning, helped me deal much easier with the pressure that I felt, as well.

Previous Page: Pencils for an ad for the Volkswagen Beetle.
Left: Steve Ditko's Peter Parker was a bit of a nebbish, which Mike reflects in this trading card recreation of that fateful meeting with a radioactive spider.
Below: Mike's layout for the cover of *Sensational Spider-Man* #8—his first issue on the book—and page 8 of the following issue. Swaaaaarm!

MM: Dude, are you just sayin' that? Don't be playin' me. If you're just jerkin' me around....

MIKE: Nope... wouldn't do that to you. I remember that from the very first conversation we had, it seemed like we were already friends...

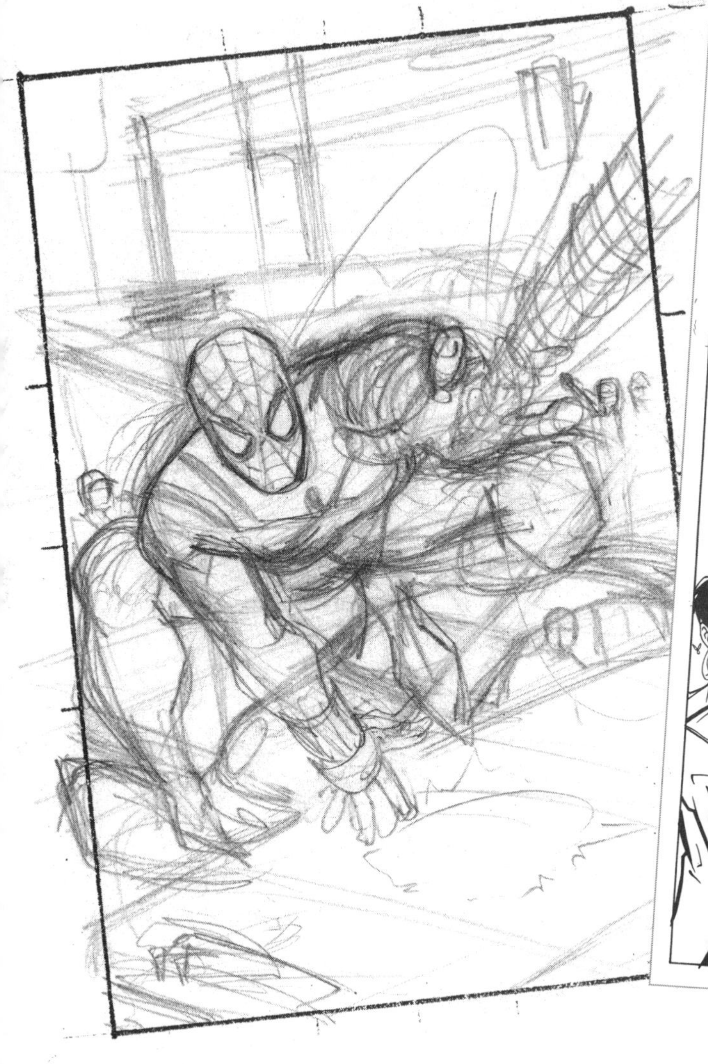

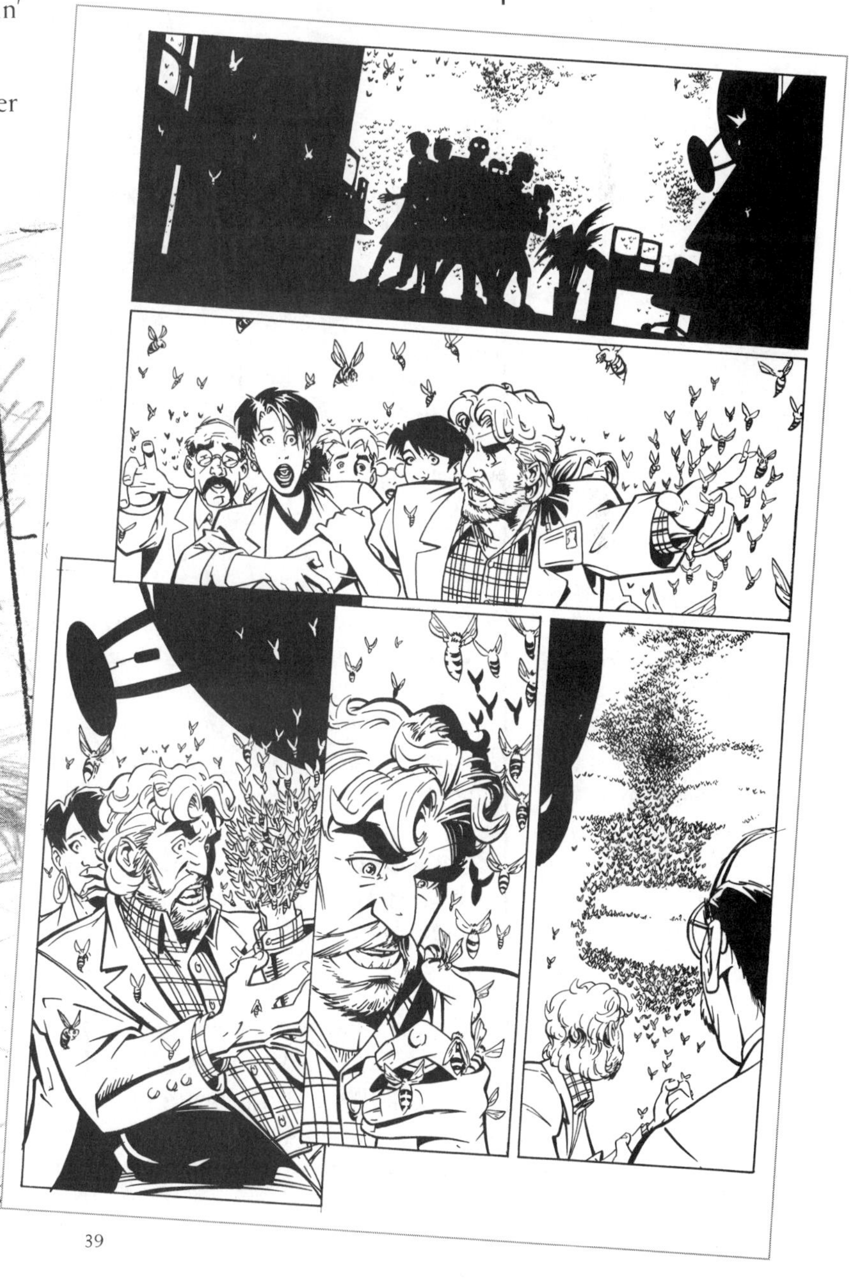

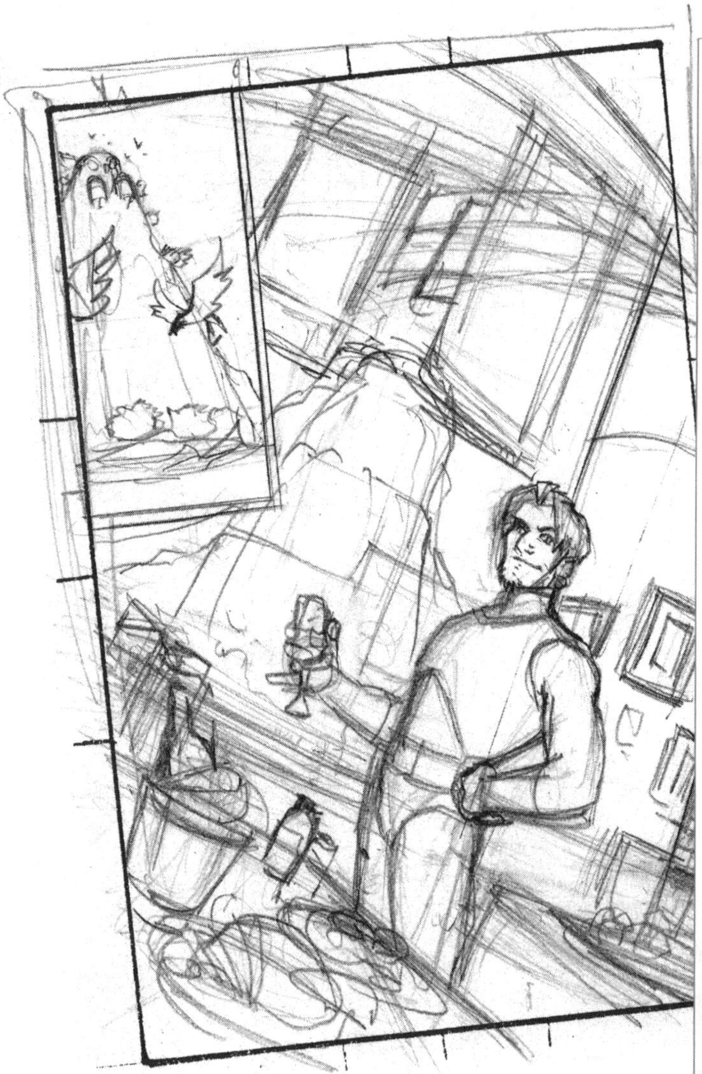

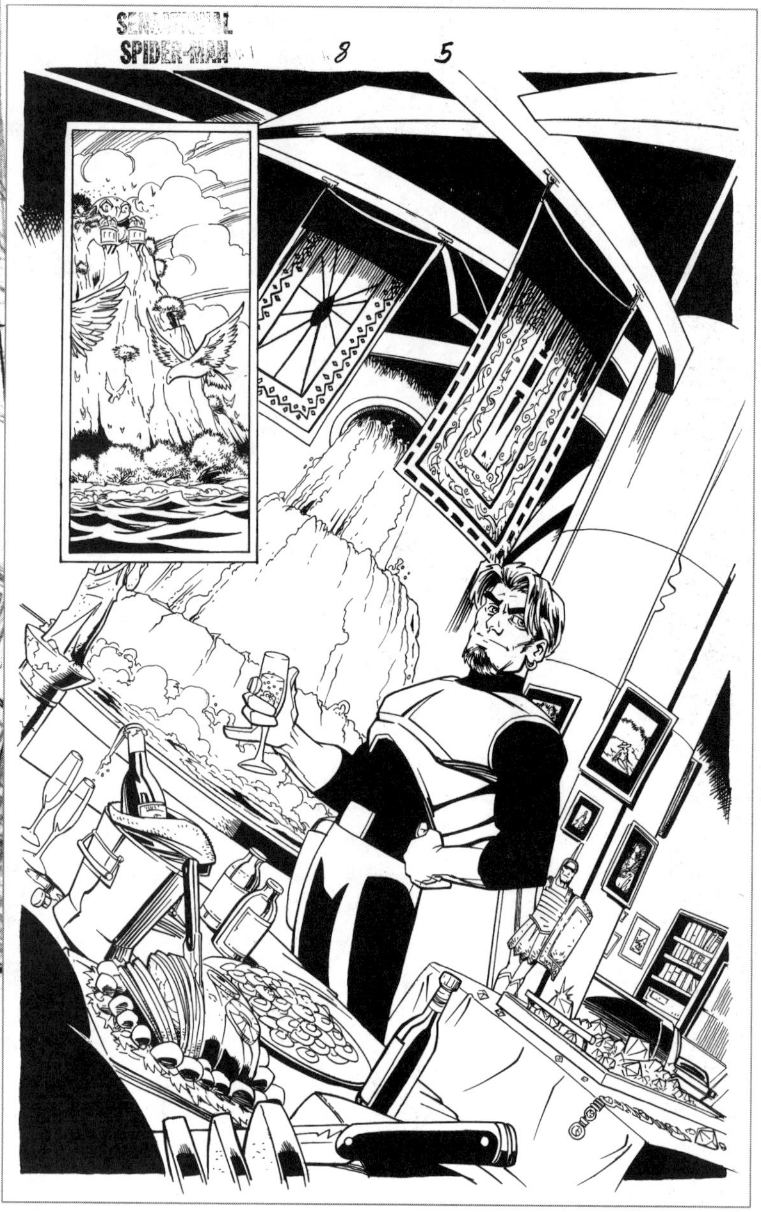
SPIDER-MAN
8
5

Above: The Looter! Layouts and finished inks from *Sensational Spider-Man* #8. Inks by Richard Case.
Next Page: Spidey in the Savage Land! Cover pencils for *Sensational Spider-Man* #13.

or like we were brothers or something. We had a lot of similar experiences and background, and we also had similar ideas on what kind of comics we like to make, so I think we connected—especially on the creative side of things—right away. Those two "transition" issues that we worked on together were so much fun that that's why, when it came time to pick a permanent writer for *Sensational*, I told Ralph that I wanted *you* to stay on so we could work together. I was pretty stunned that Marvel was allowing me to pick my own writer in the first place, but it was an easy decision after working with you for just a brief time.

MM: That's Ralph. He is one of the rare editors who is a writer himself and has been on the creative side of things. He takes into consideration the fact that the best work comes from a creative team that is happy and works well together. That doesn't happen much anymore. And yeah, I felt the same way. We really clicked. And we were both interested in bringing back some of the fun and fantasy to *Spider-Man* in those times of grim, post-*Dark Knight* angst. I was energized by our conversations... and we talked everyday! I had worked the previous two years on *Web of Spider-Man* and *Spectacular* with Steve Butler, Luke Ross, and Sal Buscema and aside from a few instances with Sal—who was great!—no one really wanted to collaborate. They just wanted me to tell the story and tell them what to draw. You brought so much to the table of what you would like to draw and I think that made it that much more fun! Brothers. Yeah, I felt the same way.

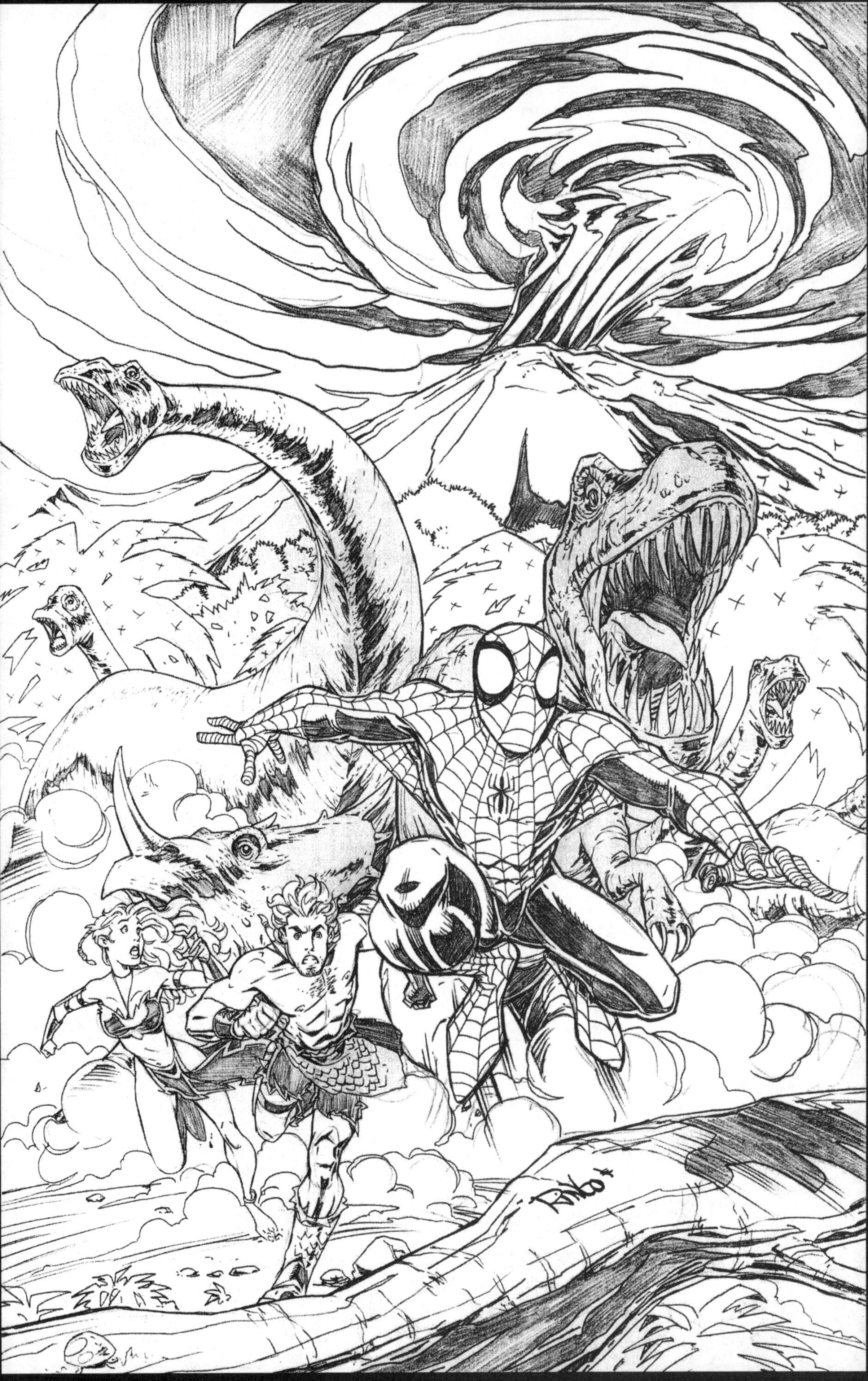

Below: Mike shows a long and strange—pardon the pun—journey in these layouts for a two-page spread for *Sensational Spider-Man* #23.
Next Page: Cover pencils for *Sensational Spider-Man* #23.

Your take on Spider-Man, too, was refreshing. Your version of Spidey hearkened back to Ditko in that you made him more wiry, less muscular. He looked more agile, more frenetic, younger, and, I always say, bouncier! Are there any memories from that time that stand out; stories you enjoyed, things that frustrated you? Would you like me to leave the interview so you can tell people what you *really* think of me?

MIKE: Would you, please...? No, seriously—I think we were really in sync on that book, and what stands out to me is that I had a blast working with you on *Sensational*. The give and take, the generosity you showed me in being so willing to cater the stories to what I was interested in drawing, the fun with the guest-stars like Doctor Strange, the super-fun story with Ka-Zar and The Savage Land, and the wonderful humor in our depiction of The Looter. There was so much that was fun about working on *Sensational*; it was a great time. The frustrating parts, for me, would be having to curtail what we wanted to do with the book to have to conform to the several crossover stories that had to run through all the Spider-Man titles. Although we ended up ultimately enjoying the stories we crafted within the parameters set for those stunts, it was still a little frustrating to have subject matter foisted on us that we had to fit in the book. But that sort of tripped up the momentum that we would be building with the stories we were doing; everything would have to be dropped for these crossovers. Other than those speed bumps, though, Ralph was very hands-off and let us do whatever struck out fancy on *Sensational*, which made for a very fun working atmosphere.

MM: While I think we probably could've gone on for another year or so on *Sensational*, our run on *Spider-Man* was cut short when

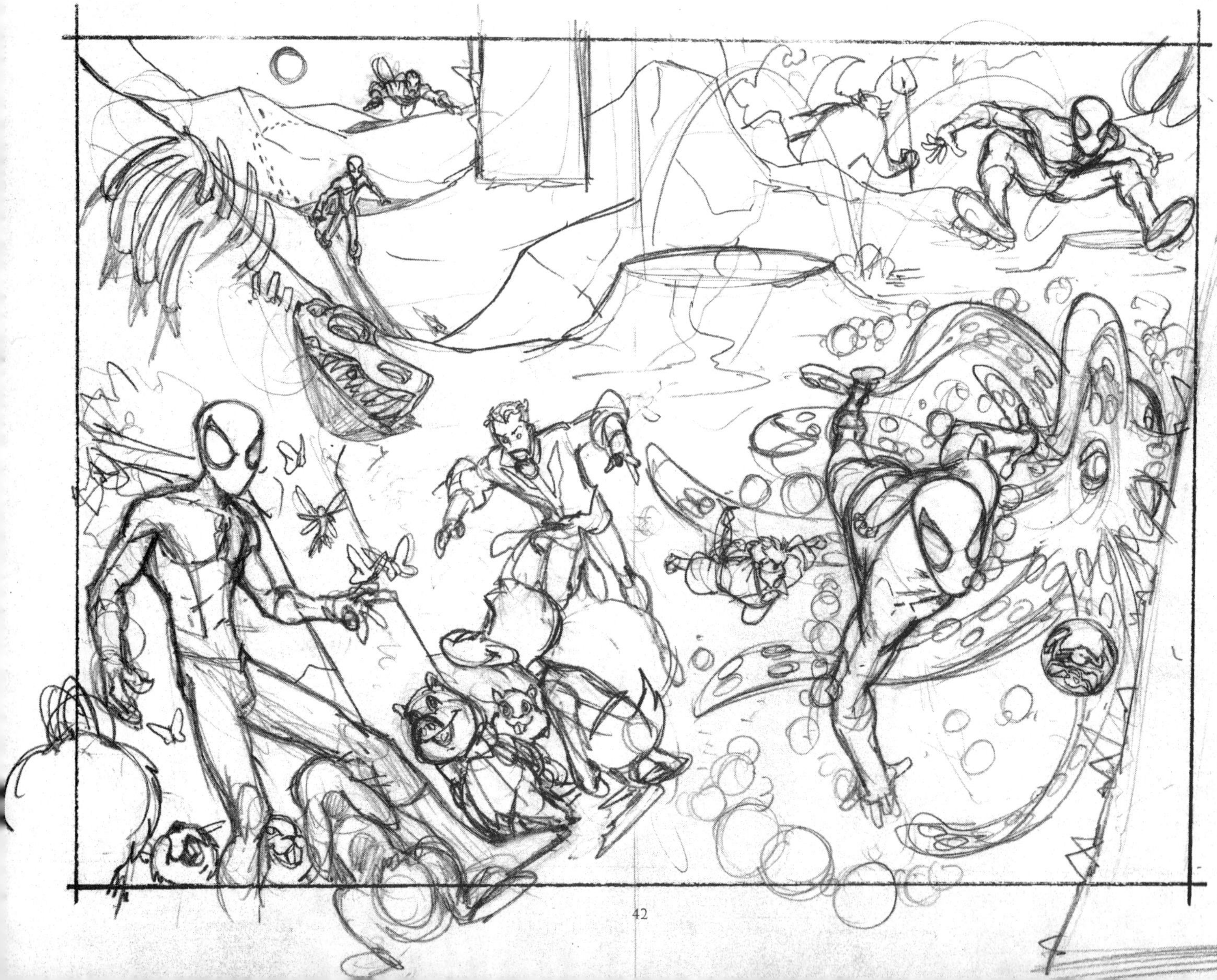

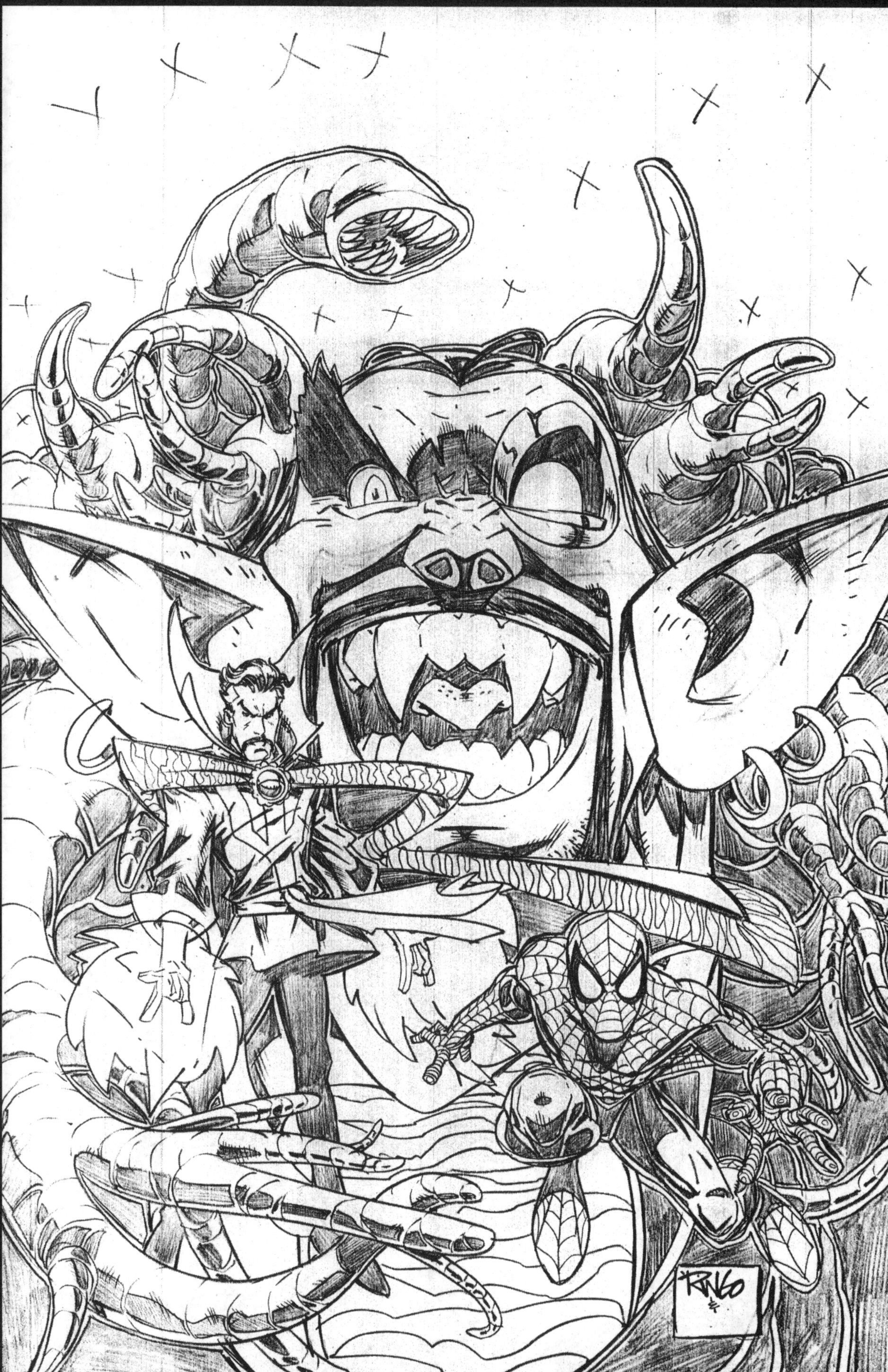
RINGO

ALL BLEED ART MUST EXTEND TO SOLID LINE

KEEP ALL LETTERING INSIDE BROKEN-LINE BOX

Book ______ Issue ______ Story Page # ______ Line Up Page # ______

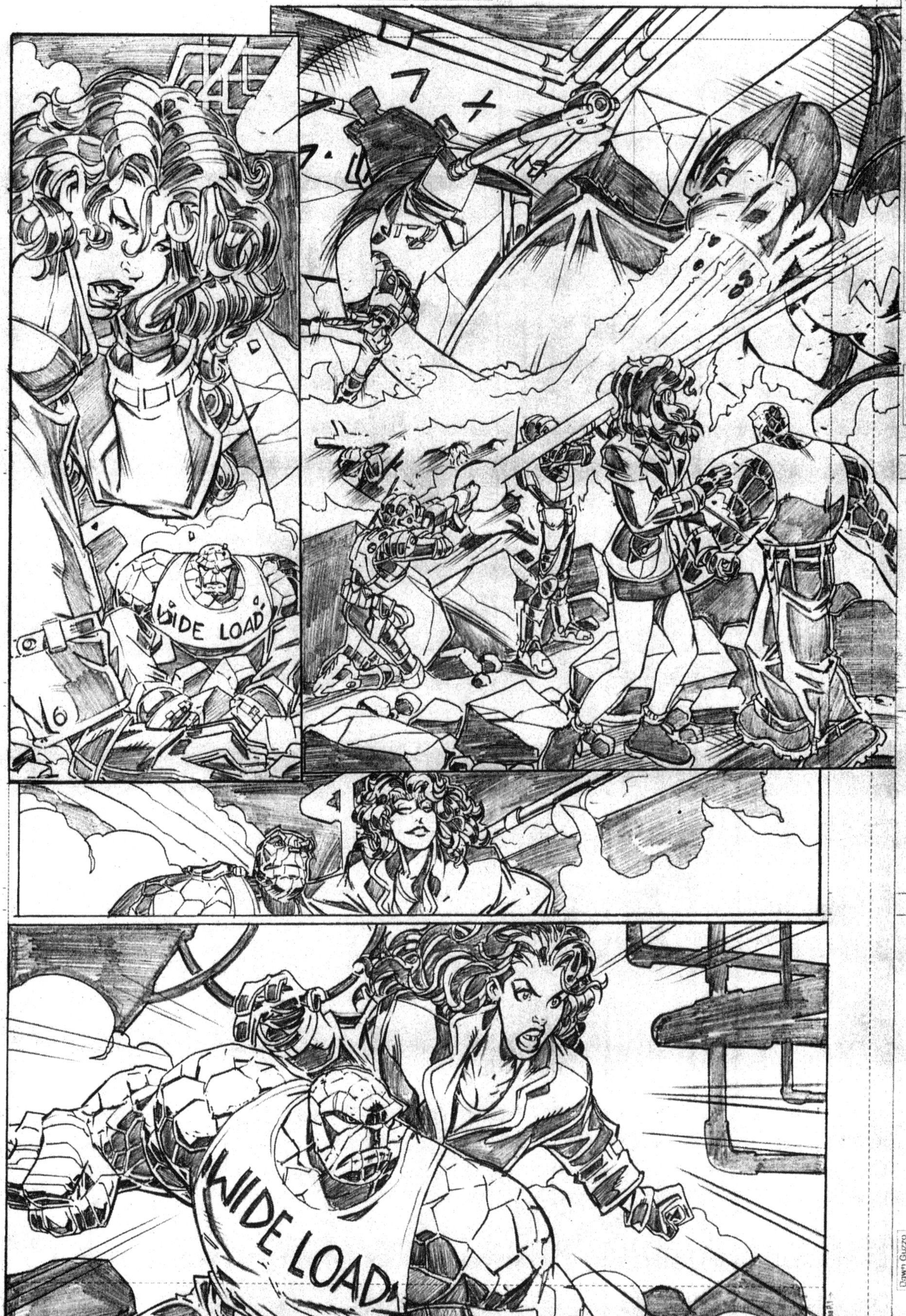
WIDE LOAD
WIDE LOAD

#6570 P.O. 64453 03/27/98

Strathmore

Dawn Guzzo

INSTRUCTIONS FOR DOUBLE PAGE SPREAD: CUT AS SHOWN, ABUT PAGE EDGES, TAPE ON BACK. **DO NOT** OVERLAP.

CUT LEFT-HAND PAGE AT THIS LINE

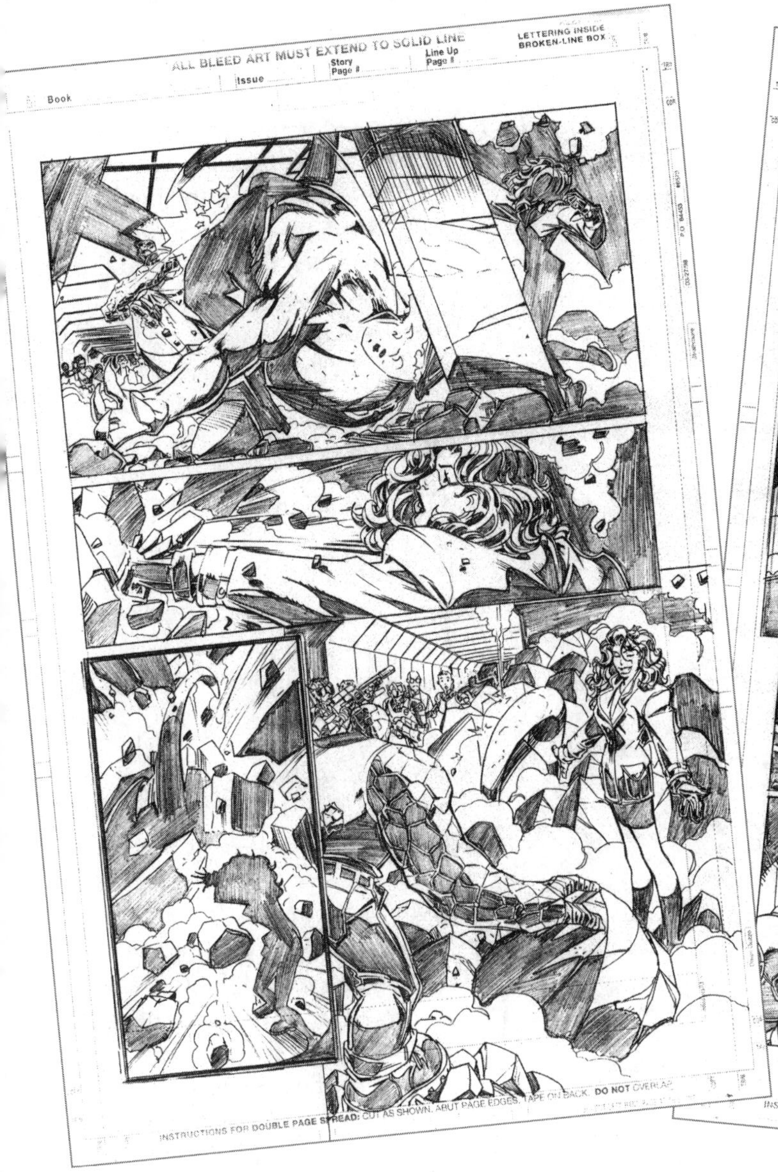
ALL BLEED ART MUST EXTEND TO SOLID LINE
LETTERING INSIDE BROKEN-LINE BOX

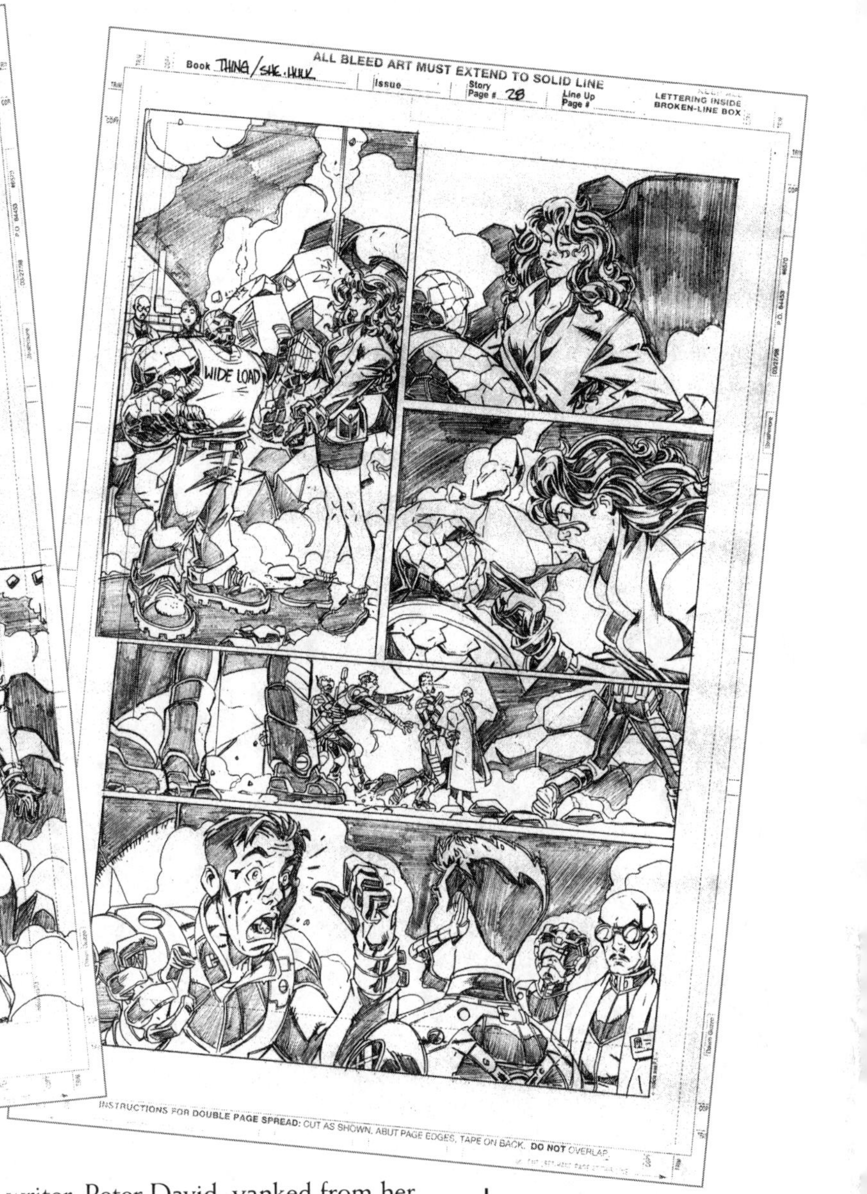
ALL BLEED ART MUST EXTEND TO SOLID LINE
LETTERING INSIDE BROKEN-LINE BOX
WIDE LOAD

they decided to do a re-launch of all the Spider-books and we were given our walking papers. Should we talk about *The Hulk*?

MIKE: Well, we can talk about the end of *Sensational* and the *Hulk* fiasco in the context of the tumultuous times at Marvel during those days when they were in the midst of their bankruptcy problems, which really caused havoc at all levels in the company and affected every one of us in some way. So, yeah... let's talk about it.

MM: It sucked.

MIKE: [*laughs*] Yeah... it did. Very much. But that whole period was pretty chaotic. They canceled *Sensational*, and in the wake of that, Bob Harras decided that he wanted to install us as the creative team on *Hulk*. You'll have to correct me if I'm getting any of this wrong, but the *Hulk* editor, Bobbie Chase, didn't take too kindly to having her star writer, Peter David, yanked from her control and having a new creative crew foisted on her. I don't think she cared so much about me being on the book... but I think she had issues with you. And things just didn't work out between the two of you. So I ultimately declined to work on the book as well, because I had no idea who the new writer would ultimately be, and I didn't want to be in the middle of all that political stuff anyway. *That* led to a whole series of aborted projects. I was supposed to finish a *She-Hulk/Thing* special you had written and Bryan Hitch never finished—I think he did about half of it—but after only drawing a few pages, I was told to stop because the project was being scrapped and the editor was being let go. The same thing happened on an *Alpha Flight* fill-in I was supposed to draw. I did a couple of pages of layouts, and then the editor called me to tell me to stop, because the book was being

Previous Page and Above: Mike's unused pencils for pages 26-28 of *Thing & She-Hulk: The Long Night*—a one-shot special which was eventually finished by Ivan Reis.

Below: One of Mike's few bright spots during his first stint with Marvel, post-*Sensational* cancellation: *X-Men #1/2*. Inks by Brad Vancatta.

Next Page: Cover art for the first *Tellos* trade paperback collection, *The Joining*.

X-Men ™ and ©2006 Marvel Characters, Inc. Jarek, Koj, Serra ™ and ©2006 Todd Dezago & Mike Wieringo.

canceled and *he* was being fired. So it was a very chaotic and unsure time then.

MM: Actually, I was fairly good friends with Bobbie Chase and we were in constant contact through this whole debacle. As it went, Bob Harras felt that Peter had been on *The Hulk* too long, solid sales and stories notwithstanding, and ordered Bobbie to give him his walking papers. Bobbie and Peter had had a long and comfortable run—and friendship—on this book and this was the first time that Bob had steamrolled over Bobbie—something he had been doing with more and more frequency over the past few months. Before Bobbie had even talked to Peter, Bob had given the book to us. I suddenly found myself caught in a power struggle between the editor and the editor-in-chief. Bobbie called me, a few times in tears, to tell me that she really didn't know what to do. She was going to quit. She resented everything about this. I tried to get them on the same page, but Bob would tell me one thing and Bobbie another. I told Bobbie that, to make things easier for her, I would remove myself from the situation. Out of solidarity, you came with us. Three weeks later, Bobbie was gone and Bob Harras gave the book to somebody else.

MIKE: In the wake of all that crap, I was being offered other projects—I was on an exclusive contract with Marvel at the time—that were... shall I say, very sub-par. The writing on those proposals was so bad that I just couldn't bring myself to draw them. So I felt kind of aimless, and I tried to get out of my contract. Marvel wasn't hearing it, so I spent about six or eight months in limbo... not working, because Marvel and I were going back and forth with letters—me saying, "I quit," and Marvel saying, "We refuse to allow you to quit your contract." So I just didn't work for anyone during that time. I wouldn't work on the ratty stories that Marvel was offering, and no one else could hire me with my contract still in effect. The *one* project that I worked on during that time that was at all enjoyable was the *X-Men #1/2* you and I did together, which was a kind of "alternate X-Men" story with the Children of the Atom in a fantasy/medieval setting. We enjoyed working on that kind of subject matter so much, that's what led us to start talking about creating something fantasy-related of our own, which ended up being *Tellos*.

X·MEN   1/2   13

MM: Well, I know all of what happened with *Tellos* and I think that we've both answered this question about a ka-billion times, but I'll go for it: So how did *Tellos* come about?

MIKE: The short-version answer is that *Tellos* came about because of one marathon phone call we had one day. The *long* version is that the seeds for what became *Tellos* were planted during our experience working on the aforementioned *X-Men* #1/2. It ostensibly set the X-characters in a fantasy setting, and as it turned out, we're both fantasy fans. We began talking about fantasy novels and comics we'd read, and during the course of one very long conversation, we came up with a premise that ended up being *Tellos*. At the time, I was coming to the end of my contract period at Marvel. I had been talking with Jeph Loeb about a project he was pushing at DC that involved the Legion of Super-Heroes and the Teen Titans. It was a very cool project, and I was pretty excited about it. I worked up a ton of character designs and studies of both teams to hopefully help get the project through... and just because I've always had a soft spot for both the Legion and the Titans. I thought the

project was a fantastic idea, but for whatever reason, DC decided to pass on it. I was highly frustrated about that, and that, combined with the stuff I'd just gone through with Marvel, I decided to just say "to hell with it" and pursue doing something creator-owned with you—in specific, *Tellos*. So I spent a lot of time doing character designs based on our various conversations and plotting sessions. I must have spent about two or three months just working on building the visual look of *Tellos*, more time than I'd ever spent on that kind of work for any other project before or since. It was a blast. And then... we got started.

MM: Having done a lot of theater, I have always related our relationship—and especially our collaboration on *Tellos*—as akin to the "yes, and..." concept of improv, where you take whatever the other guy puts out there and build on it, never negating or contradicting what the other guy brought. We built that story from the ground up, always adding and building. I knew we wanted to create a landscape that was continually shifting and changing so that we could never get bored with the kind of story we were telling or where we were. You brought in the anthropomorphic aspect, I

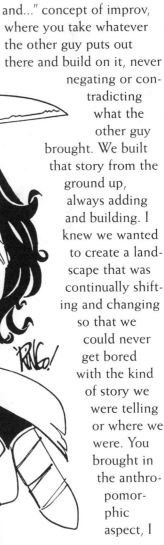

Below and Next Page Bottom: Early character designs for the Tellos cast: Serra, Hawke & Rikk, and Koj & Jarek. This designs show a bit more of an anime influence—particularly Hawke—than the end results do.
Next Page: The sparks fly in the world of Tellos, while Jared's primal self defeats Mark's primal self. *Tellos* #10, page 13. Inks by Rob Stull.

threw in the boy for readers to identify with. You added a pirate queen—who turned out to be pretty identifiable with our female readers as well!—but it was you who came up with the name Tellos. What the hell was that?!

MIKE: Well, if you ask Erik Larsen, it's one of the stupidest names for a comic book ever. [*laughter*] But the name Tellos, if I remember correctly, was a play on the words "tell us"—as in "tell us a story." And so the magical fantasy realm of Tellos came from "tell us." I know it's kind of silly, but despite what Erik thinks, I think it's a pretty cool name.

MM: We were both pretty elated about not only the prospect of doing our own book, but about a fantasy book specifically. I know that we were both pretty happy with the premise and our cast of characters; your designs were hands down the most gorgeous things I'd ever seen you do. Were there any elements or ideas that you felt we missed out on or that you wished we had incorporated into the story?

MIKE: There's nothing that I have any *regrets* about not making their way into the story, no. I remember I had the idea that there would be things—subtle things that wouldn't be very clear as to what they were until the initial story was finished—that I brought up that didn't make their way into the book except for the titan/giant in the first issue. I had the idea that there would be some elements occurring in the book that would represent certain aspects of Jared's brain function. The titan/giant that appeared in the first issue was a representative of Jared's lower, or subconscious, brain functions—the more reptilian portions of his brain that regulated bodily function. They were supposed to be big, almost mindless, lumbering creatures. Then there were to be occasional streaks of light or energy rolling across the sky that would represent the EKG monitor or the monitor of Jared's comatose brain activity. There were also supposed to be birds Jarek and company would encounter that would occasionally speak broken phrases that would strike a chord with Jarek... like something he should be remembering but couldn't. It was all to hint at, or allude to aspects of the idea that Jared/Jarek was in a coma in his waking life, and that these elements were breaking through into the fantasy realm of Tellos that he had created in his subconscious mind.

MM: Oh, yeah, well... um, for anyone that *hasn't* read *Tellos* yet, umm, you didn't hear

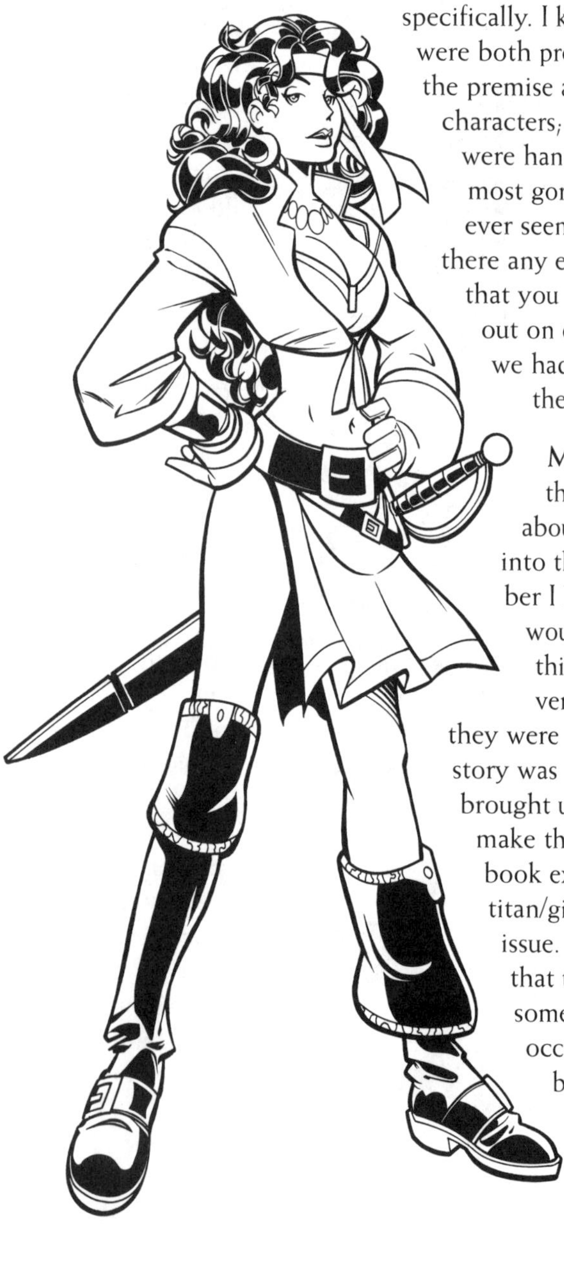

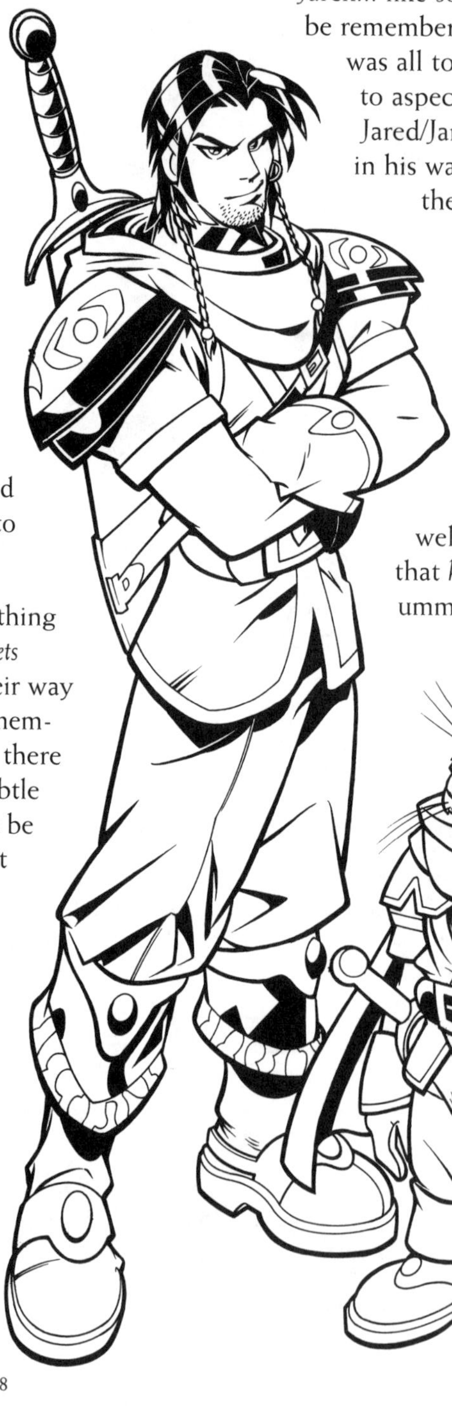

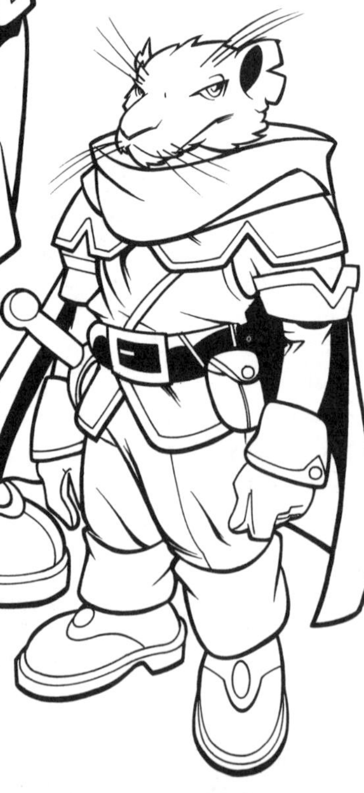

that, it never happened, it was all a dream.... Also, these are not the droids you're looking for.

How was that? Think it worked...?

MIKE: [*laughs*] I have to doubt that anyone who's buying this and reading it *hasn't* read *Tellos* yet. If I'm wrong, I apologize....

MM: Who's your favorite *Tellos* character?

MIKE: It's hard to choose.... I love them all, but if I had to make a hard choice, I'd have to go with Koj. I love animals, and I think that tigers are probably the most beautiful and regal animals in the world. I first thought of making Koj a lion, but the truth is that tigers are much bigger than lions and they're also some of the most lethal and efficient hunters and killers on earth. Male lions just lay around for the most part and allow the females of the pride to do all the hard work. The male lion gets all the press, but the tiger is the more *truly* regal and formidable, and they're on the brink of extinction. That these gorgeous, reclusive, and fierce creatures might disappear from the world is a truly heartbreaking thing to me. So with that in mind, I wanted to model Koj on the tiger as more a tribute than anything else.

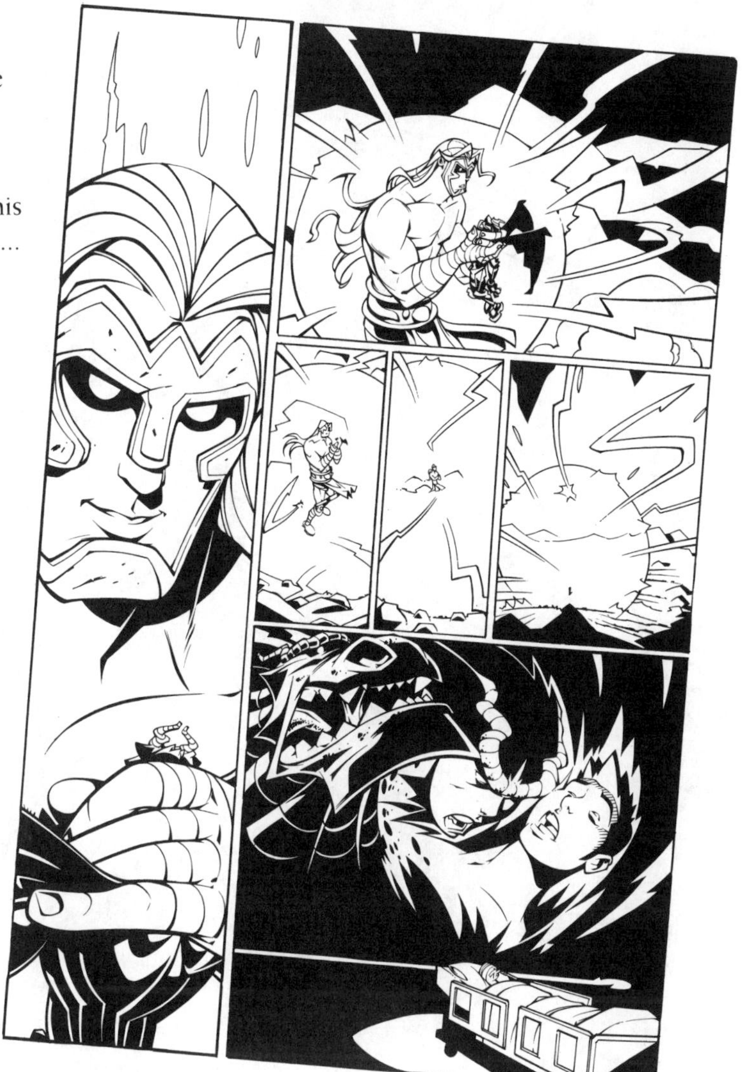

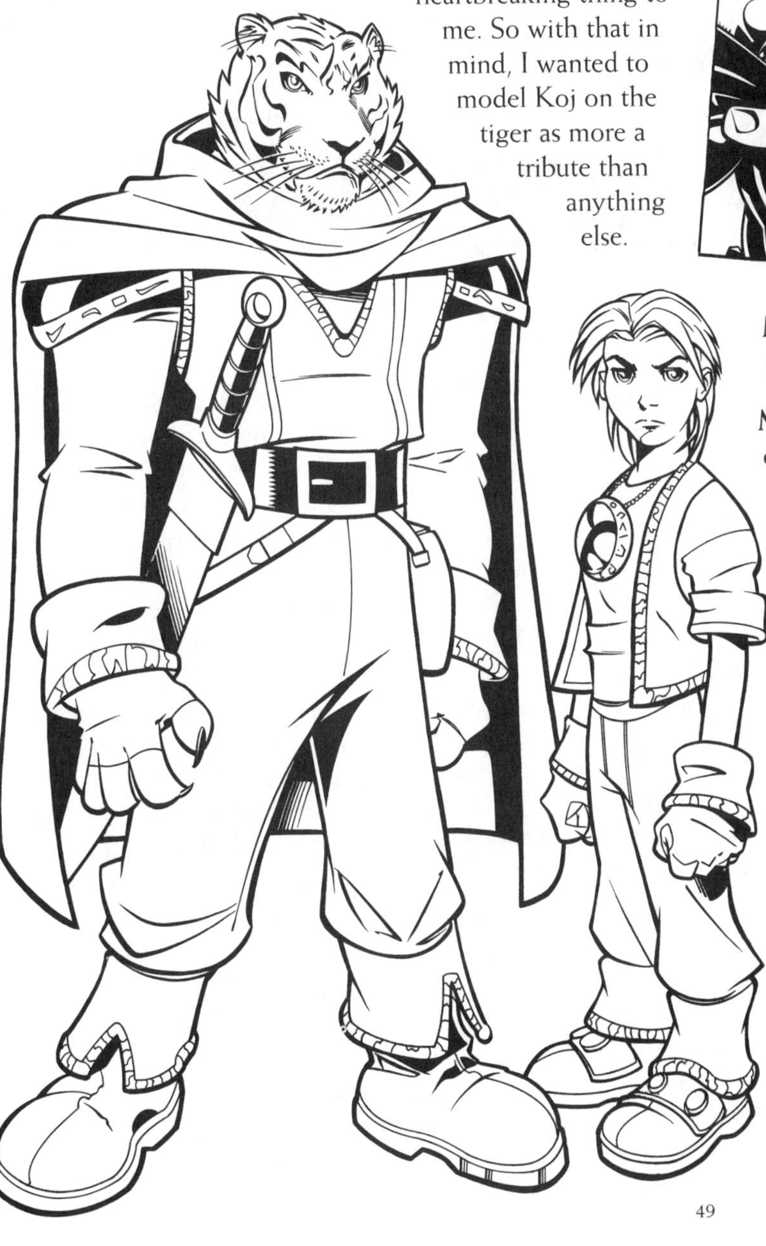

MM: Who's your second?

MIKE: That would have to be Jarek/Jared. He's the other half of Koj. They're the catalyst for the entire story, so they're forever connected. So it's an easy choice to pick Jarek as my second favorite.

MM: And, of course, one look at the comments/messages on your website/blog proves that, though you put your indelible mark on the likes of Spidey, the FF, Flash, and Superman, what your legions of loyal fans are waiting for most is... *more Tellos*!

MIKE: We will make that happen. That's a fact. As to the exact *timing* of that fact... that's up in the air. But you and I both love this book and these characters so much that it's impossible to *not* revisit them. They're just too dear. It is very gratifying to have so many people state over and over how much they want to see more *Tellos*; it happens online all the time, and at every show we go to, doesn't it? I've been very surprised at the percentage of people who talk about how much they loved the book and how much they want to see more. It seems like they grow in number with each show I attend.

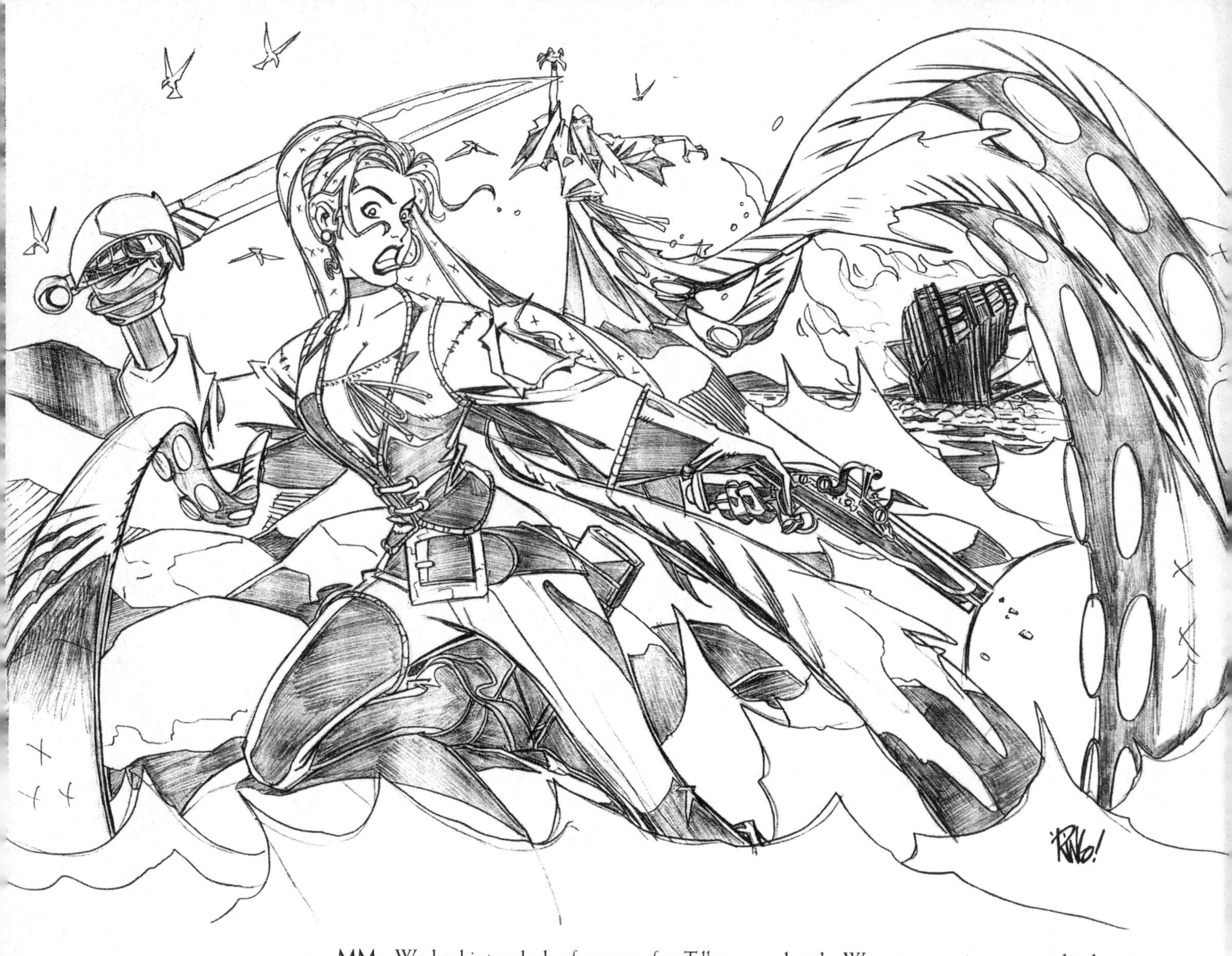

Above: There has to be more Tellos, if only to get more stories like this! **Next Page:** Serra takes a break from the action in these pencils for an alternate cover of *Tellos* #2.

MM: We had intended, of course, for *Tellos* to be an ongoing comic—and an ongoing adventure. You and I have plotted far enough into the future of these characters—and others—for us to be cranking out *Tellos* tales for quite some time. Unfortunately, the state of the industry meant that we needed to end *Tellos* early—and truncate our first story slightly. Though you've talked about this a bit in other forums, would you like to do more *Tellos*?

MIKE: Absolutely, I would. I can't think of anything else I'd rather work on than *Tellos*. It's our baby, and who doesn't want to lavish love and attention onto their baby?

Certainly there were market forces that precluded our continuing the original *Tellos* series in the manner that we wanted to, yeah, but I think there were—and we've discussed this—many things that were also contributing factors to the early end of our book. We were paying pretty high rates for coloring, inking, and lettering at that time. The production costs of the book were just too high to sustain on what the sales had settled to at that point. We were also charging about 49¢ less than almost all other Image titles. We decided that when we first started the book, that if we only charged $2.50 instead of $2.99, the book would sell more because folks would like the lower price point. I think at the end of the day, it didn't make a bit of difference one way or the other—people just didn't notice—and we were cutting ourselves out of additional revenue. We increased the price to the full $2.99 on the last couple of issues, and no one blinked an eye. I think that the lessons we've learned about the business of producing a creator-owned book in this market, as well as an increased savvy about web marketing and also—and this is pretty important—an increase in knowledge of the nuts and

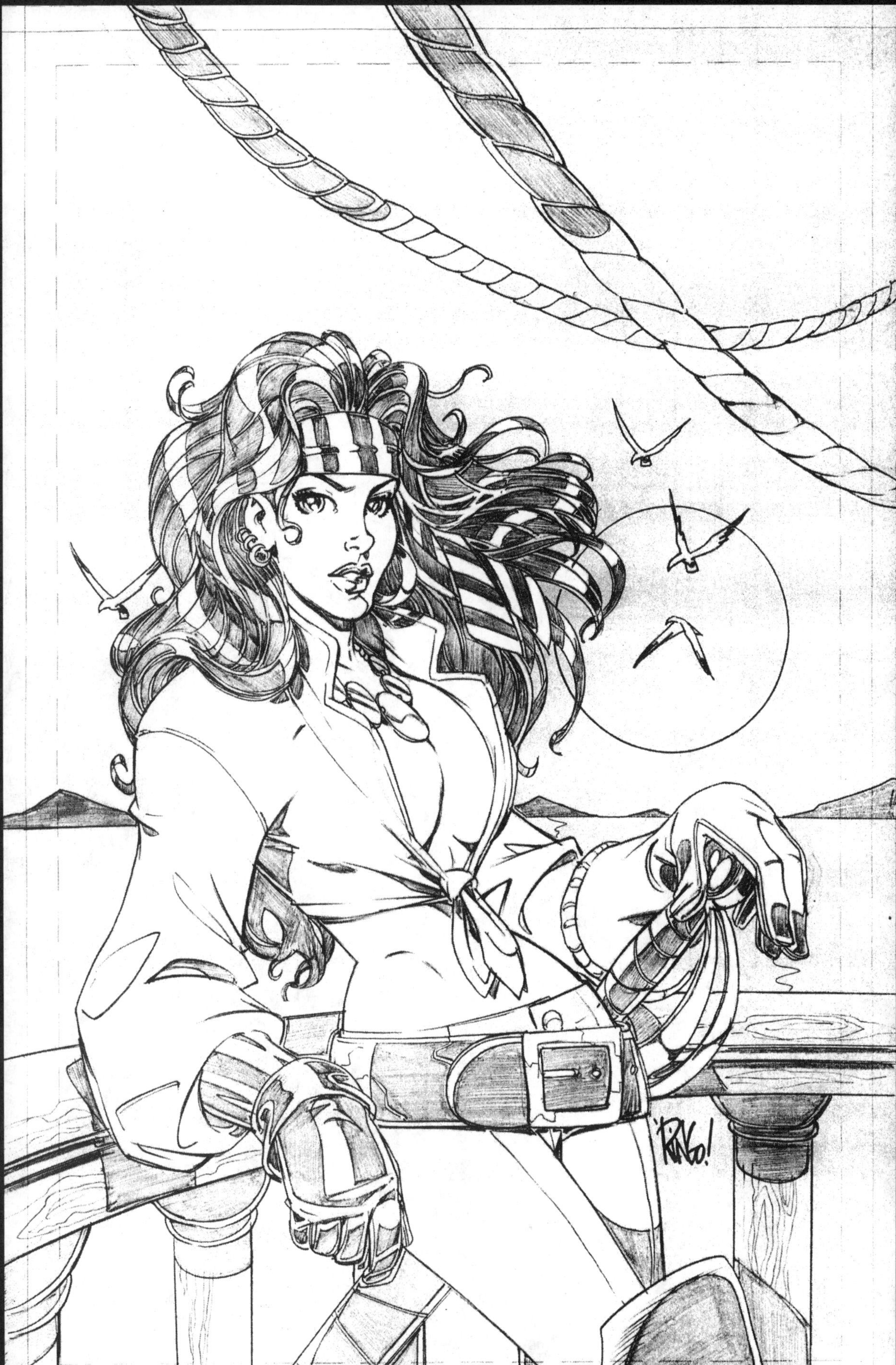
RINGO!

Below: During the end of its run, *Tellos* was published through Gorilla Comics—an imprint of Image. This panel is from Gorilla's *Tellos* preview. **Next Page:** Layouts for *Gen 13: Bootleg* #13.

bolts of other aspects of comic book production on our part will allow us to more effectively produce and market the book when we get to do more *Tellos*. And we *will* do more *Tellos*.

You've learned a lot about lettering, and I've learned a lot about digital inking, as well as becoming more comfortable with physically hand-inking my own work at this point. And there are so many immensely talented young folks out there who color very well and don't charge an arm-and-a-leg for their work. So I'm pretty optimistic about our ability to effectively and affordably produce the book when we finally get the time... well, when I finally get the time. That's the big hurdle at this point. I'm exclusively contracted to Marvel at this point, and they keep me pretty busy. So it's a matter of finding the time to do what we need to do to get more of our baby out there.

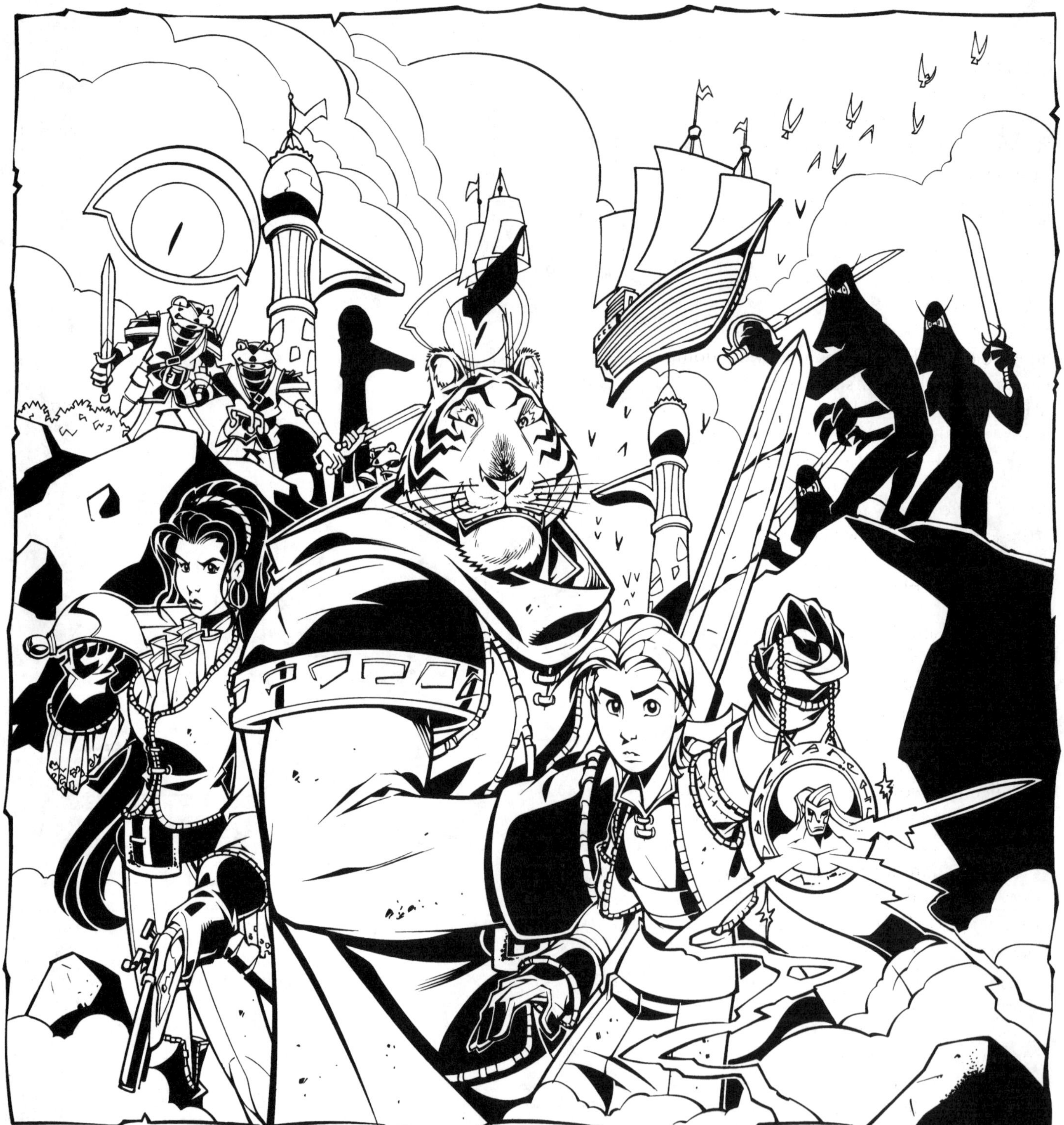

MM: Anything else you wanna say about *Tellos?*

MIKE: Well, I suppose I'd just like folks who haven't tried the book to seek out the trades and read it. You and I both know how much love and effort we put into *Tellos,* and I think it shows.

MM: Somewhere in there—and neither you or I can remember whether it was during *Sensational Spider-Man* or *Tellos*—you wrote and drew an issue of *Gen 13: Bootleg,* featuring everybody's favorite, Grunge. How did that come about?

MIKE: Well, I'm pretty sure it wasn't during *Tellos.* If I remember correctly, I didn't work on anything else during the period we were doing *Tellos,* other than maybe some covers for people here or there. I'm thinking the *Gen 13: Bootleg* was done during *Sensational.* Anyway, how it came about was that over my early years of working in comics, I'd done stuff for WildStorm at times—mostly trading cards and pin-ups—so I had a bit of a relationship with the editorial folks there. Scott Dunbier was the head honcho at the time, and we'd see each other at cons and also talk on the phone once in a while, and we'd always talk about working on something more substantial than trading cards or pin-ups together. One day Scott called and asked me if I'd be interested in both writing and drawing an issue of the *Bootleg* book they were doing. At the time, *Gen 13* was WildStorm's signature book—their most popular title—so they had this spin-off book going. I had never written anything for actual publication before, and it's something I've always wanted to explore, so I said yes.

MM: We've already talked about the fact that you used to write and draw your own comics as a kid, but this was the first time your were going to write and draw something professionally. How did you approach the writing side of it?

MIKE: Actually, I approached it the same way I did the personal comics I did as a kid, that being that I made it up as I went along. [*laughter*] I had a basic idea of what I wanted the story to be, so since I was drawing it myself, I didn't see the real need to write out a script. But Scott Dunbier wanted me to submit a script so that I could get paid for the writing side of the comic. Now, this was before we had a computer in the studio I shared with the other guys, and I didn't have one at home, either, so I hand wrote the script very quickly and faxed it off to WildStorm and Scott. I don't think I actually followed every detail of the hand-written script in the final comic, but I wanted to give Scott the physical script he needed. I remember that while I was just getting started on the *Gen 13* book, I was called to jury duty. I reported to the courthouse and brought my drawing materials along. I was never called to actually serve on an active jury, so while waiting for the entire day in the jury pool room, I just concentrated on doing layouts, and ended up laying out about half the book while I was there. The lack of rigid structure in creating the book was actually a lot of fun.

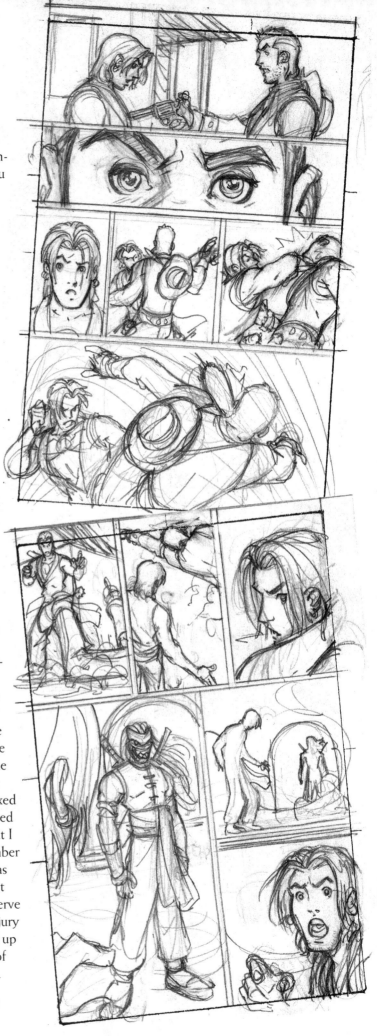

Interlude: Tellos Gallery

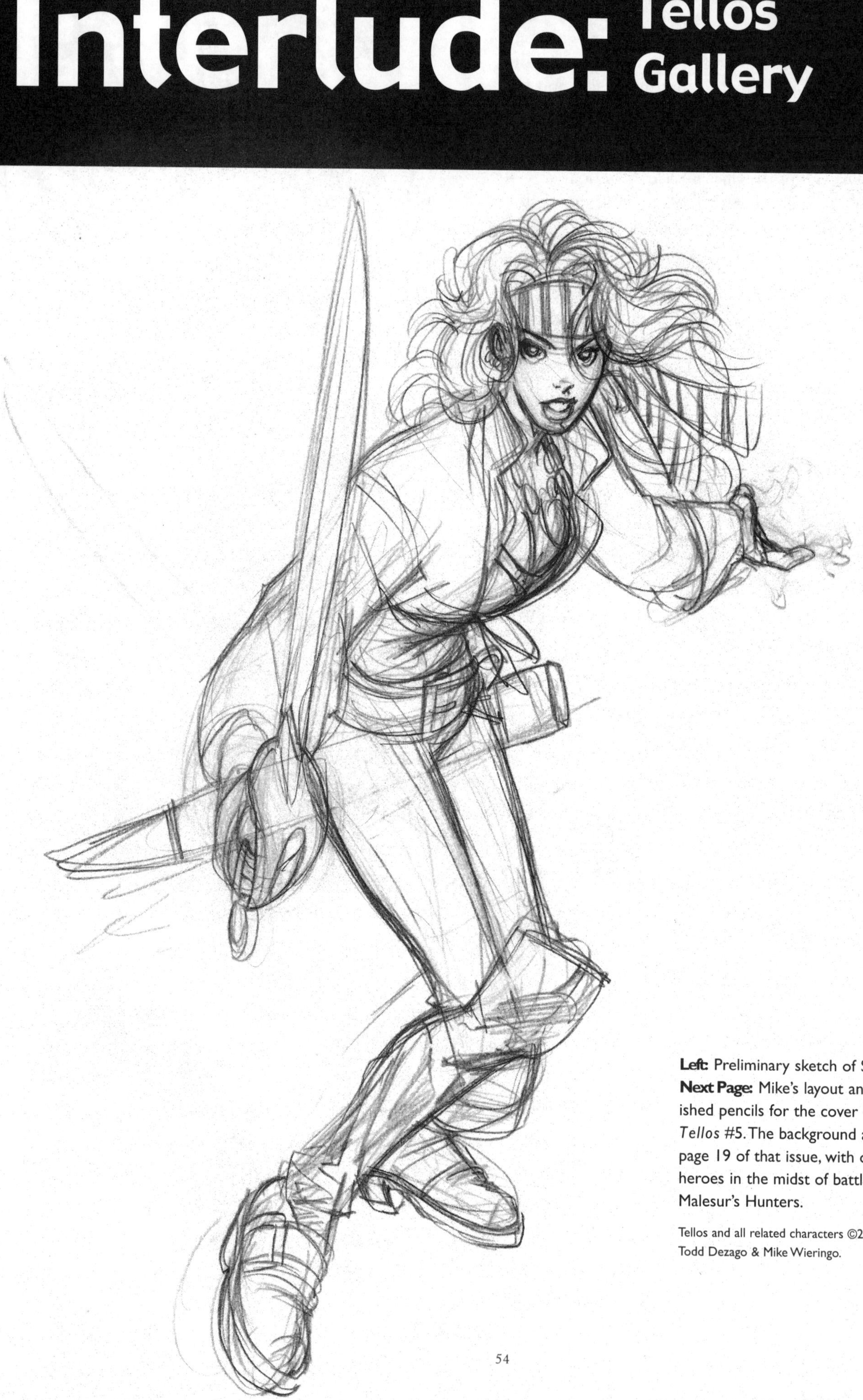

Left: Preliminary sketch of Serra.
Next Page: Mike's layout and finished pencils for the cover of *Tellos* #5. The background art is page 19 of that issue, with our heroes in the midst of battle with Malesur's Hunters.

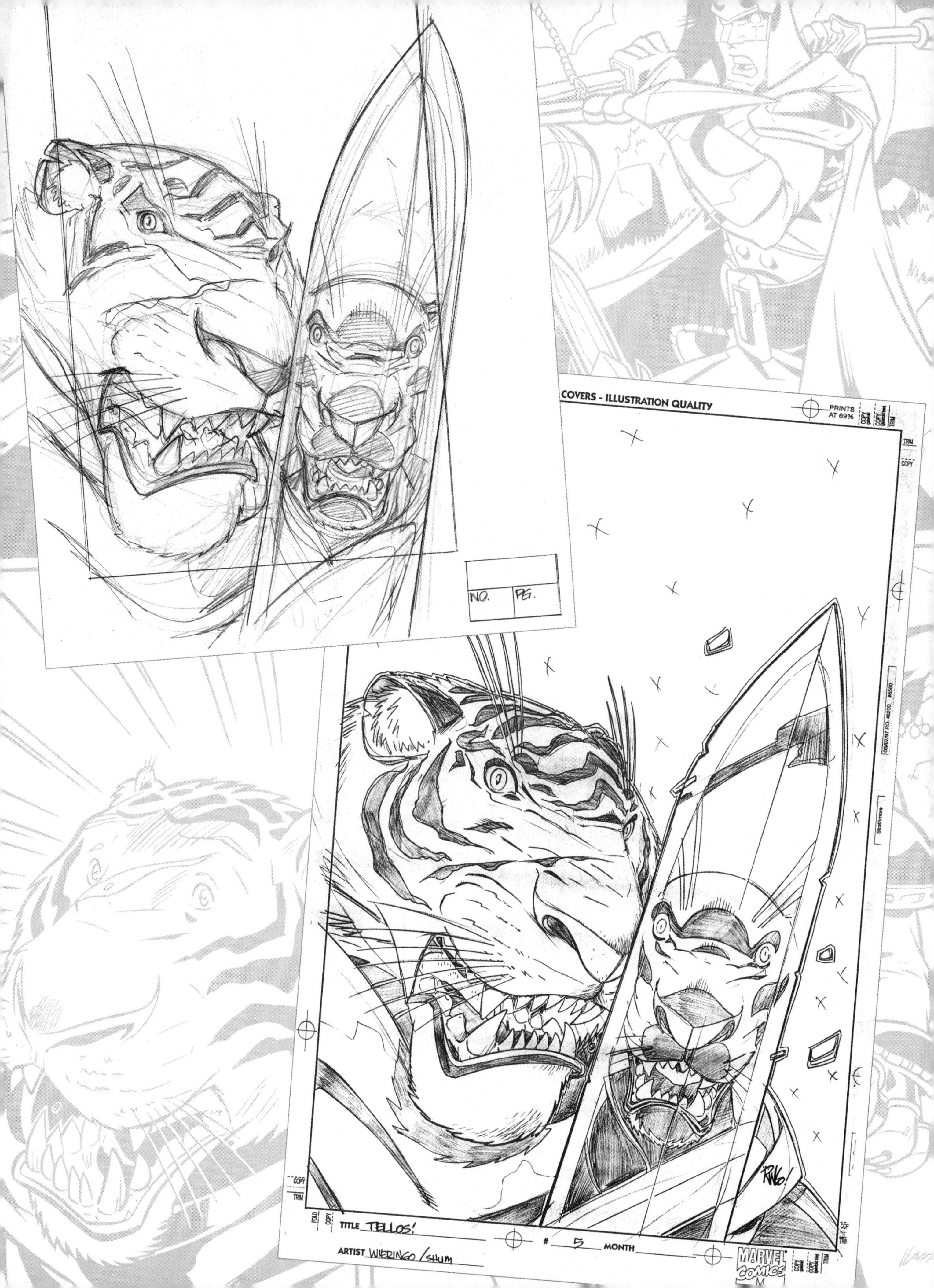
NO.
PG.
COVERS - ILLUSTRATION QUALITY
PRINTS AT 69%
TRIM
COPY
Strathmore
RINGO!
TITLE TELLOS!
5 MONTH
ARTIST WIERINGO / SHUM
MARVEL COMICS

This Page: The sketch of Rikk was drawn at 8½" x 11" size before Mike added the figure to the cover pencils of *Tellos* #4.
Next Page: Preliminary model sketch of the good doctor's alter ego, and preliminary sketches of the lemms for *Tellos* #8. Panel 4 of page 7 from that issue—shown just above the sketches—shows some of the end results.

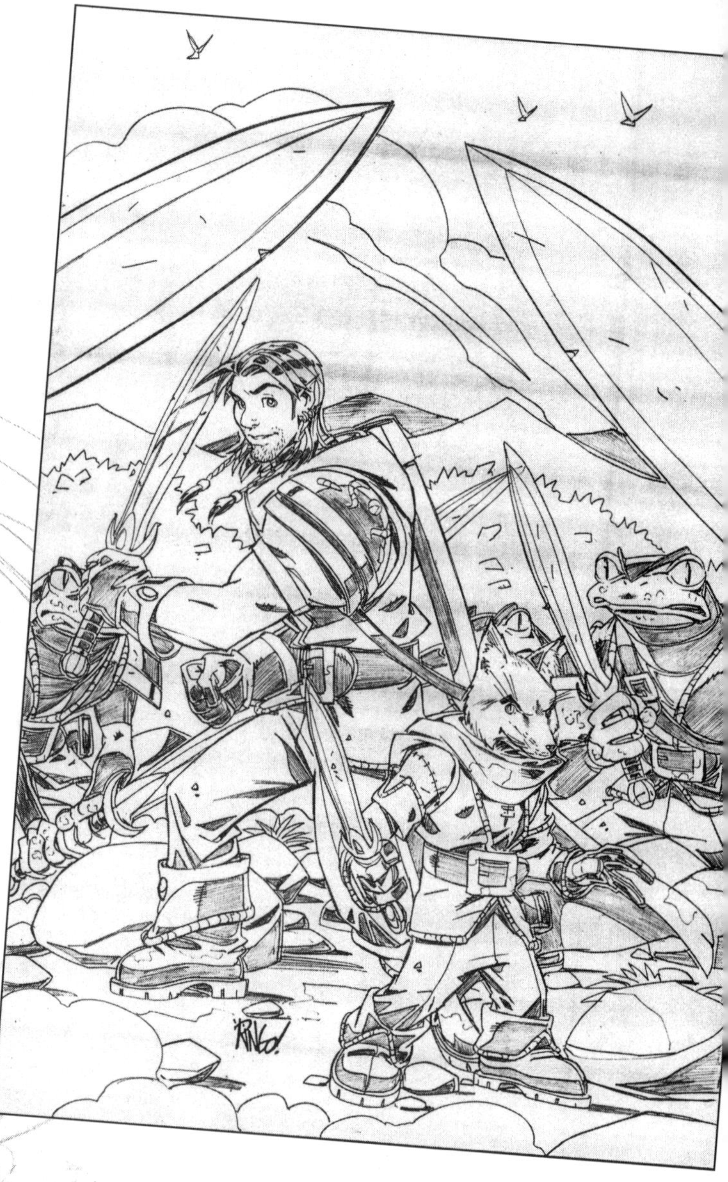

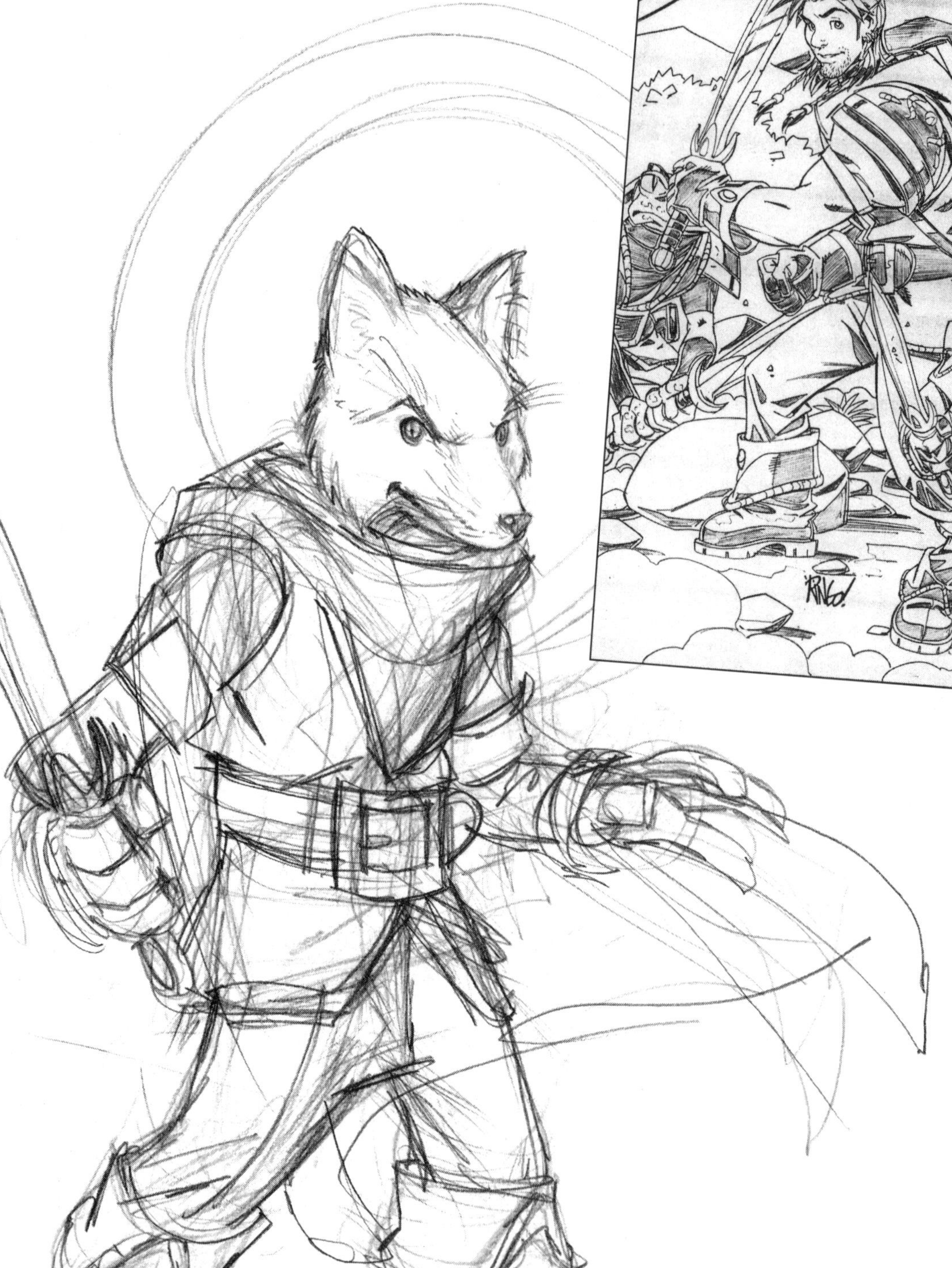

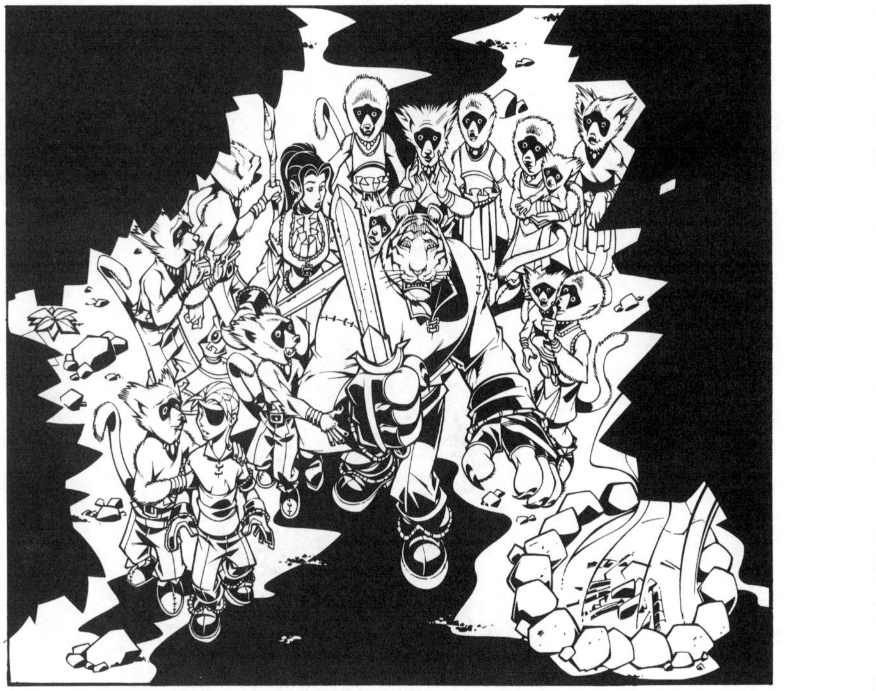

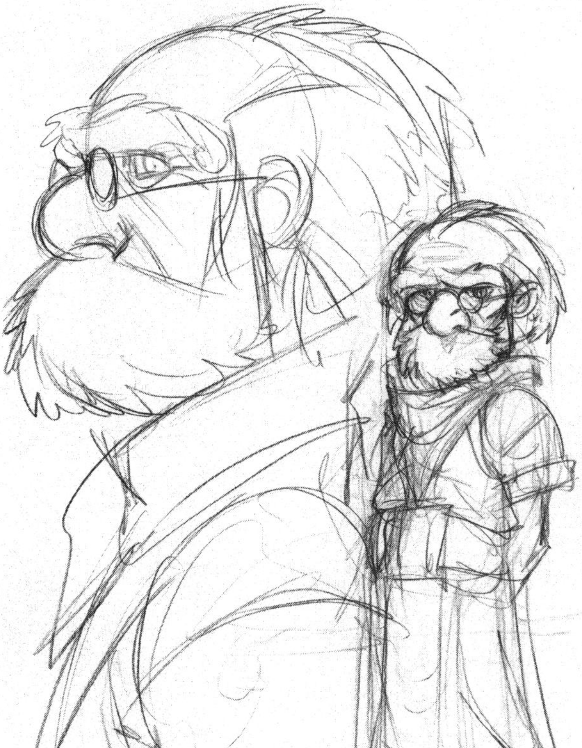

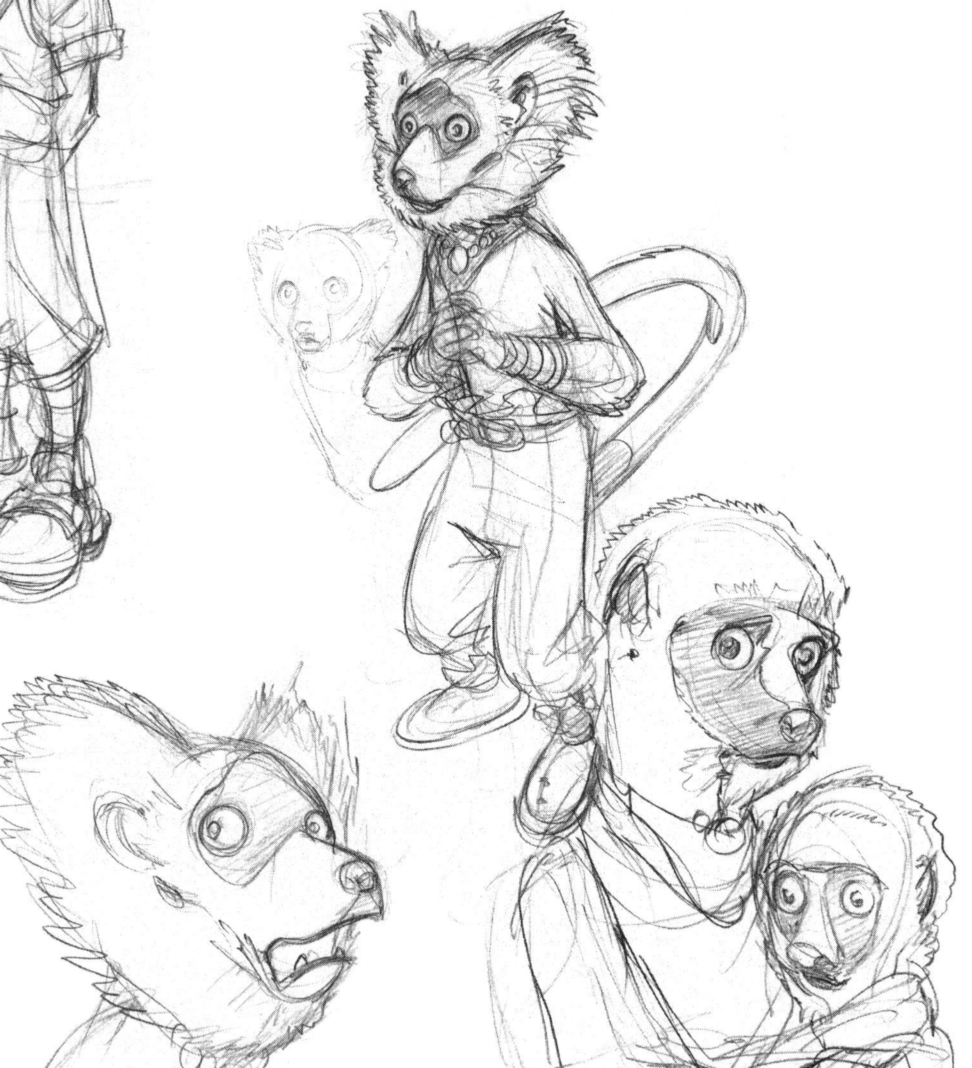

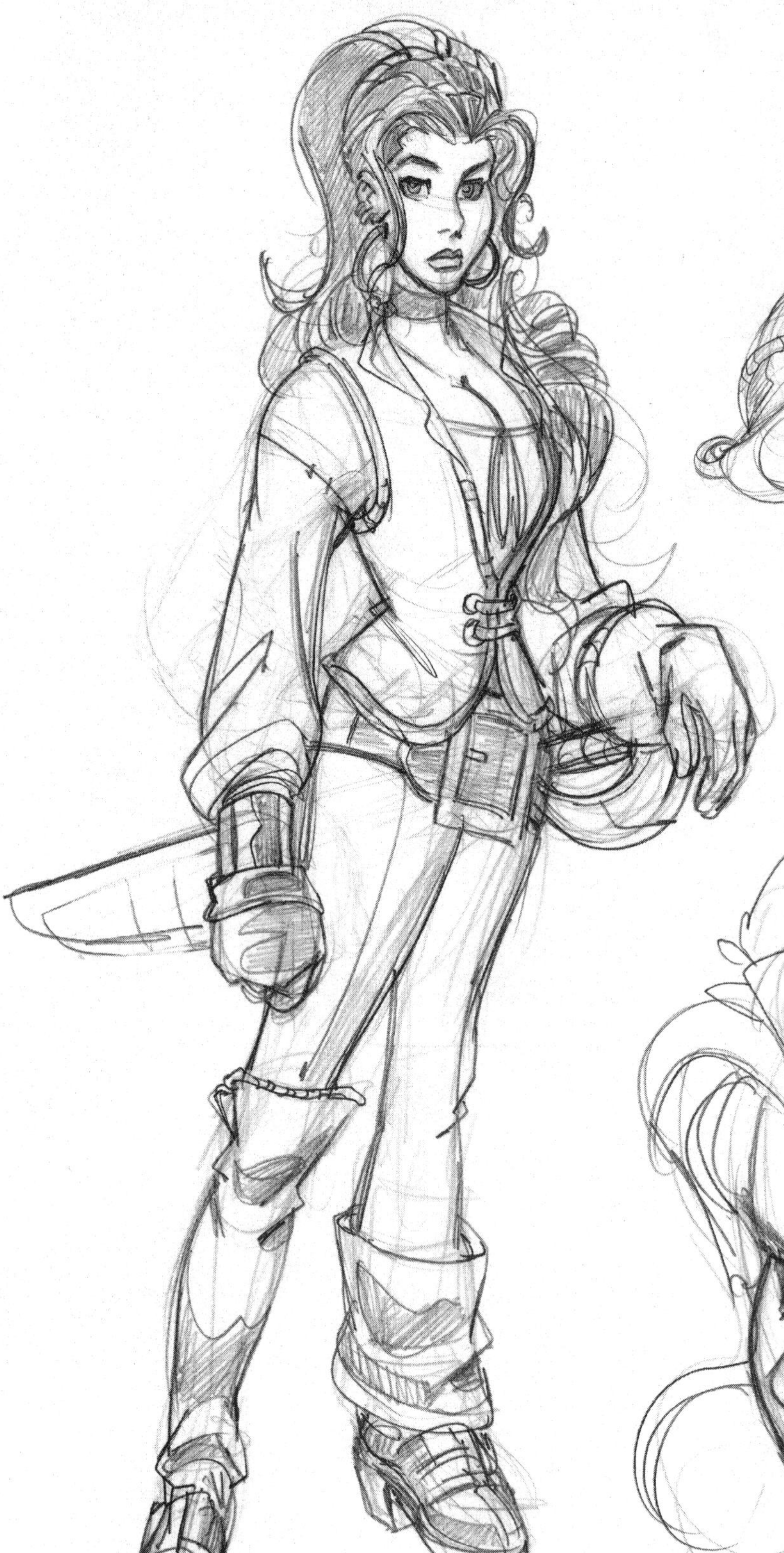

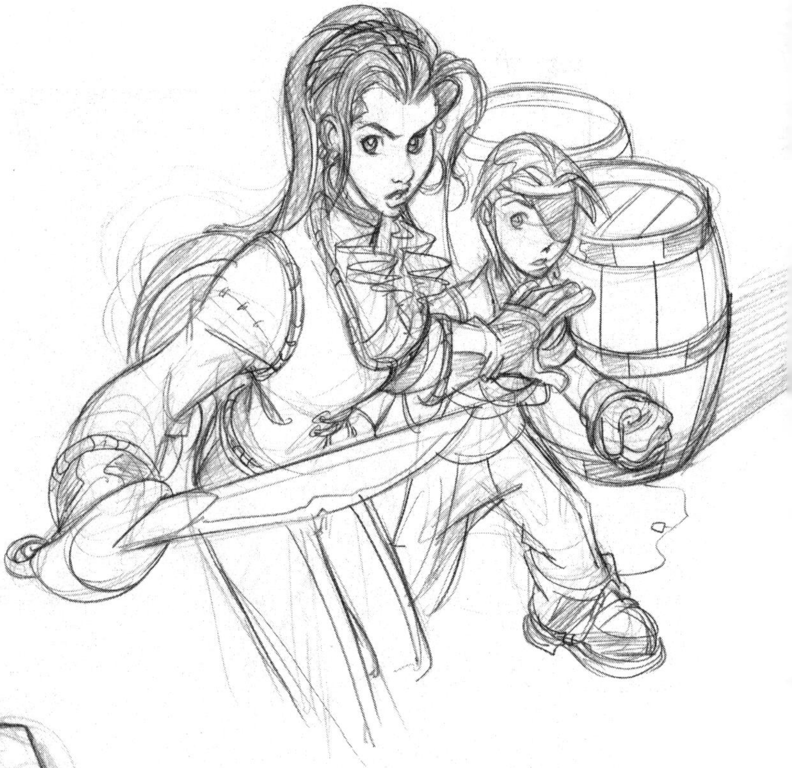

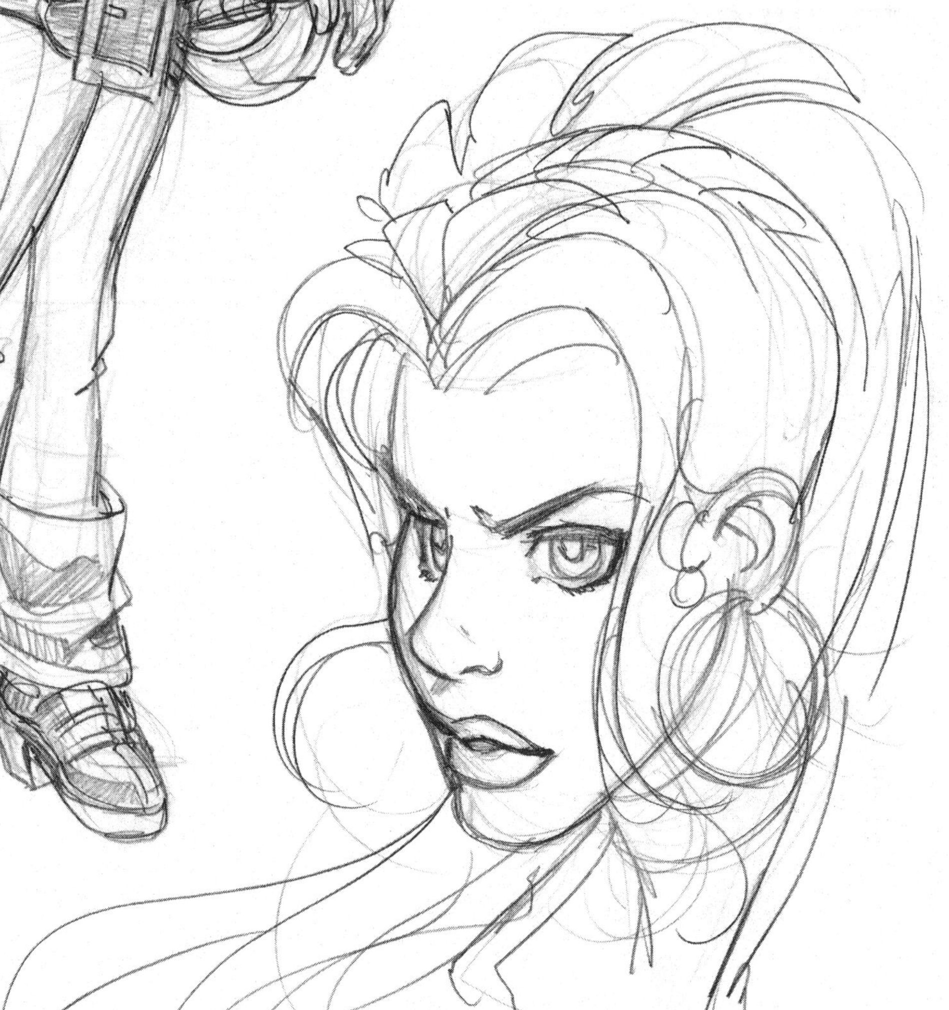

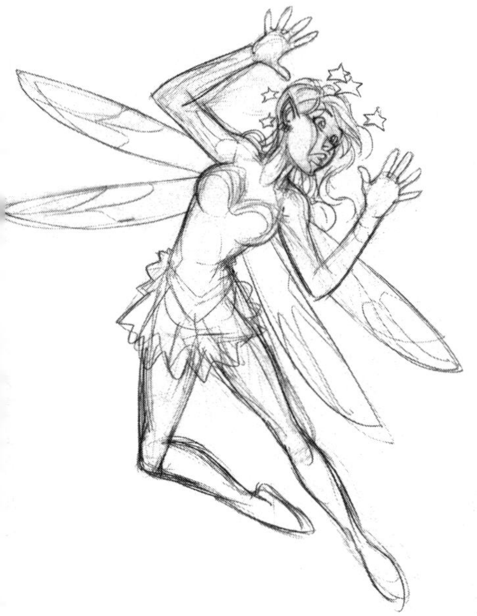

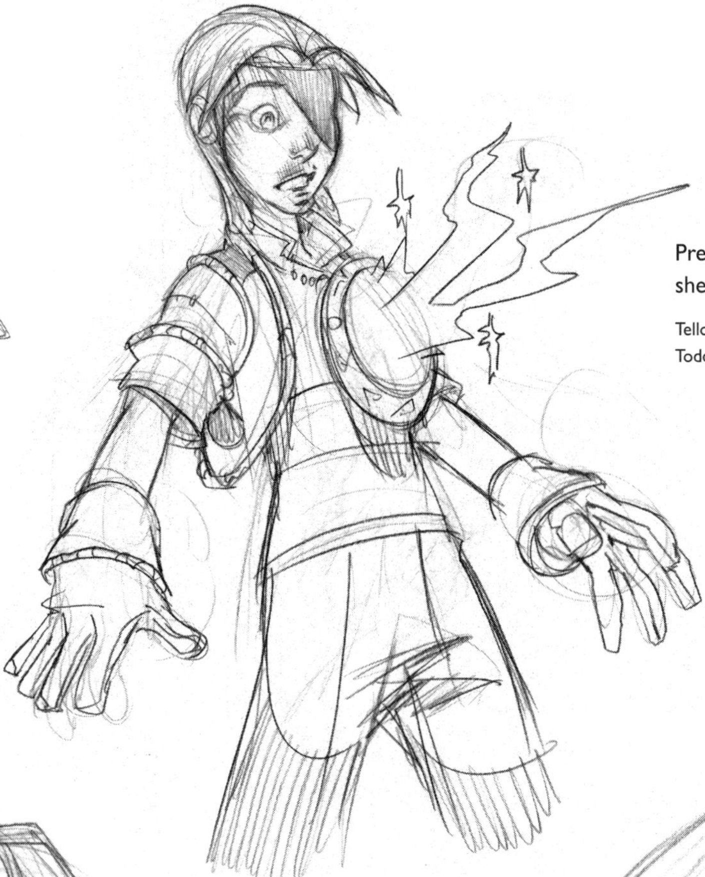

Preliminary sketches and model sheets of the *Tellos* cast.

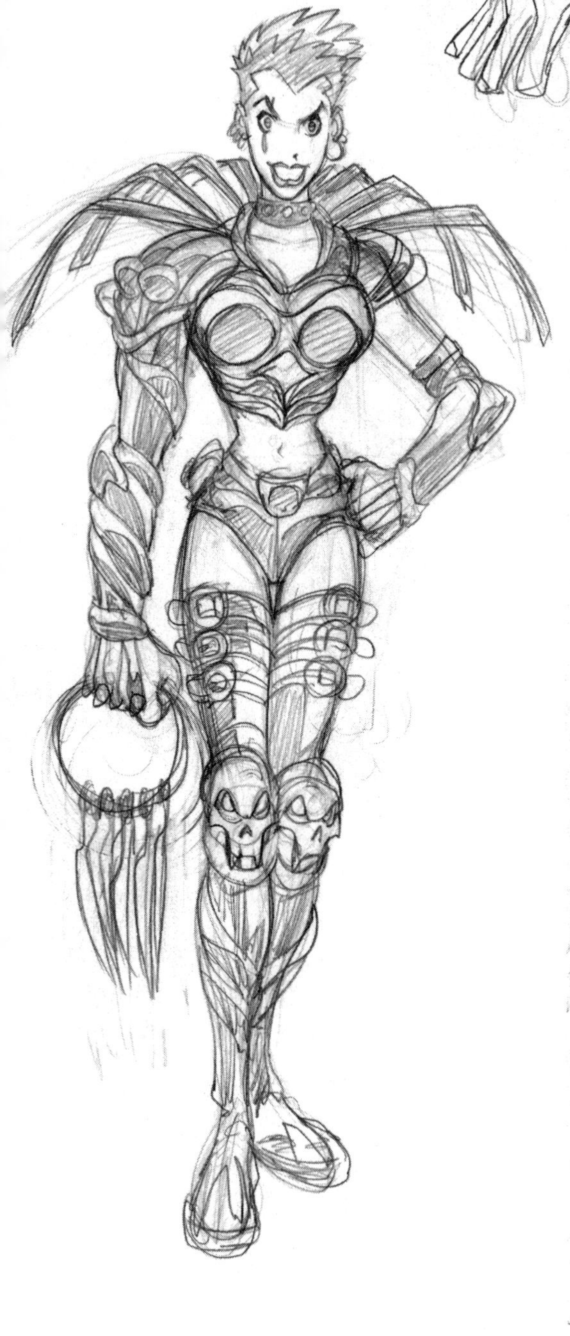

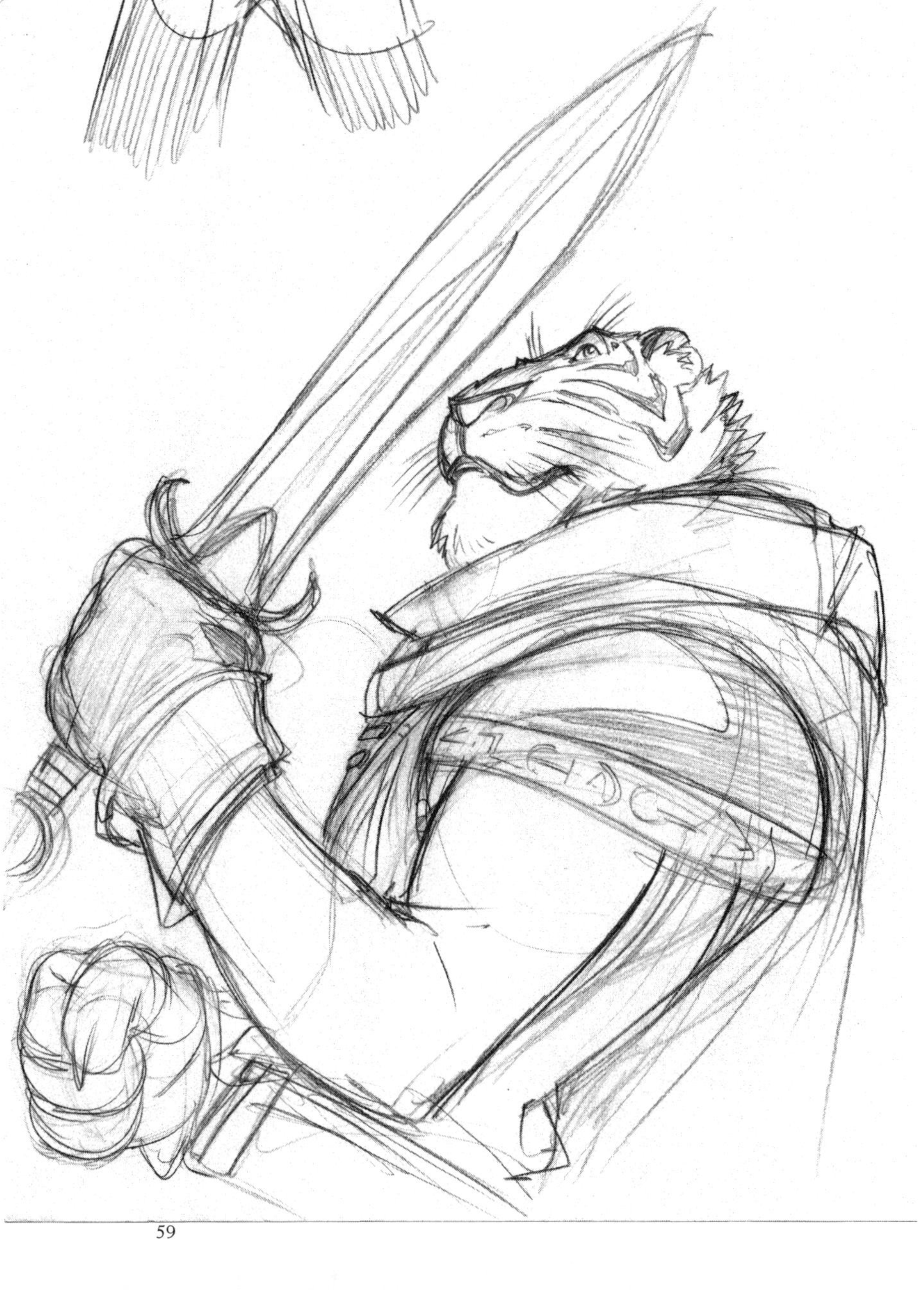

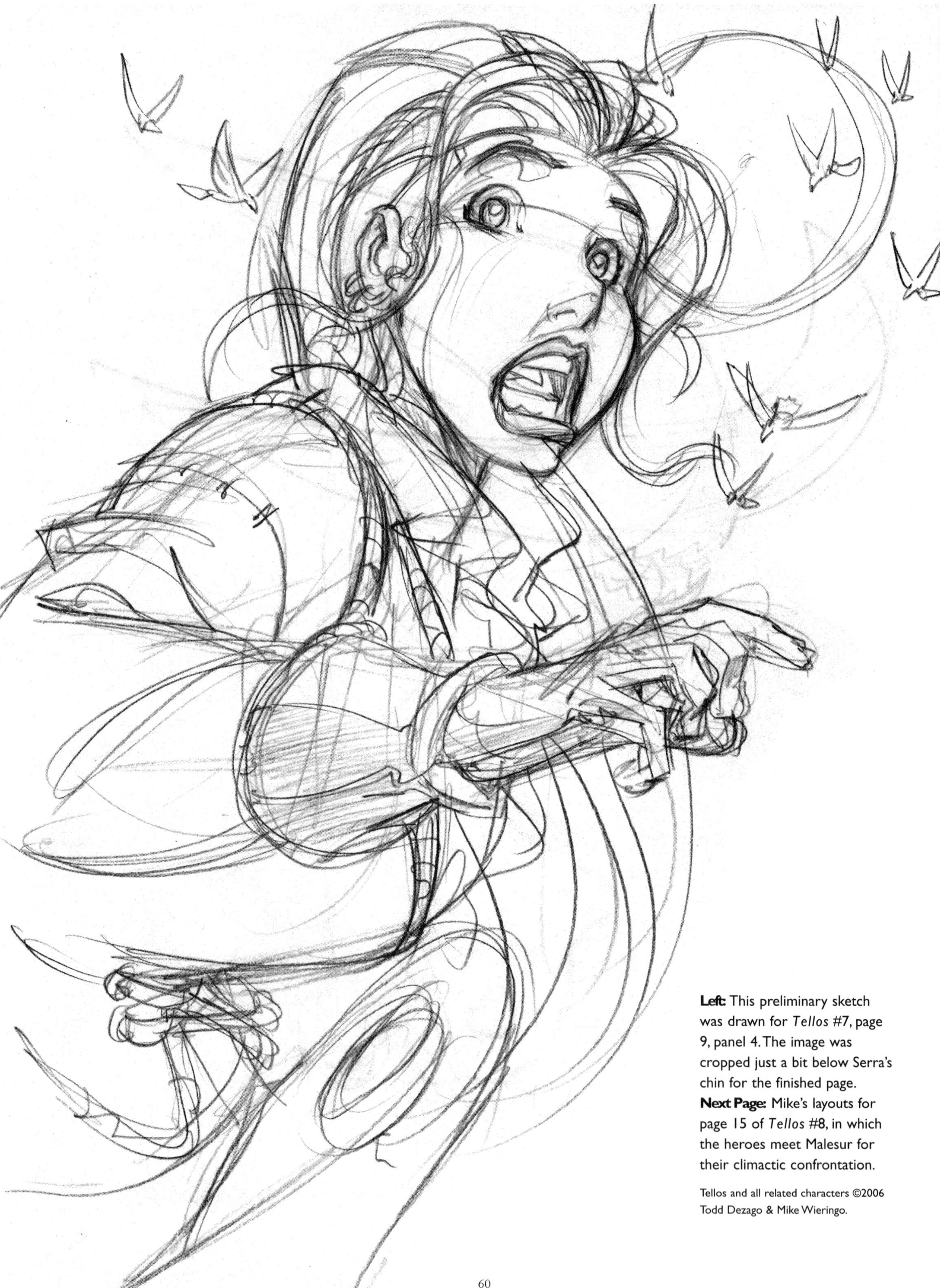

Left: This preliminary sketch was drawn for *Tellos #7*, page 9, panel 4. The image was cropped just a bit below Serra's chin for the finished page.
Next Page: Mike's layouts for page 15 of *Tellos #8*, in which the heroes meet Malesur for their climactic confrontation.

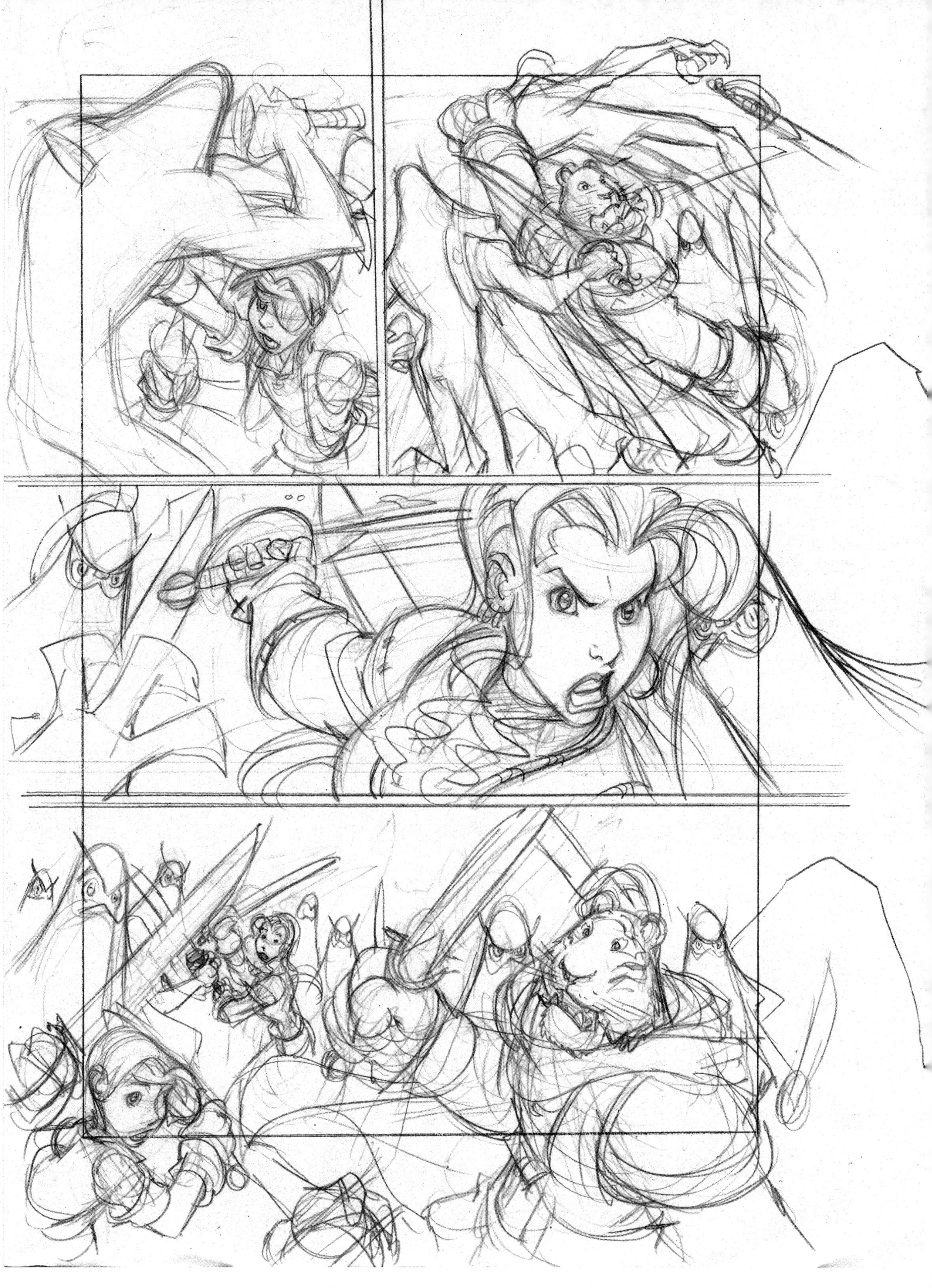

Part 6: Classic Characters in a "Non-Classic" Style

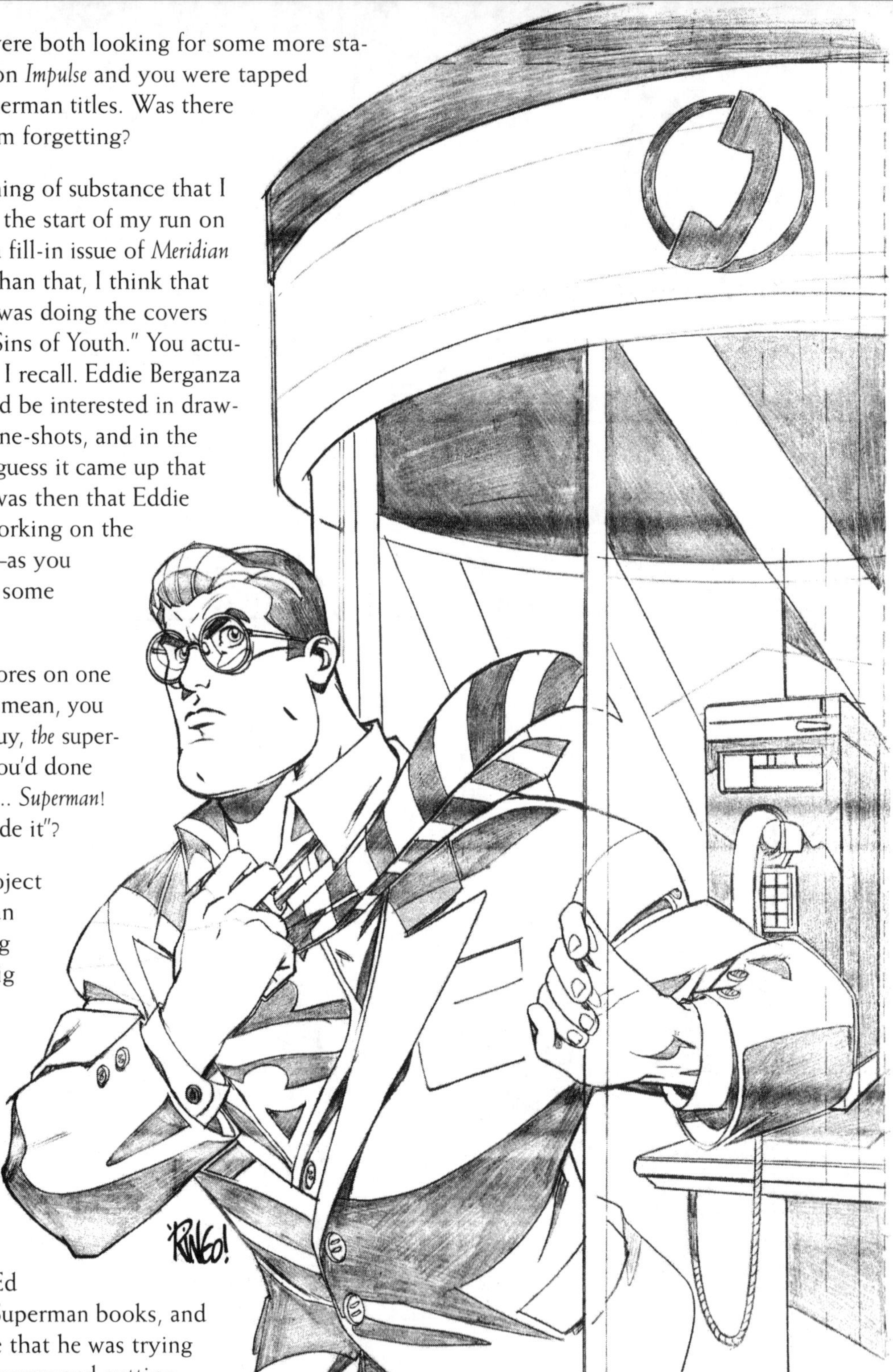
RINGO!

MM: After *Tellos* ran down, we were both looking for some more stable work. I was already working on *Impulse* and you were tapped to be the artist on one of the Superman titles. Was there anything in-between there that I'm forgetting?

MIKE: Nope. I can't recall anything of substance that I did between the end of *Tellos* and the start of my run on *Adventures of Superman*. There was a fill-in issue of *Meridian* for CrossGen comics, but other than that, I think that when *Tellos* was winding down, I was doing the covers for a DC 5th week stunt called "Sins of Youth." You actually wrote one of those books, as I recall. Eddie Berganza had called me to ask me if I would be interested in drawing the covers for that series of one-shots, and in the conversation about the covers, I guess it came up that *Tellos* was going to be ending. It was then that Eddie asked me if I'd be interested in working on the Superman title. I said yes, since—as you said—we were both ready to get some steady income going again.

MM: Was taking over the art chores on one of the Superman titles exciting? I mean, you were gonna be drawing the big guy, *the* superhero, the one that started it all! You'd done Spidey over at Marvel, but, dude... *Superman*! Did you feel like you'd really "made it"?

MIKE: Like just about every project I've started, working on Superman felt entirely intimidating. The big drawback to working on these big icons is that they come with a huge built-in fanbase, and they have certain expectations and prejudices about those characters. It's very hard to measure up to those feelings—especially when you don't have a very... classic, I guess you could say, style. I also felt a bit intimidated by the fact that Ed McGuiness was the *man* on the Superman books, and Eddie told me when he hired me that he was trying to give the books a more high-energy and cutting-edge cartoony style, so that's why he had Ed on *Superman*, and that's why he wanted to put me on

Adventures of Superman. I think I made a mistake in that I felt as though I needed to try to incorporate a bit of what Ed was doing into my own work in terms of how big he was drawing Superman—and I think that was wrongheaded. I think it hampered me to a great degree. But to the core of your question, like most of the big characters I've worked on, I felt like I was a bit of a fraud and that I didn't deserve the shot—exactly the opposite of feeling as though I'd "made it."

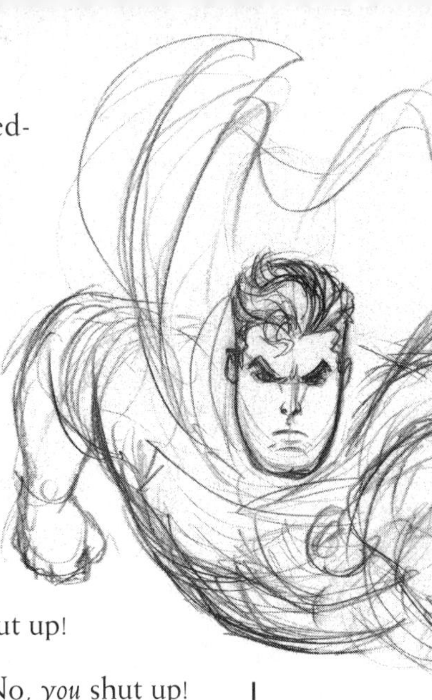

MM: You *are* wrongheaded.

MIKE: No, *you* are.

MM: Shut up!

MIKE: No, *you* shut up! [*laughter*]

MM: While working on *Sensational Spider-Man* we were faced with several occasions when a crossover with the other Spider-Man books was... ahem... necessary. And it was frustrating in that we had to set aside our stories, plans, and sub-plots for a month—or two, or three, or four—and that we were also only telling a quarter of

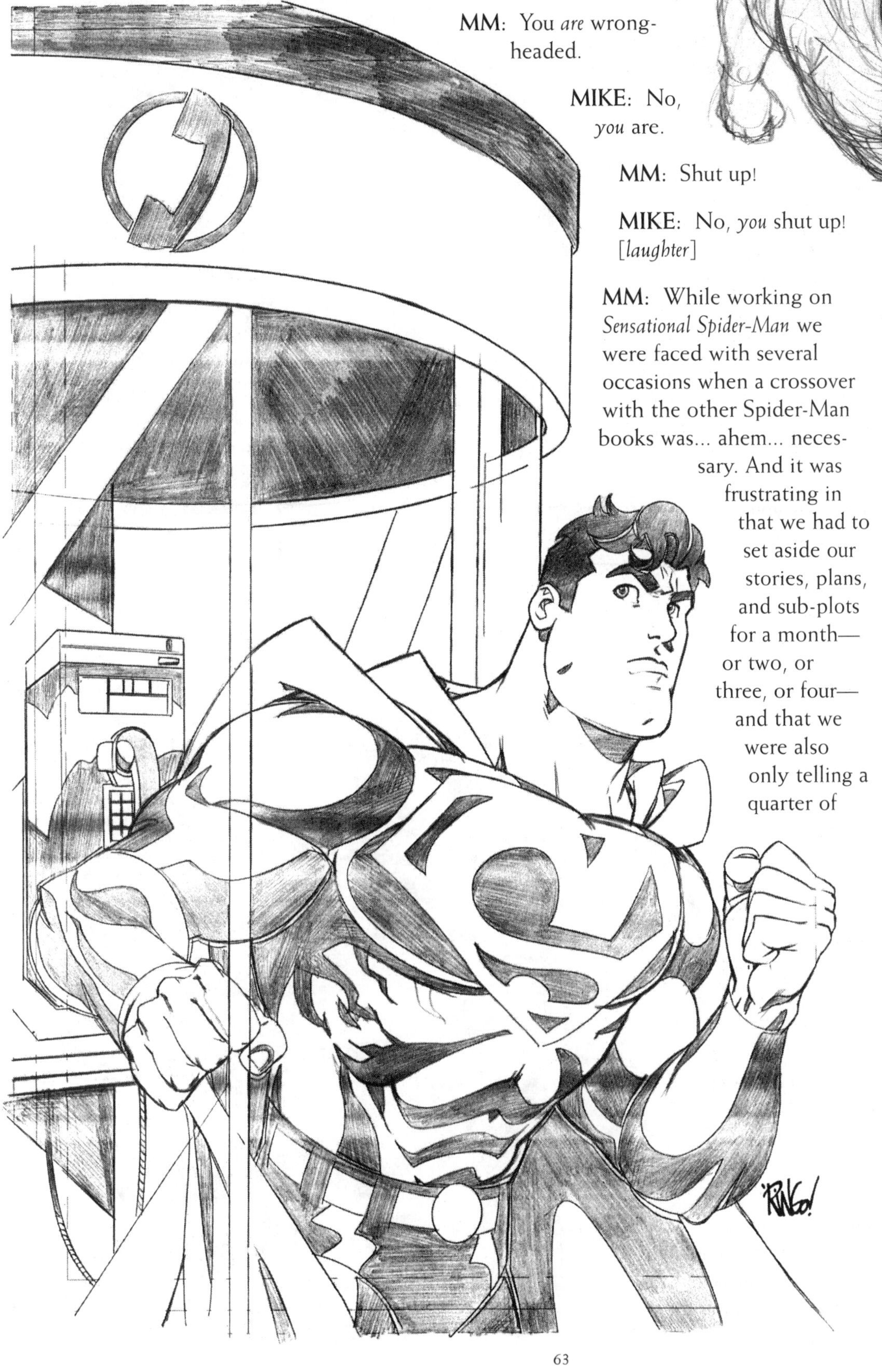
'RINGO!

Left: Presto change-o! Cover pencils for *Adventures of Superman* #598 and *Superman: Man of Steel* #120.
Above: Superman layout sketch.

the story, a chapter without a resolution, without a conclusion to build to. That can be very frustrating. At the time, the Superman books were *only* that, a continuing crossover from one title to the next. How was that?

MIKE: It was utterly devoid of any creative fulfillment. I wasn't privy to any of the story points to the other books, which made my work on *Adventures of Superman* like being partially blind. I had no idea what I was in the middle of, so I was always off-balance. It's one of the main reasons I didn't stay on the book any longer than I did. I just had no real hope of enjoying anything I was working on. Probably more than at any other time in my career, I felt like just a cog in a machine... like a pencil for hire with no creative input whatsoever.

MM: Did you have any opportunity to voice this frustration? Did DC look for something else for you, to give you something that you could actually sink your teeth into and flex your storytelling muscles?

MIKE: Not really. I voiced some concerns to Eddie about the writing and inking on the book, that I was dissatisfied with both, but he never really did anything permanently about it. I remember he assigned a different inker on one issue to sort of appease me, I suppose, and I told him how much I really loved what he had done. I think it was Lary Stucker. The very next issue, Lary was gone again, and I was back to getting inks I was unhappy with. I don't think that Eddie ever took much stock in anything I had to say as far as wanting even a modicum of control to the visuals. I certainly couldn't have story input, but the other things that Eddie told me I *could* have, like being assigned to another of the Superman titles or having a new permanent inker, never came about. The situation just wasn't what I wanted it to be, so I left.

Below: More iconic cover art, this time for *Adventures of Superman* #591 and 596, respectively.
Next Page: During Mike's all-too-short stint on *Adventures of Superman*, he was able to show his take on the never-ending struggle between Superman and Darkseid. Layouts from *Adventures of Superman* #595.

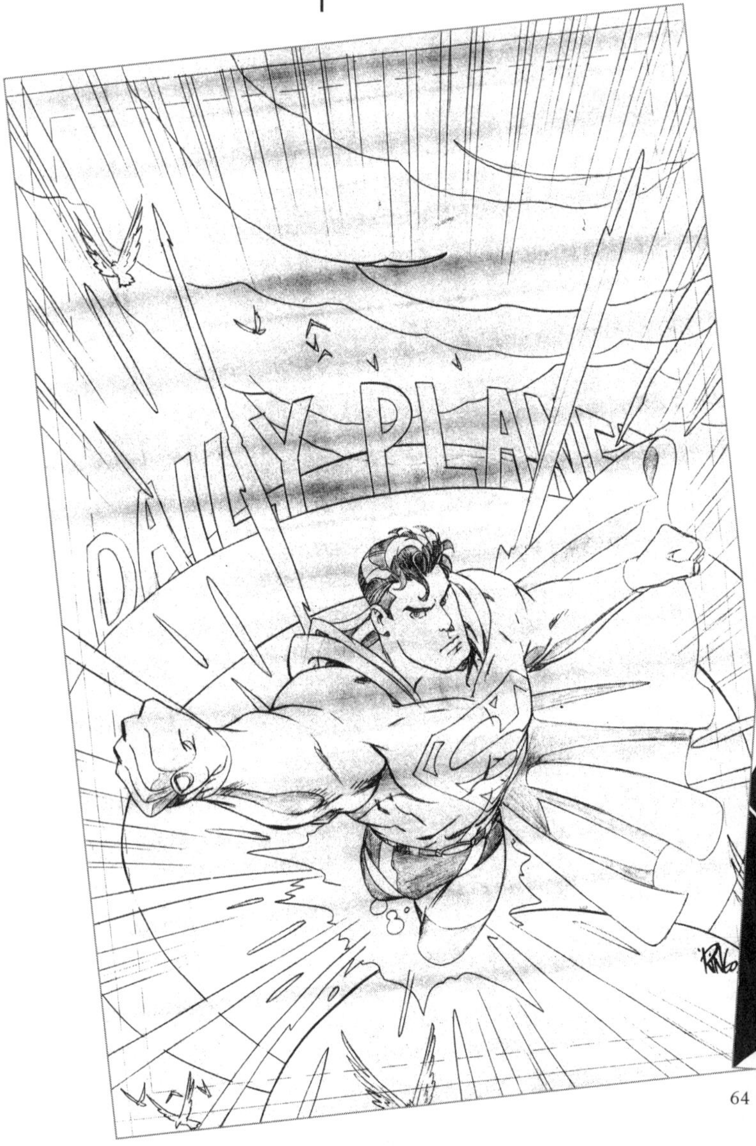

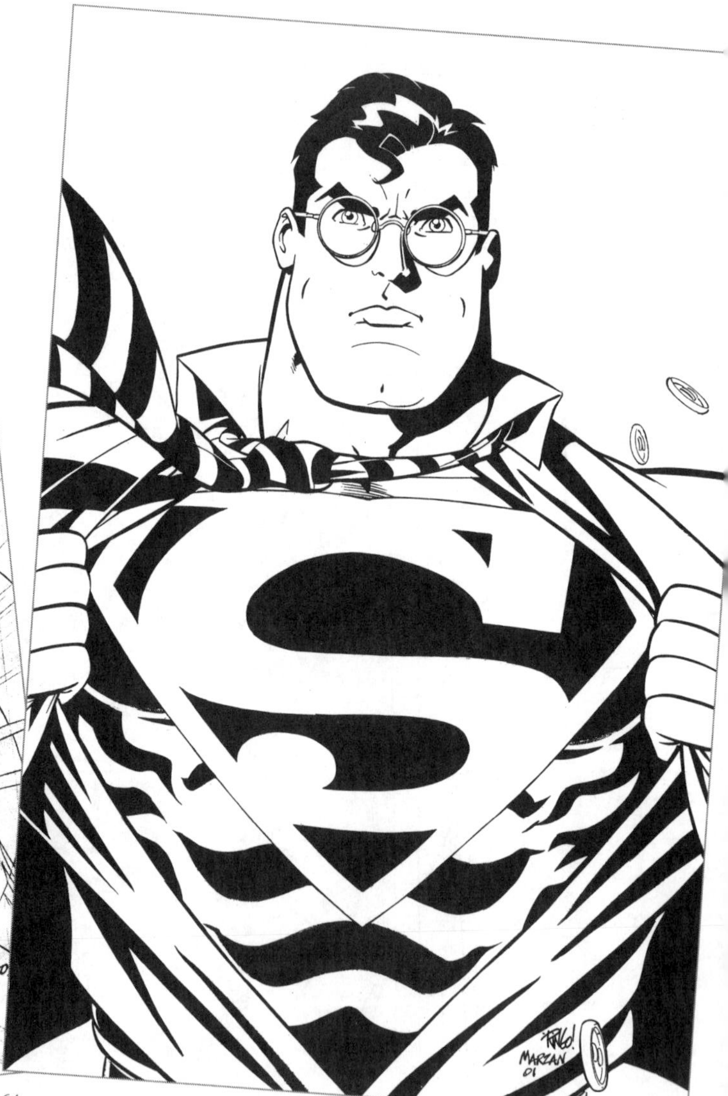

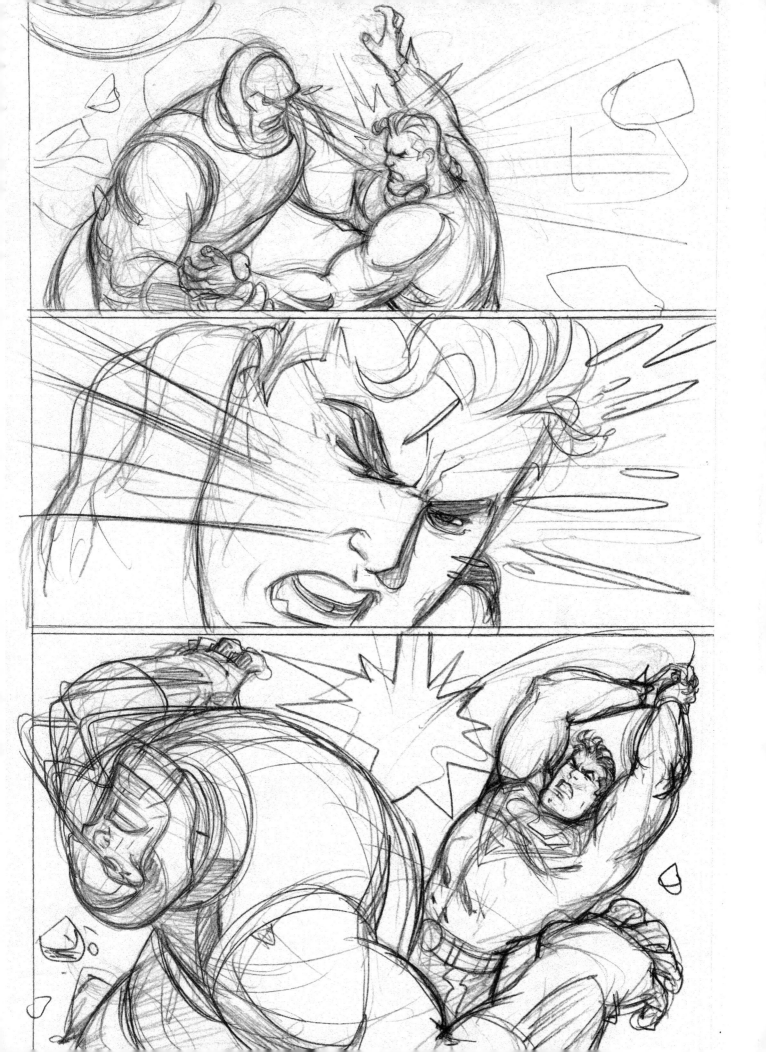

DAILY

Above: Mr. Kent goes to Washington... but he doesn't like what he finds!
Next Page Top: Reed and Franklin spend some quality time together. In trying to capture the best expression for Reed in panel 2, Mike drew a couple of studies first.
Next Page, Bottom Left: A fun sketch exploring the playful (mostly) relationship between Ben and Johnny.

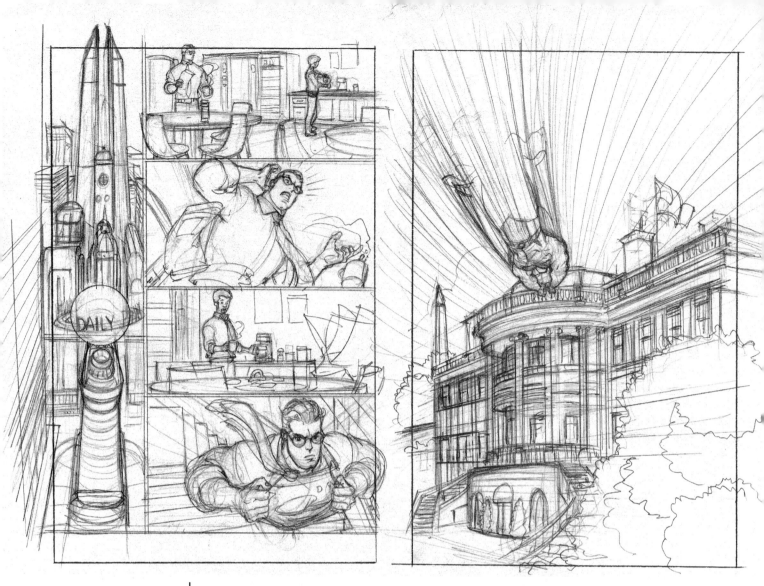

MM: So at this point you ended up going over to Marvel to start the *Fantastic Four* with Mark Waid. Was this a conscious decision to leave DC or was that just where the work was?

MIKE: I quit *Adventures of Superman* without actually having anything else lined up. I don't know if I've ever done that before, but I just couldn't take it anymore. The straw that broke the camel's back, so to speak, was when I got the script for the big 600th anniversary issue of *Adventures of Superman*, and rather than it being about some big, grand Superman adventure, it was a story about [then-President] Lex Luthor getting implanted with some chip that made him take on the persona of *Alex* Luthor, a criminal mastermind who wore a bad wig tilted to one side. The story was nothing like I thought a big anniversary issue should be; it was silly and—to my mind—a waste of an opportunity to do something special. So I had had enough and after reading the script, and put in my notice telling Eddie that the anniversary issue would be my last. I don't know how this happened, but word got out that I was off the book... perhaps through the Internet, I dunno. But it wasn't long after my quitting *Adventures of Superman* that I got the call from Tom Brevoort offering me the penciling gig on *Fantastic Four*. I jumped at it immediately.

MM: And, of course, that was with the awesome—and our pal—Mark Waid, someone with whom you'd worked before and who you could count on for exciting, solid stories. Were you psyched? Did you guys talk about what you were gonna do? Or did he already have things planned out?

MIKE: I was brought on the title before the book was offered to Mark to write. Tom told me that there were several folks that they were thinking of to write *FF* and

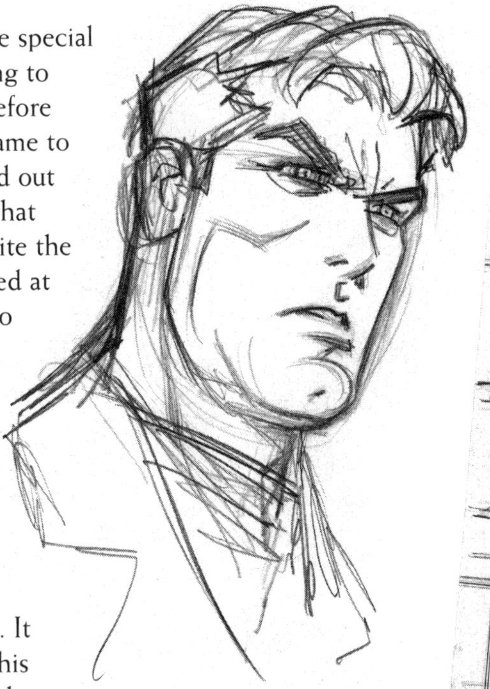

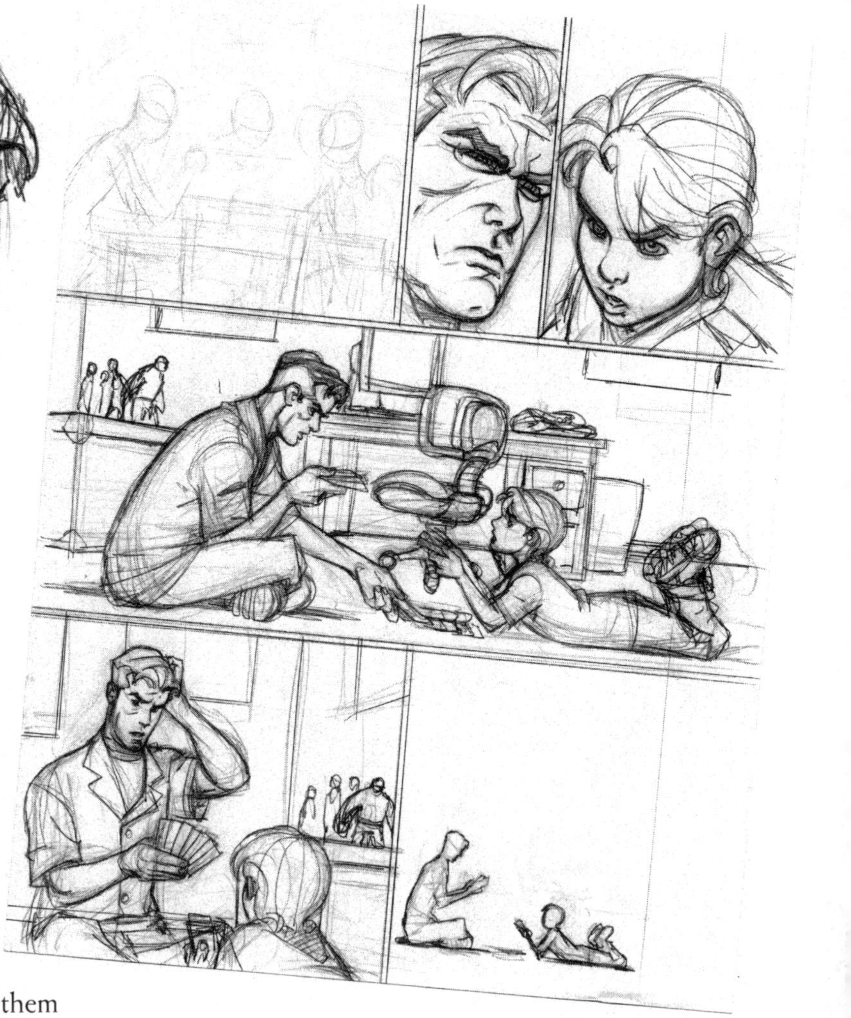

that there was one special guy he was waiting to hear back from before he revealed his name to me. When I found out it was Mark and that he'd agreed to write the book, I was thrilled at the opportunity to work with him again. Mark and I spoke on the phone at length, and he gave me an overview of what he had in mind for the title. It sounded terrific; his ideas to bring back the emphasis on family and exploration again was something that really clicked with me. Mark then wrote a great long treatment that I was able to read, and he had so many wonderful ideas for the direction of the book that I knew this was going to be something special. Actually, Mark didn't get around to using every one of the ideas he laid out in the overview... and some of them were doozies. But it was very exciting to be in on this book and this creative team.

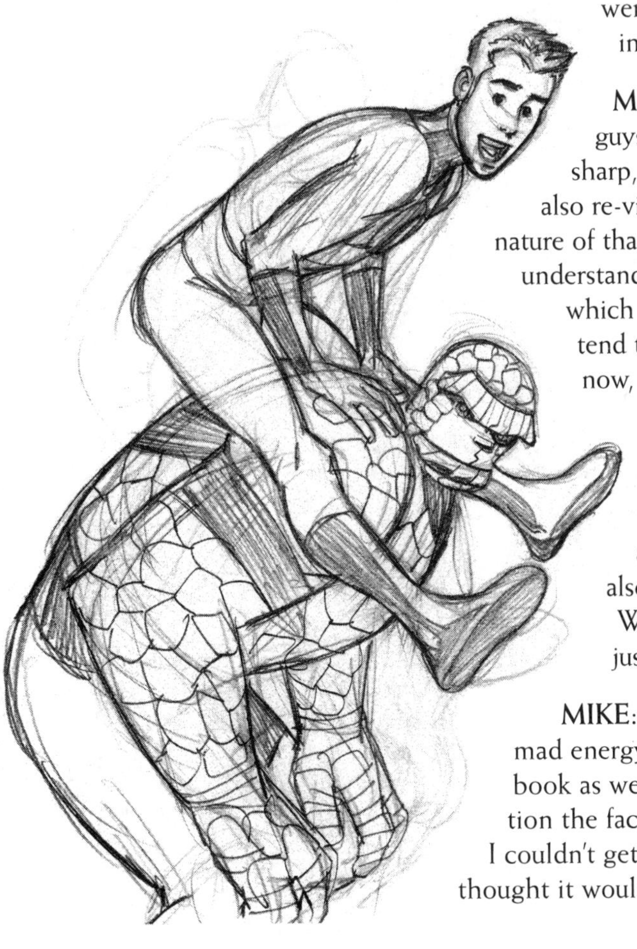

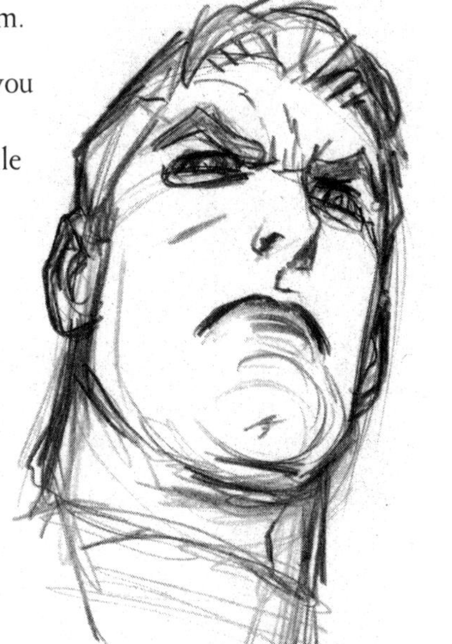

MM: It really was a stellar run! And you guys did a fantastic job of presenting sharp, progressive, and unique stories while also re-visiting/re-establishing the essential nature of that book—family strength and understanding—without going all retro, which is what a lot of writers and artists tend to do. Looking over those issues now, you threw in some Kirby-esque devices and apparati here and there, but much of it looks, well... Ringo-esque. New and smoother. It was a great balance, giving it a taste of Jack, but also saying, "C'mon, let's move along." Was that a conscious effort or were you just getting the page done?

MIKE: I knew going in that I was never going to be able to match that mad energy and brilliant design that Jack Kirby brought to the *Fantastic Four* book as well as everything else he drew in his wonderful career. Not to mention the fact that even if I *tried* to match those design elements in a Kirby style, I couldn't get any work done; that stuff is just too complicated in nature. So I thought it would serve me well to try to work out something more streamlined and

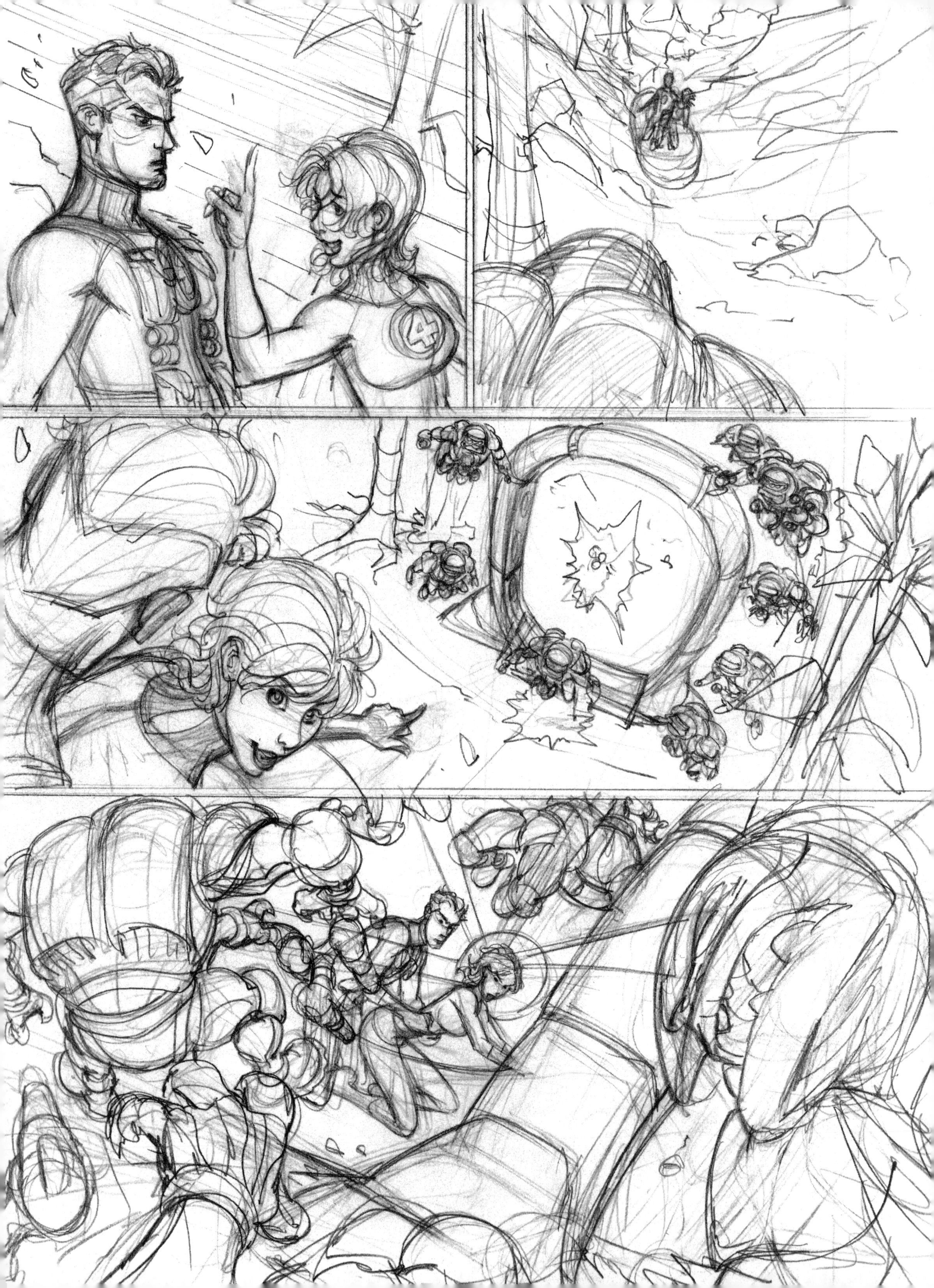

modern in design—something I could do quickly and would still look nice on the page. I can only hope that it worked.

MM: In that this was your second run on an ongoing book with Mark, with several years in-between for both of you to grow and hone your respective crafts, how was this collaboration different? Or were things pretty much the same, without any need for that "honeymoon period"?

MIKE: I think the biggest difference is that when we were working on *Flash*, I was a completely new, untried penciler. I didn't have the years of experience and work under my belt I had going into *FF*. So Mark didn't have much of an idea of what I was capable of—especially in the beginning, my first several issues. There were times, after the first half or so of my work with Mark on *Flash*, when he finally felt comfortable with calling me and talking out various scenes. He'd call to consult with me about what I felt comfortable with in conveying what he wanted to depict in certain scenes; he'd discuss with me how to best work it out without driving me nuts in the process by asking for something I wasn't capable of. By the time we were working on *Fantastic Four* together, he was very comfortable with calling me and talking things out. It seemed very natural at that point, because in point of fact, not only had we been working partners in the past, we'd become friends, as well. So there's now a very comfortable level of discussion between us—not only about work subjects, but now we can just talk about anything. So that's another difference when it came to working on *FF*. Mark wasn't learning about a new artist and a new person, we were buddies and former co-workers.

MM: You got to draw all sorts of stories there: some great family stuff, character interaction, a fun Spidey guest star, and, of course, you guys finished up your run with

Previous Page: Reed and Sue go exploring. Layouts for *Fantastic Four* vol. 3 #68, page 8.
Below: Spidey gets in on the fun. This layout was drawn at a full 8½" x 11" for panel 2 of *Fantastic Four* #512, page 5 (during Mark and Mike's run on FF, the numbering reverted back to that of the first volume).

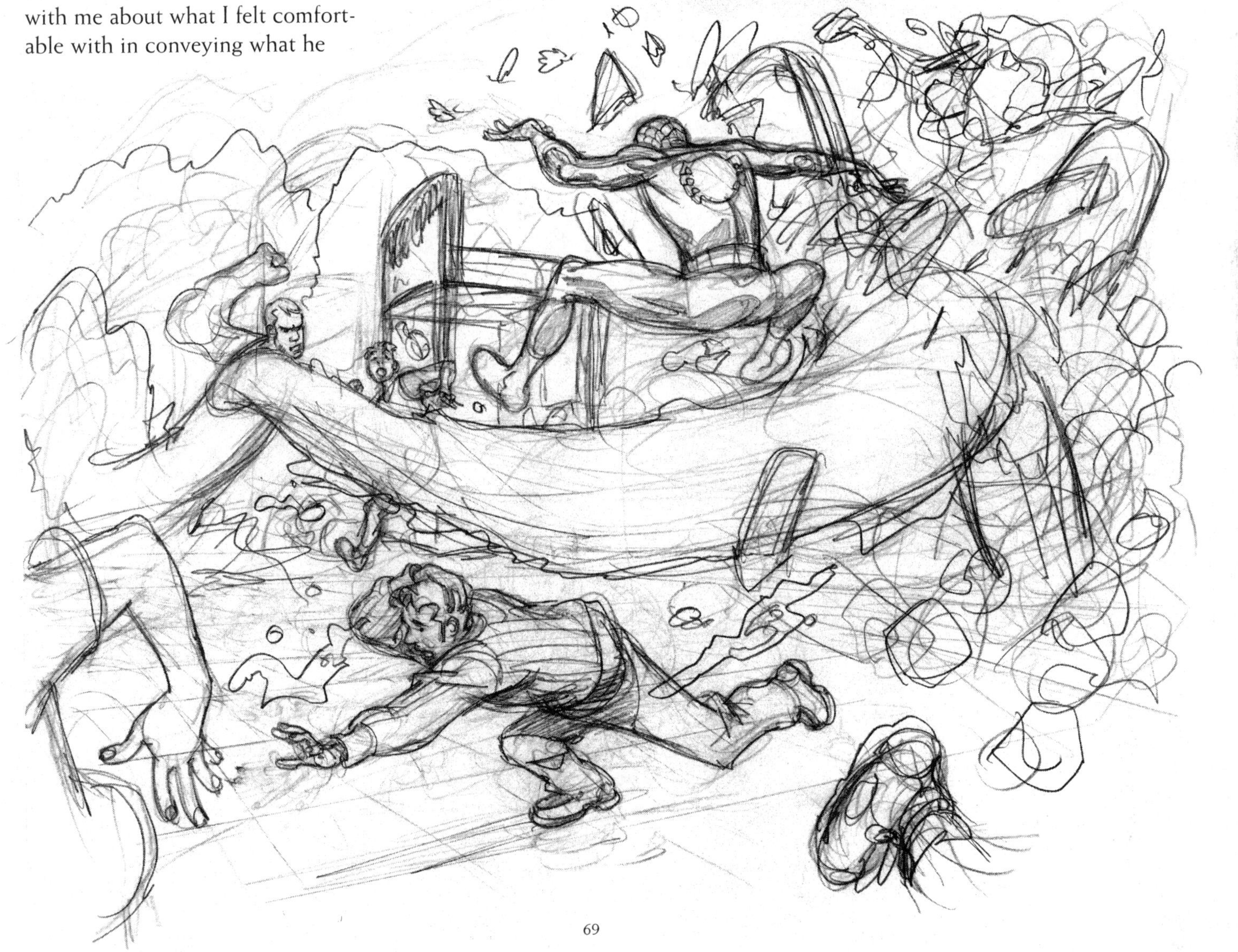

Below: The dramatic return of Dr. Doom! **Next Page:** In an interesting twist on the Galactus saga, Johnny becomes the herald of Galactus. Layouts for *Fantastic Four* #521, page 20, panel 1.

a truly cosmic tale that was filled with both the interstellar grandeur and the world-threatening suspense that *is* the Fantastic Four! Were there any FF villains or characters that you didn't get to draw along the way?

MIKE: The *Fantastic Four* comic has such a rich history that there are certainly a lot of characters I didn't get to draw, but I don't have any regrets. I think it was Mark's intention to avoid cycling through all the various villains and characters that it seems that every creative team before us went through. It became rote to sort of try to emulate the magic of what Jack and Stan did in their original run, but who can really match that...? So Mark stuck with just the "big two" of FF antagonists: Dr. Doom and Galactus. They were integral to major, defining story arcs for our run, and along the way, I got to draw Medusa, Lockjaw, and Crystal in Attillan on the moon as well as Alicia Masters. I'd be lying if I said it wouldn't have been cool to get to draw such characters as Blastaar, Annihilus, The Watcher, and The Impossible Man, but if it would have meant compromising the integrity of the stories that Mark was telling just for the sake of working in characters I might have liked to take a crack at, it certainly wouldn't have been worth it. So, ultimately, I'm satisfied.

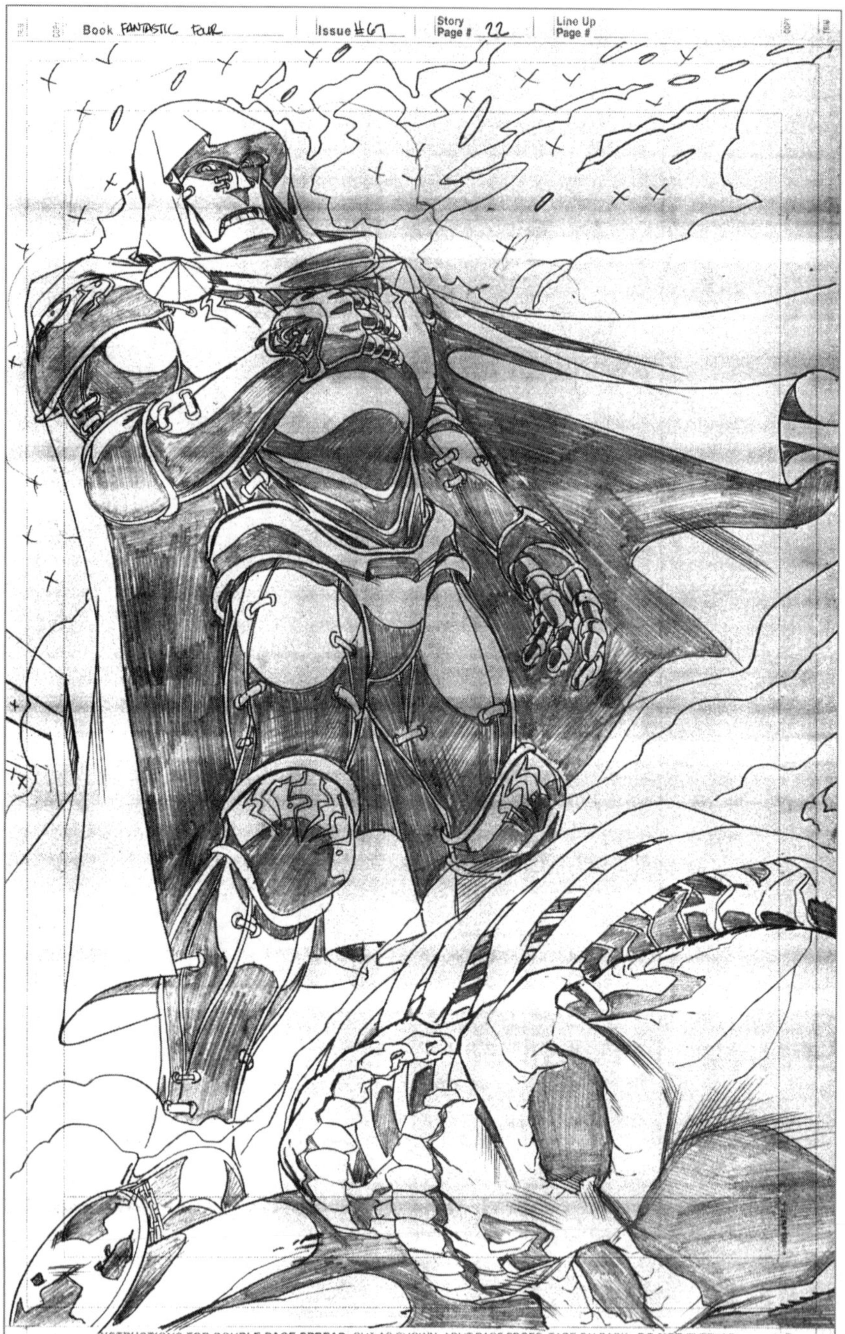
Book FANTASTIC FOUR
Issue #
Story Page # 22
Line Up Page #
INSTRUCTIONS FOR DOUBLE PAGE SPREAD: CUT AS SHOWN, ABUT PAGE EDGES, TAPE ON BACK. DO NOT OVERLAP

MM: There was a slight rumor of controversy surrounding the two of you leaving the book; first you were leaving, then you were gonna hang around for a while, then you weren't. Can you tell us what happened there or is it moot?

MIKE: Well, everyone with an Internet connection and an interest in super-hero comic books knows about that situation, I guess. The then-publisher at Marvel, Bill Jemas, decided that he wanted another direction for the *FF* book, even though what Mark was doing was very popular. Mark had no interest in that, so Jemas decided he'd remove him from the title and install a writer that he'd found from the theater biz to take over. I read the first script, and had no interest in this new direction... it just didn't make any sense. So I decided to leave the book as well, as a way of supporting Mark, really. I started talking to the folks at DC about working with Mark on the *Legion of Super-Heroes* title he was going to start writing, but they were reticent to offer me a contract, which is what I wanted. By the time they finally came through with a contract offer, I'd committed to [*FF* editor] Tom Brevoort that I'd draw two transition issues of *FF* written by someone other than Mark or the new writer as a bridge to the new direction.

That kind of soured the folks at DC on me, so they pulled the contract. They didn't want me to do those two issues, but I'd promised Tom I would, and I didn't want

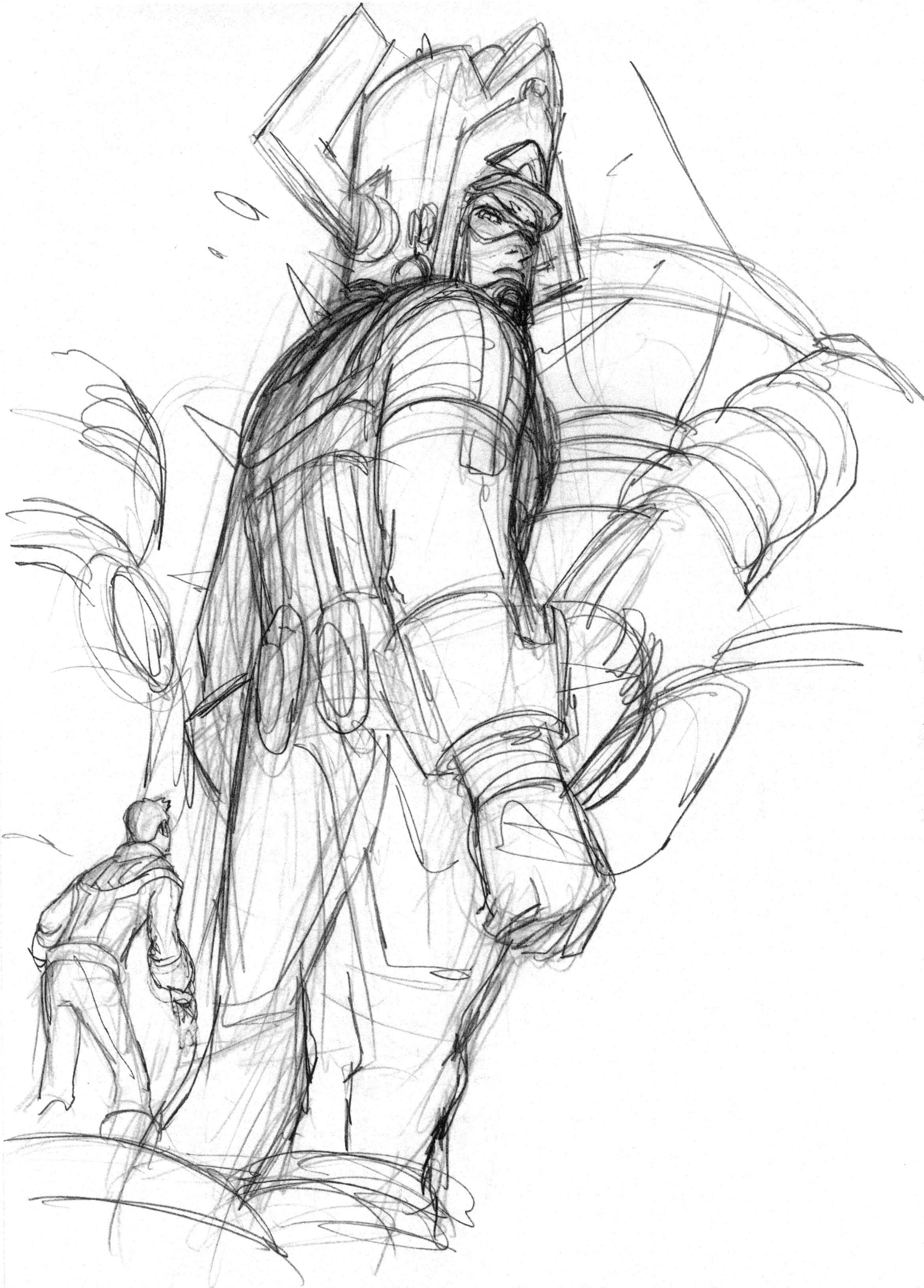

Right: Layouts for *Friendly Neighborhood Spider-Man* #4, page 22.
Below: Layouts for *Friendly Neighborhood Spider-Man* #5, page 14. In this issue—a wonderful standalone story told through flashbacks—Mike was able to draw quite a few villains from Spidey's rogue's gallery.
Next Page: Spidey evolves... which leads to new powers and a new costume. Not exactly what Mike had been looking forward to drawing. Layouts for *Friendly Neighborhood Spider-Man* #3, page 14.

Mary Jane Parker, Morlun, Rhino, Spider-Man ™ and ©2006 Marvel Characters, Inc.

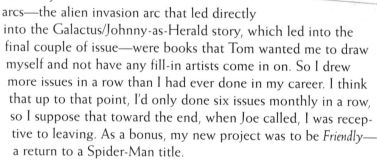

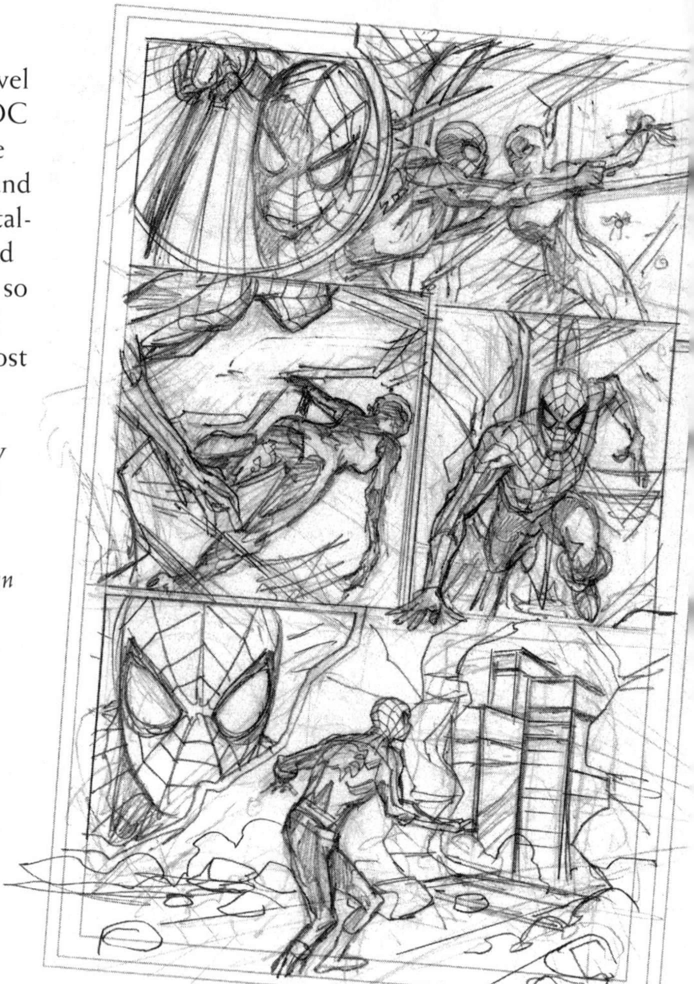

to break a promise. Fortunately, Marvel made up the loss of the contract at DC by offering me one with them. In the meantime, Jemas changed his plans and decided to launch his *FF* idea as a totally new book, and Mark was reinstated as writer on the main *FF* comic. And so we were back to work, with a several month blip for me, but Mark never lost a step in the whole debacle.

MM: And was the next thing *Friendly Neighborhood Spider-Man*? Or was there something in-between there?

MIKE: *Friendly Neighborhood Spider-Man* was the next thing. Joe Quesada called me to say that they were looking to make a change in the creative team. His idea was that to try to keep some heat on the book, that they needed some new blood to come in and take over. I was, I guess, getting a little fatigued by working on the [*FF*]—especially in the last push on the final eight issues of the book.

The story arcs—the alien invasion arc that led directly into the Galactus/Johnny-as-Herald story, which led into the final couple of issue—were books that Tom wanted me to draw myself and not have any fill-in artists come in on. So I drew more issues in a row than I had ever done in my career. I think that up to that point, I'd only done six issues monthly in a row, so I suppose that toward the end, when Joe called, I was receptive to leaving. As a bonus, my new project was to be *Friendly*—a return to a Spider-Man title.

MM: You hadn't worked with Peter David before, had you? Did you two connect, talk over story, or chat to get on the same page?

MIKE: We had a discussion in a three-way conference call with Tom Brevoort, but it was mostly one-sided. Peter told me how he worked—how he prefers to write full script and has his own ideas. He told me that I could suggest some characters I'd like to draw and he'd try to work them in, but for the most part, I got the feeling it was a situation where he had his own ideas, and he wanted to implement them without much feedback. So I felt that it was an atmosphere where I would be most appreciated as a "silent partner." Beyond that, I called him a couple of times to clarify things in the script on different occasions, but it was hit or miss as to whether he'd be home. I remember one time, by the time he got back to me, I'd already talked the situation over with the editor and moved on. Not much communication, no.

MM: When we took over *Sensational* we had to deal, for several issues, with the end of "The Clone Saga" and Ben Reilly in a different Spider-Man costume. But that changed soon enough. With *Friendly Neighborhood* you hardly had a chance to draw him before he took on that Tony Stark-designed spider-armor and then Peter began revisiting his old *Spider-Man 2099* canon. Is it frustrating to be drawing a Spider-Man book and not be able to draw Spider-Man?

MIKE: It is... it was. Especially since the way the book was pitched to me was that it would be—of the three monthly Spider-Man titles—the more traditional, classic version of the character. I was looking forward to drawing stories that hearkened back to the glory days of the book... more the Ditko and Romita era than what actually happened. It was disappointing... but I understood that there are things that the company feels it needs to do to garner excitement and sales for their books. And, to be honest, it worked with the "The Other" crossover event. *Friendly*

came out of the gate with fantastic sales. And when they decided, after that stunt, to go with a new costume design, I actually thought the new design was pretty cool. I just didn't like the way I drew it; I didn't do it justice. My work is more suited to the classic costume. And the 2099 stuff... well, that's really what ultimately drove me to leave the book. It just wasn't my cup of tea.

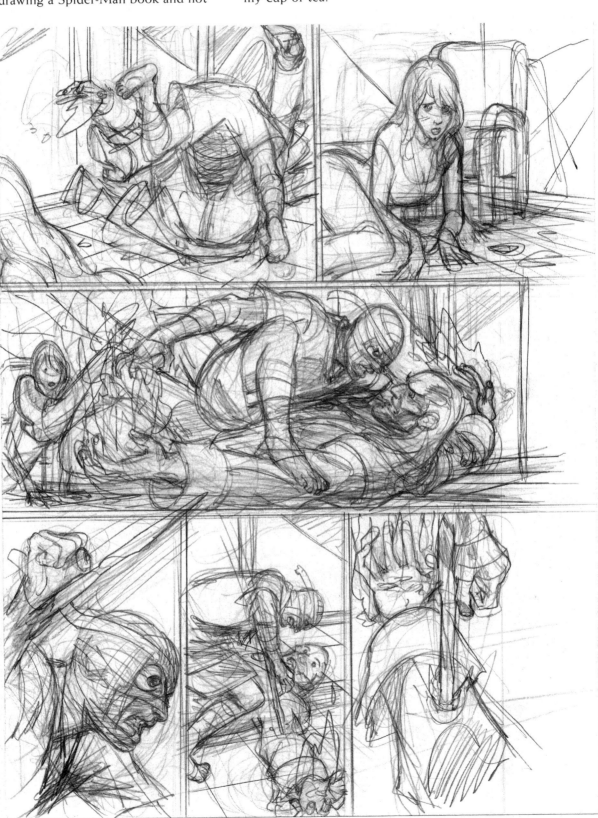

73

Part 7: Storytelling and the Creative Process

MM: We've already talked about where *Tellos* came from, so let's talk about one of the action scenes from *Tellos* #4. I remember this being fun 'cause the idea was to leave the other three characters—Jarek, Koj, and Serra—in a cliff-hanger at the end of issue #3 and introduce these two totally new characters, Hawke and Rikk, here. And these guys were fun!

MIKE: They were fun... but I remember being a little reticent to break the flow of what had been set up at the end of issue #3 by breaking to a couple of new characters and an entirely new setting. It didn't take me long to fall in love with Hawke and Rikk, though, and in the end, I think that the break-away to them and Luftholde was a brilliant idea.

MM: As you said earlier, in preparing for *Tellos* you did a *lot* of sketches and designs of both characters and locales as we kept talking and watching *Tellos* take shape. You designed some really fantastic places—buildings, palaces, etc.—many that we didn't even get a chance to use... yet.

When you drew the floating city, I knew that we needed to plot some action there—what an opportunity! And then we got thinking about all the possibilities—and the realities—a floating city would offer. Where would they get their water...?

MIKE: Yeah... I guess I'm going to sound like a constant sour-puss, but I wasn't all that thrilled with the idea of the huge collection funnels—which makes perfect sense, really, for a floating city to collect water and store it for use by the citizenry. And the idea of the big water sluices not only didn't particularly appeal to me, but they intimidated me, as well. I think that sometimes my lack of desire to work on certain stories or scenarios might stem from self-doubt or feelings of artistic inadequacy. I dunno... but again, in the end, this setup turned out to be a fun, super-appealing, and effective story.

MM: I think, too, that this was the first chapter where you really weren't sure exactly what was going to happen. We had, of course, talked a lot about the overall story and had beaten out a lot of the scenes, but this diversion was gonna be really new—and, I hoped, exciting—for you.

MIKE: Well, even though we had pretty much charted out the overall flow of the major storyline, there was still a lot of fluidity in what we were doing issue to issue, so I'm pretty sure it was your idea to insert the introduction of Hawke and Rikk at the time we did and in the manner we did. And yes, it ended up being fun, despite whatever reservations I had beforehand.

MM: Before we get into the plot-to-page stuff, I wanna warn everybody, as I do with every artist I work with, that my plots are kind of dense. A frustrated artist

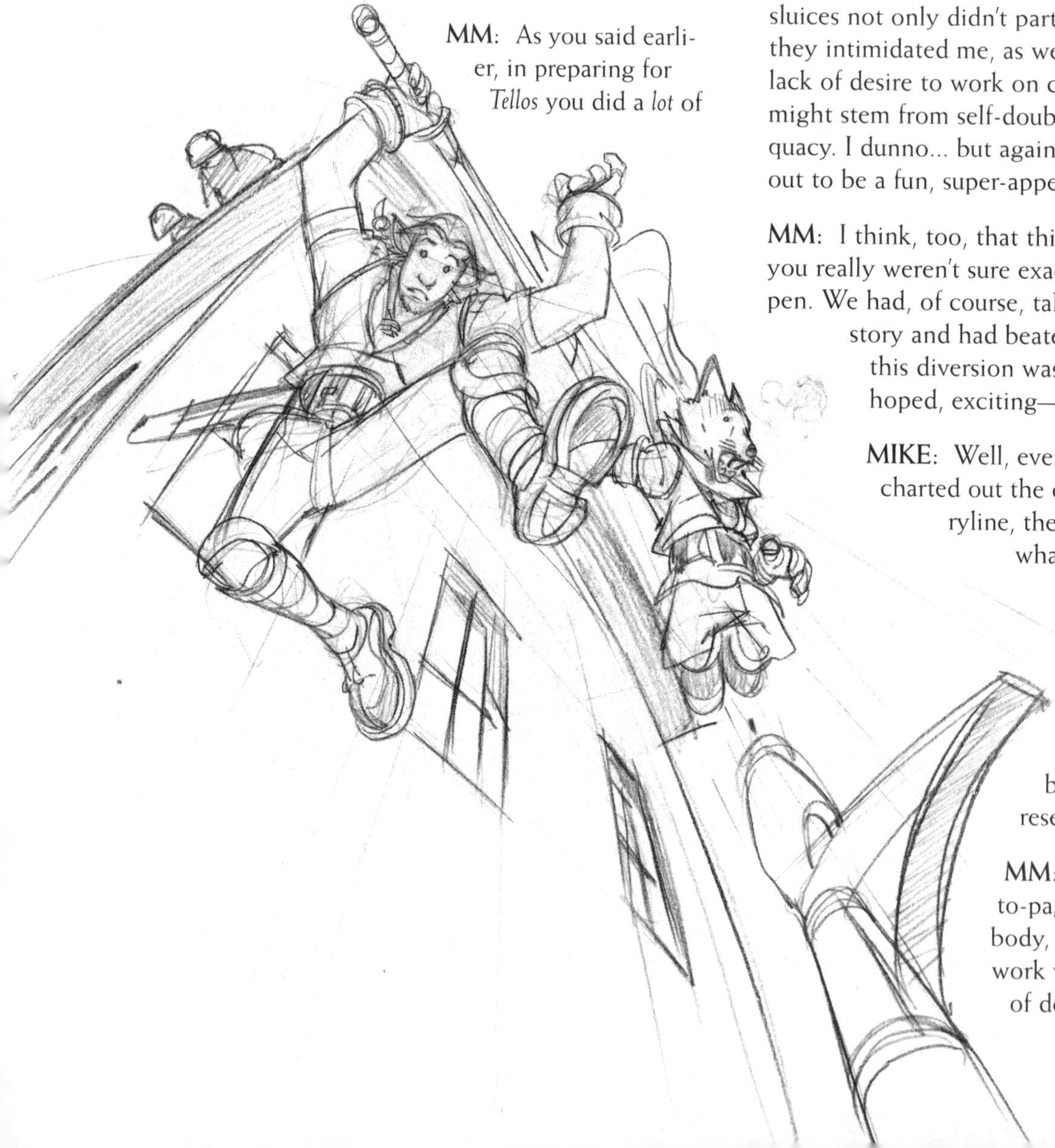

myself, I'm just putting down what I'm seeing in my head—how I imagine it *might* play out. I always tell the artist that it's definitely *not* written in stone, they can interpret it however they see fit; they are, after all, the visual storytellers.

So these are pages 11 and 12 of *Tellos #4*, where our two hapless thieves, Rikk, a fox, and Hawke, an Ulf, are on the run from the local constabulary and realizing that they've run out of options. This is the stuff you said you weren't looking forward to drawing, right?

MIKE: Yep. I was wracking my brain for a way to depict the sluices. I kept thinking of elevated wooden or metal waterways on stilts of some sort, and that was just not something that was thrilling me to draw. I can't remember if we talked it out—we probably did... we talked out every little detail of the book, but that was one of the most fun things about the whole experience from start to finish—but eventually it was decided that the sluices would be of stone, and built into the architecture of the buildings of Luftholde itself. Not only did that make more sense, in that the sluice-ways would have to be something utterly permanent and a part of the Luftholde way of life, but they were more fun to draw as well. I also doubted my own ability to depict the perspective that it was going to take to pull off the scenes with the waterways, but in the end, it turned out rather well, if I say so myself. Like I said before, a lot of my negative feelings about drawing certain things, I think, comes from my lack of certainty in my own abilities.

MM: Yeah, you've gotta stop that.

MIKE: I try. It's something I struggle with just about every day.

MM: I throw in a lot of cinematic, camera angle stuff and tell you—actually beg you—not to use it. You are a master of pacing. The two pages prior to these two just build and build the suspense, and then

when we get here, man, it just cuts loose! I remember when you faxed the pages over to me, I was just amazed at how frenetic they were, how they just carried you right along, right through! You, as the reader, were *on* that waterslide!

MIKE: One of the things I ultimately loved—and *still* love—about this scene is that it was not only challenging, but it pushed me to come up with shots that would convey as much of a sense of reckless movement and danger as was possible in a 2-D medium. Hawke and Rikk plummeting pell-mell down the water sluices with the sheriff and his men chasing them and firing at them... it was all very tough to do, but in the end very rewarding.

TELLOS #4
plot

From over the ARITAUR'S shoulder as the INNKEEPER points to a back door, telling him that that's where the culprits have snuck out.

Cut to; As HAWKE and RIKK race up the back stair, RIKK looking over his shoulder in fear, HAWKE looking over his should in anger at his trouble-prone partner, asking him if that's an Aritaur chasing them?! On the landing a few steps above we can see a shuttered window.

From outside; as HAWKE flings the shutters open, his expression changing from hope to despair. Behind him, RIKK wears the same face.

PAGE ELEVEN
Wide; from over HAWKE'S head/shoulder as he looks out on the rooftops of Luftholde, and more importantly, the system of flume-like troughs that snake and weave in and around the buildings, carrying water to the denizens of this ground-waterless town. HAWKE is defeated, telling RIKK that they are totally screwed--

--and inside, as the rampaging CAPTAIN of the GUARD, spies them on the landing, a terrified RIKK telling HAWKE that it's gonna hafta do as he shoves his Ulfen partner out the window!

On them falling toward the nearest trough, still a good 10 or 15 feet down, HAWKE shouting in surprise and anger at RIKK.

SPLASH!

And Wide; as the two zoom down the flume, caught up in the flow, coughing and sputtering, as the ARITAUR leans out the window ominously.

And from inside; as he turns and angrily barks orders at several of his GUARD, telling them to get after them, find them!

PAGE TWELVE
Cut to; Wide shot, as HAWKE and RIKK slide uncontrollably down the biggest waterslide in history, as a panicking HAWKE sees that the trough splits up ahead, telling RIKK to "Go left! Go left!" RIKK: "My left or your left?!"

On them, their expressions both of wide-eyed excitement, as HAWKE yells, "They're the same thing!"

From below as a cadre of GUARDSMEN track the two thieves progress, keeping up with them and trying to discover how to overtake them.

On HAWKE and RIKK as an infuriated HAWKE finally finds the words to berate his kleptomaniacal friend, asking him if they're being chased because he stole that sphere that he expressly told him NOT to steal?!?!

Same shot as the two look with surprise as two or three arrows whiz between them from below, RIKK meekly admitting, "Okay, maybe a little..."

Previous Page: Hawke and Rikk leap into action... or, rather, away from the action.
Above: Part of Todd's plot for *Tellos #4*. Todd describes the action, the emotions involved, and adds bits of dialogue, but Mike is free to tweak things as he sees fit.
Next Two Pages: Pages 11 and 12 of *Tellos #4*. Inks by Rob Stull.

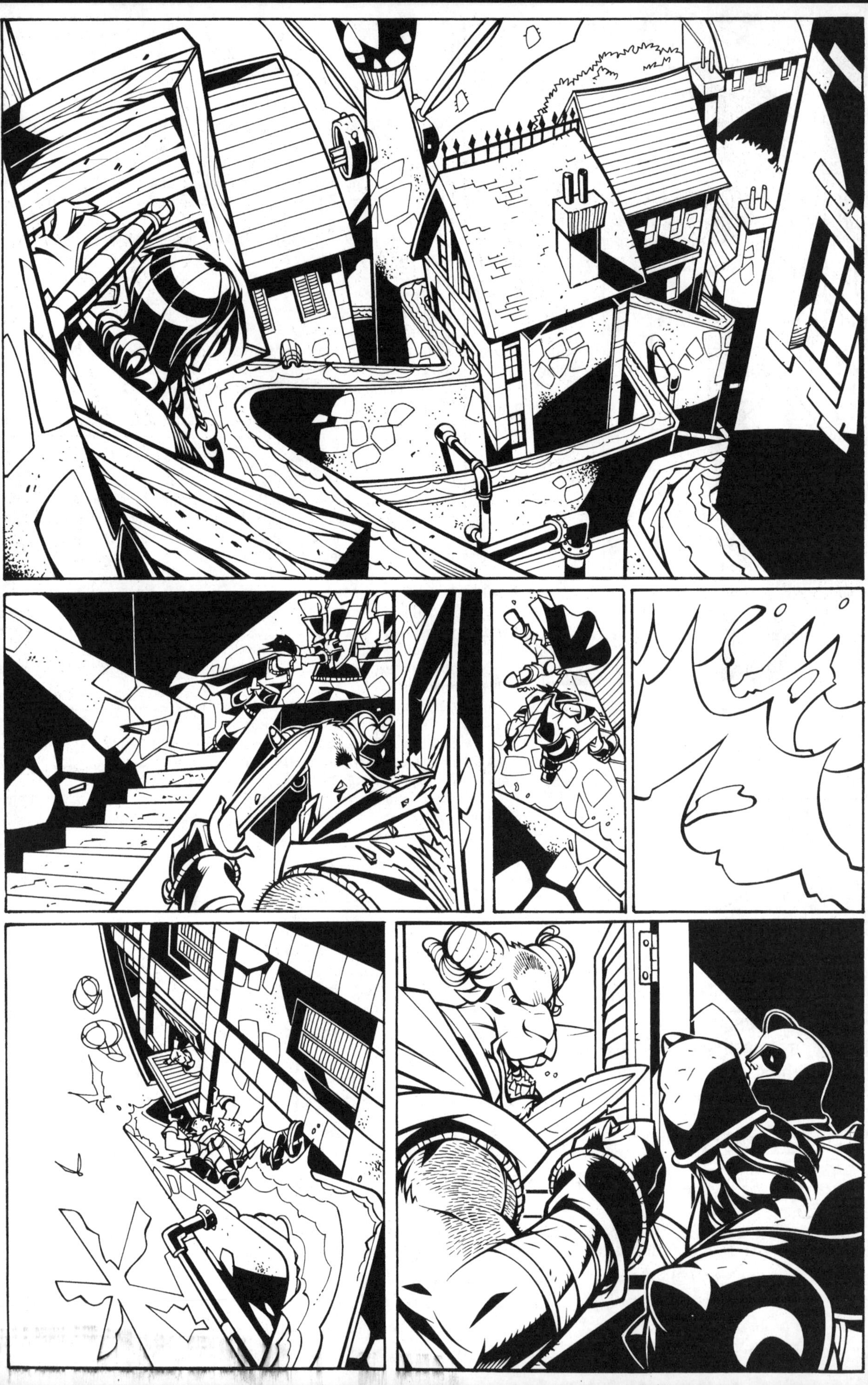

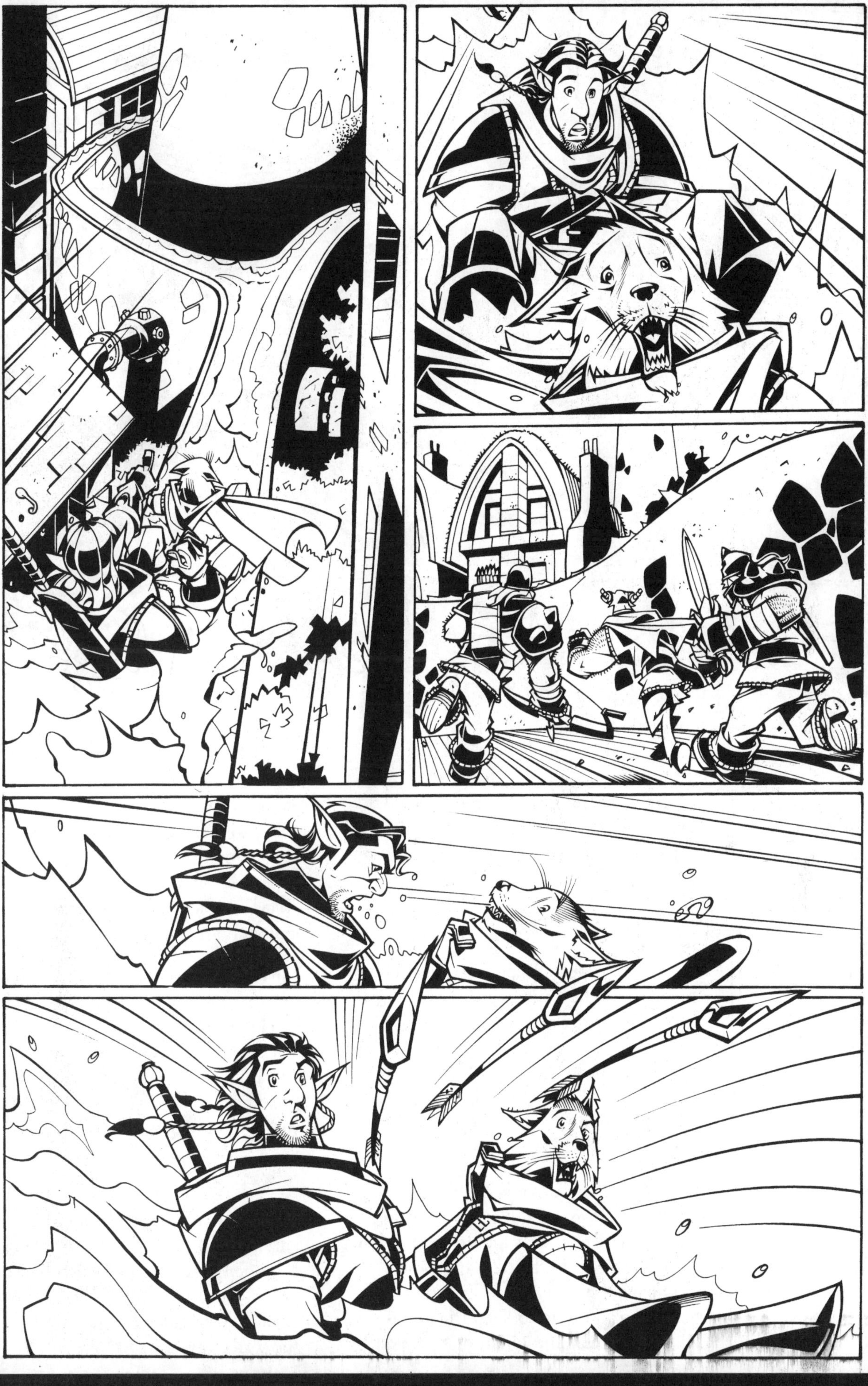

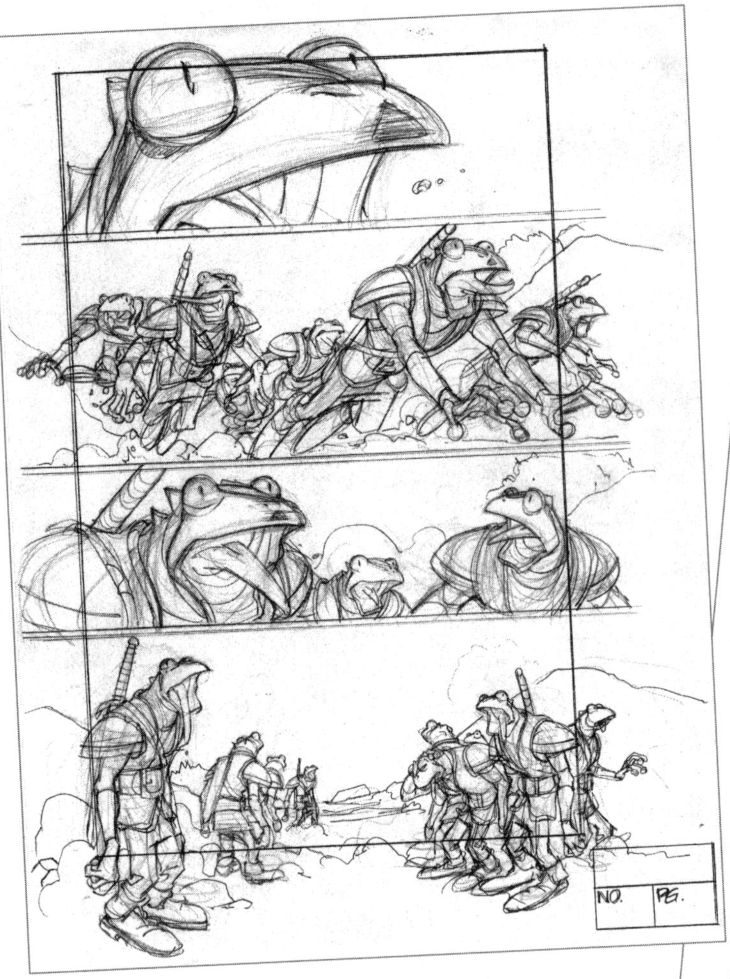
NO.
PG.

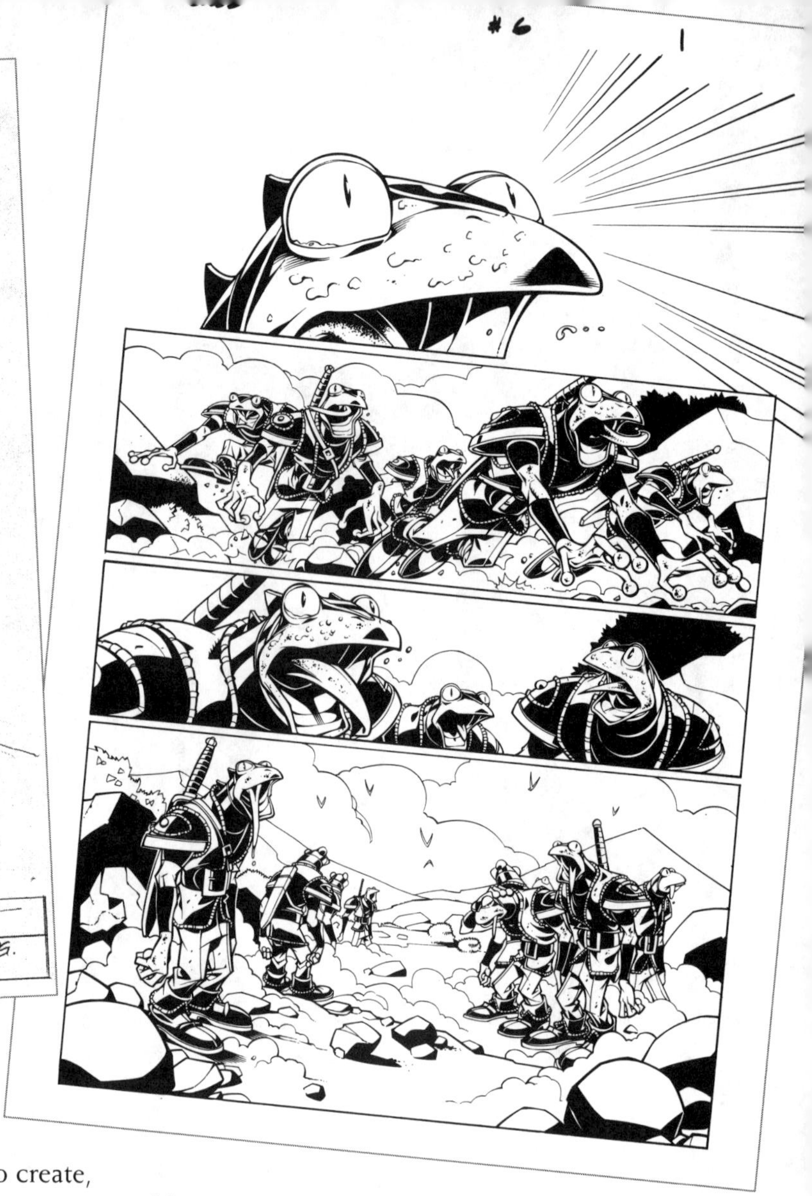
#6
1

Above: I love me some frog soldiers. Mike's layout and the finished inks of the opening page of *Tellos* #6.
Next Page: Part of Todd's plot to *Tellos* #9.
Next Two Pages: Mike's layouts for pages 13 and 14 of *Tellos* #9. Panel 4 of page 13 was later changed to a wider shot over Serra's left shoulder.

I know that for all the action scenes in *Tellos*, we wanted to make things as kinetic as possible, to try to create, in essence, something that someone could look at and immediately see it filmed or animated in a movie, almost shot for shot. I think we were successful.

MM: Yeah, why aren't they making this into a movie?!!

I should especially point out panel 5 on page 11: The crazy, vertiginous angle, the energy of the action, and you even managed to include the angry Aritaur sticking his head out the window to encapsulate the entire scene in one panel! And you're telling me that was mostly subconscious...?

MIKE: No... not entirely. One of the things that slows me down in producing pages is that I'm always mulling over what the best and most effective shot is for every panel on every page. I struggle with that, and also trying to keep the storytelling very clear and incorporating everything I can from panel to panel to make a very smooth, convincing storytelling transition for the page. Especially on a book that's all-ages like *Tellos* is, which is going to be read by as many children as adults, most likely.

MM: Children and adults that could also be enjoying the movie together...! [*laughter*]

The next page is just pure energy! It's not just the speed lines that hurtle Hawke and Rikk—and the reader—along at breakneck speed! The facial expressions, the body language, everything screams velocity! And it's so very clear and easy to follow.

MIKE: Thanks, man... I did my job, then! I'm most happy, I think, with the over-the-shoulder shot in the first panel, which really conveys the sense of gravity, depth and peril that the guys are in barreling down the waterways.

MM: My dad reads everything I write, and has commented a time or two on this or that artist's busy and oft-times confusing storytelling. But Dad's a seasoned pro now and can manage through just about anything. My mom, on the other hand, would get lost or frustrated, not knowing where to read next, telling me, sorry, but that she couldn't get through it. Never on *Tellos* though. She said that you made it easy for her to follow.

MIKE: That's wonderful to know. I think you might have mentioned something about that to me some time ago. It's one thing to be able to make things read well for kids—they're kind of programmed to connect to comics, anyway—but to also have clarity in the storytelling for someone who's not a regular comic reader and might not fully appreciate the language of panel-to-panel storytelling in all its myriad, bizarre forms—at times from so many artists, it seems—that's very gratifying.

MM: Let's break down a more emotional scene—one that highlights your storytelling in a more intimate moment. We'll go with pages 13 and 14 from *Tellos #9*, where, as the ultimate battle between the forces of good and those of evil are waged above, one of our heroes has fallen.

MIKE: That was intense. Those last two issues were very emotional, and as close as we are to the *Tellos* characters, that was a very powerful and wrenching scene to draw.

MM: Earlier in the interview, I commented on how easy it is for you to improv, to fall into a funny voice—in some cases, a funny face—and do these hilarious monologues. I think that that plays a huge part in your artwork as well. The emotions, the drama, the acting that you're able to put into your characters, their faces, brings *so much* more to the story! I've said time and again how I've been able to leave out dialogue because you were able to convey in their faces exactly what I had intended for that character to say. Do you use a mirror when you draw? Or do you have any reference books for that?

MIKE: Well, I think that stems a lot from the fact that I'm a wannabe actor. I always wish I had become an actor rather than an artist, but I didn't have the looks or the comfort level at performing in front of people to have any

realistic thought of even trying it. But I've channeled that into my drawing work. I think that's helped me to be able to depict emotional scenes pretty effectively, especially when I'm really connected to the story I'm drawing. If it's something close to my heart and I'm, in a sense, feeling the emotions written in a particular scene, then it's easier for me to do. And this scene in particular was something very special and meant a lot to me... so I guess that helped.

I *do* use a mirror on occasion, but not all that often. I suppose if it's a particularly complicated facial expression, or it's something I'm wanting to make a bit more realistic than my usual style is, I'll perhaps use a mirror. I don't have any books for facial expressions. That would be a good thing to have, if one even exists!

MM: What amazes me is that you haven't killed me yet. There are times, in my rambling descriptions, in the heat of the moment, I'll suggest not one, but two different expressions, different emotions—sometimes completely

---

TELLOS #9
plot

PAGE 13

Wide; as SERRA and RIKK race across the craggy landscape toward where HAWKE fell, his body battered and bloodied, his feathers twisted and bent.

On the three of them as SERRA is overcome with emotion, unsure what to do as she looks down at the broken HAWKE. On the verge of panic, tears roll down her cheeks. RIKK cradles his head, reassuring him, telling him to take it easy, it's gonna be alright.

Close on HAWKE, weak, in pain, but happy, knowing that he did the right thing, as he jokes that he wishes somebody'd've let him know that that MALESUR-MONSTER could shoot beams'a energy outta his eyes...

On the three of them, as SERRA tries to calm him, speaking softly, soothingly, telling him to lay still, that he going to be--

And on SERRA, startled and horrified, as her eyes finally rest on the gaping wound in HAWKE'S chest, her words choked off in her throat.

And close on them as HAWKE struggles to talk, beginning to tell SERRA his now all-too-obvious secret, as SERRA cuts him off, telling him that he was stupid to think that this would change her feelings for him. Wings?! She loves him for who he is, not what he looks like! We had so many fights over... wings?!

PAGE 14

Close on HAWKE as he now strains to speak through a jolt of pain, as he coughs, a trickle of blood on his lips, as he begins to tell her that it's more than that, that--

Close on the two of them, SERRA leaning in close, HAWKE, realizing that there's little time left, gazing deeply into her eyes, telling her that the loves her so much...

...close on RIKK, watching, a tear rolling down his furry face...

...on him and SERRA as he thanks her for making his life so happy...

Wide; on them, tiny in the foreground, as the giant MALESUR and OGE K'TION wage an epic battle above them, as the three of them look up, HAWKE proudly saying, "See... I toldja I could get that... Amulet to Jarek..." RIKK is telling him that he saved them all--

PAGE 15

On them as RIKK and SERRA look back to see that HAWKE has died.

On SERRA, sobbing now, whispering his name over and overÖ

And then they both step back in surprise as his body is suddenly enveloped in a bright and serene light--

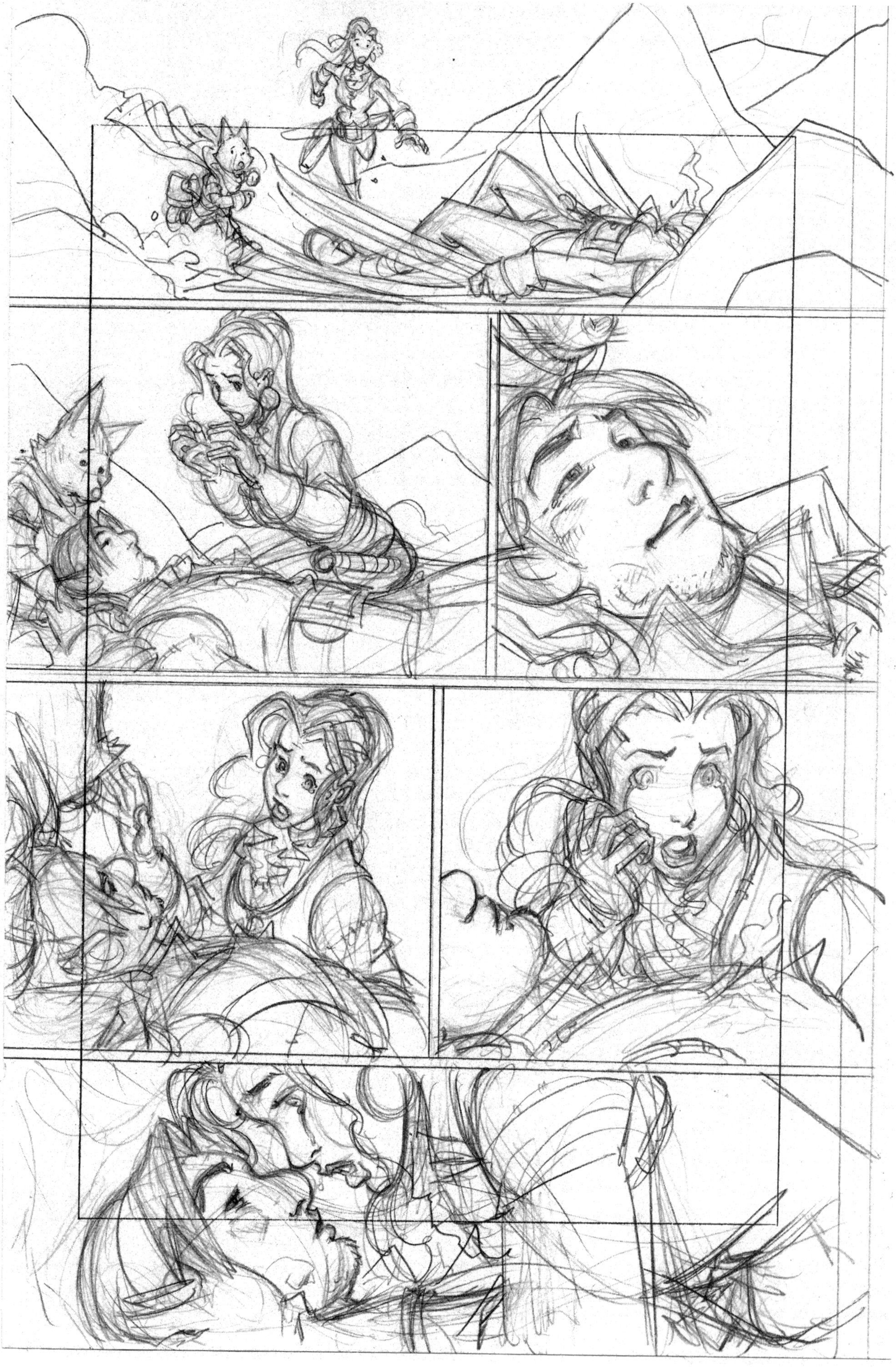

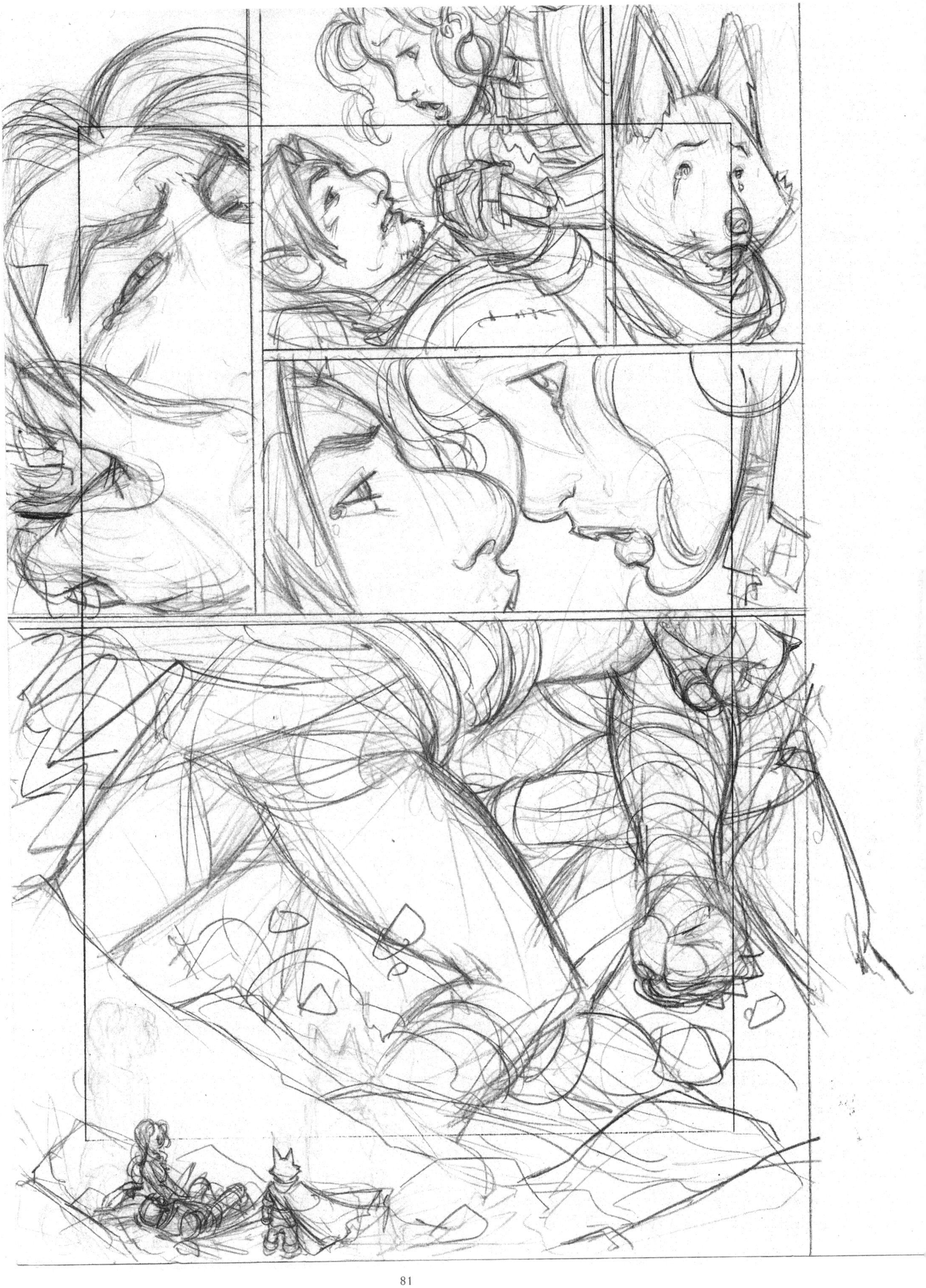

contradictory of each other—and you somehow manage to get 'em both in there! I don't know anyone else who could do that—or put up with it!

MIKE: I have no problem with trying to draw two different emotions/expressions on a face at the same time. I love drawing faces, and it's challenging and rewarding to try for something like that. Now, if you were to write multiple *actions* in the same panel—which is what some writers who don't understand what the limitations of comics actually are—then you and I might have a problem... heh.

MM: And this scene has you running all over the emotional spectrum. Serra alone ranges from her initial shock to hope to horror to comforting support to professions of love. Pacing-wise, you continue to play the angle while bringing the camera in closer and closer, making the reader a part of this sad, yet incredibly intimate moment.

MIKE: Yeah... and that's just it. I wanted to have the "camera" gradually close in on these two people who are so connected to each other in a way they're not to anyone else, and who are in essence, saying goodbye to each other. I wanted to get that intimate feel of two people who are, for that moment, blocking out the rest of the world... tuning out the chaos around them to concentrate their love on each other in that final moment. Then the last panel pulls way back to show that very chaos that's going on as Hawke points out that he'd accomplished his mission. I tried to be as cinematic as possible with it, but y'know, it was all there in the plot. You're just as adept with plucking the emotions in *me* with your writing, which only helps me to draw it on the page. I think that's the thing that made the book so strong—the fact that we were in constant contact, and always playing off one another creatively. That, and the fact that we both love these characters so much.

MM: Yeah, true dat. And I really like the way that Hawke distracts them... and then uses that distraction to slip away. When they turn back, he's gone.

Because I've sat next to you at countless conventions and shows, I know that you're very appreciative and encouraging of young artists. What advice do you give to nascent artists who are eager to show you their stuff?

MIKE: Huh... well, I guess first and foremost—from a personal point of view—I'd say to keep in mind that I'm still always learning myself, and my opinions on any hopeful's work is purely subjective. I've got my own likes and dislikes as far as comic art goes, and my opinion might differ completely from another professional.

From a more nuts-and-bolts perspective, I'd advise aspiring artists to

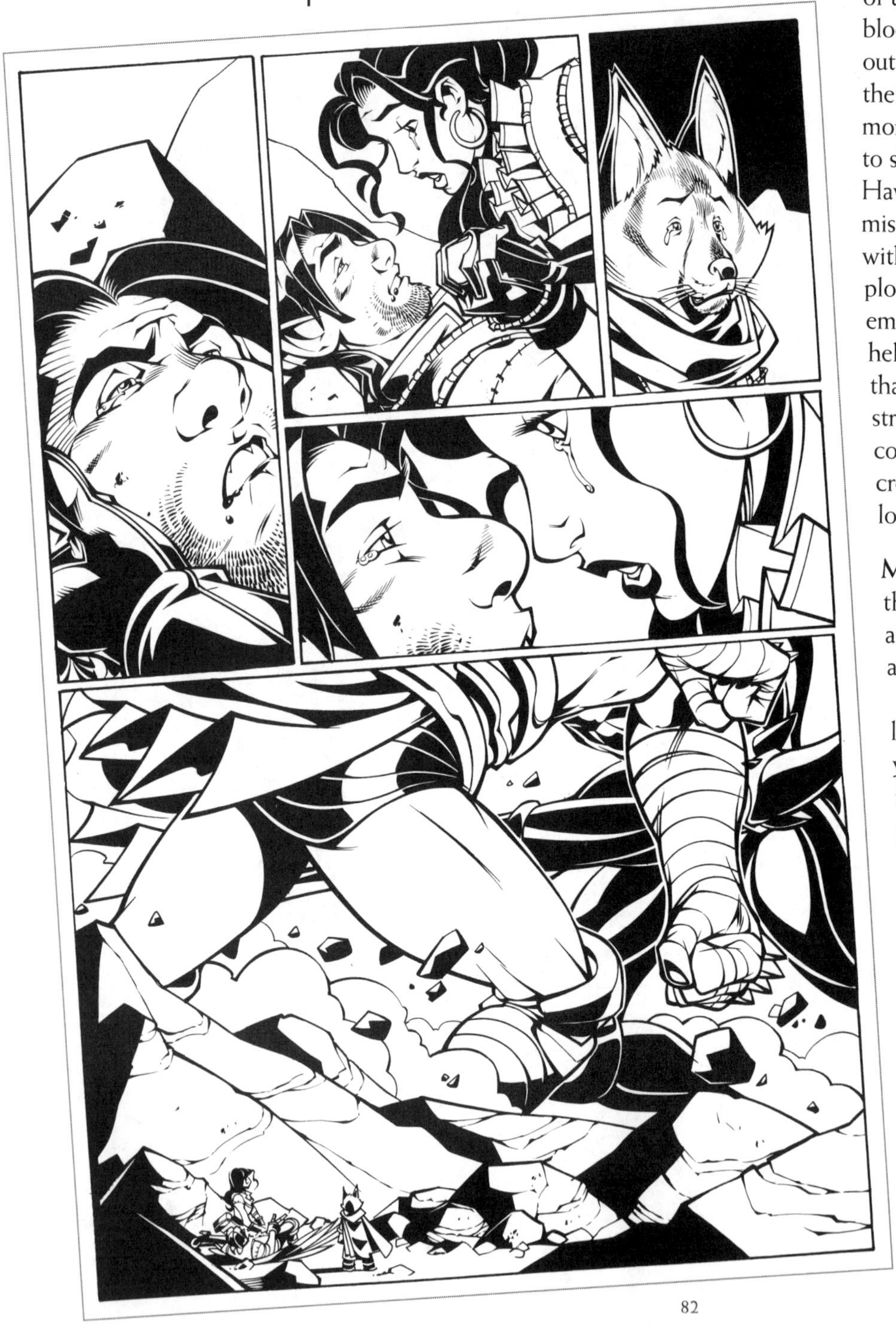

Below: The inked version of page 14. Notice panel 1 was redrawn at a slightly wider angle in order to better portray Hawke's painful expression.
Next Page: A happier scene, but equally emotional, as Jarek and Koj are reunited—though the dream soon becomes a nightmare.

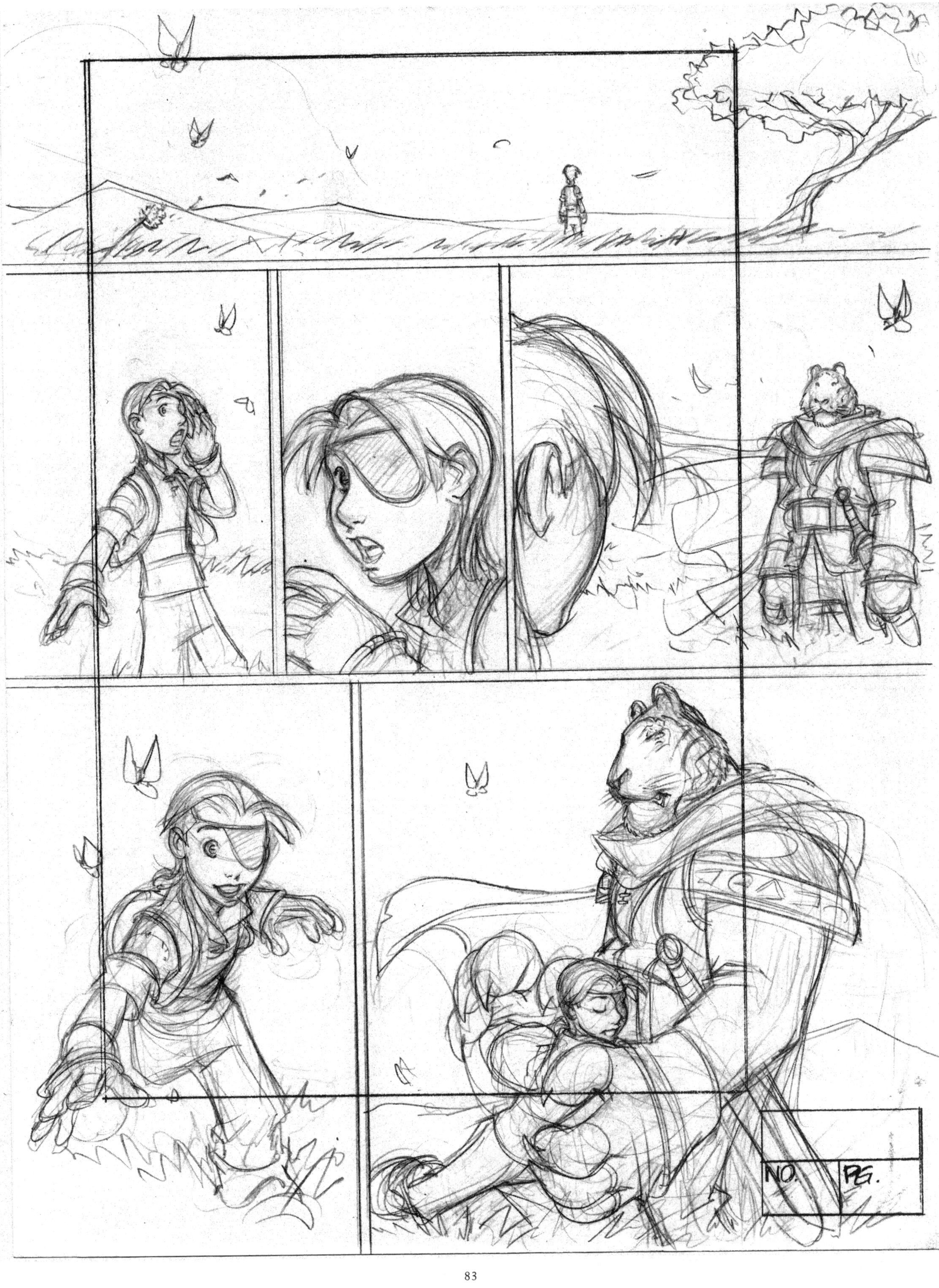
NO.
PG.

Below: Okay, so you can draw a big super-hero brawl. But can you draw normal people in everyday situations. The events of *Tellos* were set in motion by an unfortunately all too common occurrence—a car crash. *Tellos* #10, page 1. Inks by Rob Stull.

have around six or so pages of their best work to show, that has a mix of quiet, human character stuff in with some cool super-hero action of whatever subject they're planning on using in their portfolio—whether it's guys in capes, or pirates, or fantasy... whatever it may be. They need to show that they can draw normal scenes as well as the more high-action stuff. Also, concentrate on depicting clear, easy to read storytelling. Comics are all about storytelling, and that's just as important to show in samples as it is to show how well you can draw. It wouldn't hurt to have some pin-up stuff included as well, although it's not necessary. But I think being able to show that you can do dynamic cover and/or pin-up work is a good thing. But don't have *only* that kind of thing in the portfolio—the storytelling samples are more important.

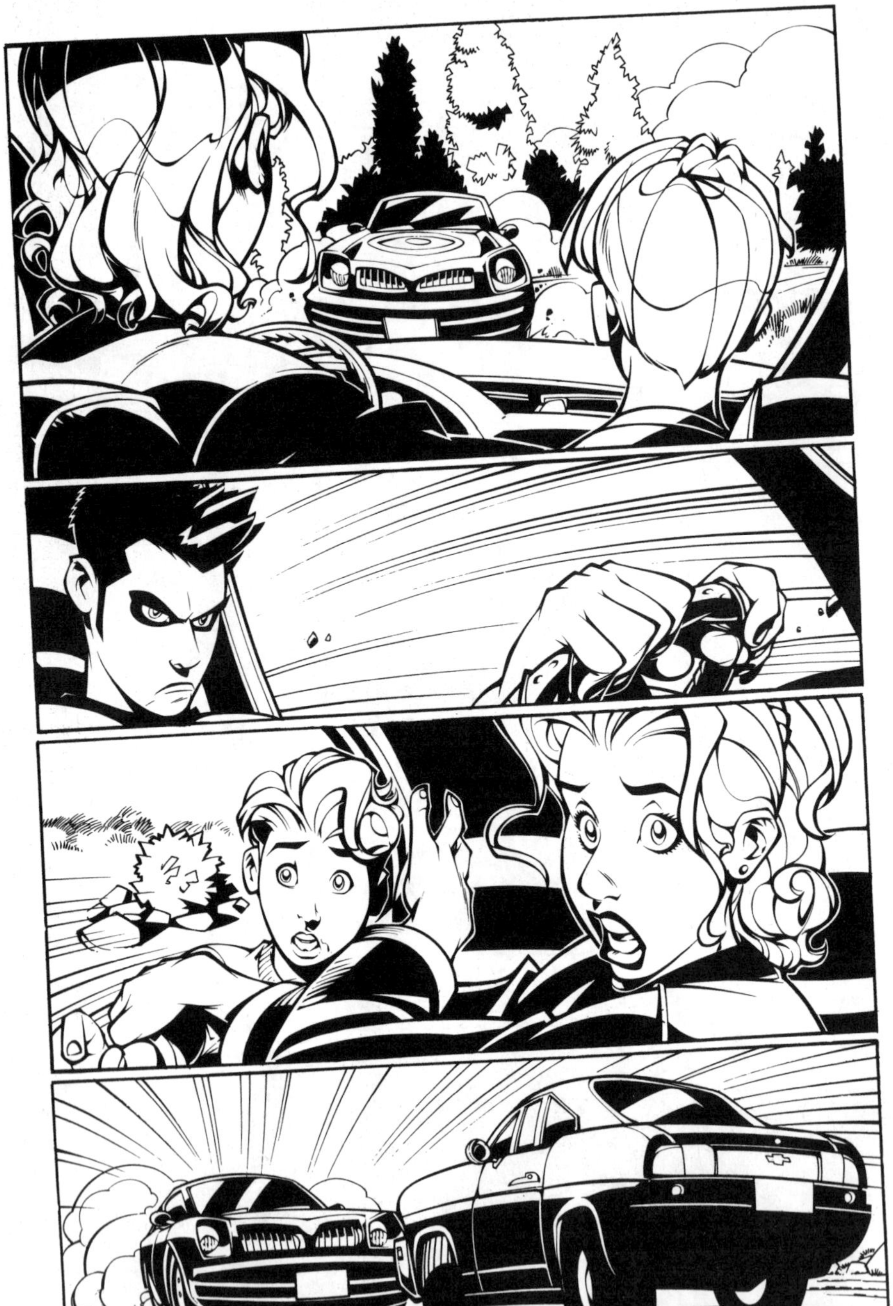

It's very important to keep in mind that no matter what the criticisms—or praise—might be, it should be accepted with poise and grace. No one will do themselves any good arguing or trying to explain away problems that someone evaluating their portfolio might point out. I don't think anyone who agrees to do a crit is out to hurt anyone's feelings or to crush someone's spirit, so don't take any negative criticism personally. It's just the personal point of view of that particular individual, and as I said, the next person looking at the work may have a completely opposite opinion. However, I think the artist should think about whatever advice is given, and use it to constantly improve their work. I think when editors see prospective artists always striving to get better and showing that they're driven to improve all the time, that's when they really take notice and get excited about the promise that artist might have.

MM: Any final thoughts?

MIKE: I suppose I'd end with the thought that I wish the industry and its fan base would be a bit more willing to embrace more diversity in both subject matter/genre as well as art styles. I'm a huge fan of the European comics market, where it seems like anything and everything goes. There are folks with very cartoony/animated styles that work on serious, dark material. There's a huge market there for comedy and humor material. There's a huge market for fantasy and science-fiction. You know as well as I do from our trip to France back in 1999—or was it 2000?—how amazing and pervasive the comics industry is over there. I suppose it's a form of envy, but I really wish we had more of a taste of what they have there over here in the States. Good stories are good stories, and good art is good art.... I think there's room for everything and enjoyment to be had for all in diversity. Long underwear shouldn't necessarily be King.

'Ringo!

Mike Wieringo

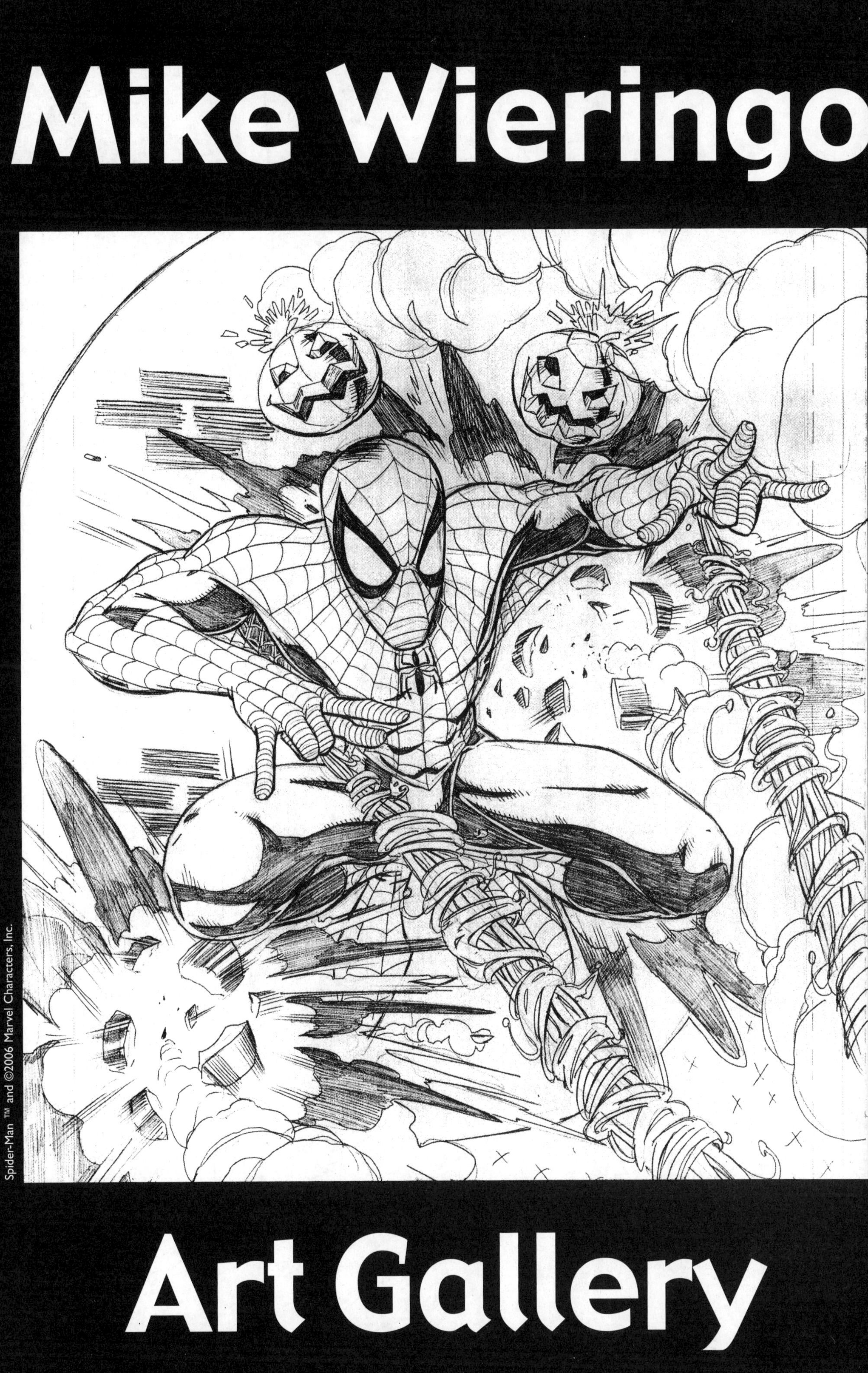

Art Gallery

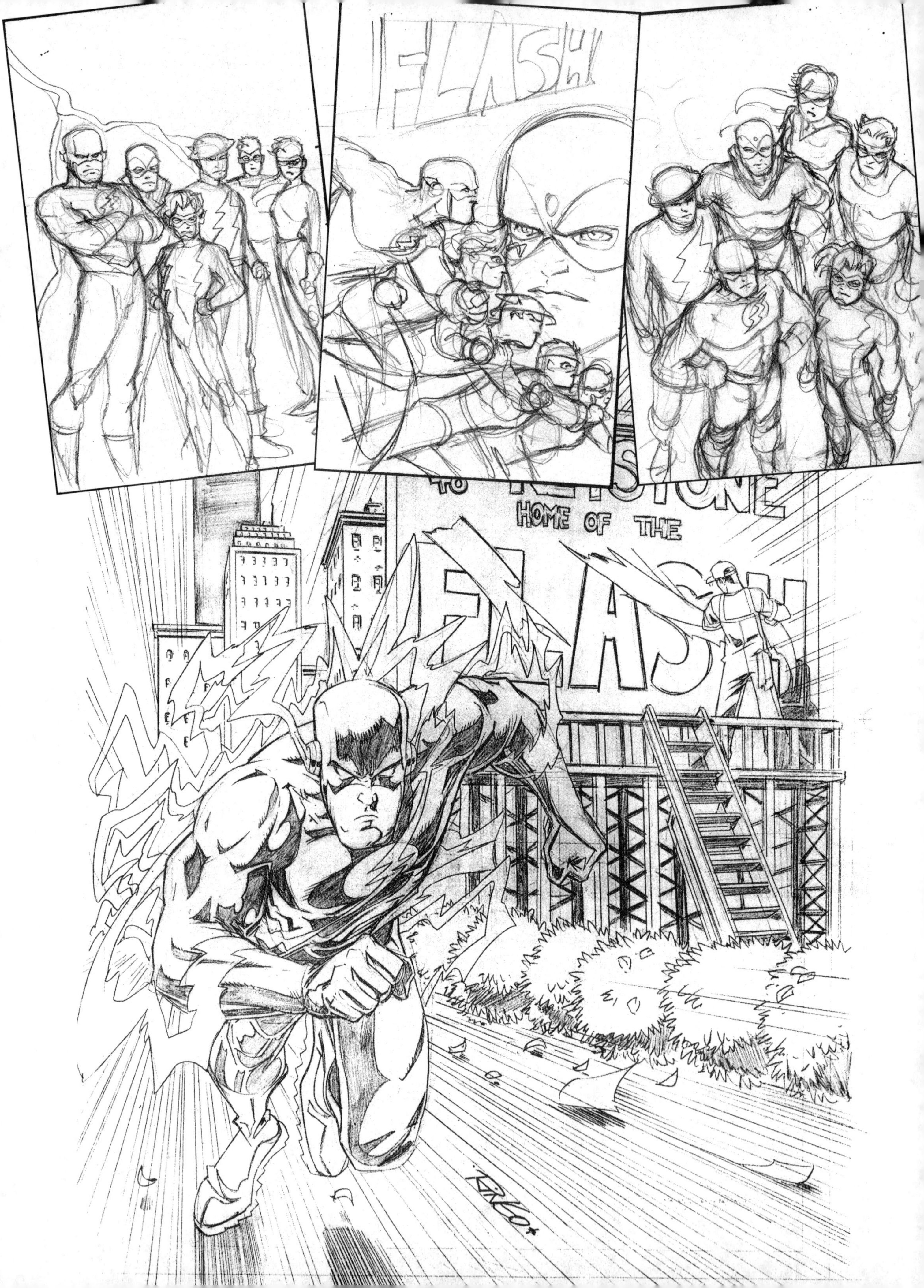
FLASH
HOME OF THE

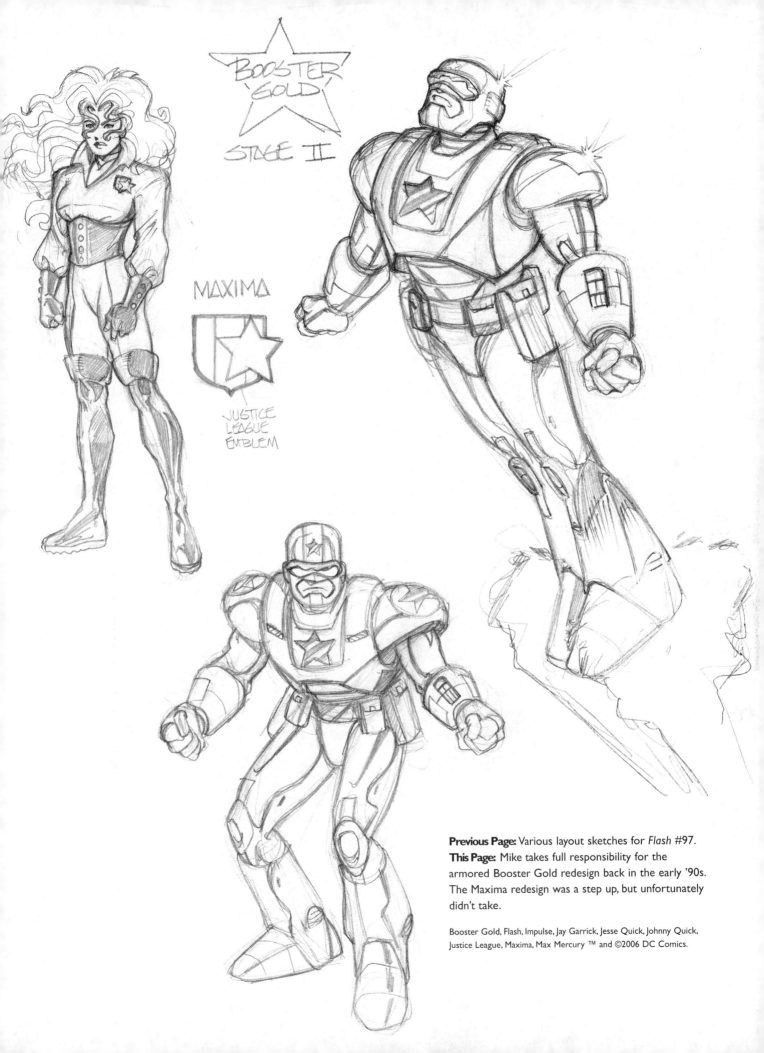

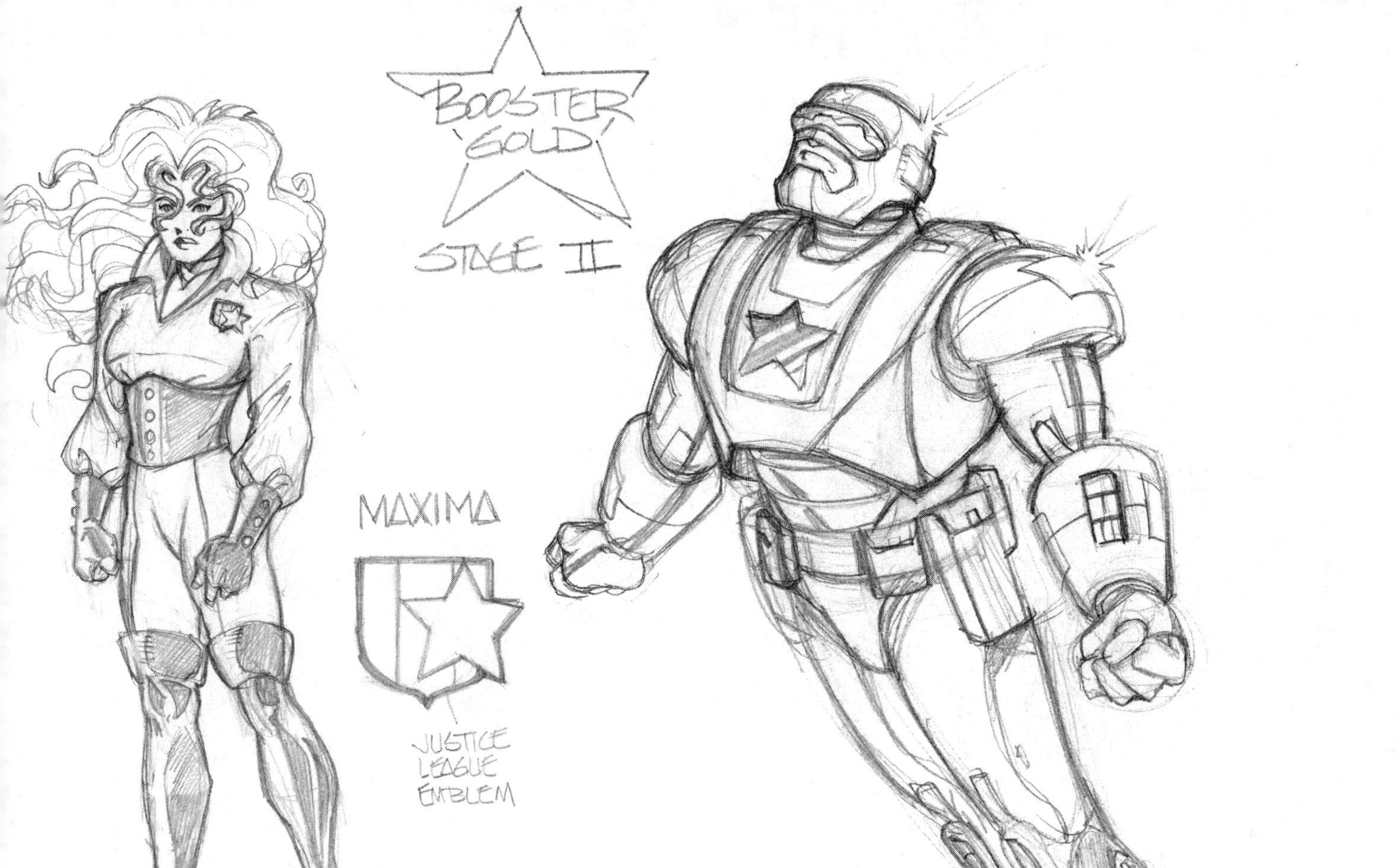
BOOSTER GOLD
STAGE II
MAXIMA
JUSTICE LEAGUE EMBLEM

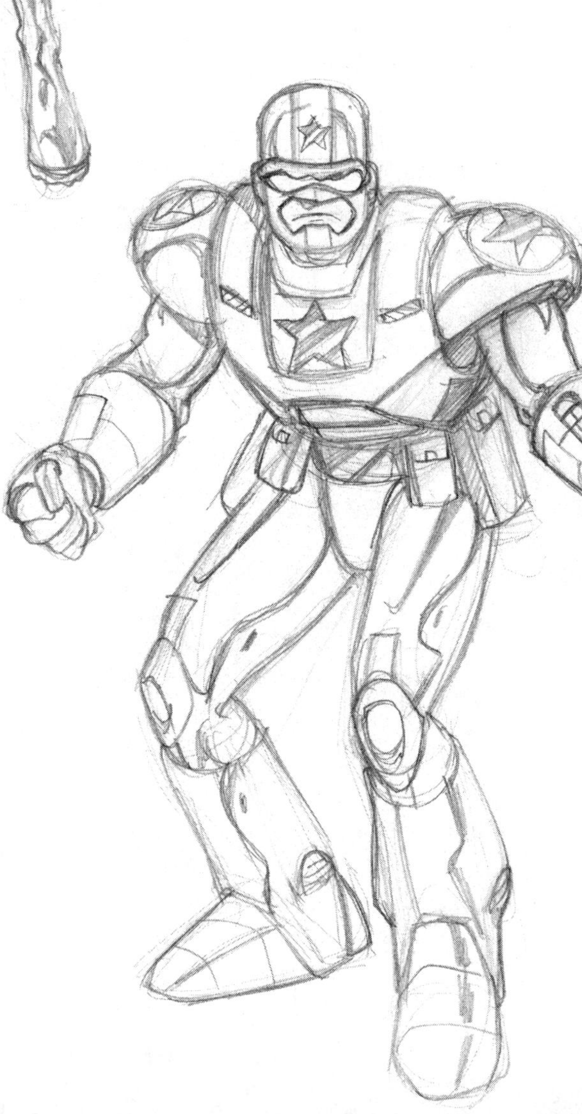

Previous Page: Various layout sketches for *Flash* #97.
This Page: Mike takes full responsibility for the armored Booster Gold redesign back in the early '90s. The Maxima redesign was a step up, but unfortunately didn't take.

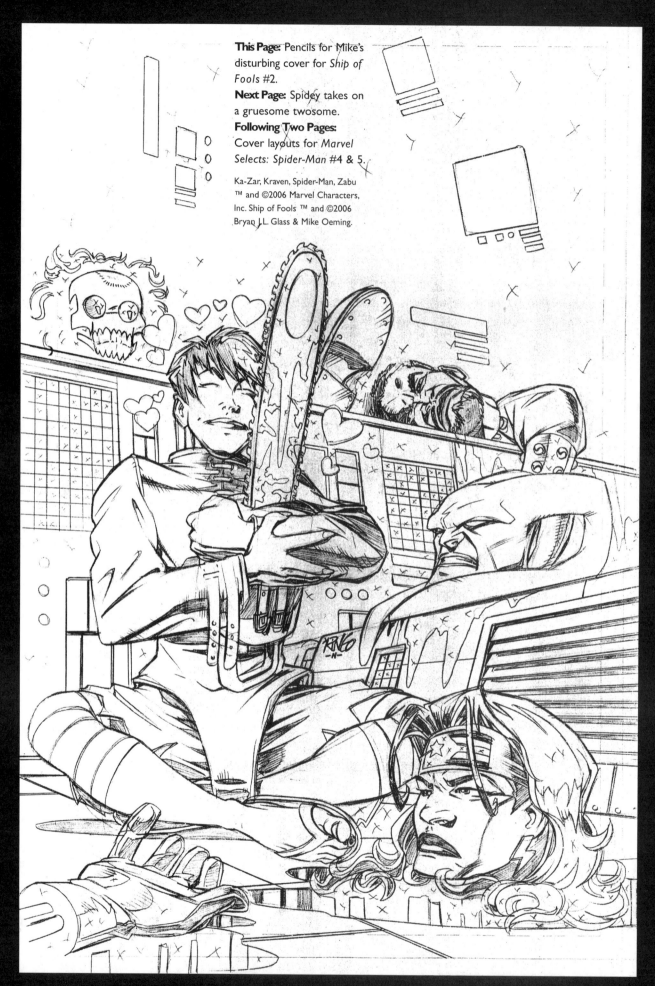

This Page: Pencils for Mike's disturbing cover for *Ship of Fools* #2.
Next Page: Spidey takes on a gruesome twosome.
Following Two Pages: Cover layouts for *Marvel Selects: Spider-Man* #4 & 5.

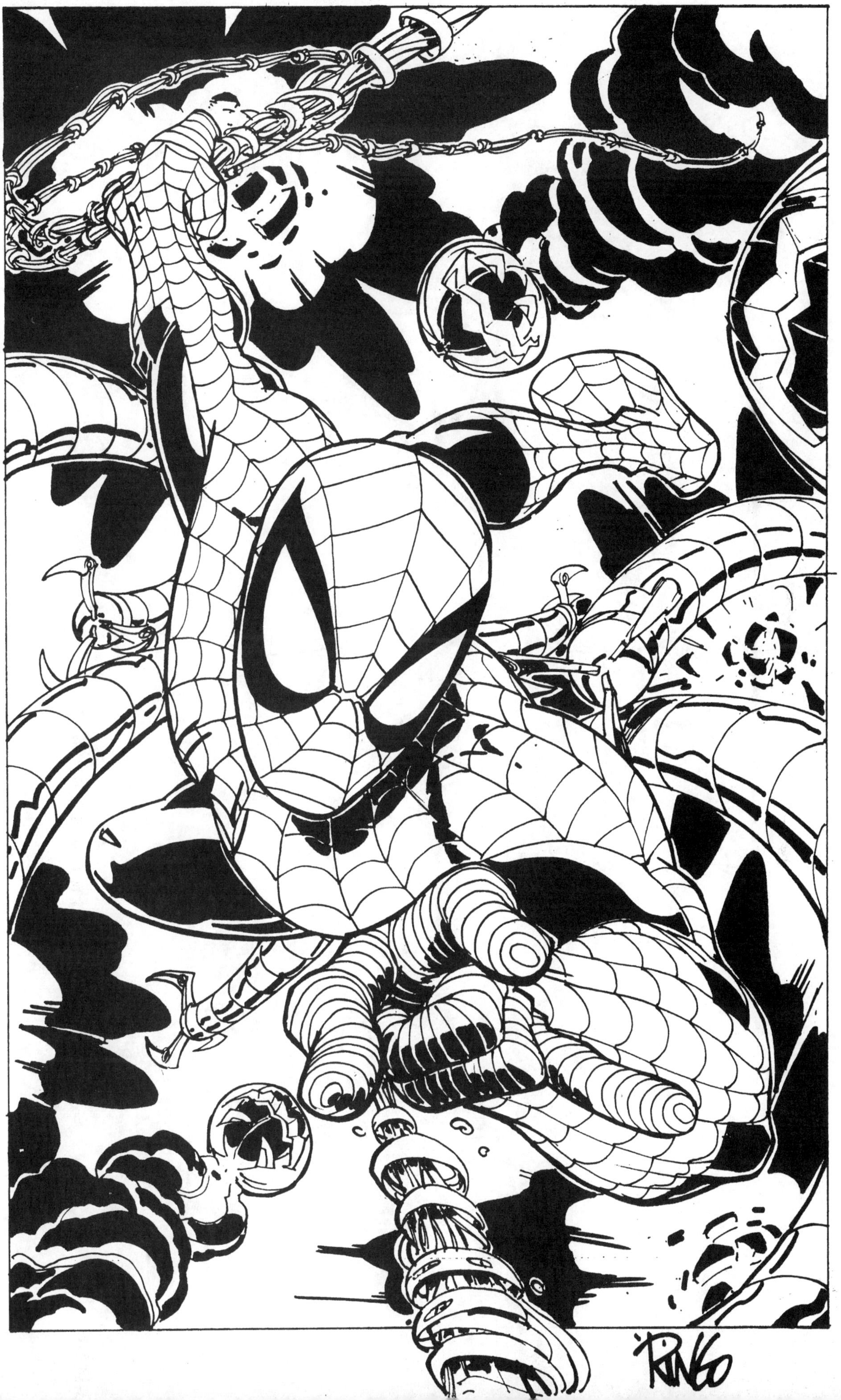
RINGO

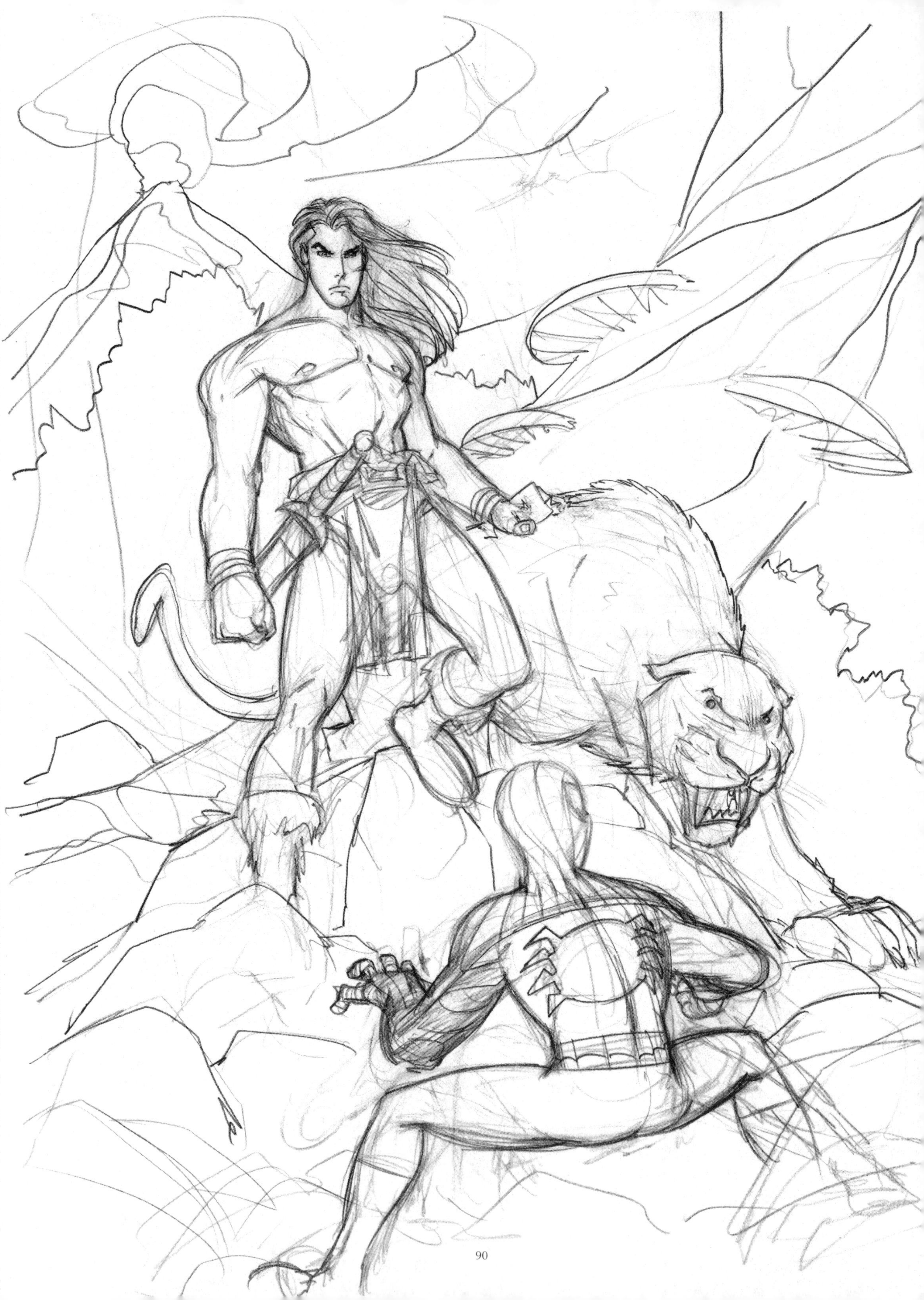

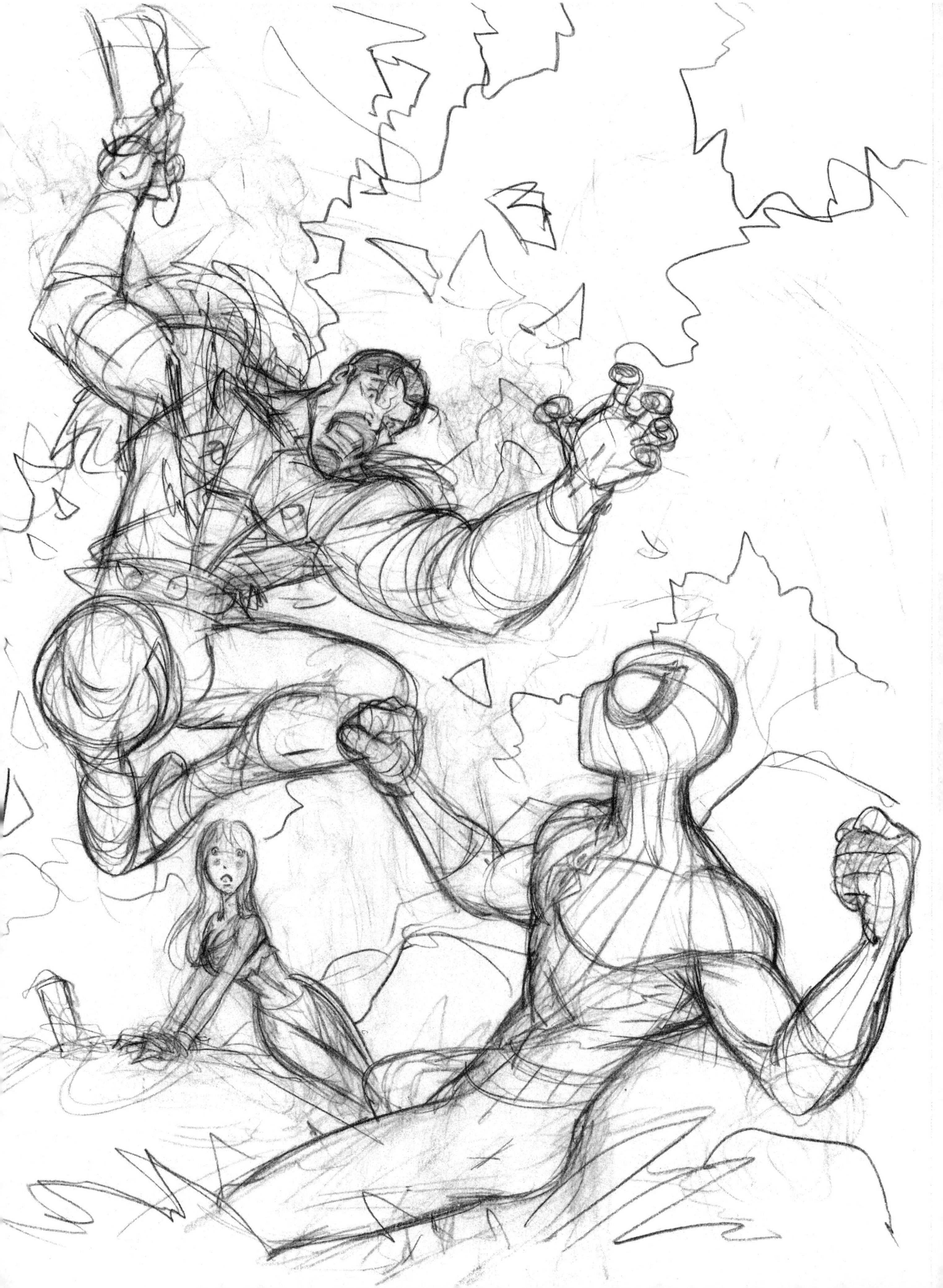

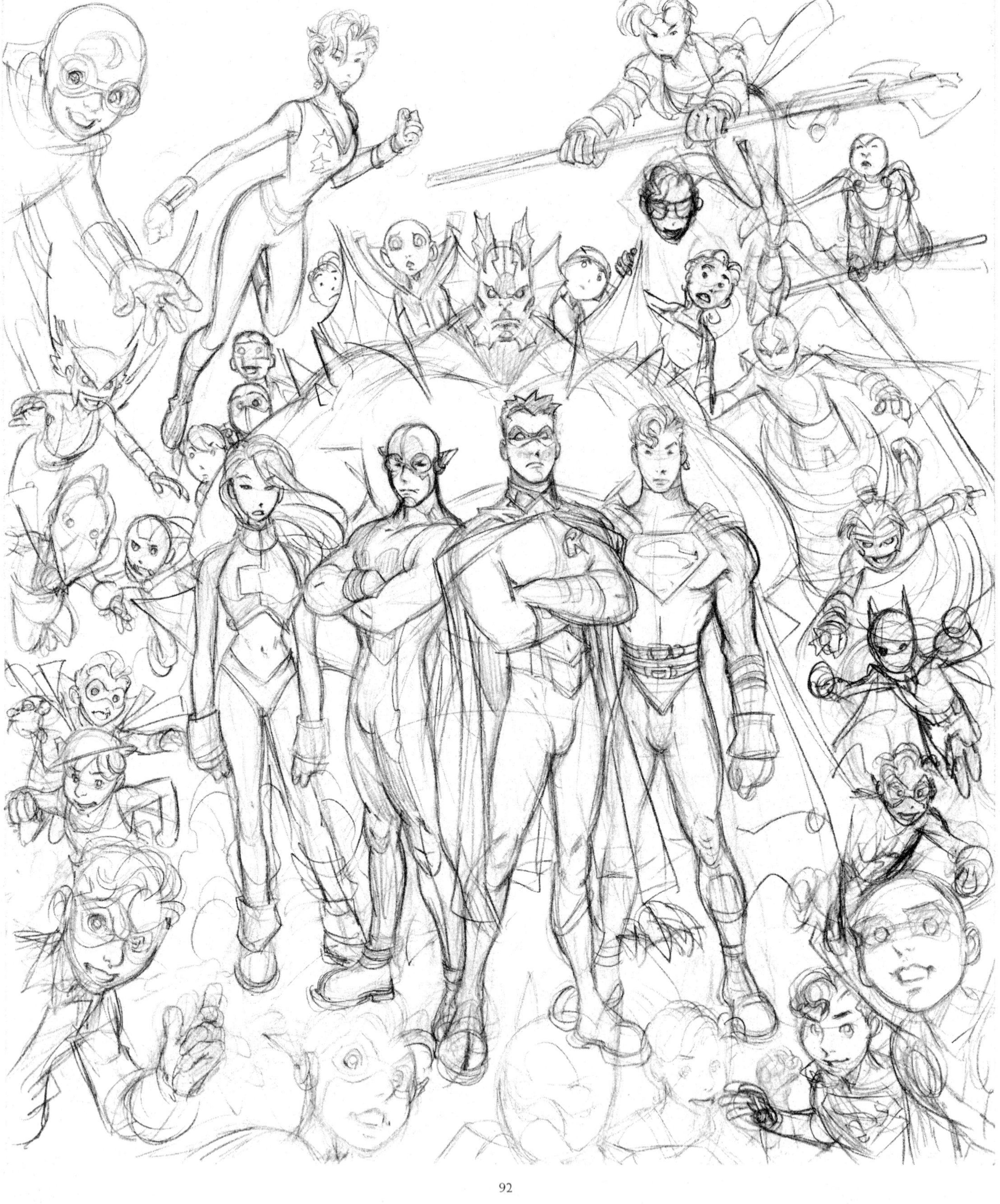

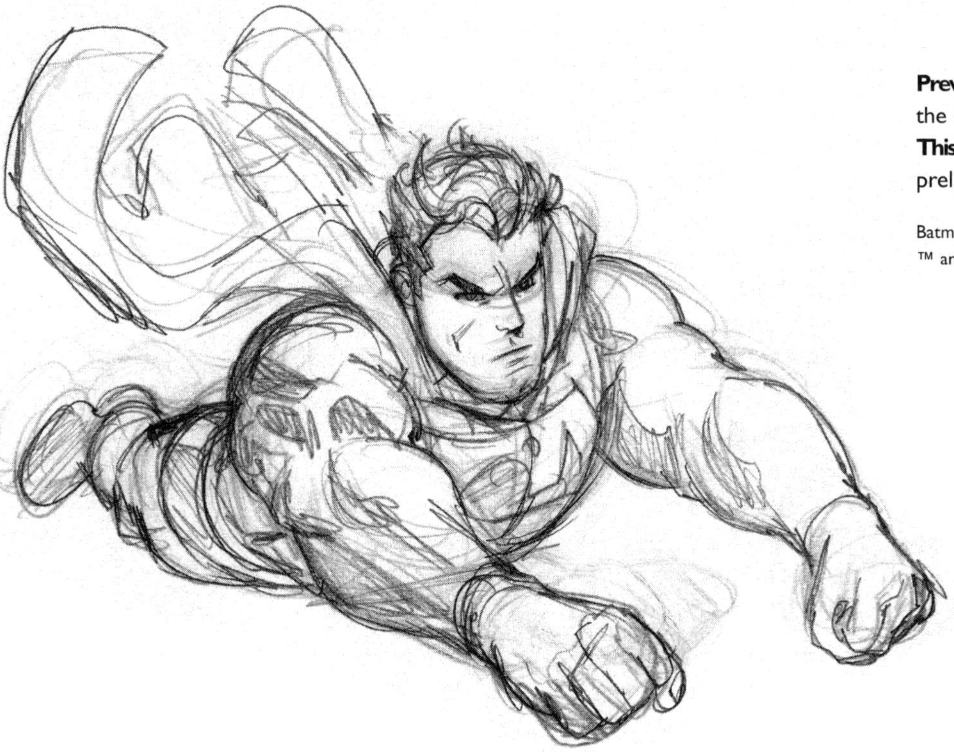

Previous Page: Mike's layout for the *Sins of Youth* tpb collection.
This Page: Superman preliminary sketches.

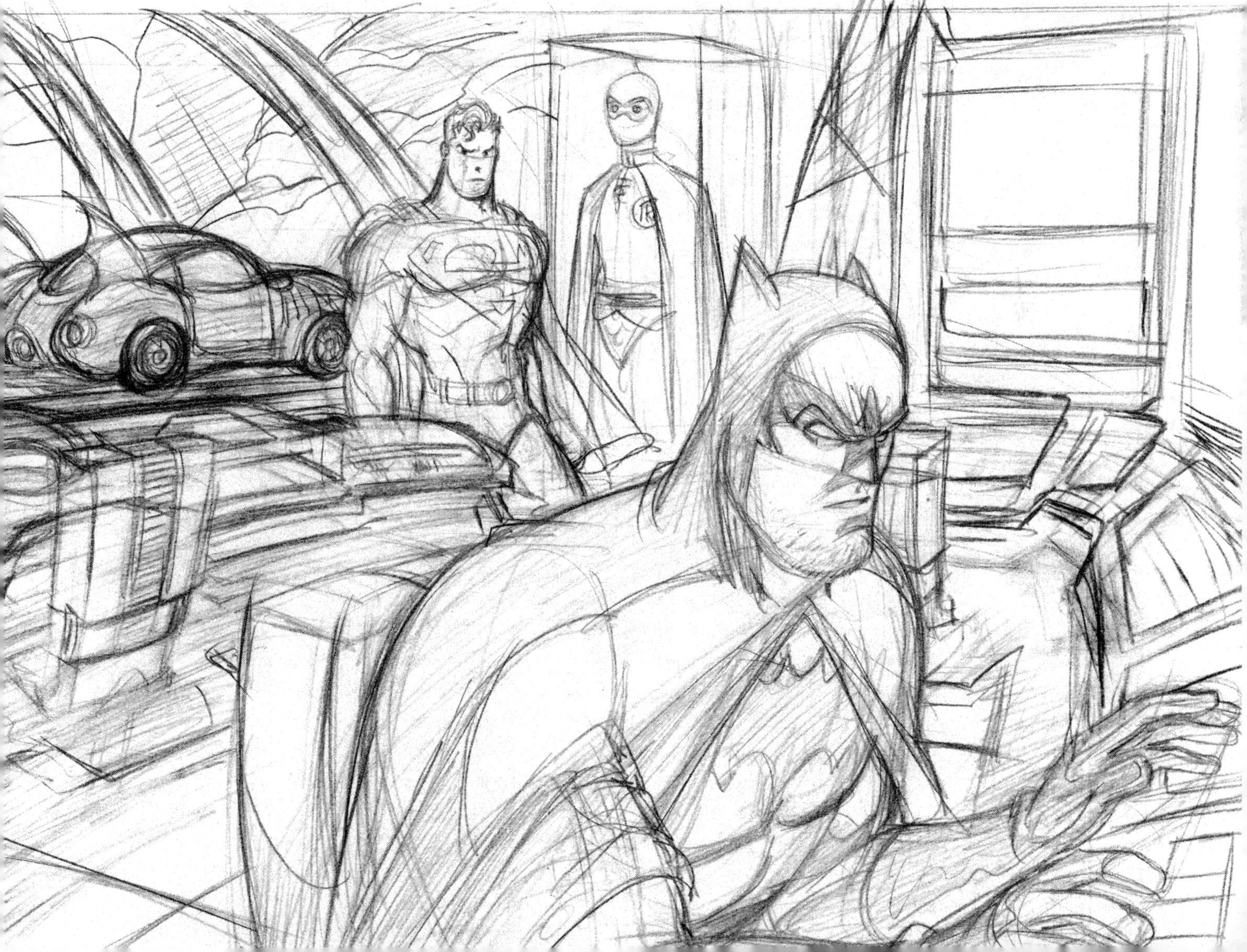

This Page: Cover art for *Fantastic Four* #509 and #510—inks by Karl Kesel—and a pencil drawing of the team.
Next Page: A nice Invisible Woman drawing and a FF "bonus page" layout of the Thing taking in a little R-'n'-R. The background image is page 12 of *FF* #68—featuring a nice interaction between Sue and Ben. Inks by Karl Kesel.

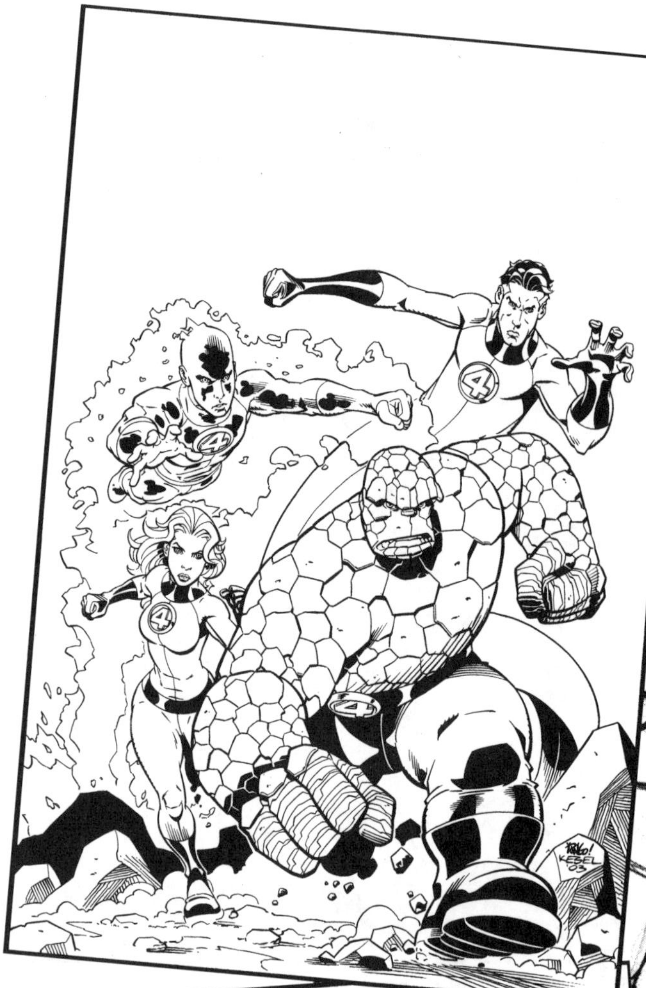

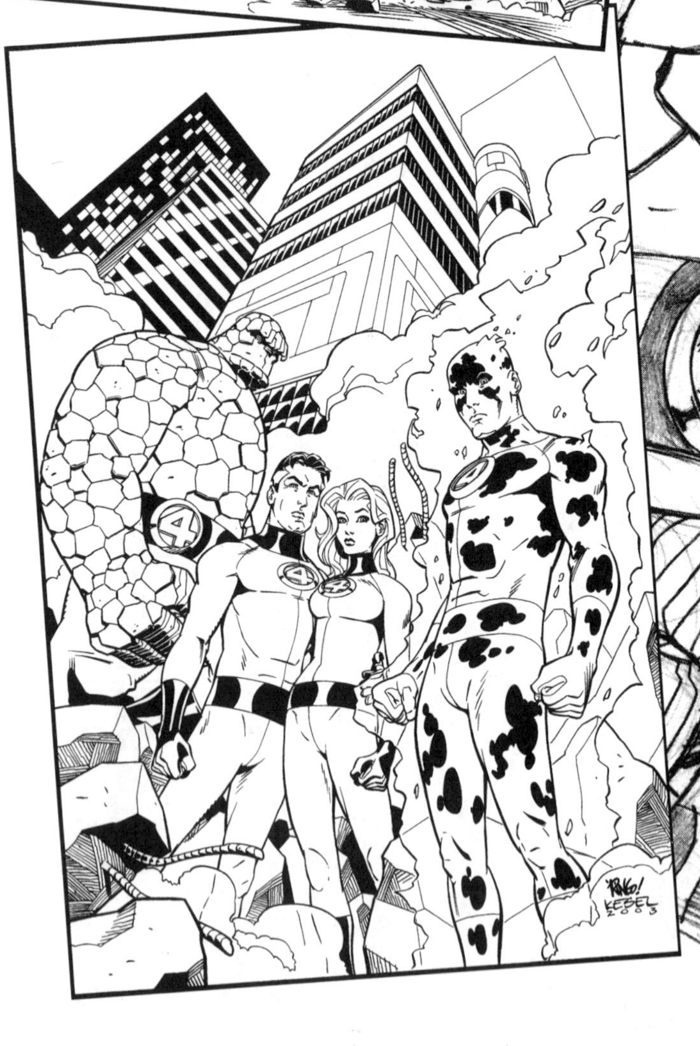

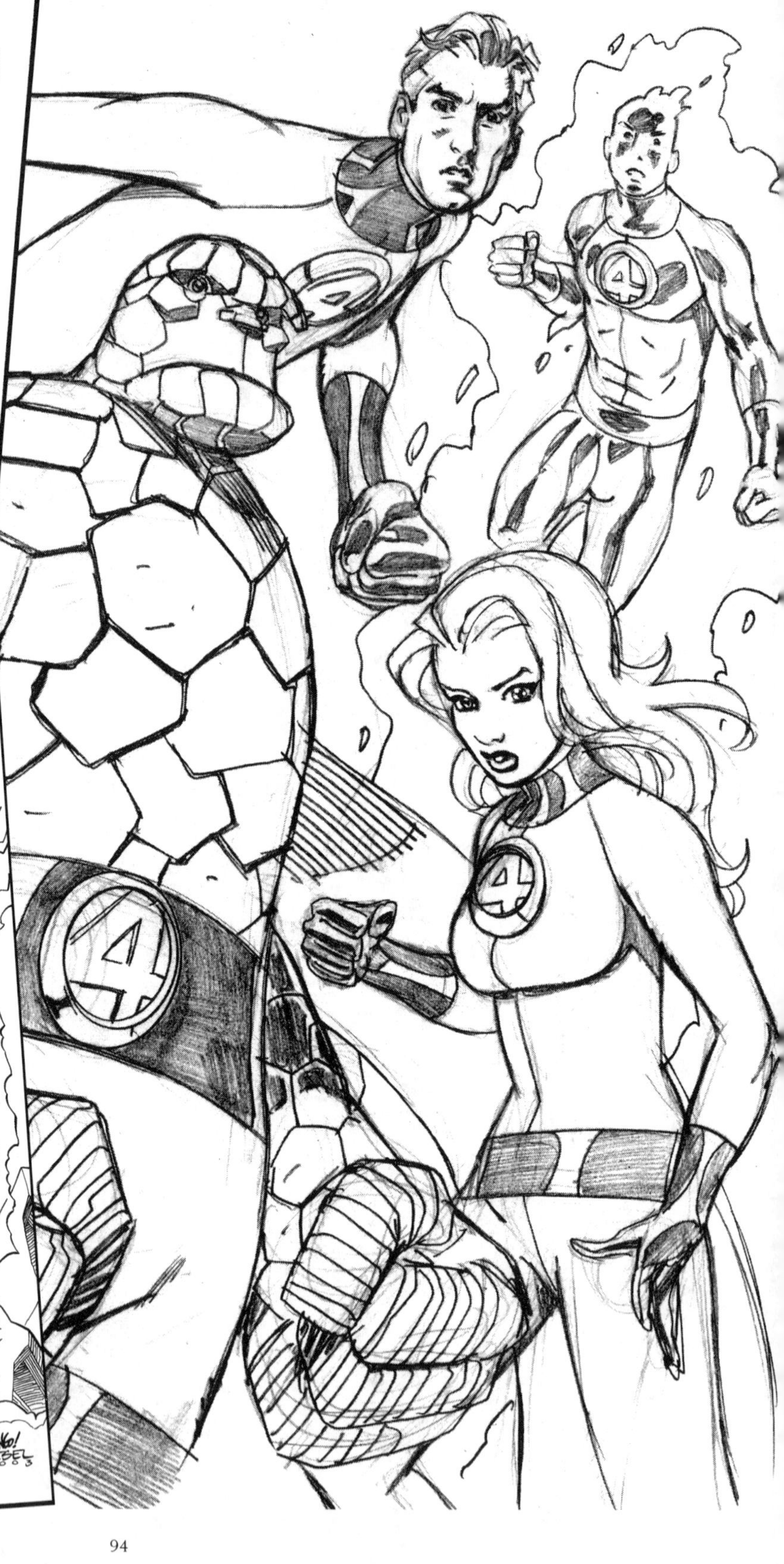

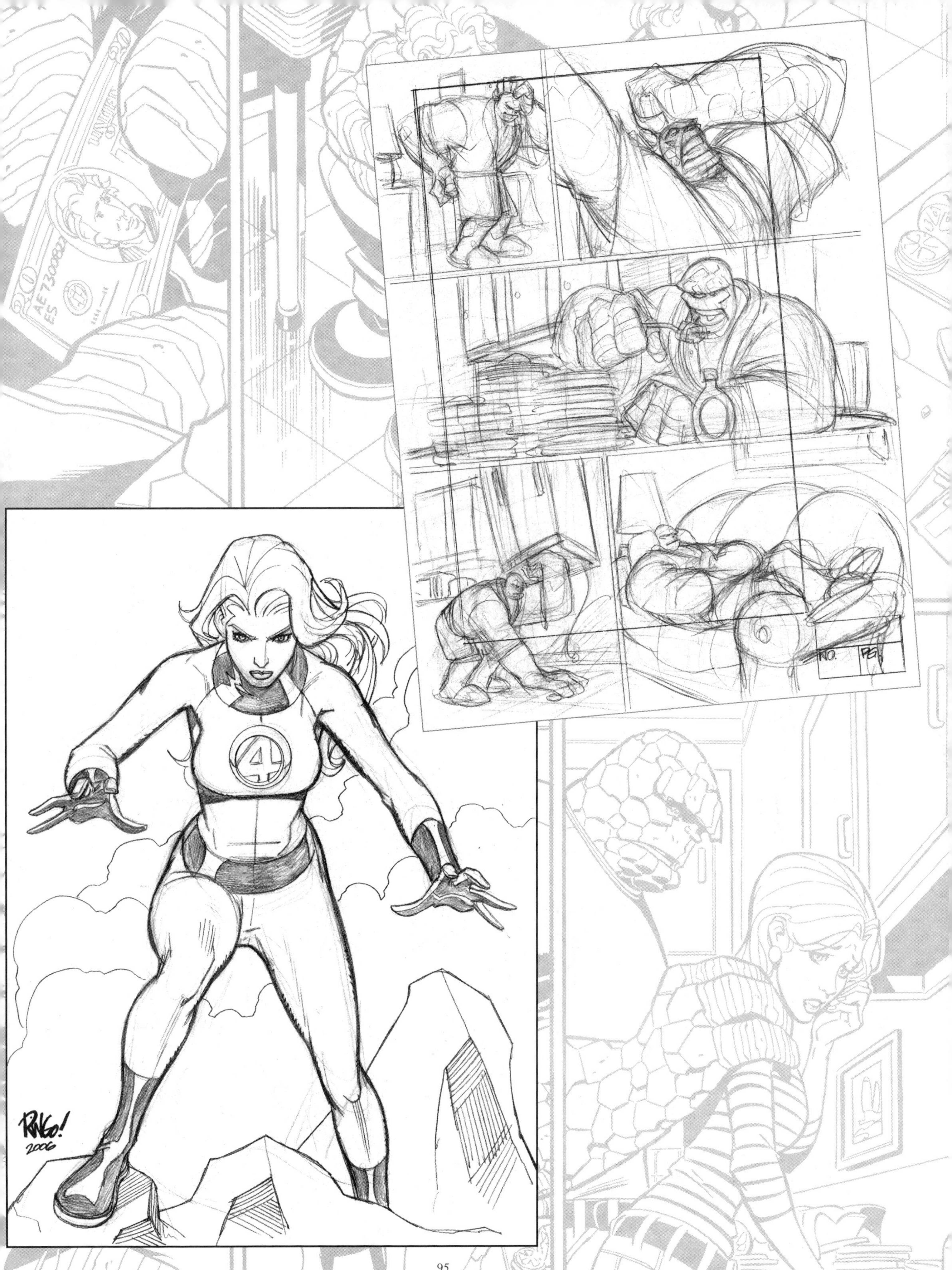
NO. PG.
RINGO!
2006

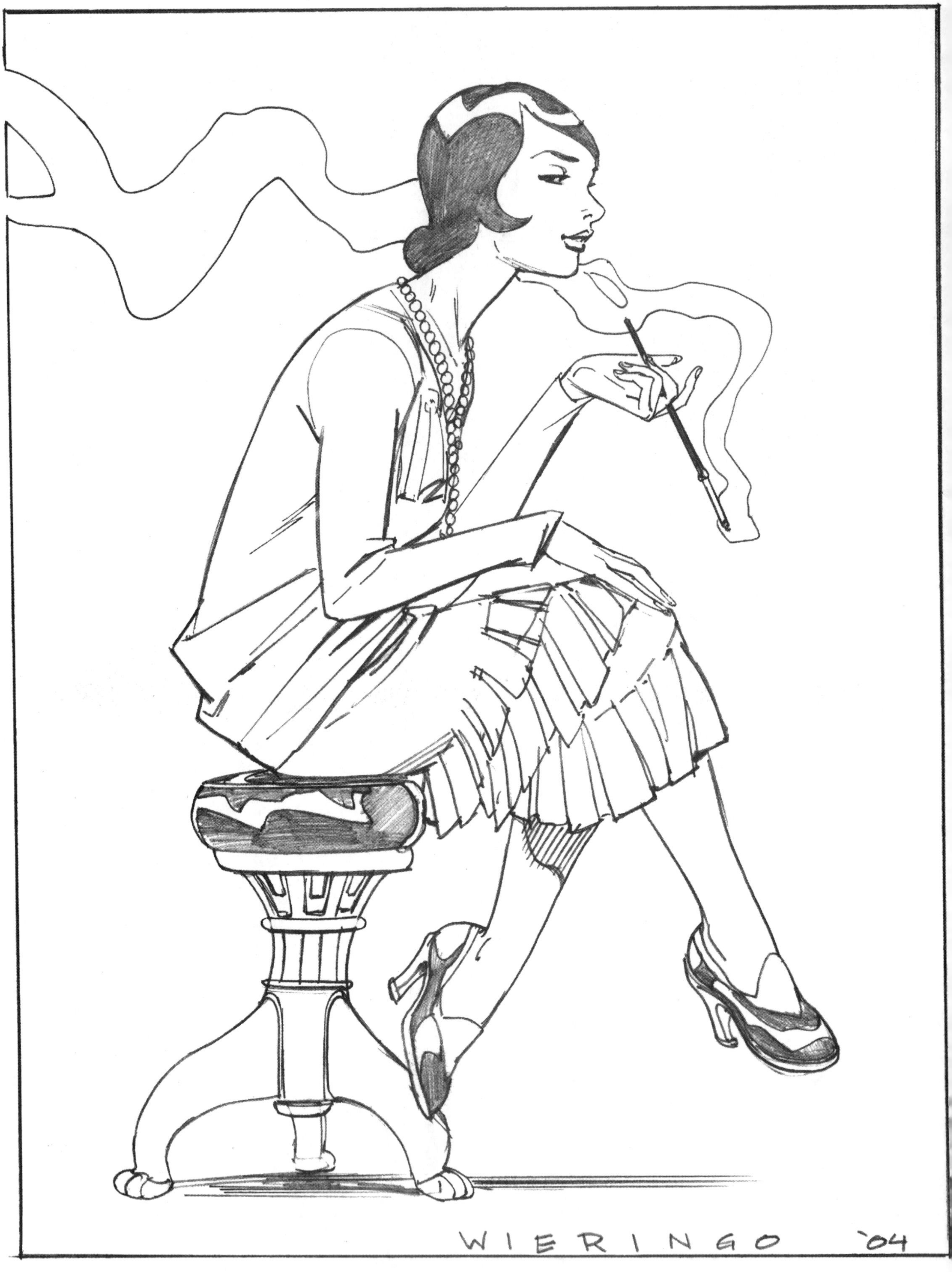
WIERINGO '04

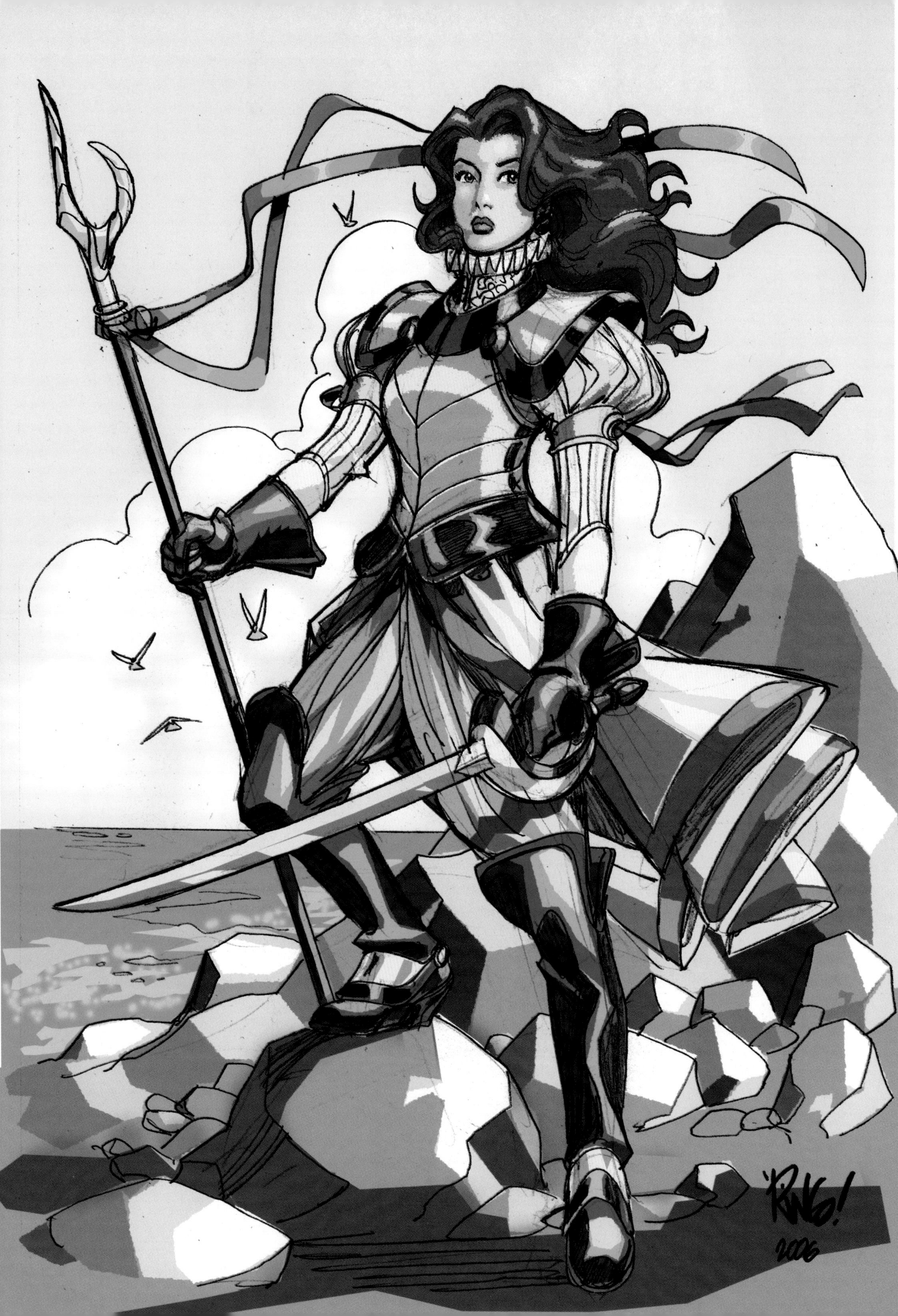
2006

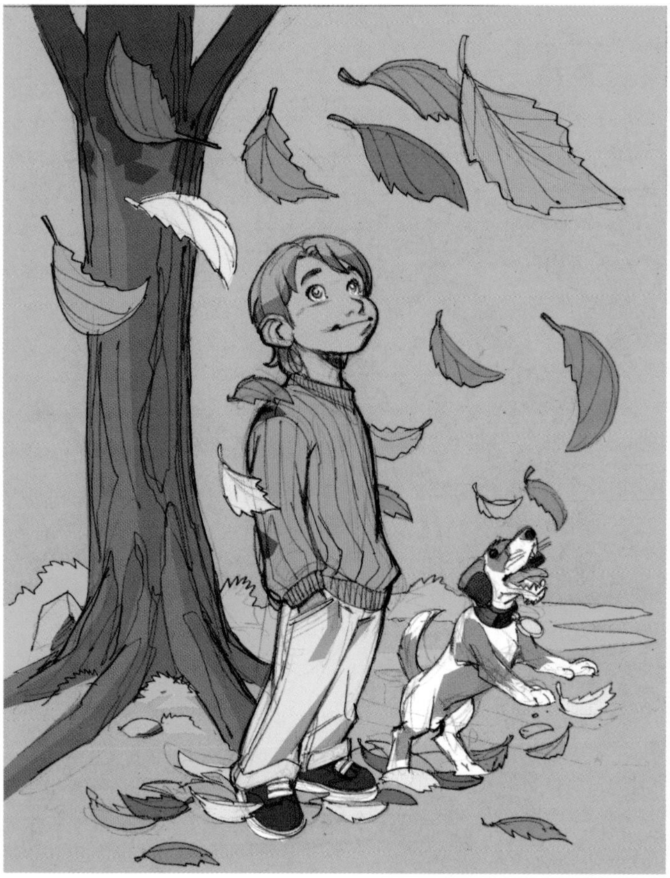

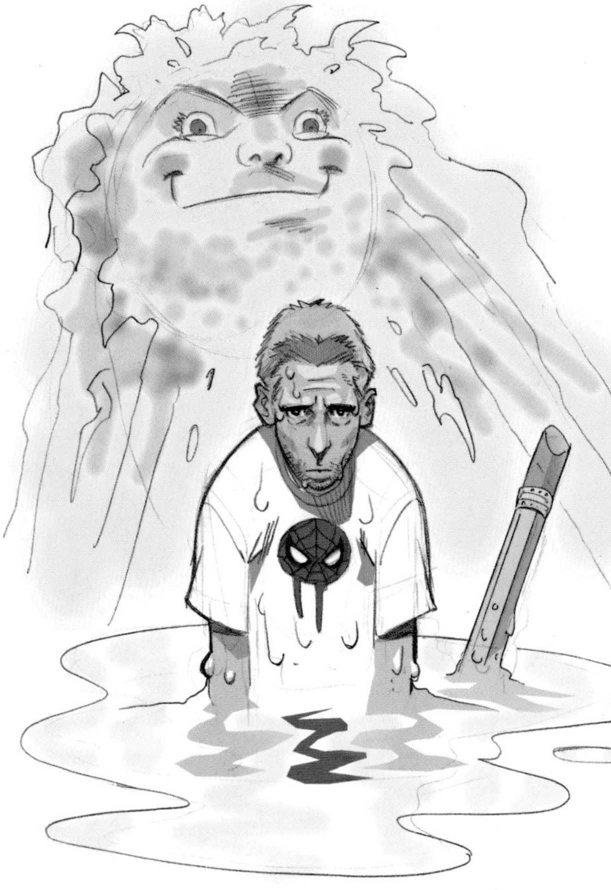

This Page: Artwork from Mike's always interesting blog—at *www.mikewieringo.com*—where Mike posts semi-daily sketches of whatever is on his mind.
Next Page: Artwork done for a relief effort to help victims of Hurricane Katrina.

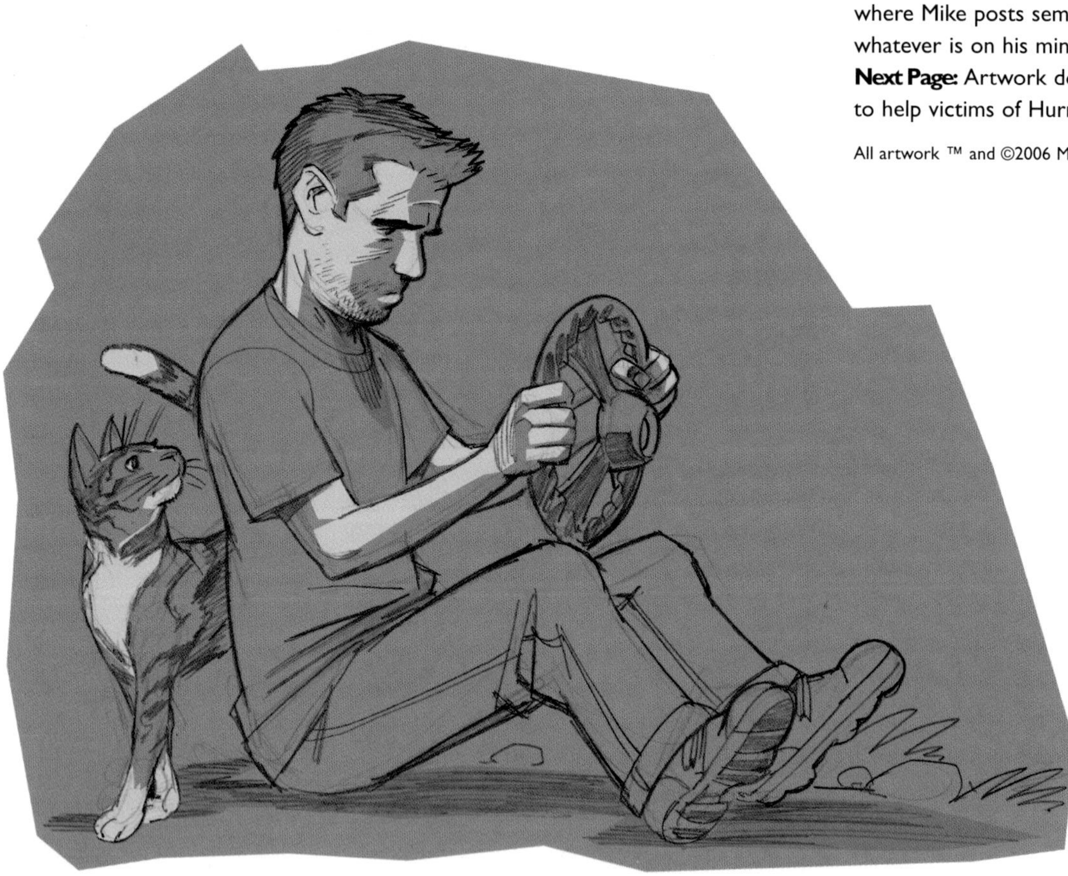

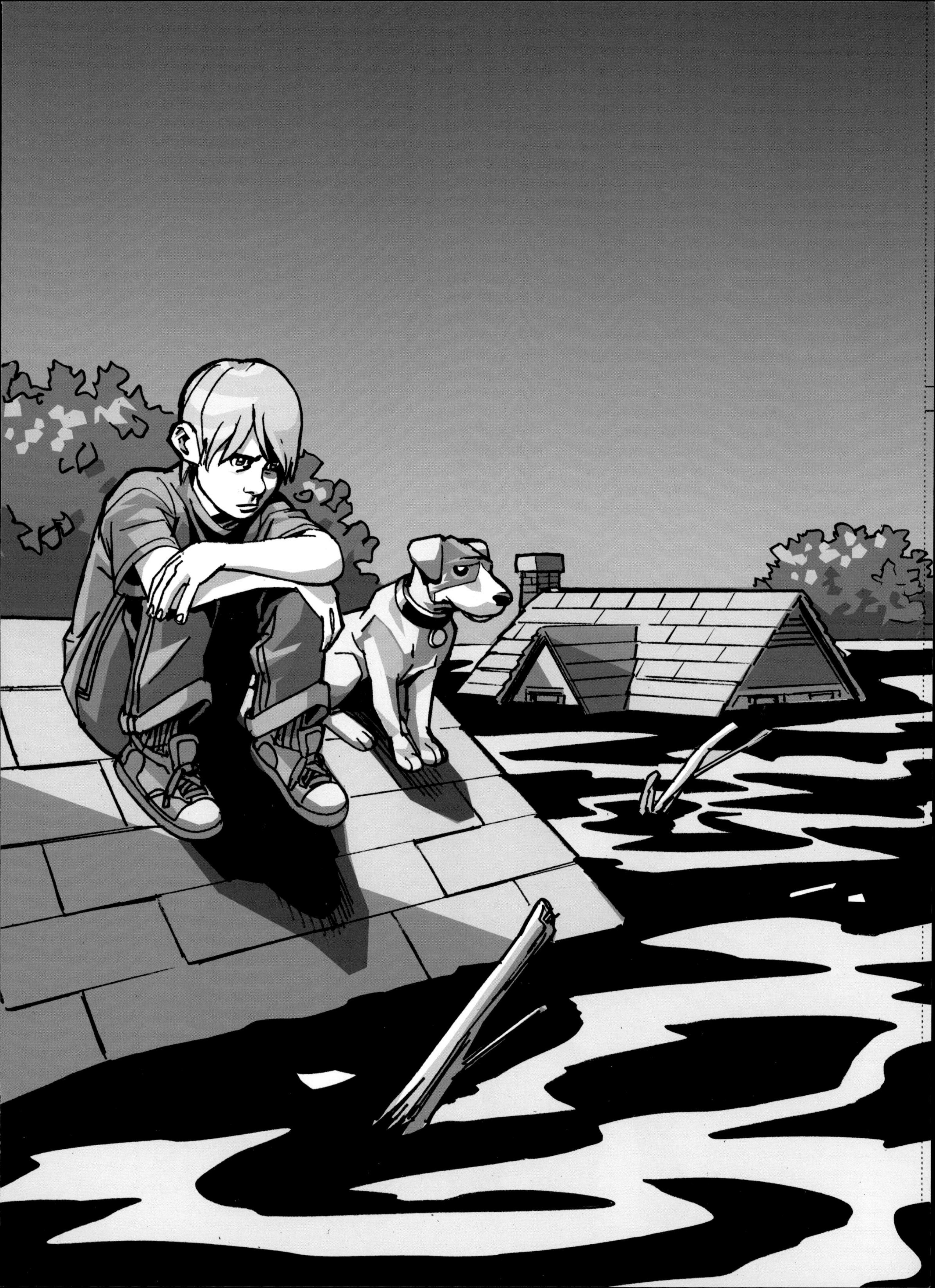

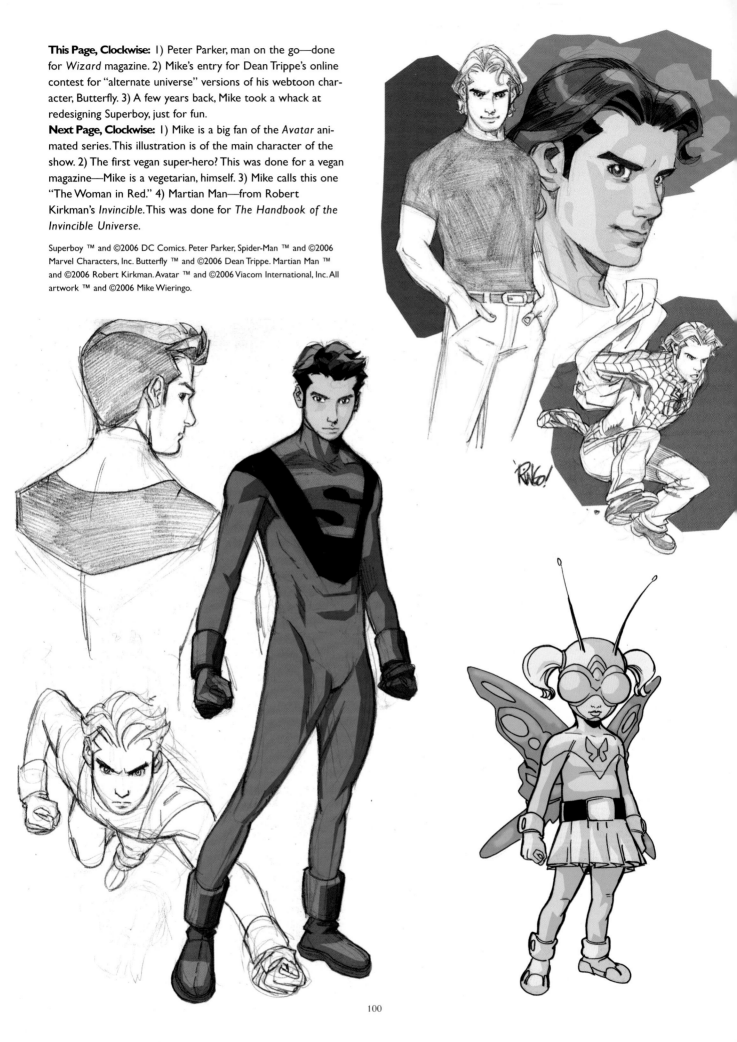

This Page, Clockwise: 1) Peter Parker, man on the go—done for *Wizard* magazine. 2) Mike's entry for Dean Trippe's online contest for "alternate universe" versions of his webtoon character, Butterfly. 3) A few years back, Mike took a whack at redesigning Superboy, just for fun.

Next Page, Clockwise: 1) Mike is a big fan of the *Avatar* animated series. This illustration is of the main character of the show. 2) The first vegan super-hero? This was done for a vegan magazine—Mike is a vegetarian, himself. 3) Mike calls this one "The Woman in Red." 4) Martian Man—from Robert Kirkman's *Invincible*. This was done for *The Handbook of the Invincible Universe.*

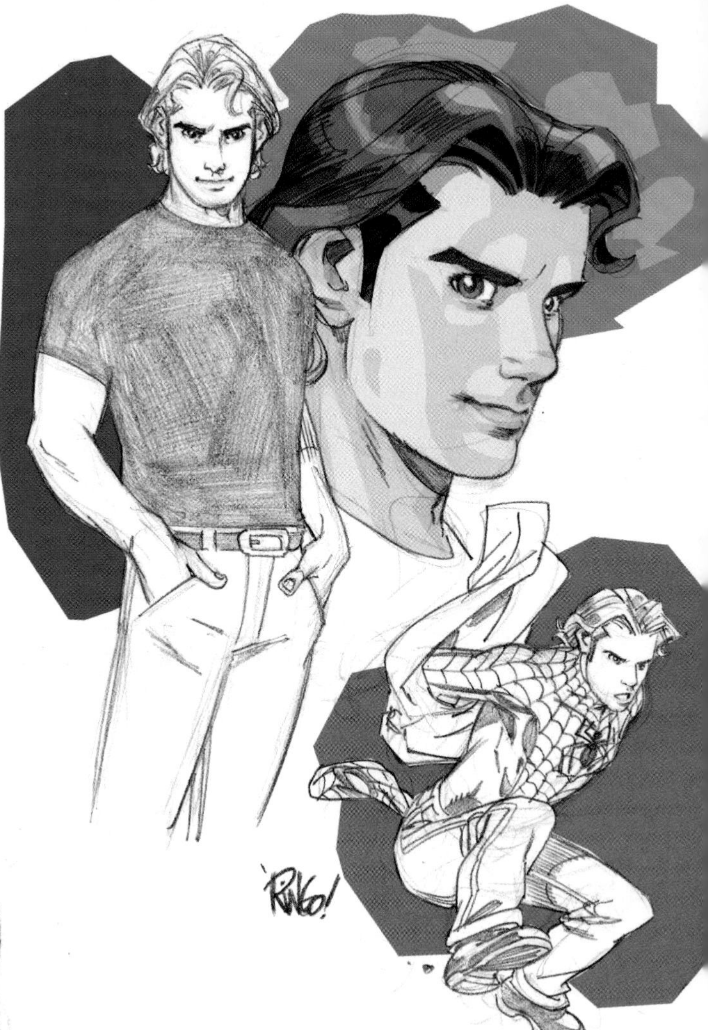

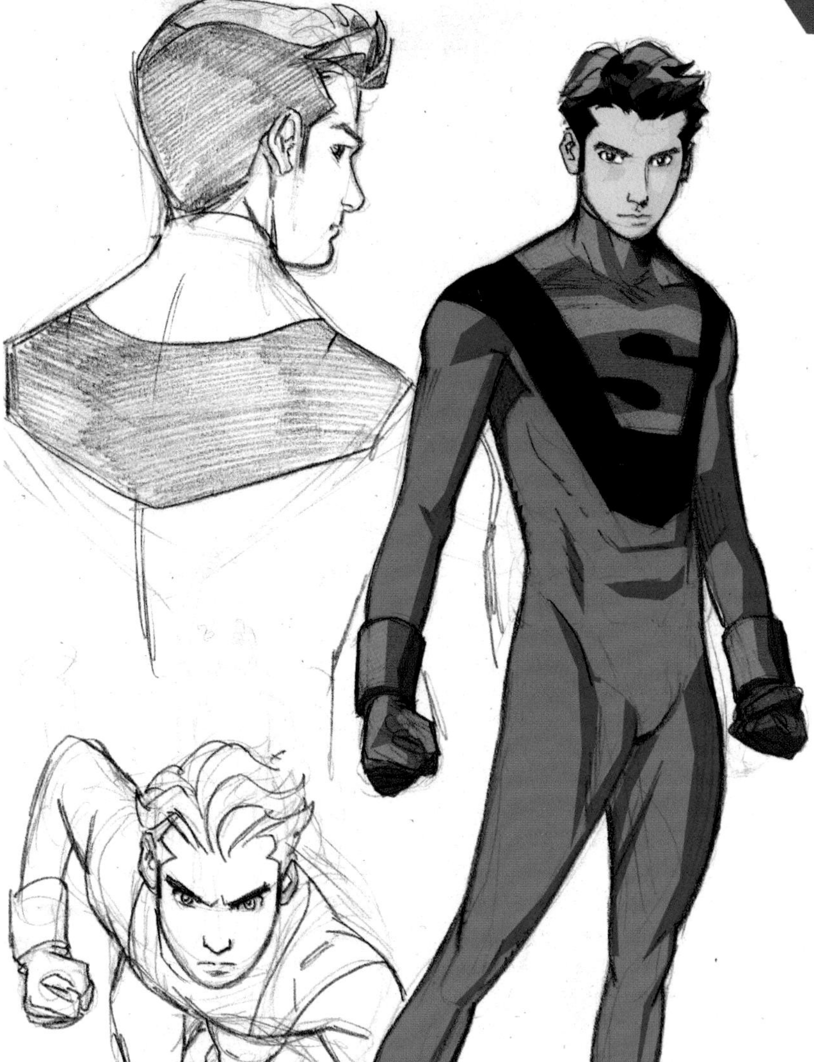

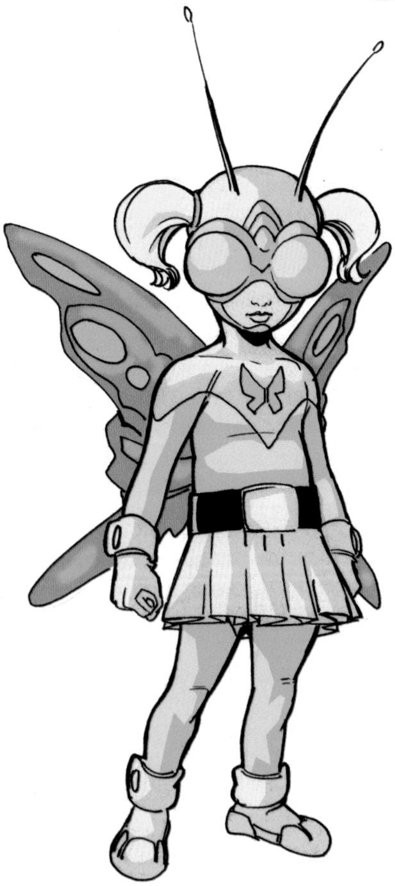

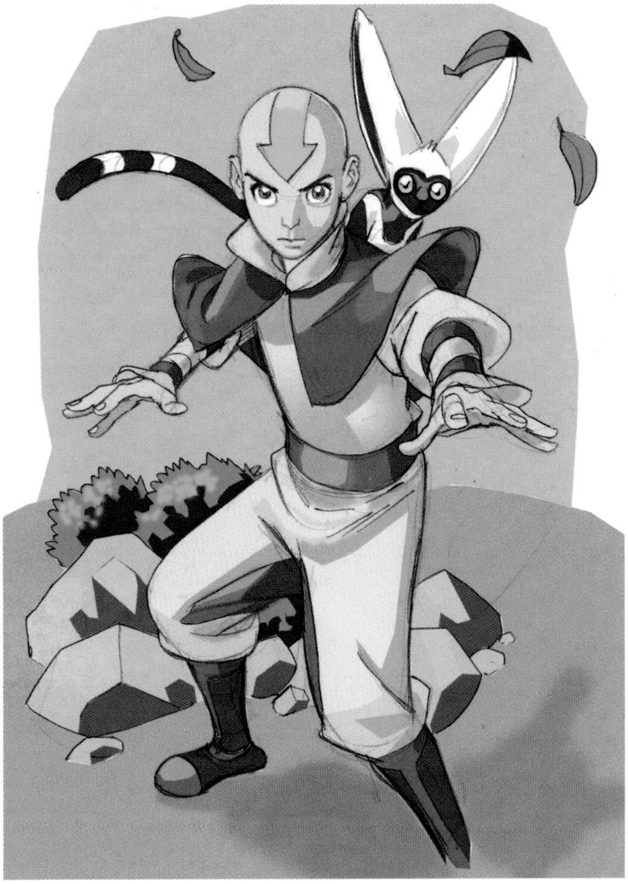

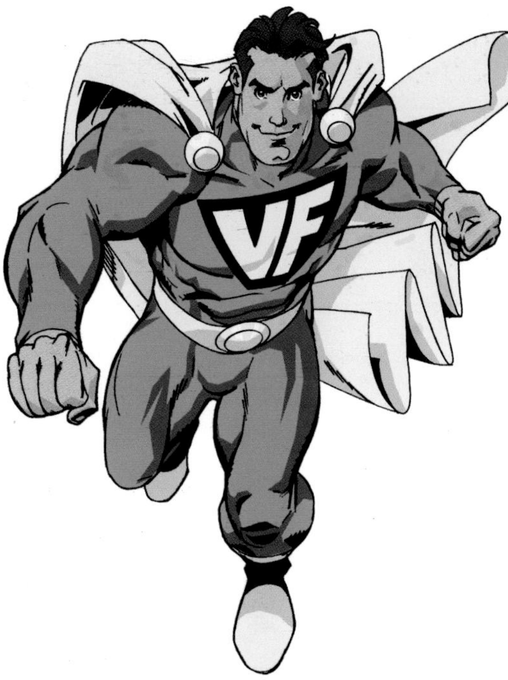
VF

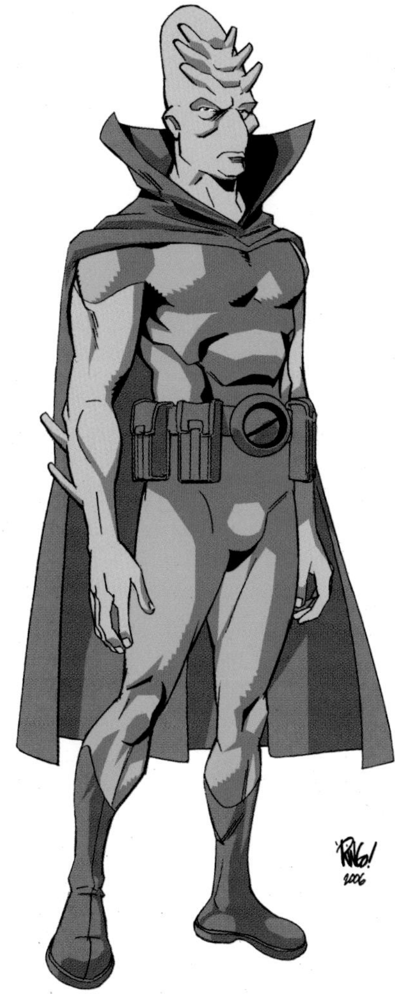

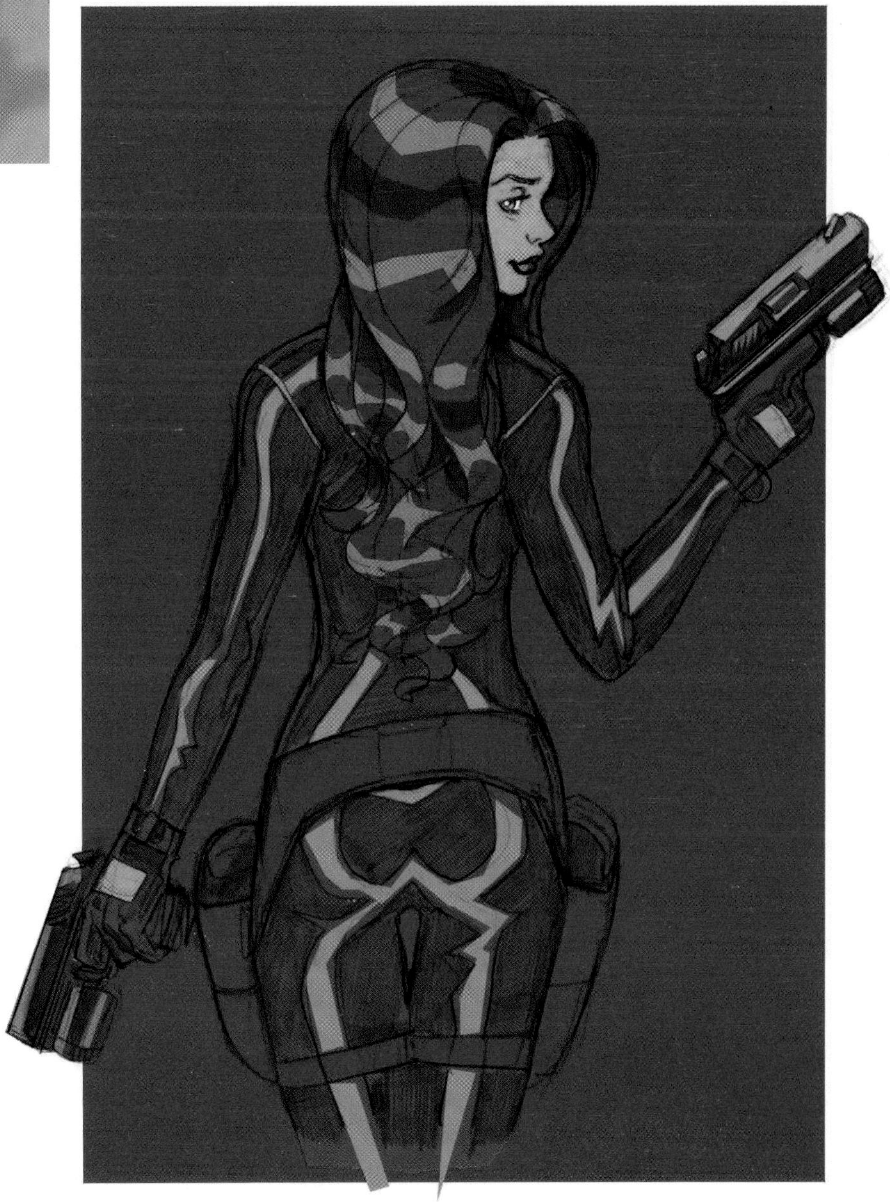

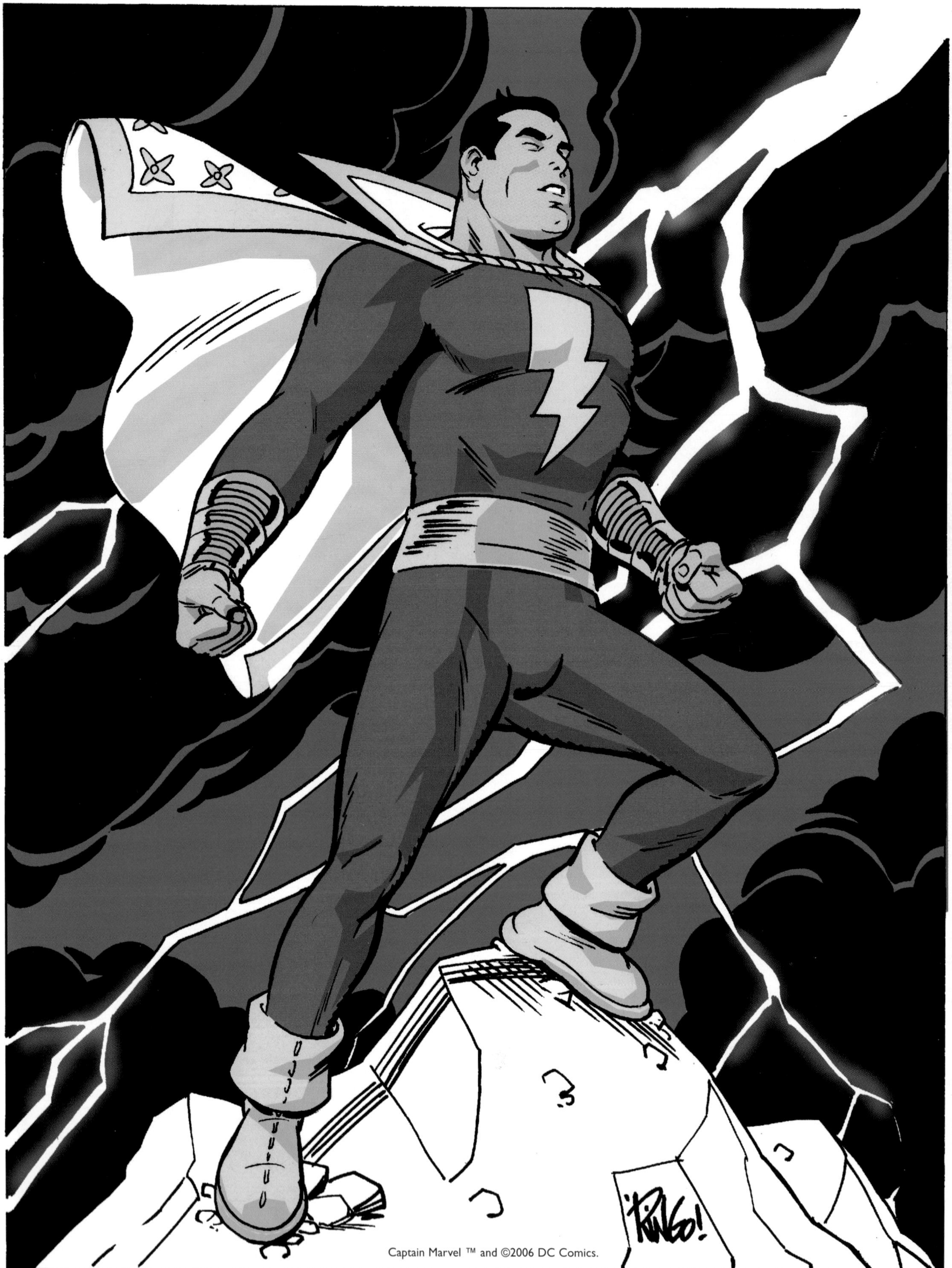
RINGO!

FOR MARK — A GREAT WRITER AND A GREAT FRIEND...

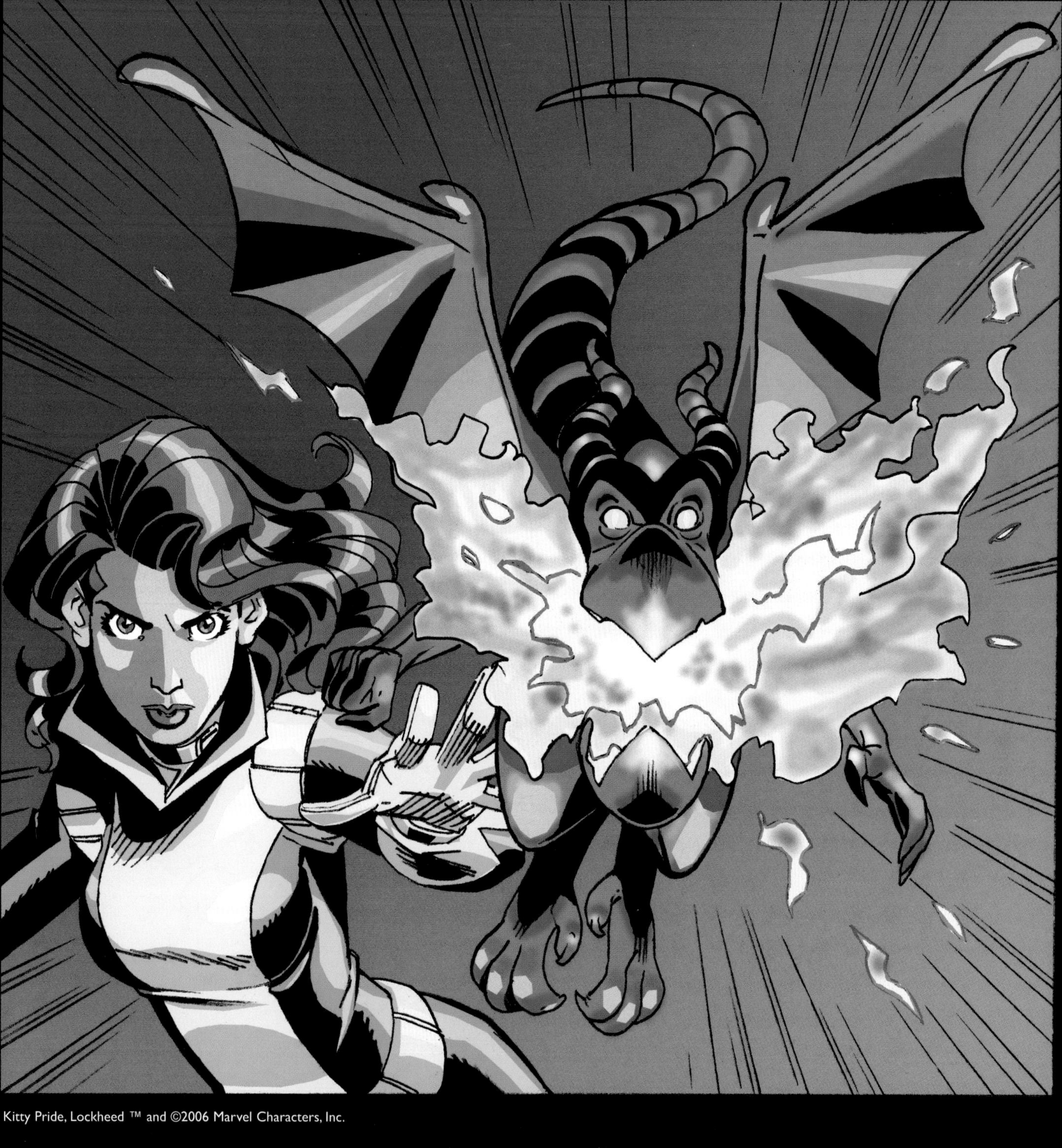

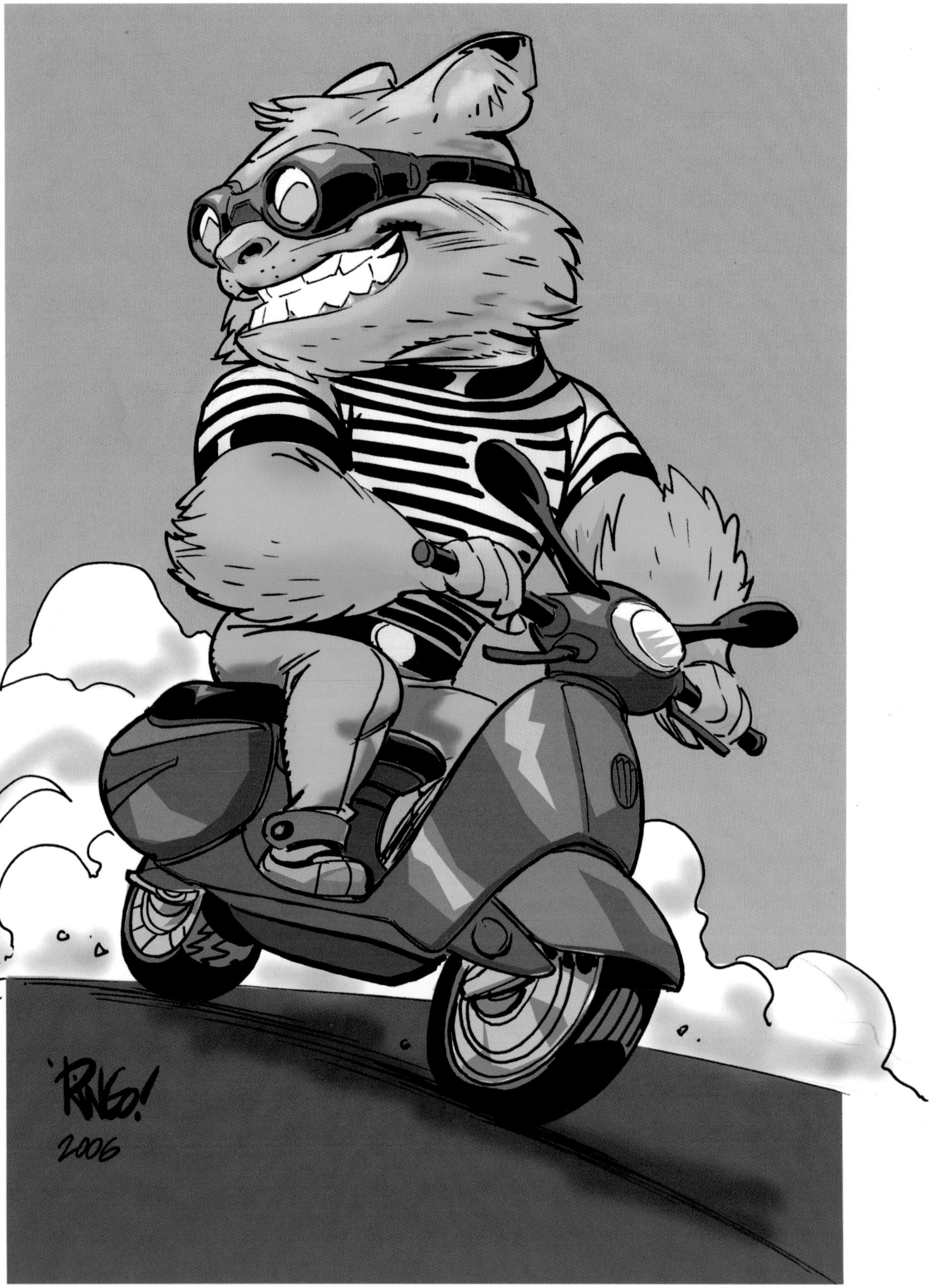
'RINGO!
2006

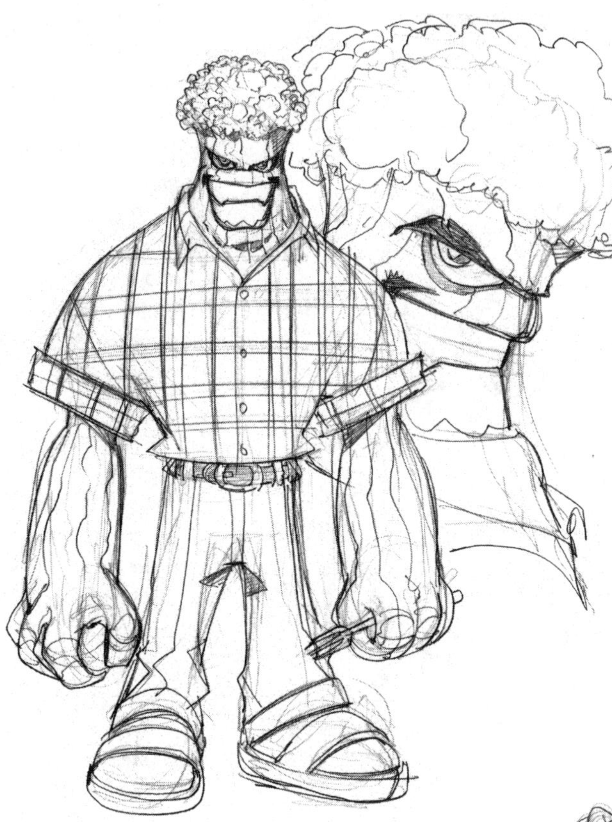

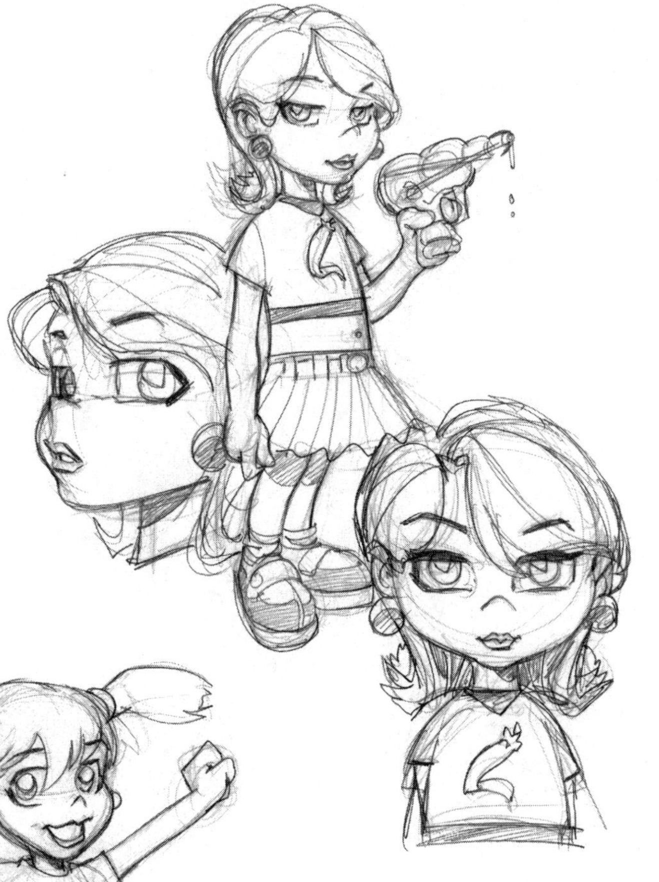

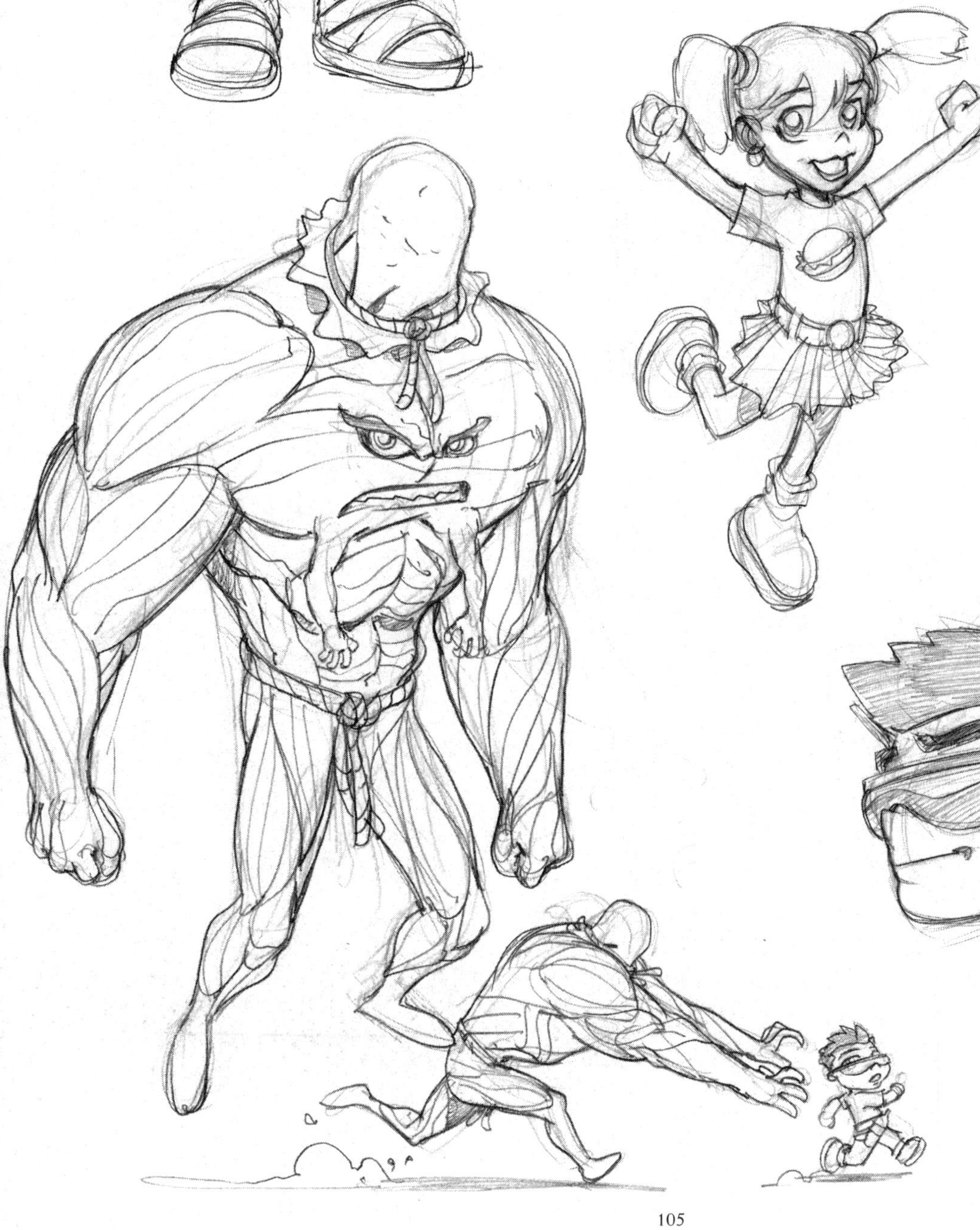

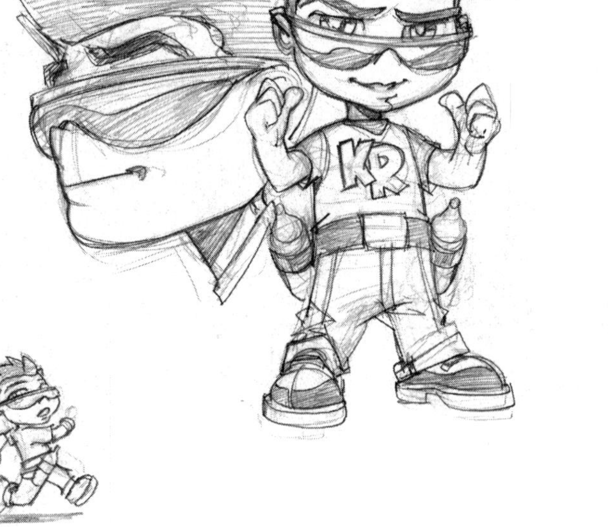
KR

Previous Page: That's one bad motor scooter.
This Page: Character designs for an online entertainment site, back during the Dotcom Boom.

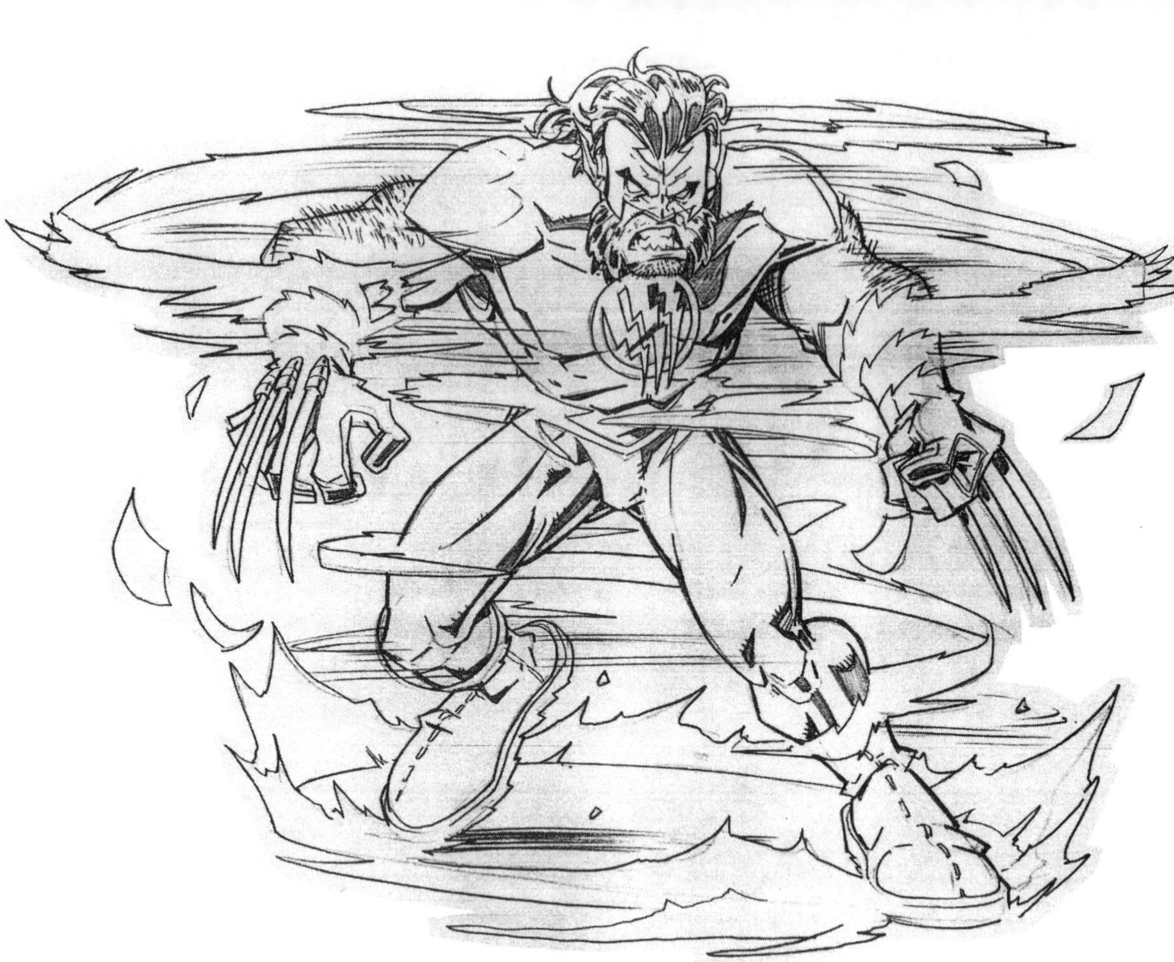

This Page, Clockwise: 1) A few years back, *Wizard* asked what you would get if you crossed Flash with Wolverine? 2) How about Spider-Man and the Atom? 3) And the inspiration came from the DC/Marvel Amalgam crossover series. This is one of Mike's layouts from the *Spider-Boy*—mixing Spider-Man and Superboy—book.
Next Page: 1) Mike drew this preliminary sketch for a Malibu-proposed Captain Marvel/Prime crossover book, back before Marvel bought the company. 2) The Atom vs. Ant-Man!

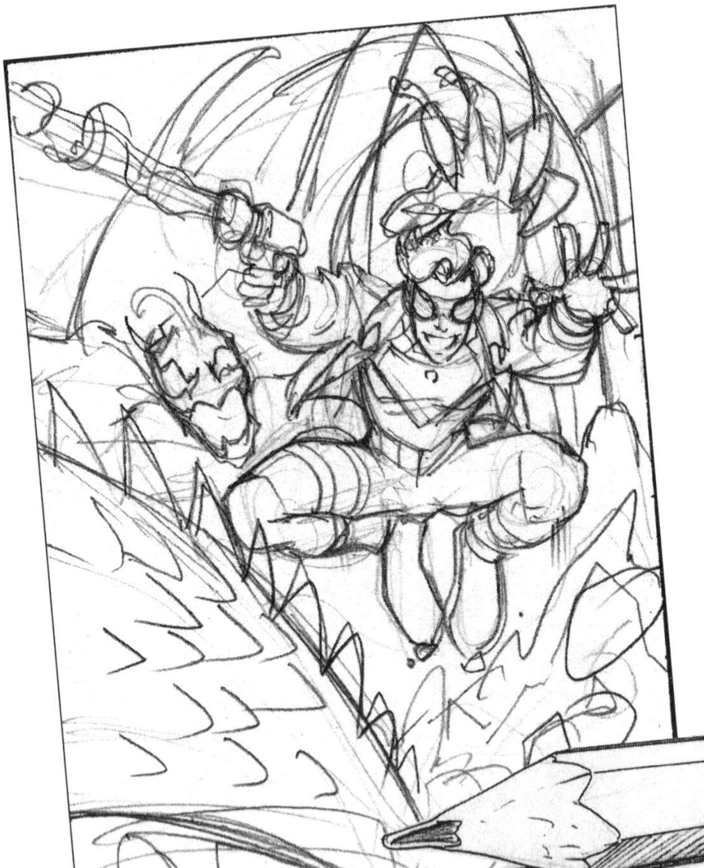

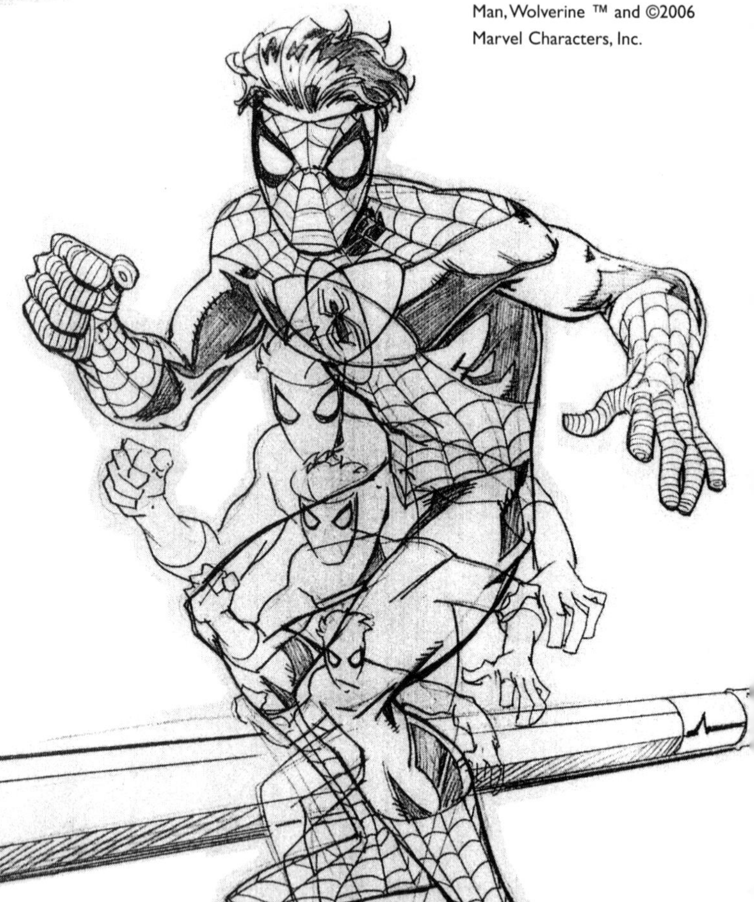

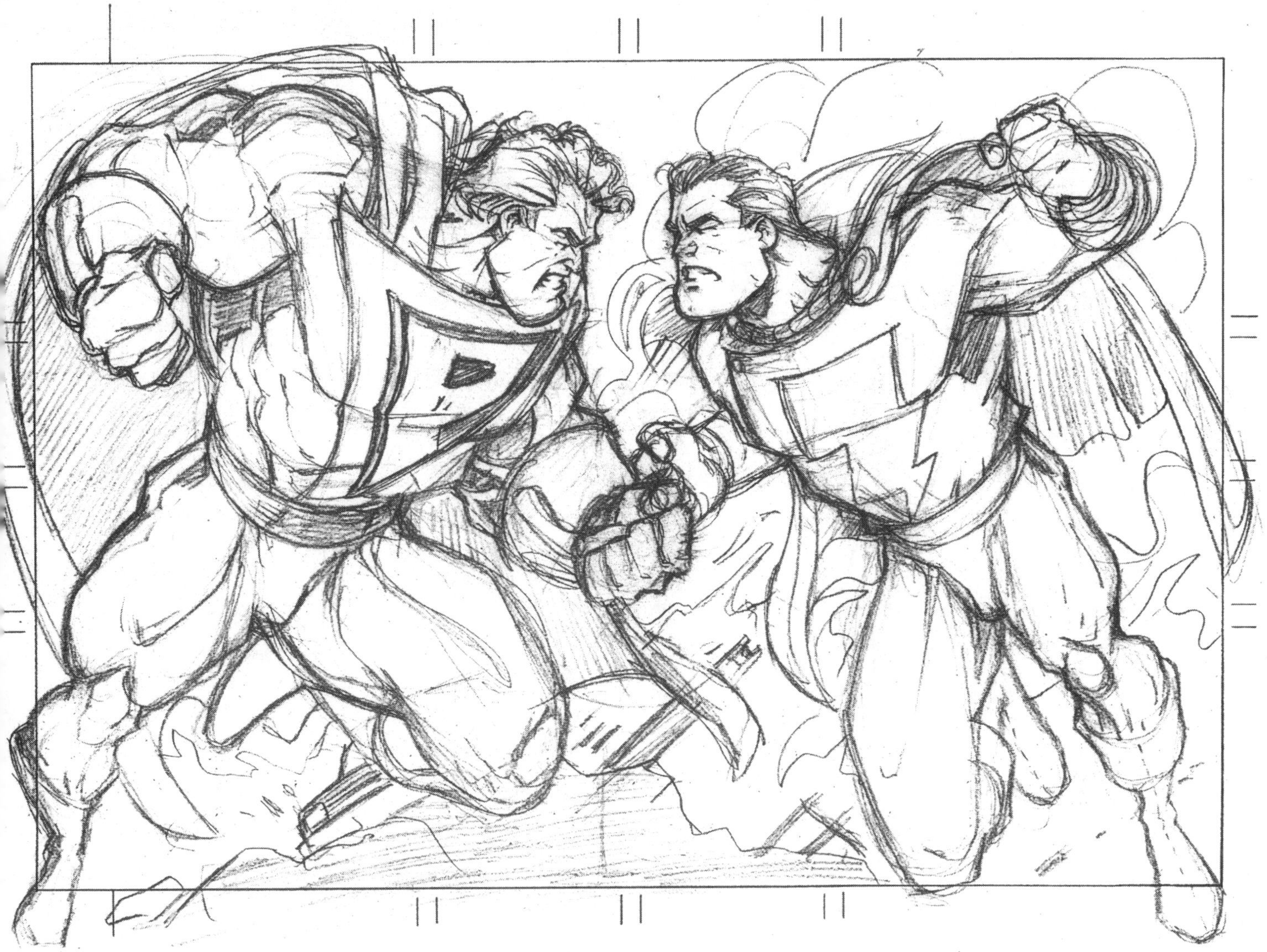

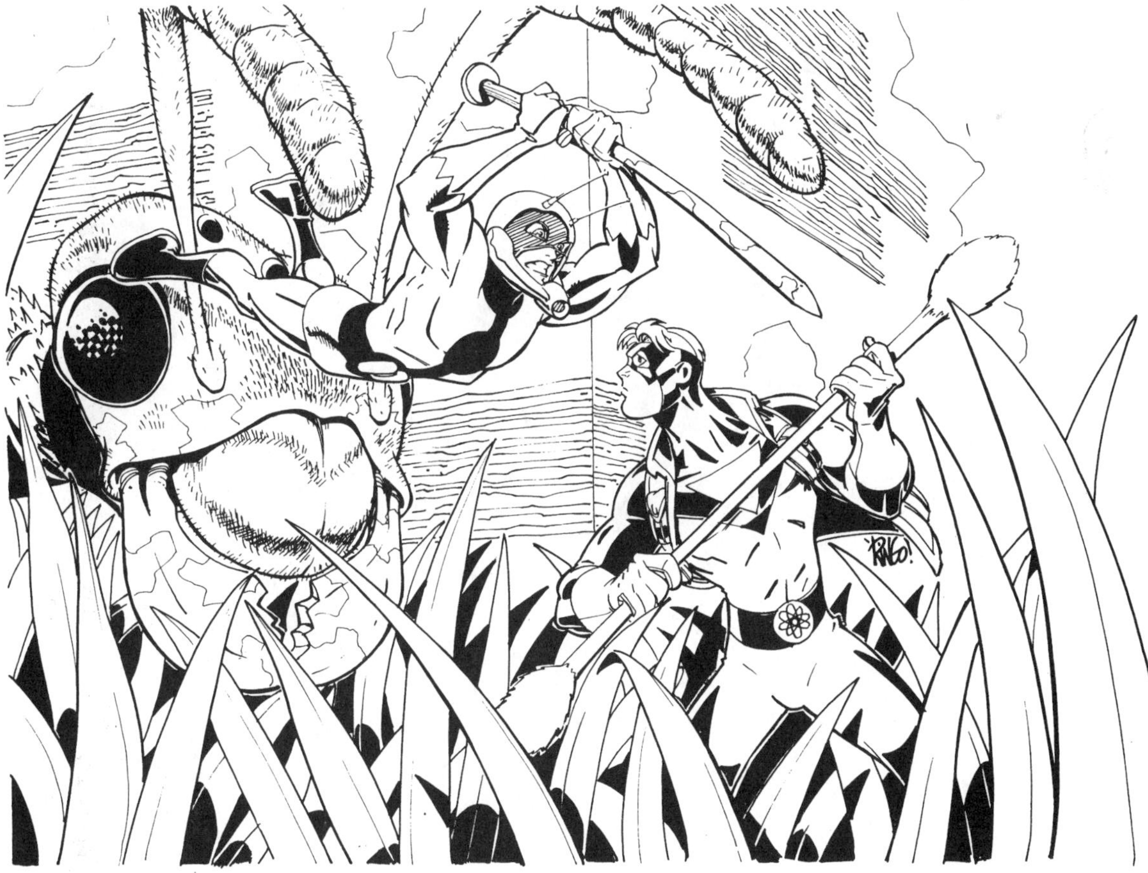

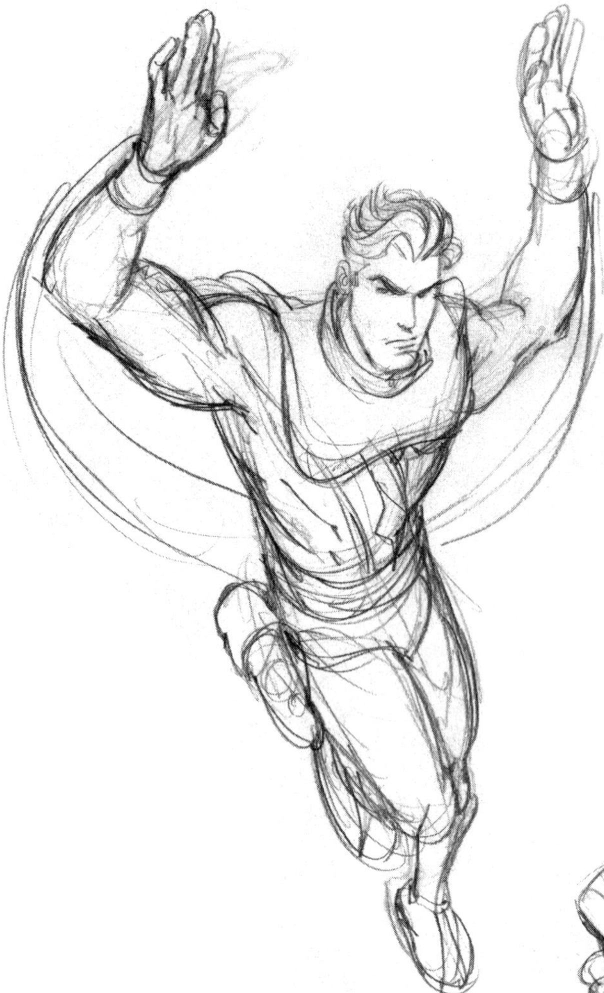

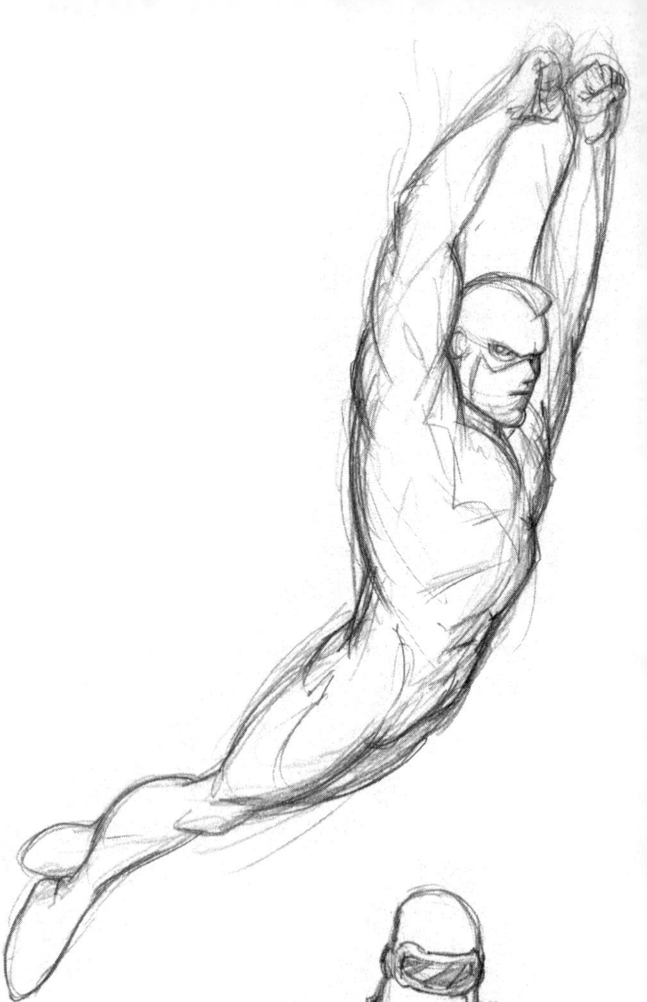

This Page and Next: During Mike's last stint at DC, he was to be the pin-up artist for a proposed *Freedom Fighters Secret Files* one-shot. Needless to say, the book fell through, but he drew some great preliminary sketches for it. **Next Two Pages:** Mike's pencils for the back cover art for *Leave it to Chance* #13, and two layout options for *Thing & She-Hulk: The Long Night* cover—which Mike ended up not drawing for the published book.

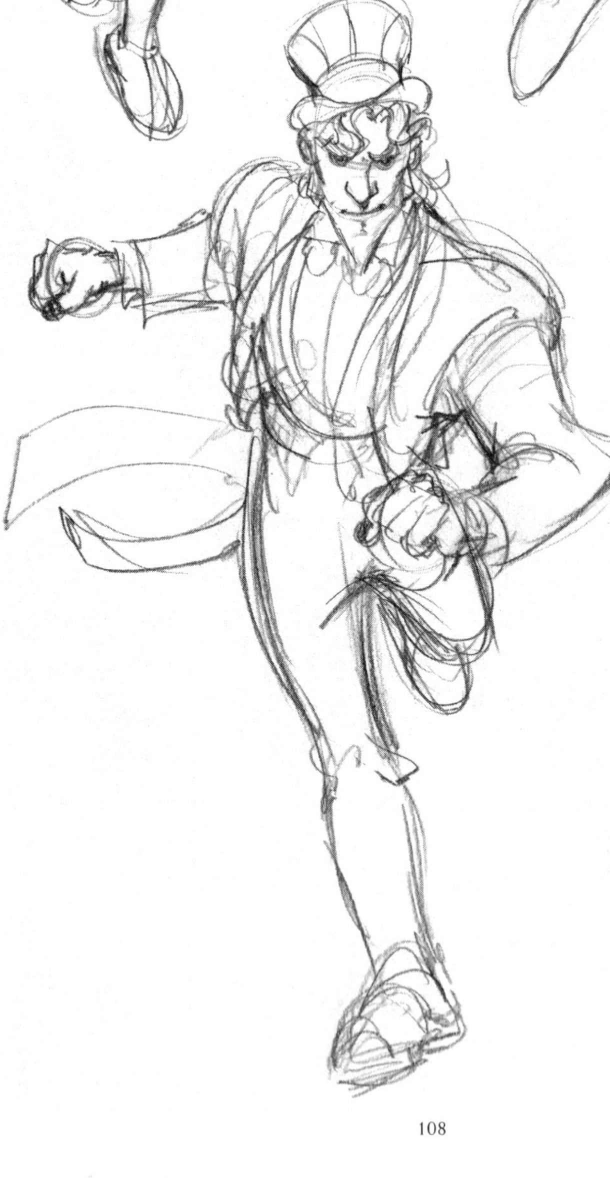

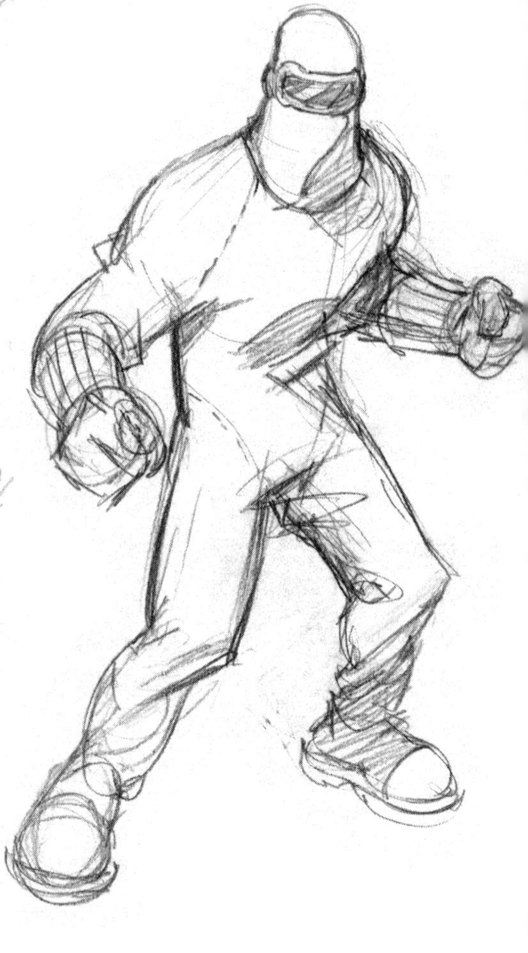

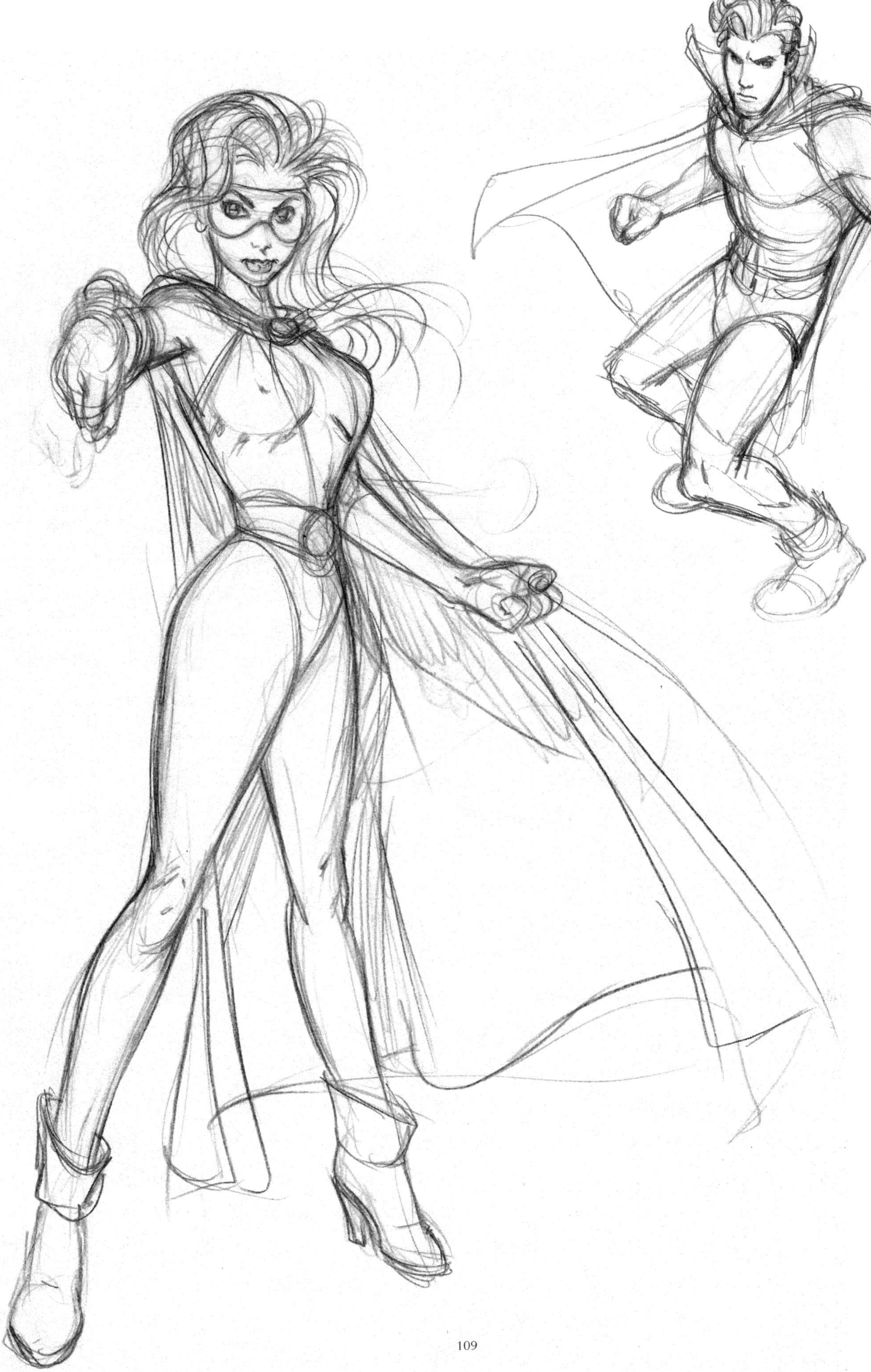

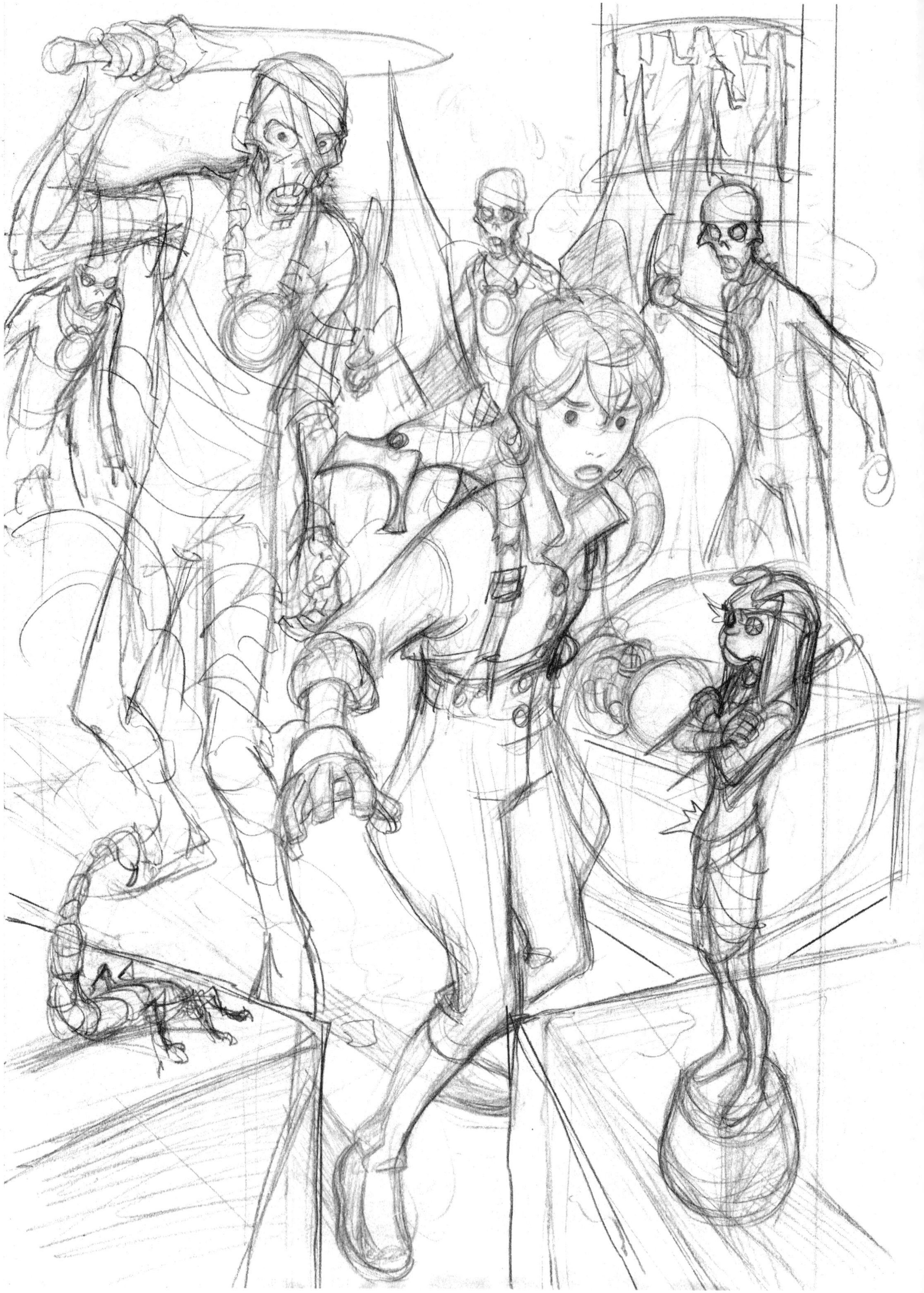

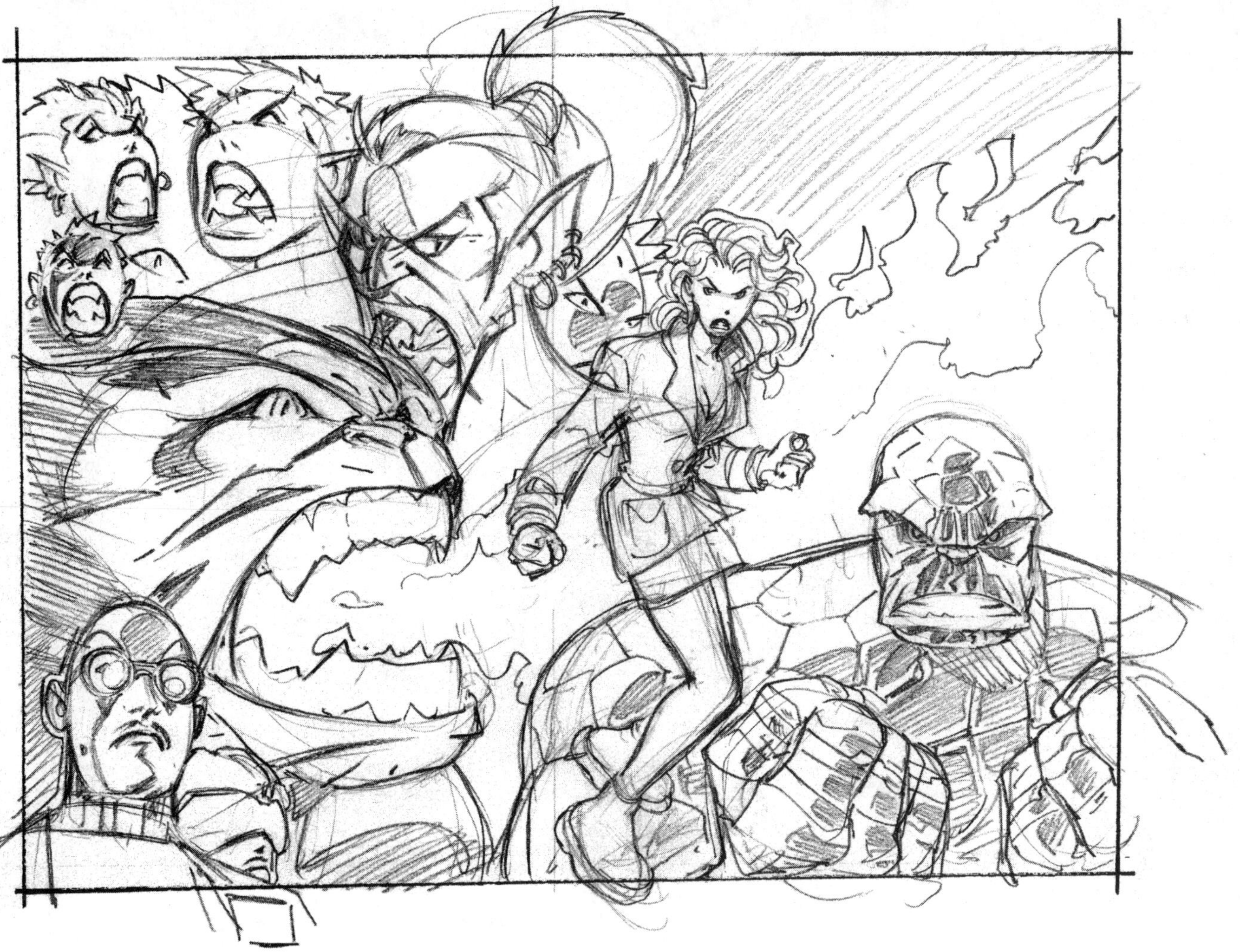
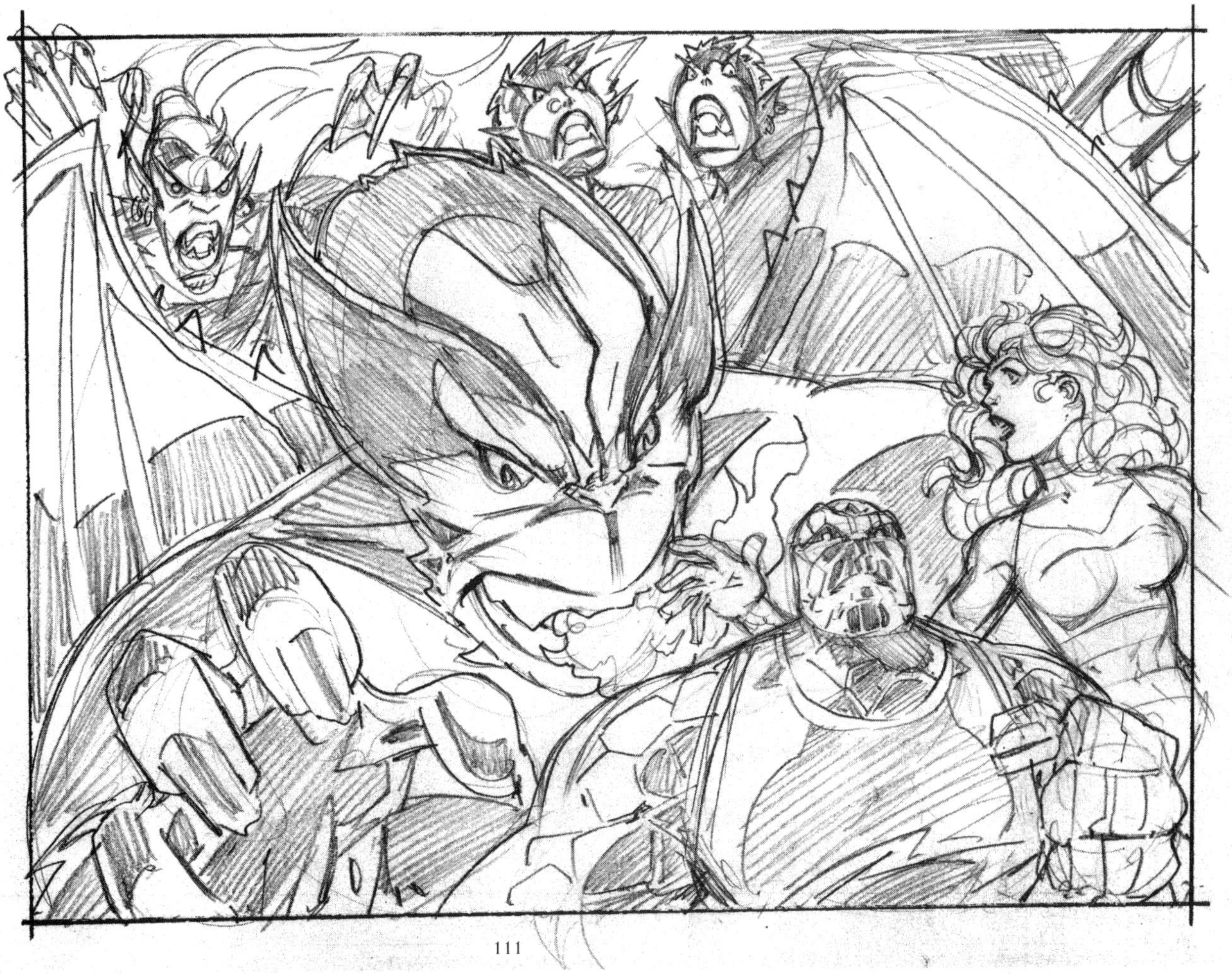

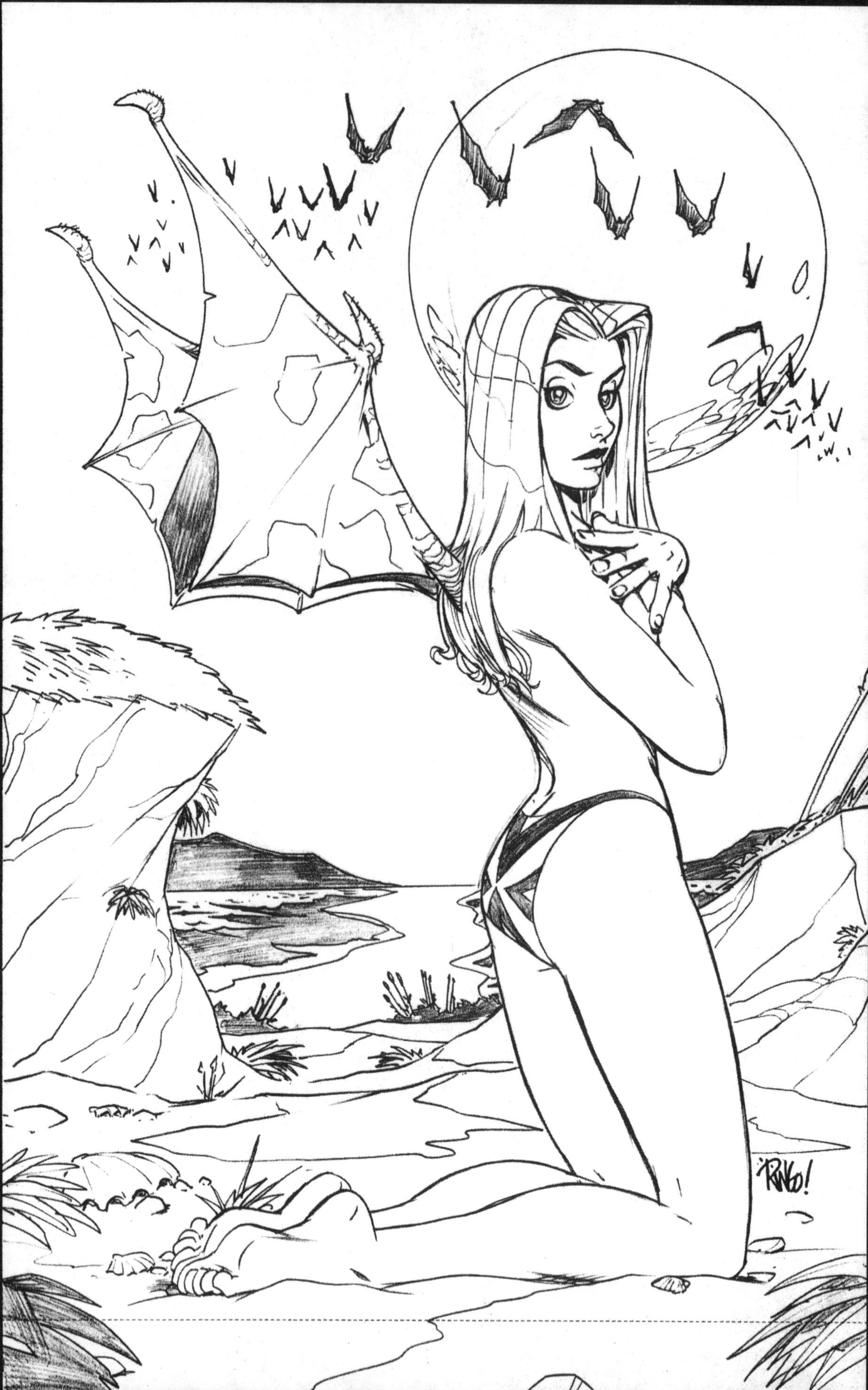
RINGO!

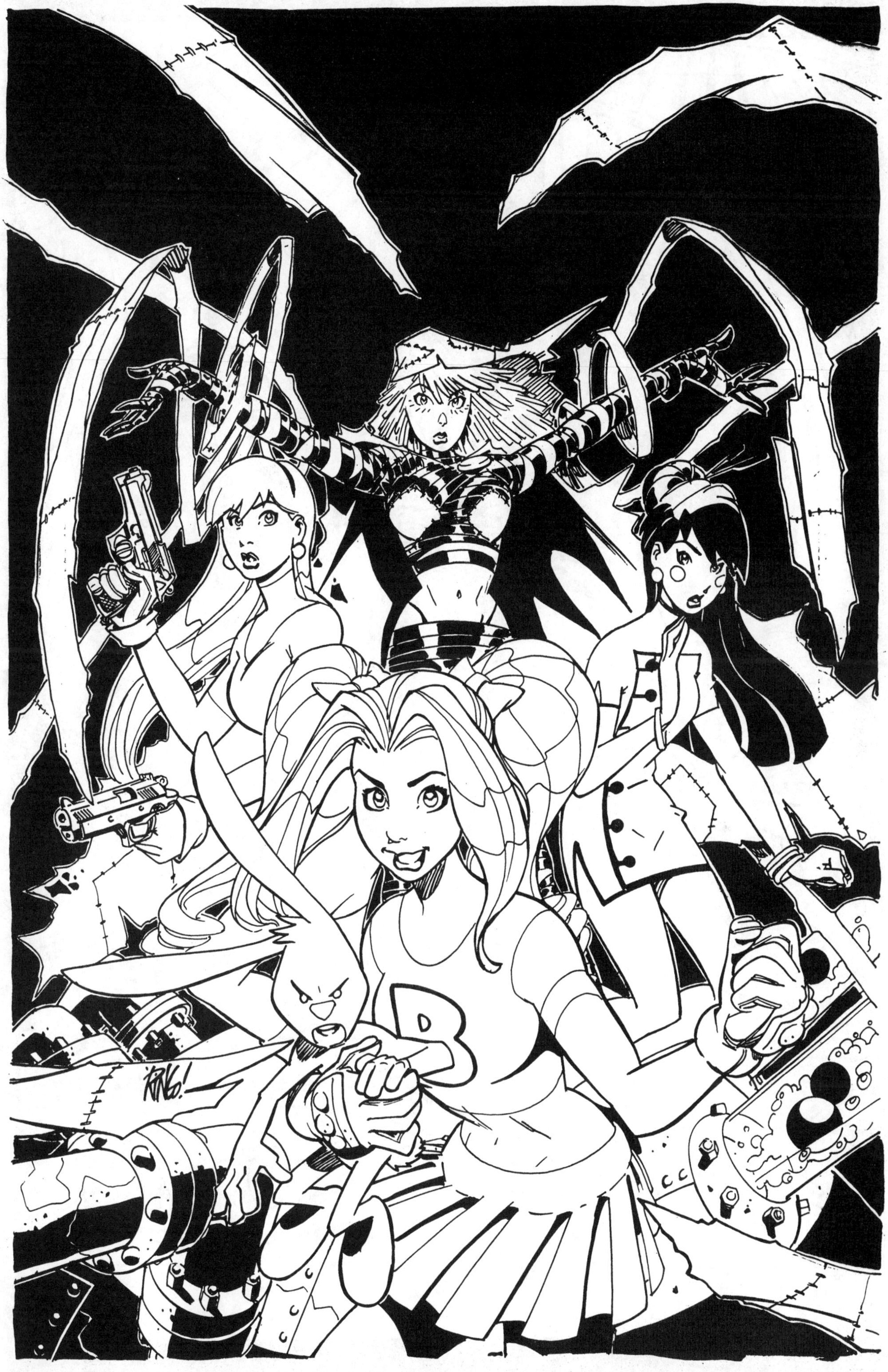

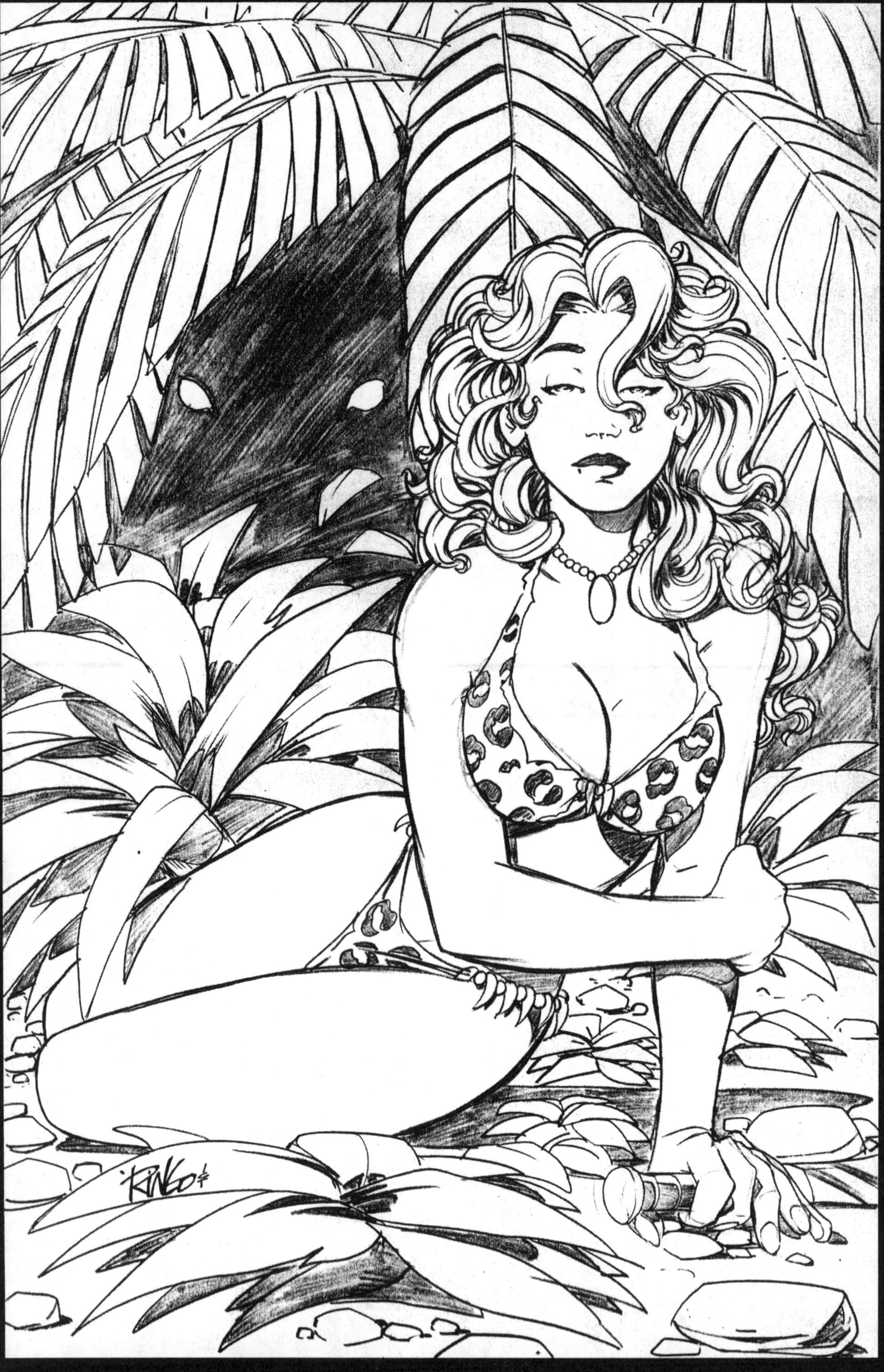

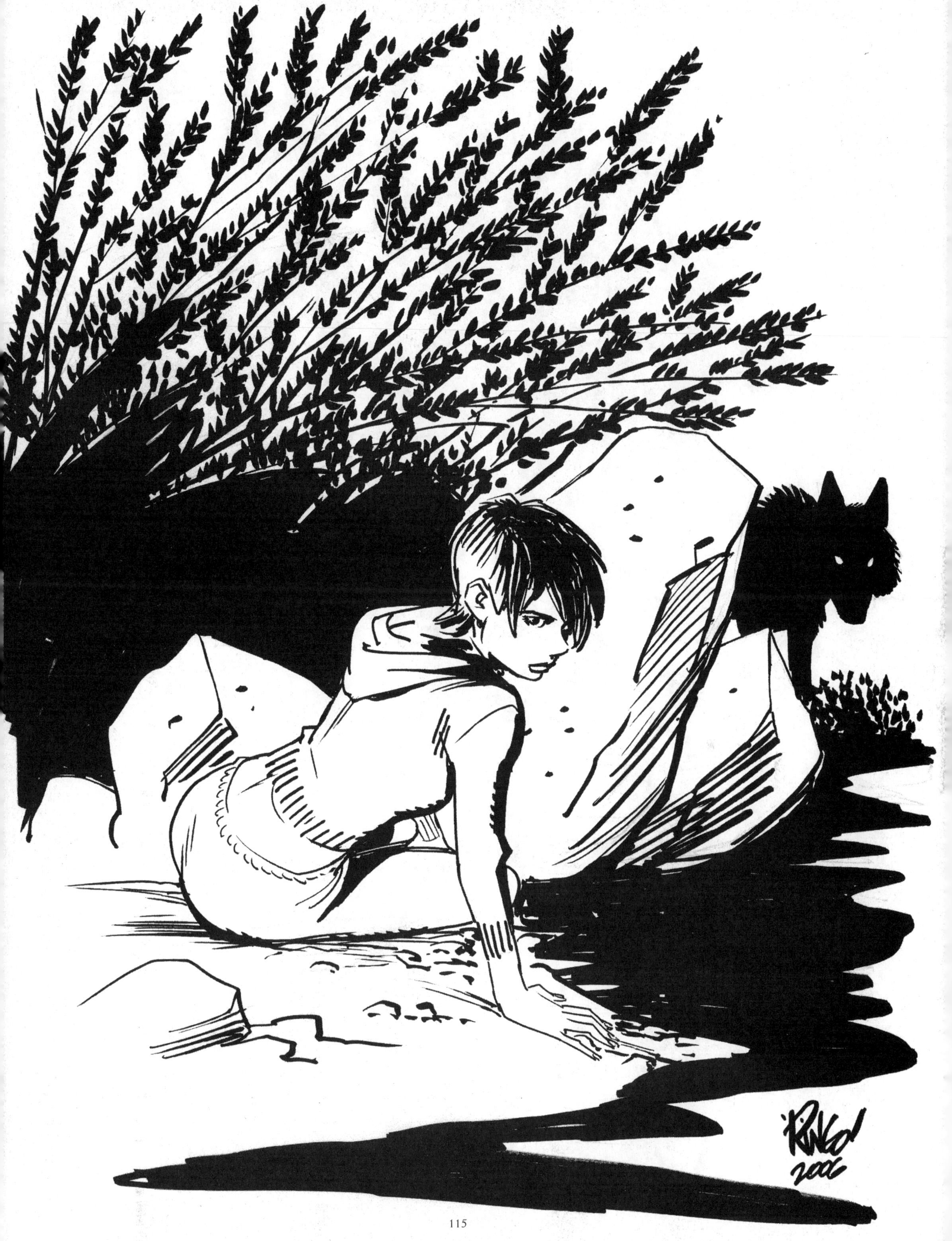
Ringo!
2006

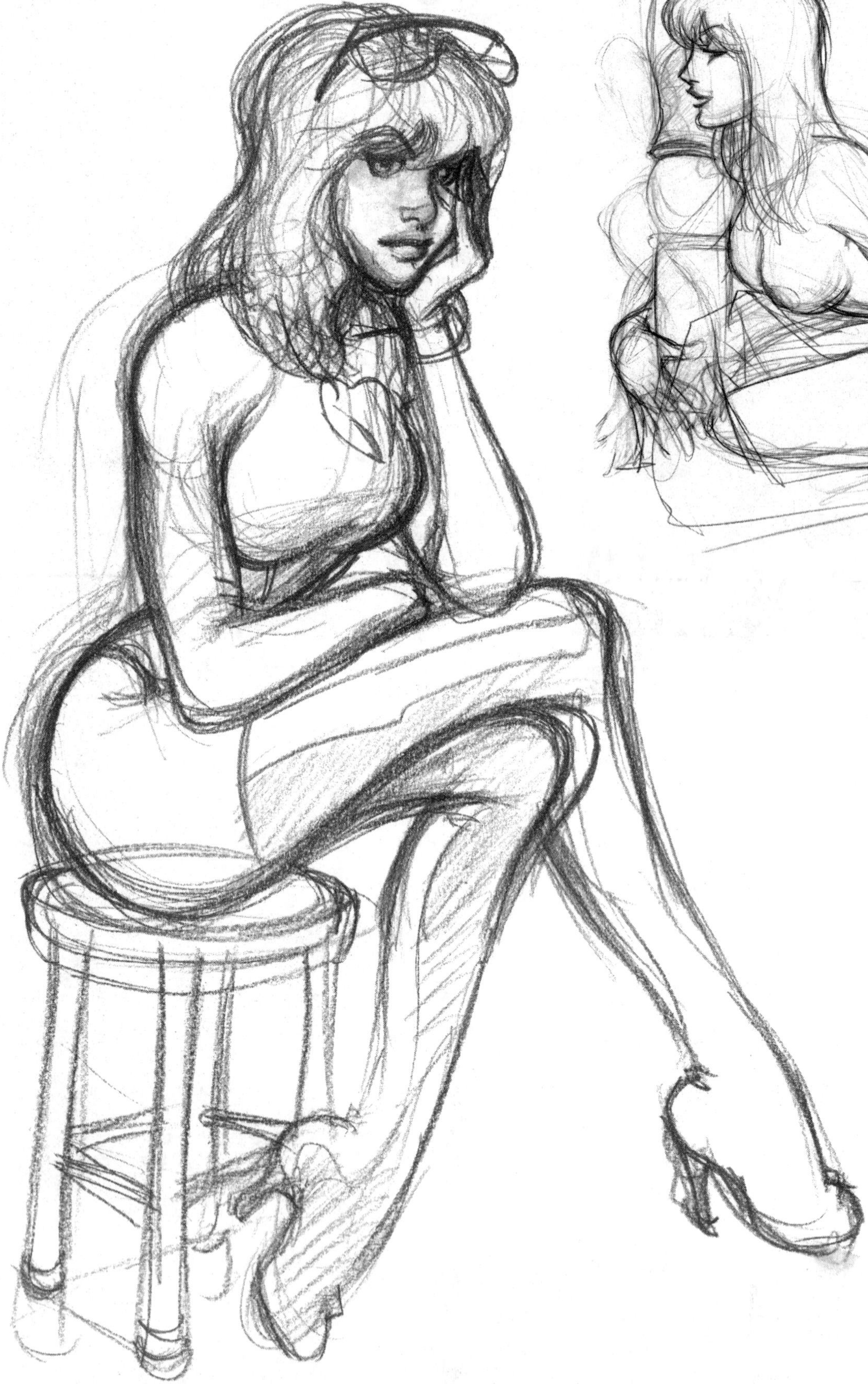

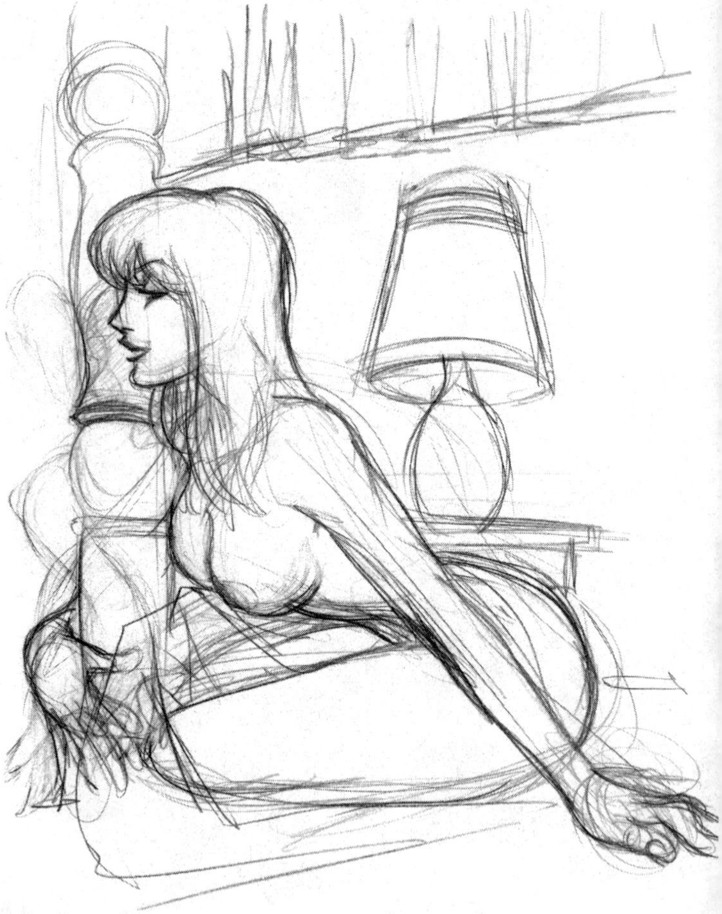

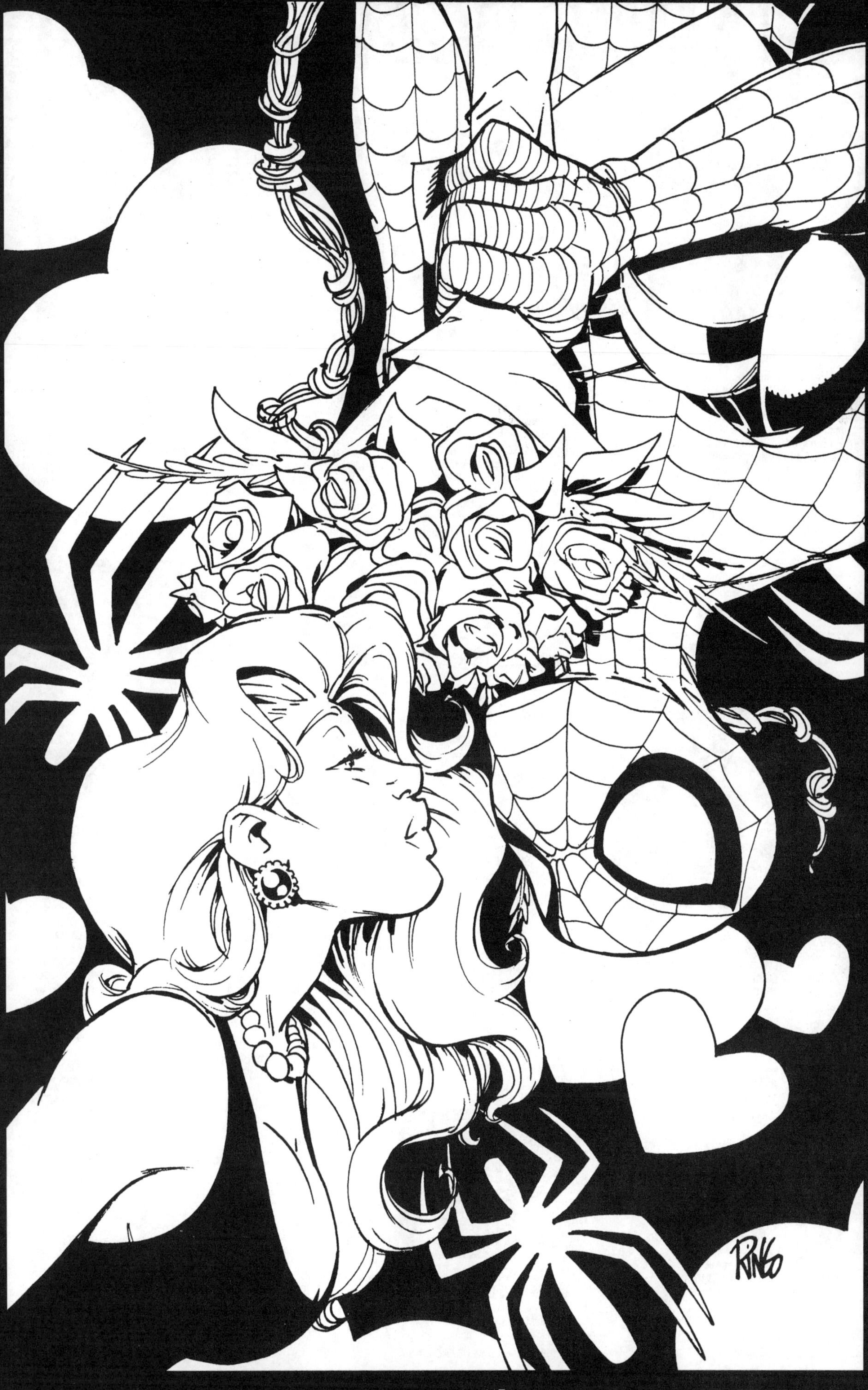
RINGO

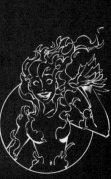

THE TWOMORROWS LIBRARY

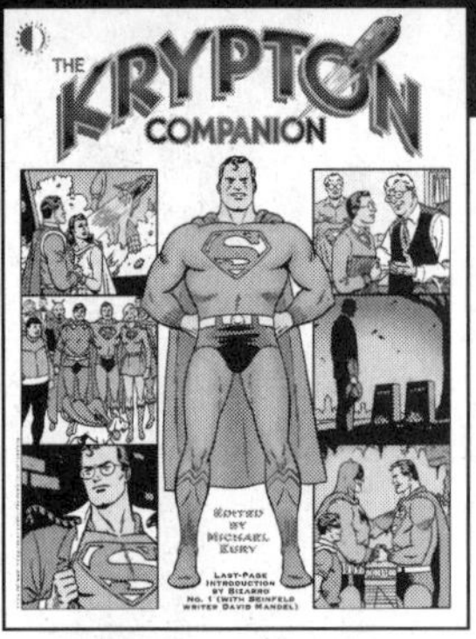
The KRYPTON COMPANION

THE KRYPTON COMPANION

Unlocks the secrets of Superman's Silver and Bronze Ages, when kryptonite came in multiple colors and super-pets flew the skies! Features all-new interviews with **NEAL ADAMS, MURPHY ANDERSON, NICK CARDY, JOSÉ LUIS GARCÍA-LÓPEZ, KEITH GIFFEN, JIM MOONEY, DENNIS O'NEIL, BOB OKSNER, MARTY PASKO, BOB ROZAKIS, JIM SHOOTER, LEN WEIN, MARV WOLFMAN,** and others, plus tons of rare and unseen art! By **BACK ISSUE MAGAZINE'S** Michael Eury!

(240-Page Trade Paperback) **$29 US**

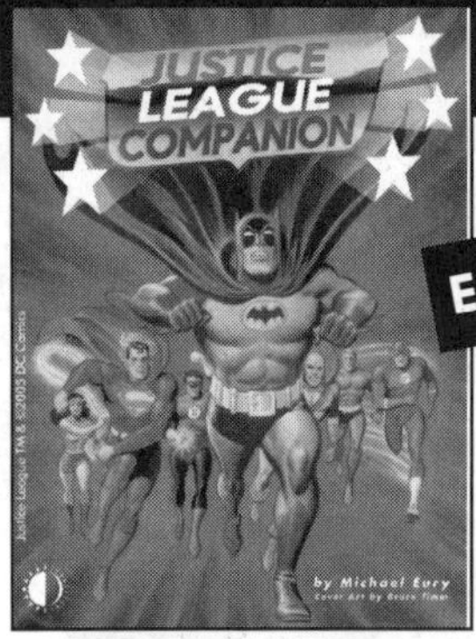
JUSTICE LEAGUE COMPANION
by Michael Eury

JUSTICE LEAGUE COMPANION VOL. 1

A comprehensive examination of the Silver Age JLA by **MICHAEL EURY**, tracing its development, history, and more through interviews with the series' creators, an issue-by-issue index of the JLA's 1960-1972 adventures, classic and never-before-published artwork, and other fascinating features. Contributors include **DENNY O'NEIL, MURPHY ANDERSON, JOE GIELLA, MIKE FRIEDRICH, NEAL ADAMS, ALEX ROSS, CARMINE INFANTINO, NICK CARDY,** and many, many others. Plus: An exclusive interview with **STAN LEE**, who answers the question, "Did the JLA really inspire the creation of Marvel's Fantastic Four?" With an all-new cover by **BRUCE TIMM** (TV's Justice League Unlimited)!

(224-page trade paperback) **$29 US**

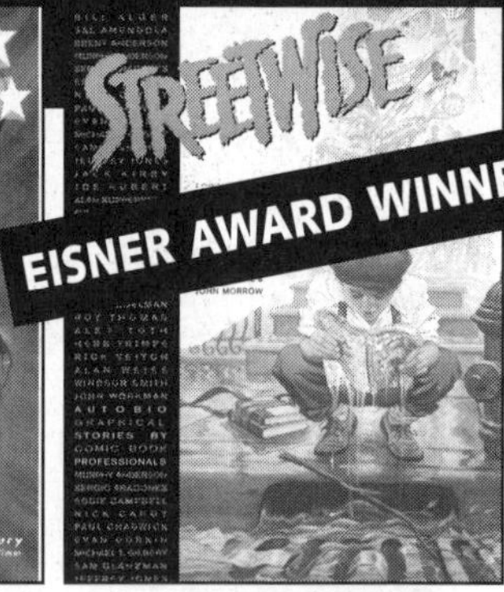
STREETWISE
EISNER AWARD WINNER!

STREETWISE
TOP ARTISTS DRAWING STORIES OF THEIR LIVES

An unprecedented assembly of talent drawing **NEW** autobiographical stories:

- Barry **WINDSOR-SMITH** • C.C. **BECK**
- Sergio **ARAGONÉS** • Walter **SIMONSON**
- Brent **ANDERSON** • Nick **CARDY**
- Roy **THOMAS** & John **SEVERIN**
- Paul **CHADWICK** • Rick **VEITCH**
- Murphy **ANDERSON** • Joe **KUBERT**
- Evan **DORKIN** • Sam **GLANZMAN**
- Plus Art **SPIEGELMAN**, Jack **KIRBY**, more! Cover by **RUDE** • Foreword by **EISNER**

(160-Page Trade Paperback) **$24 US**

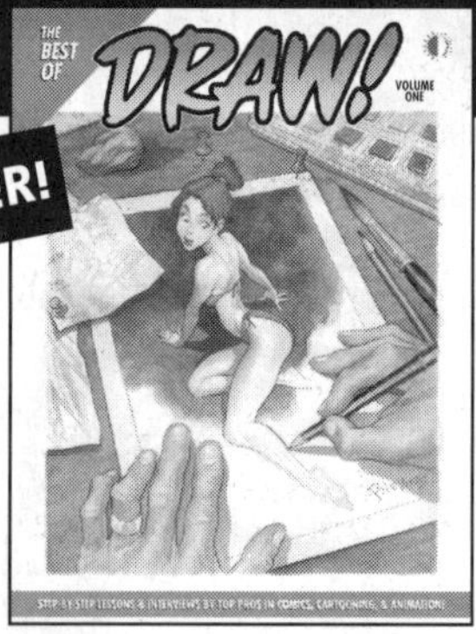
THE BEST OF DRAW! VOLUME ONE

BEST OF DRAW! VOL. 1

Compiles material from the first two sold-out issues of **DRAW!**, the "How-To" magazine on comics and cartooning! Tutorials by, and interviews with: **DAVE GIBBONS** (layout and drawing on the computer), **BRET BLEVINS** (drawing lovely women, painting from life, and creating figures that "feel"), **JERRY ORDWAY** (detailing his working methods), **KLAUS JANSON** and **RICARDO VILLAGRAN** (inking techniques), **GENNDY TARTA-KOVSKY** (on animation and Samurai Jack), **STEVE CONLEY** (creating web comics and cartoons), **PHIL HESTER** and **ANDE PARKS** (penciling and inking), and more!

(200-page trade paperback) **$26 US**

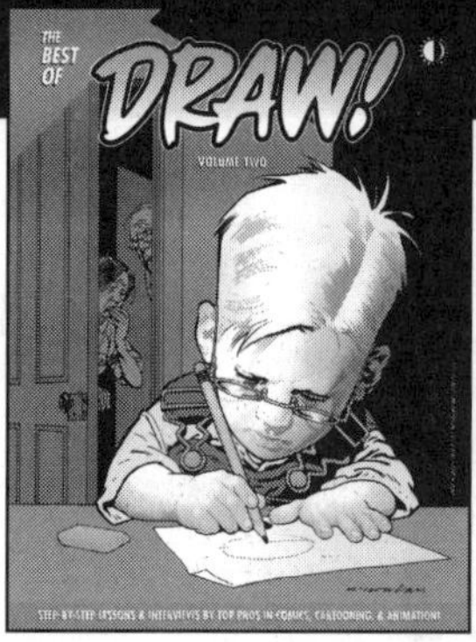
THE BEST OF DRAW! VOLUME TWO

BEST OF DRAW! VOL. 2

Compiles material from issues #3 and #4 of **DRAW!**, including tutorials by, and interviews with, **ERIK LARSEN** (savage penciling), **DICK GIORDANO** (inking techniques), **BRET BLEVINS** (drawing the figure in action, and figure composition), **KEVIN NOWLAN** (penciling and inking), **MIKE MANLEY** (how-to demo on Web Comics), **DAVE COOPER** (digital coloring tutorial), and more! Cover by **KEVIN NOWLAN**!

(156-page trade paperback) **$22 US**

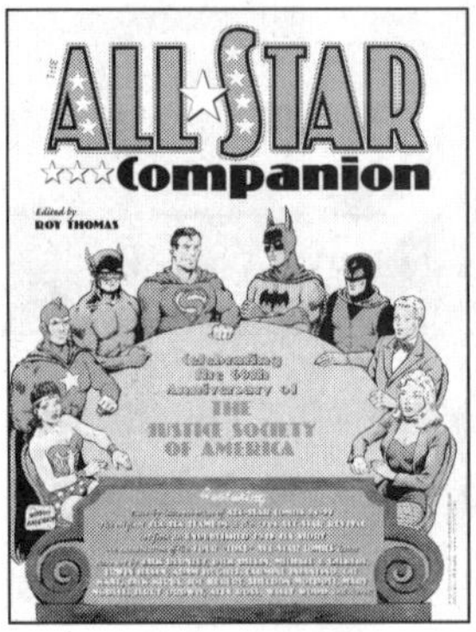
ALL-STAR Companion
ROY THOMAS

ALL-STAR COMPANION VOL. 1

ROY THOMAS has assembled the most thorough look ever taken at All-Star Comics:

- Covers by **MURPHY ANDERSON!**
- Issue-by-issue coverage of **ALL—STAR COMICS #1—57**, the original **JLA—JSA** teamups, & the **'70s ALL—STAR REVIVAL!**
- Art from an unpublished **1945 JSA** story!
- Looks at **FOUR "LOST" ALL-STAR** issues!
- Rare art by **BURNLEY, DILLIN, KIRBY, INFANTINO, KANE, KUBERT, ORDWAY, ROSS, WOOD** and more!!

(208-page Trade Paperback) **$26 US**

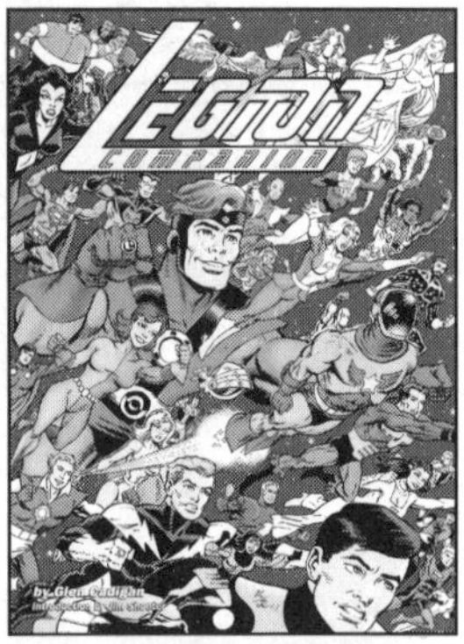
LEGION COMPANION

THE LEGION COMPANION

- A history of the Legion of Super-Heroes, with **DAVE COCKRUM, MIKE GRELL, JIM STARLIN, JAMES SHERMAN, PAUL LEVITZ, KEITH GIFFEN, STEVE LIGHTLE, MARK WAID, JIM SHOOTER, JIM MOONEY, AL PLASTINO,** and more!
- Rare and never-seen Legion art by the above, plus **GEORGE PÉREZ, NEAL ADAMS, CURT SWAN,** and others!
- Unused Cockrum character designs and pages from an **UNUSED STORY!**
- New cover by **DAVE COCKRUM** and **JOE RUBINSTEIN**, introduction by **JIM SHOOTER**, and more!

(224-page Trade Paperback) **$29 US**

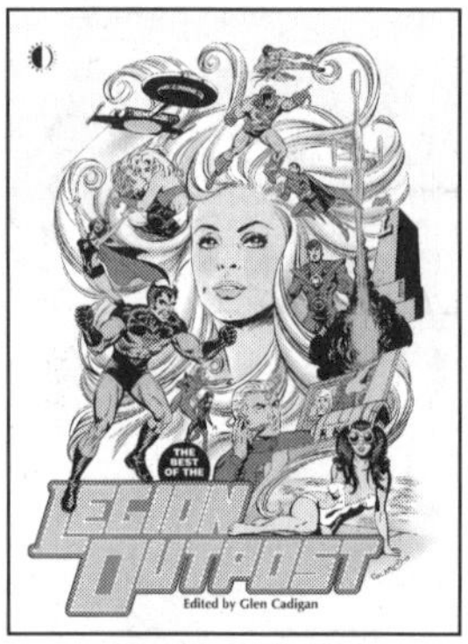
THE BEST OF THE LEGION OUTPOST
Edited by Glen Cadigan

BEST OF THE LEGION OUTPOST

Collects the best material from the hard-to-find **LEGION OUTPOST** fanzine, including rare interviews and articles from creators such as **DAVE COCKRUM, CARY BATES,** and **JIM SHOOTER**, plus never-before-seen artwork by **COCKRUM, MIKE GRELL, JIMMY JANES** and others! It also features a previously unpublished interview with **KEITH GIFFEN** originally intended for the never-published **LEGION OUTPOST** #11, plus other new material! And it sports a rarely-seen classic 1970s cover by Legion fan favorite artist **DAVE COCKRUM!**

(160-page trade paperback) **$22 US**

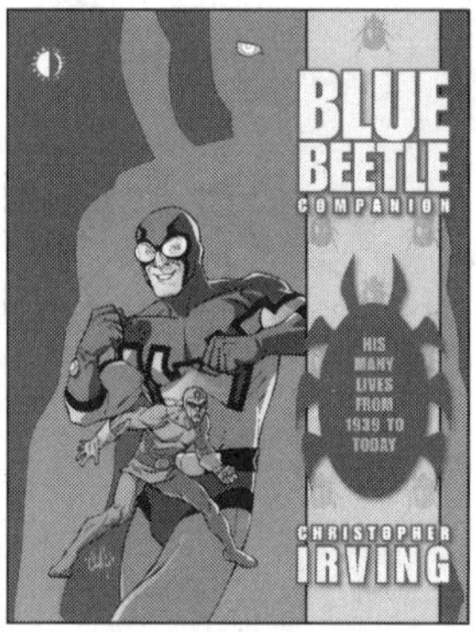
BLUE BEETLE COMPANION
HIS MANY LIVES FROM 1939 TO TODAY
CHRISTOPHER IRVING

BLUE BEETLE COMPANION

The history of a character as old as Superman, from 1939 to his tragic fate in DC Comics' hit **INFINITE CRISIS** series, and beyond! Reprints the first appearance of The Blue Beetle from 1939's **MYSTERY MEN COMICS #1**, plus interviews with **WILL EISNER, JOE SIMON, JOE GILL, ROY THOMAS, GEOFF JOHNS, CULLY HAMNER, KEITH GIFFEN, LEN WEIN,** and others, never-before-seen Blue Beetle designs by **ALEX ROSS** and **ALAN WEISS**, as well as artwork by **EISNER, CHARLES NICHOLAS, JACK KIRBY, STEVE DITKO, KEVIN MAGUIRE,** and more!

(128-page Trade Paperback) **$21 US**

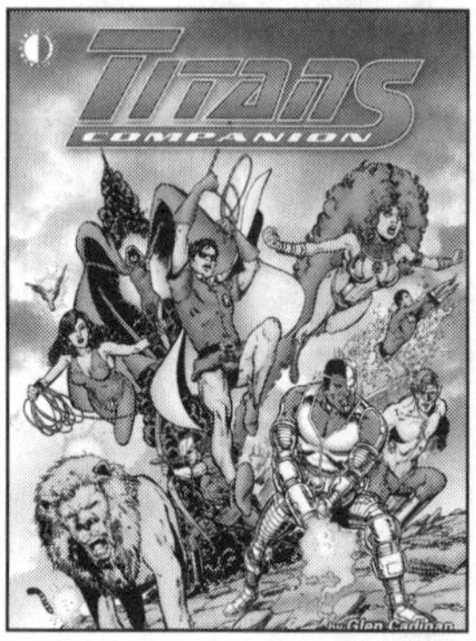
Titans COMPANION

TITANS COMPANION

A comprehensive history of the **NEW TEEN TITANS**, with interviews and rare art by **MARV WOLFMAN, GEORGE PÉREZ, JOSÉ LUIS GARCÍA-LÓPEZ, LEN WEIN,** & others, a Silver Age section with **NEAL ADAMS, NICK CARDY, DICK GIORDANO,** & more, plus **CHRIS CLAREMONT** and **WALTER SIMONSON** on the **X-MEN/TEEN TITANS** crossover, **TOM GRUMMETT, PHIL JIMENEZ & TERRY DODSON** on their '90s Titans work, a new cover by **JIMENEZ**, & intro by **GEOFF JOHNS!** Written by **GLEN CADIGAN.**

(224-page trade paperback) **$29 US**

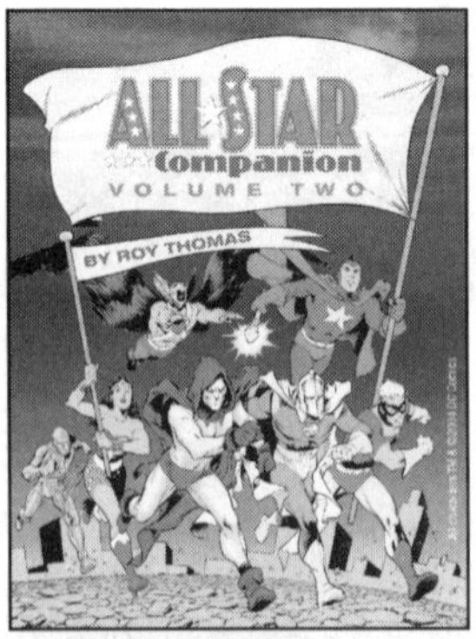
ALL-STAR Companion
VOLUME TWO
BY ROY THOMAS

ALL-STAR COMPANION VOL. 2

ROY THOMAS' new sequel, with more secrets of the **JSA** and **ALL-STAR COMICS**, from 1940 through the 1980s:

- Wraparound **CARLOS PACHECO** cover!
- More amazing information, speculation, and unseen **ALL-STAR COMICS** art!
- Unpublished **1940s JSA STORY ART** not printed in Volume One!
- Full coverage of the 1980s **ALL-STAR SQUADRON**, with scarce & never-published art!

(240-page Trade Paperback) **$29 US**

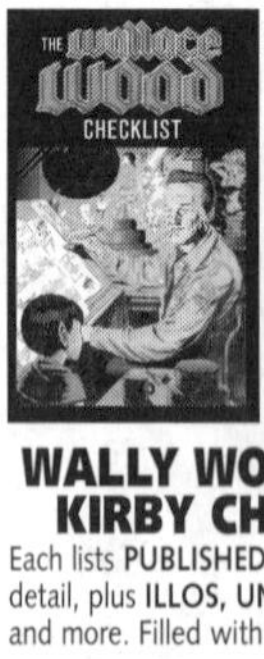
THE wallace wood CHECKLIST

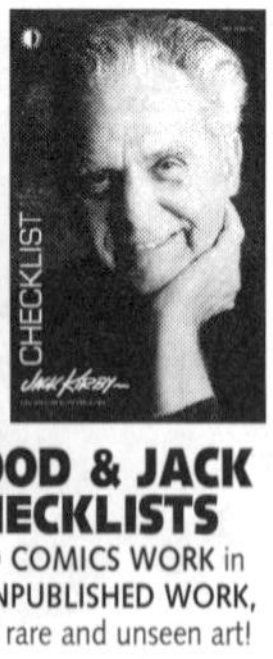
CHECKLIST

WALLY WOOD & JACK KIRBY CHECKLISTS

Each lists **PUBLISHED COMICS WORK** in detail, plus **ILLOS, UNPUBLISHED WORK,** and more. Filled with rare and unseen art!

(68/100 Pages) **$8 US EACH**

T.H.U.N.D.E.R. AGENTS COMPANION

The definitive book on **WALLACE WOOD**'s super-team of the 1960s, featuring interviews with Woody and other creators involved in the T-Agents over the years, plus rare and unseen art, including a rare 28-page story drawn by **PAUL GULACY, UNPUBLISHED STORIES** by **GULACY, PARIS CULLINS,** and others, and a **JERRY ORDWAY** cover. Edited by **CBA's JON B. COOKE.**

(192-page trade paperback) **$29 US**

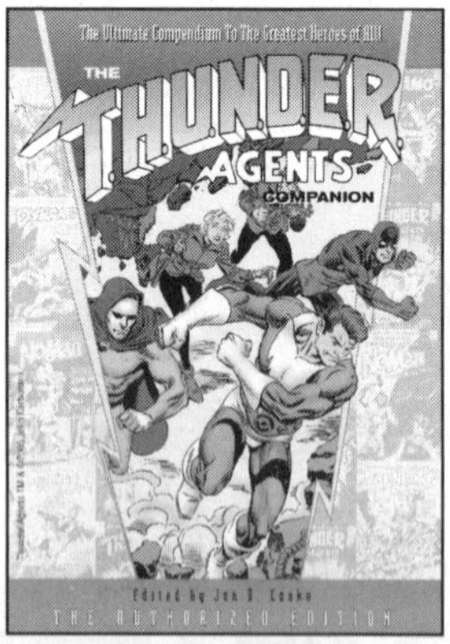
THE T.H.U.N.D.E.R. AGENTS COMPANION

Prices include US Postage. Outside the US, **ADD PER ITEM**: Magazines & DVDs, $2 ($7 Airmail) • Softcover books, $3 ($10 Airmail) • Hardcover books, $6 ($15 Airmail)

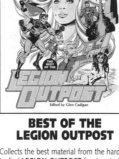

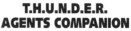

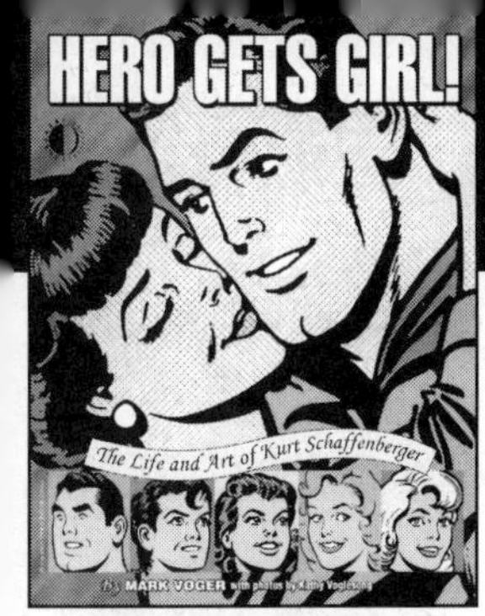
HERO GETS GIRL!
The Life and Art of Kurt Schaffenberger

HERO GETS GIRL! THE LIFE & ART OF KURT SCHAFFENBERGER

MARK VOGER's biography of the artist of **LOIS LANE** & **CAPTAIN MARVEL!**

- Covers **KURT'S LIFE AND CAREER** from the 1940s to his passing in 2002!
- Features **NEVER-SEEN PHOTOS & ILLUSTRATIONS** from his files!
- Includes recollections by **ANDERSON, EISNER, INFANTINO, KUBERT, ALEX ROSS, MORT WALKER** and others!

(128-page Trade Paperback) **$19 US**

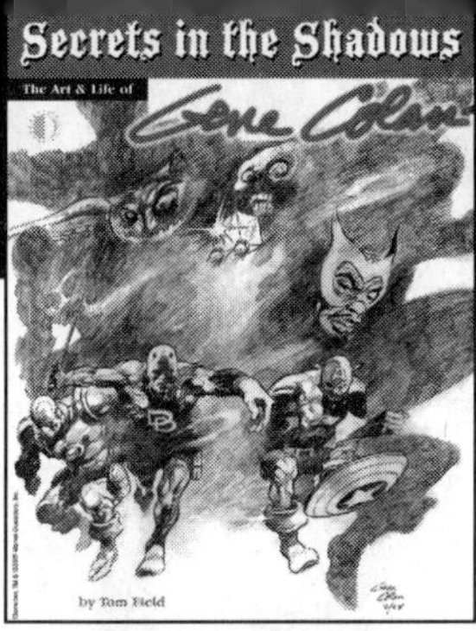
Secrets in the Shadows
The Art & Life of Gene Colan
by Tom Field

SECRETS IN THE SHADOWS: GENE COLAN

The ultimate retrospective on **COLAN**, with rare drawings, photos, and art from his nearly 60-year career, plus a comprehensive overview of Gene's glory days at Marvel Comics! **MARV WOLFMAN, DON MCGREGOR** and other writers share script samples and anecdotes of their Colan collaborations, while **TOM PALMER, STEVE LEIALOHA** and others show how they approached the daunting task of inking Colan's famously nuanced penciled pages! Plus there's a **NEW PORTFOLIO** of never-before-seen collaborations between Gene and such masters as **JOHN BYRNE, MICHAEL KALUTA** and **GEORGE PÉREZ**, and all-new artwork created specifically for this book by Gene! Available in Softcover and Deluxe Hardcover (limited to 1000 copies, with 16 extra black-and-white pages and 8 extra color pages)!

(168-page softcover) **$26 US**
(192-page trade hardcover) **$49 US**

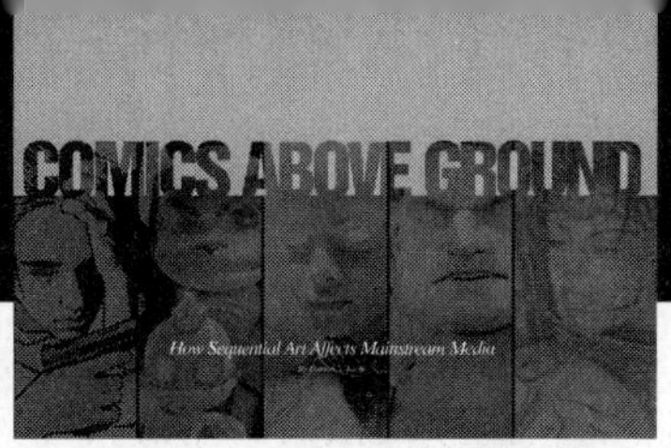
COMICS ABOVE GROUND
How Sequential Art Affects Mainstream Media

COMICS ABOVE GROUND
SEE HOW YOUR FAVORITE ARTISTS MAKE A LIVING OUTSIDE COMICS

COMICS ABOVE GROUND features top comics pros discussing their inspirations and training, and how they apply it in "Mainstream Media," including Conceptual Illustration, Video Game Development, Children's Books, Novels, Design, Illustration, Fine Art, Storyboards, Animation, Movies & more! Written by **DURWIN TALON** (author of the top-selling **PANEL DISCUSSIONS**), this book features creators sharing their perspectives and their work in comics and their "other professions," with career overviews, never-before-seen art, and interviews! Featuring:

- **BRUCE TIMM**
- **BERNIE WRIGHTSON**
- **ADAM HUGHES**
- **LOUISE SIMONSON**
- **DAVE DORMAN**
- **GREG RUCKA & MORE!**

(168-page Trade Paperback) **$24 US**

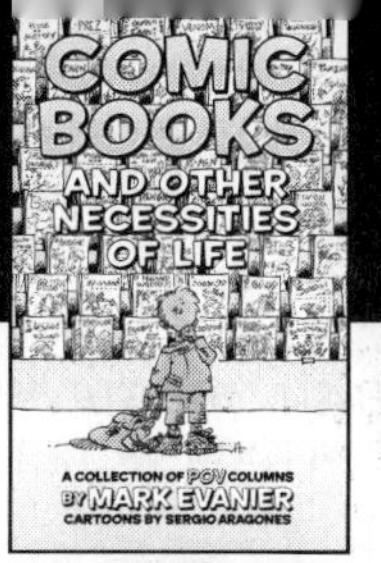
COMIC BOOKS AND OTHER NECESSITIES OF LIFE
A COLLECTION OF POV COLUMNS
BY MARK EVANIER
CARTOONS BY SERGIO ARAGONÉS

COMIC BOOKS & OTHER NECESSITIES OF LIFE

WERTHAM WAS RIGHT!

SUPERHEROES IN MY PANTS!

Each collects **MARK EVANIER'S** best essays and commentaries, plus new essays and illustrations by **SERGIO ARAGONÉS!**

(200-page Trade Paperbacks)
$17 US EACH
ALL THREE BOOKS: $34 US

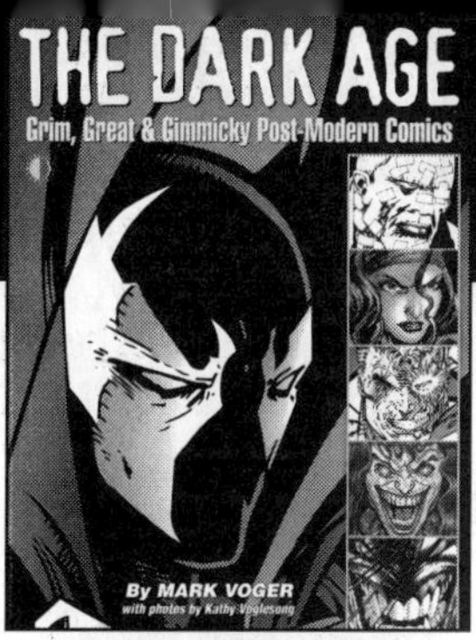
THE DARK AGE
Grim, Great & Gimmicky Post-Modern Comics
By MARK VOGER
with photos by Kathy Voglesong

THE DARK AGE

Documents the '80s and '90s era of comics, from **THE DARK KNIGHT RETURNS** and **WATCHMEN** to the "polybagged premium" craze, the **DEATH OF SUPERMAN**, renegade superheroes **SPAWN, PITT, BLOODSHOT, CYBERFORCE**, & more! Interviews with **TODD McFARLANE, DAVE GIBBONS, JIM LEE, KEVIN SMITH, ALEX ROSS, MIKE MIGNOLA, ERIK LARSEN, J. O'BARR, DAVID LAPHAM, JOE QUESADA, MIKE ALLRED** and others, plus a color section! Written by **MARK VOGER**, with photos by **KATHY VOGLESONG.**

(168-page trade paperback) **$24 US**

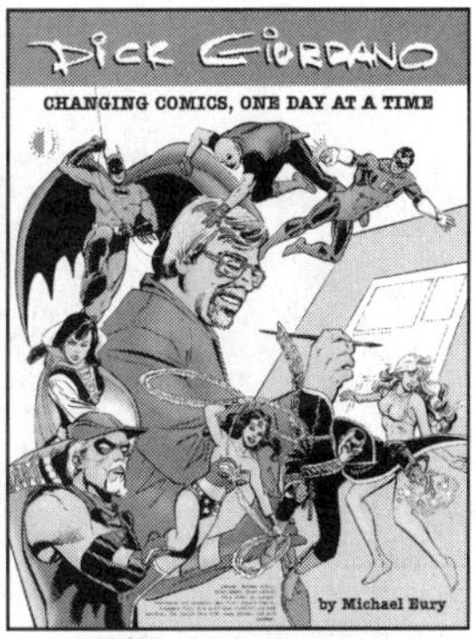
DICK GIORDANO
CHANGING COMICS, ONE DAY AT A TIME
by Michael Eury

DICK GIORDANO CHANGING COMICS, ONE DAY AT A TIME

MICHAEL EURY's biography of comics' most prominent and affable personality!

- Covers his career as illustrator, inker, and editor, peppered with **DICK'S PERSONAL REFLECTIONS** on his career milestones!
- Lavishly illustrated with **RARE AND NEVER SEEN** comics, merchandising, and advertising art (includes a color section)!
- Extensive index of his published work!
- Comments & tributes by **NEAL ADAMS, DENNIS O'NEIL, TERRY AUSTIN, PAUL LEVITZ, MARV WOLFMAN, JULIUS SCHWARTZ, JIM APARO** & others!
- With a Foreword by **NEAL ADAMS** and Afterword by **PAUL LEVITZ!**

(176-pg. Paperback) **$24 US**

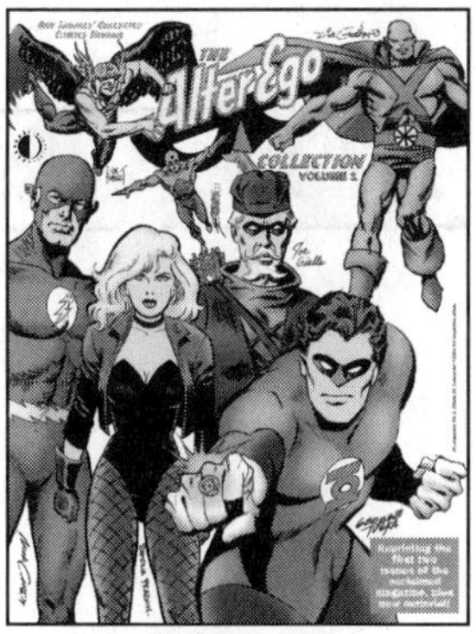
The Alter Ego Collection

ALTER EGO COLLECTION, VOL. 1

Collects the first two issues of **ALTER EGO**, plus 30 pages of **NEW MATERIAL!** JLA Jam Cover by **KUBERT, PÉREZ, GIORDANO, TUSKA, CARDY, FRADON, & GIELLA**, new sections featuring scarce art by **GIL KANE, WILL EISNER, CARMINE INFANTINO, MIKE SEKOWSKY, MURPHY ANDERSON, DICK DILLIN**, & more!

(192-page trade paperback) **$26 US**

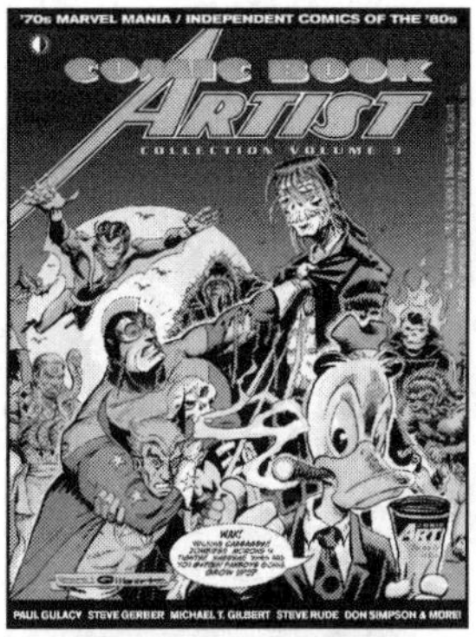
'70s MARVEL MANIA / INDEPENDENT COMICS OF THE '80s
COMIC BOOK ARTIST
COLLECTION VOLUME 3

COMIC BOOK ARTIST COLLECTION, VOL. 3

Reprinting the Eisner Award-winning **COMIC BOOK ARTIST** #7 and #8 ('70s Marvel and '80s independents), featuring a new **MICHAEL T. GILBERT** cover, plus interviews with **GILBERT, RUDE, GULACY, GERBER, DON SIMPSON, CHAYKIN, SCOTT McCLOUD, BUCKLER, BYRNE, DENIS KITCHEN**, plus a **NEW SECTION** featuring over 30 pages of previously-unseen stuff! Edited by **JON B. COOKE.**

(224-page trade paperback) **$29 US**

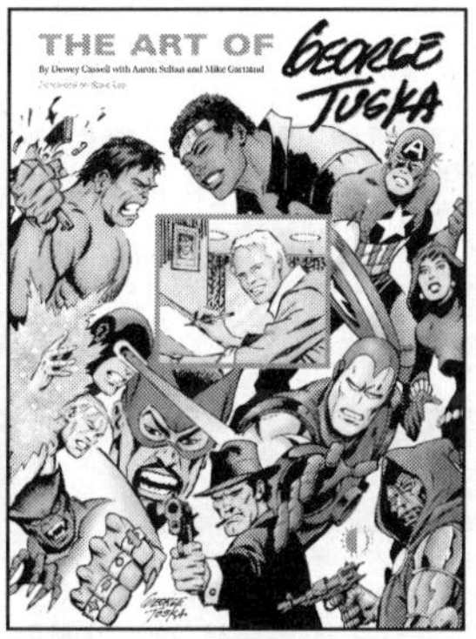
THE ART OF GEORGE TUSKA

ART OF GEORGE TUSKA

A comprehensive look at Tuska's personal and professional life, including early work with Eisner-Iger, crime comics of the 1950s, and his tenure with Marvel and DC Comics, as well as independent publishers. The book includes extensive coverage of his work on **IRON MAN, X-MEN, HULK, JUSTICE LEAGUE, TEEN TITANS, BATMAN, T.H.U.N.D.E.R. AGENTS**, and many more! A gallery of commission artwork and a thorough index of his work are included, plus original artwork, photos, sketches, previously unpublished art, interviews and anecdotes from his peers and fans, plus George's own words!

(128-page trade paperback) **$19 US**

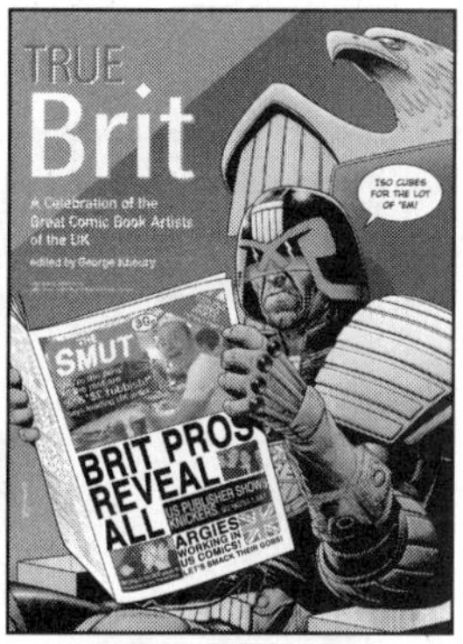
TRUE Brit
A Celebration of the Great Comic Book Artists of the UK
BRIT PROS REVEAL ALL

TRUE BRIT CELEBRATING GREAT COMIC BOOK ARTISTS OF THE UK

A celebration of the rich history of British Comics Artists and their influence on the US with in-depth interviews and art by:

- **BRIAN BOLLAND**
- **ALAN DAVIS**
- **DAVE GIBBONS**
- **BRYAN HITCH**
- **DAVID LLOYD**
- **DAVE MCKEAN**
- **KEVIN O'NEILL**
- **BARRY WINDSOR-SMITH** and other gents!

(204-page Trade Paperback with COLOR SECTION) **$26 US**

HOW TO CREATE COMICS
FROM SCRIPT TO PRINT

REDESIGNED and **EXPANDED** version of the groundbreaking **WRITE NOW! #8 / DRAW! #9** crossover! **DANNY FINGEROTH** & **MIKE MANLEY** show step-by-step how to develop a new comic, from script and roughs to pencils, inks, colors, lettering—it even guides you through printing and distribution, & the finished 8-page color comic is included, so you can see their end result! **PLUS:** over 30 pages of **ALL-NEW** material, including "full" and "Marvel-style" scripts, a critique of their new character and comic from an editor's point of view, new tips on coloring, new expanded writing lessons, and more!

(108-page trade paperback) **$18 US**

(120-minute companion DVD) **$35 US**

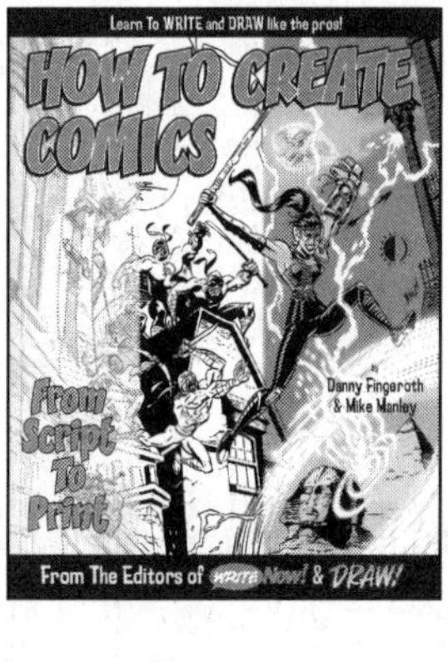
Learn To WRITE and DRAW like the pros!
HOW TO CREATE COMICS
From Script To Print
Danny Fingeroth & Mike Manley
From The Editors of Write Now! & DRAW!

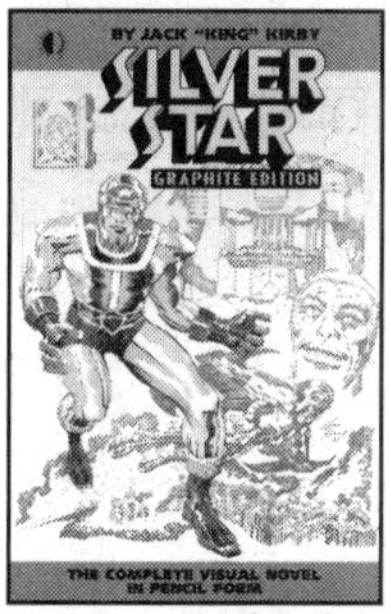
BY JACK "KING" KIRBY
SILVER STAR
GRAPHITE EDITION
THE COMPLETE VISUAL NOVEL IN PENCIL FORM

SILVER STAR: GRAPHITE

JACK KIRBY'S six-issue "Visual Novel" for Pacific Comics, reproduced from his powerful, uninked pencil art! Includes Kirby's illustrated movie screenplay, never-seen sketches, pin-ups, & more from his final series!

(160 pages) **$24 US**

CALL, WRITE, OR E-MAIL FOR A FREE COLOR CATALOG!

COLLECTED JACK KIRBY COLLECTOR, VOL. 1-5

See what thousands of comics fans, professionals, and historians have discovered: The King lives on in the pages of **THE JACK KIRBY COLLECTOR!** These colossal **TRADE PAPERBACKS** reprint the first 22 sold-out issues of the magazine for Kirby fans!

- **VOLUME 1:** Reprints **TJKC #1-9** (including the Fourth World and Fantastic Four theme issues), plus over 30 pieces of Kirby art never before published in TJKC! • (240 pages) **$29 US**

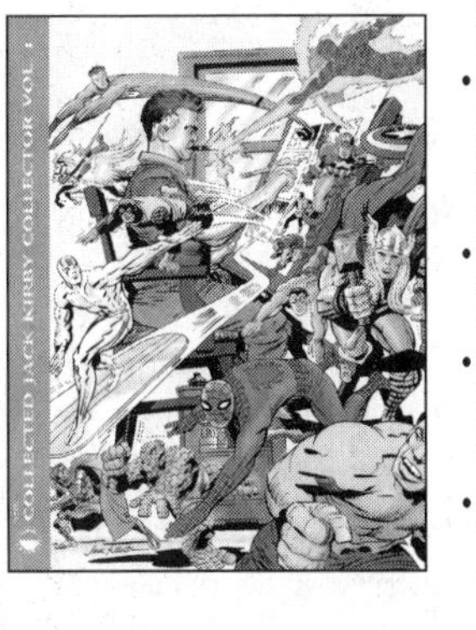
COLLECTED JACK KIRBY COLLECTOR VOL. 1

- **VOLUME 2:** Reprints **TJKC #10-12** (the Humor, Hollywood, and International theme issues), and includes a new special section detailing a fan's private tour of the Kirbys' remarkable home, showcasing more than 30 pieces of Kirby art never before published in TJKC! • (160 pages) **$22 US**
- **VOLUME 3:** Reprints **TJKC #13-15** (the Horror, Thor, and Sci-Fi theme issues), plus 30 new pieces of Kirby art! • (176 pages) **$24 US**
- **VOLUME 4:** Reprints **TJKC #16-19** (the Tough Guys, DC, Marvel, and Art theme issues), plus more than 30 pieces of Kirby art never before published in TJKC! • (240 pages) **$29 US**
- **VOLUME 5:** Reprints **TJKC #20-22** (the Women, Wacky, and Villains theme issues), plus more than 30 pieces of Kirby art never before published in TJKC! • (224 pages) **$29 US**

MODERN MASTERS SERIES

> "TwoMorrows blesses us fans with a frank, honest interview with the man himself. And it doesn't cut any corners... If you love Pérez's work, you'll definitely love this."
>
> **Comics International on MODERN MASTERS VOL. 2: GEORGE PÉREZ**

Edited by **ERIC NOLEN-WEATHINGTON**, these trade paperbacks and DVDs are devoted to the **BEST OF TODAY'S COMICS ARTISTS!** Each book contains **RARE AND UNSEEN ARTWORK** direct from the artist's files, plus a **COMPREHENSIVE INTERVIEW** (including influences and their views on graphic storytelling), **DELUXE SKETCHBOOK SECTIONS**, and more! And **DVDs** show the artist at work!

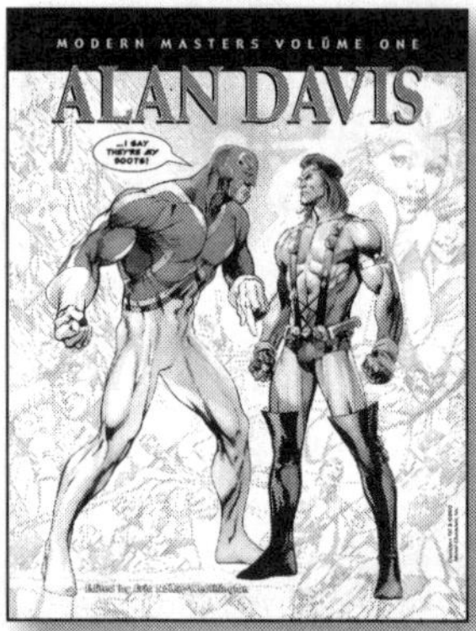
MODERN MASTERS VOLUME ONE
ALAN DAVIS

VOL. 1: ALAN DAVIS
(128-Page Trade Paperback)
$19 US

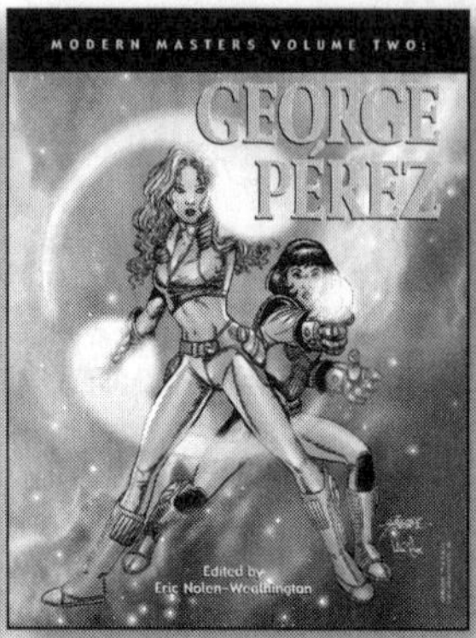
MODERN MASTERS VOLUME TWO:
GEORGE PÉREZ
Edited by
Eric Nolen-Weathington

V.2: GEORGE PÉREZ
(128-Page Trade Paperback)
$19 US

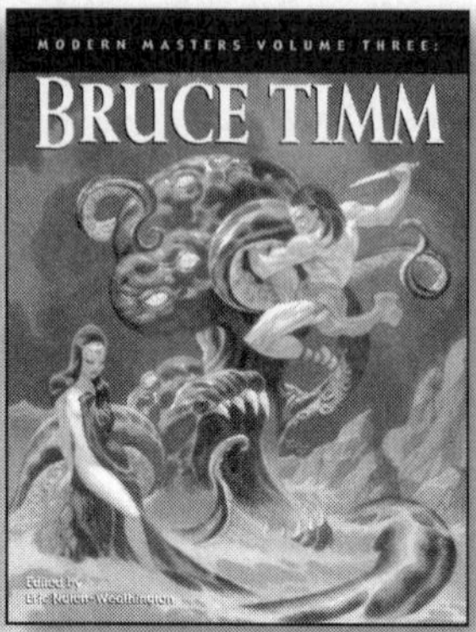
MODERN MASTERS VOLUME THREE:
BRUCE TIMM

V.3: BRUCE TIMM
(120-Page TPB with COLOR)
$19 US

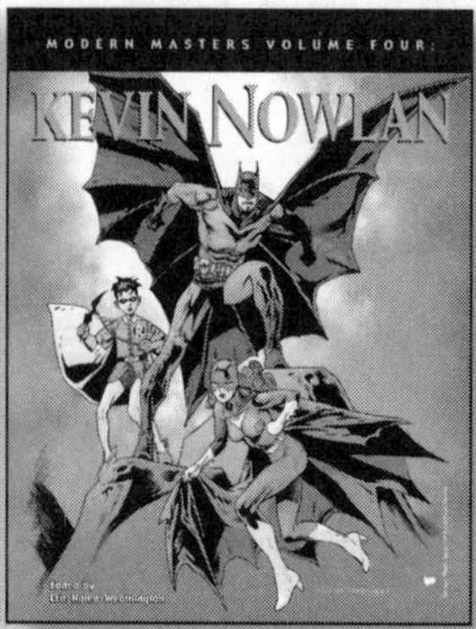
MODERN MASTERS VOLUME FOUR:
KEVIN NOWLAN

V.4: KEVIN NOWLAN
(120-Page TPB with COLOR)
$19 US

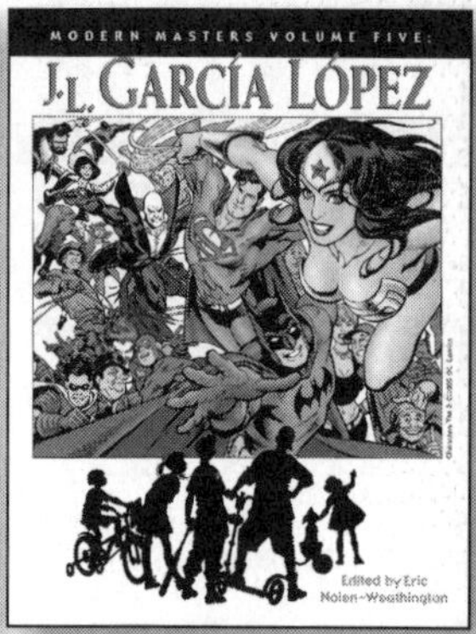
MODERN MASTERS VOLUME FIVE:
J.L. GARCÍA LÓPEZ
Edited by Eric
Nolen-Weathington

V.5: GARCÍA-LÓPEZ
(120-Page TPB with COLOR)
$19 US

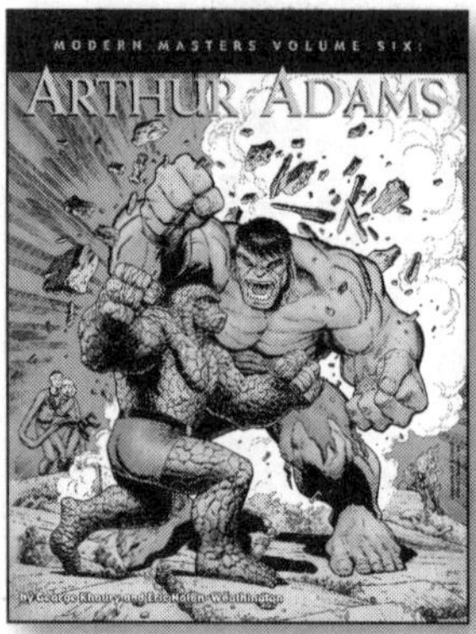
MODERN MASTERS VOLUME SIX:
ARTHUR ADAMS

V.6: ARTHUR ADAMS
(128-Page Trade Paperback)
$19 US

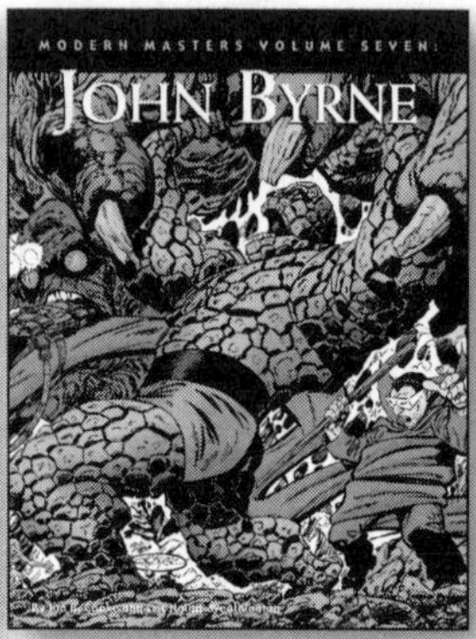
MODERN MASTERS VOLUME SEVEN:
JOHN BYRNE

V.7: JOHN BYRNE
(128-Page Trade Paperback)
$19 US

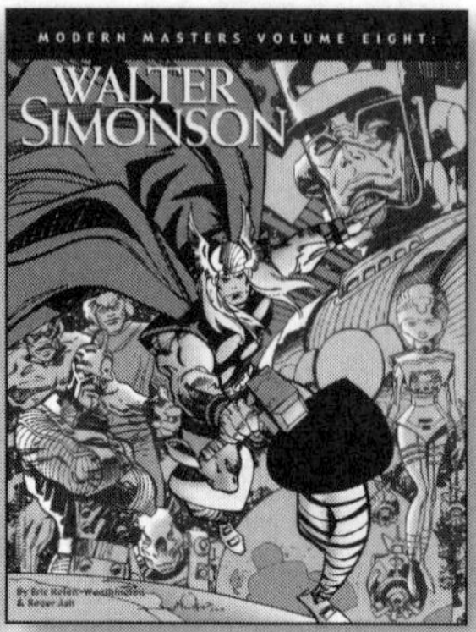
MODERN MASTERS VOLUME EIGHT:
WALTER SIMONSON

V.8: WALTER SIMONSON
(128-Page Trade Paperback)
$19 US

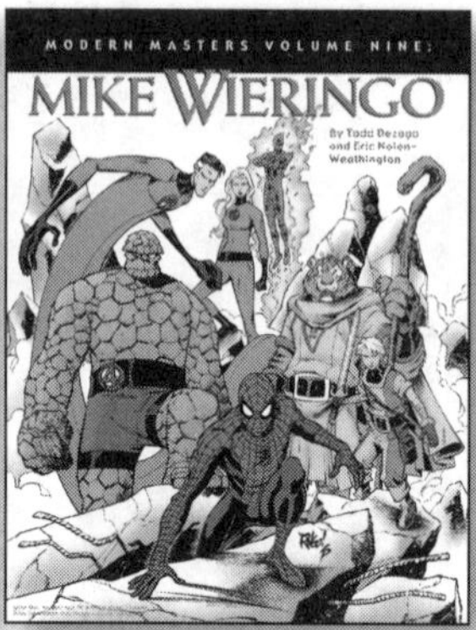
MODERN MASTERS VOLUME NINE:
MIKE WIERINGO

V.9: MIKE WIERINGO
(120-Page TPB with COLOR)
$19 US

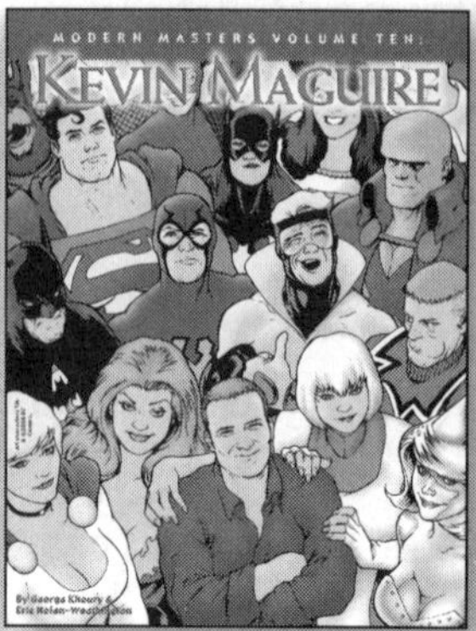
MODERN MASTERS VOLUME TEN:
KEVIN MAGUIRE

V.10: KEVIN MAGUIRE
(128-Page Trade Paperback)
$19 US

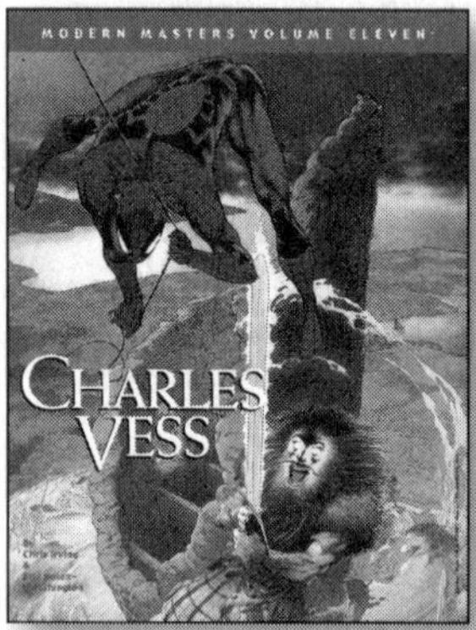
MODERN MASTERS VOLUME ELEVEN:
CHARLES VESS

V.11: CHARLES VESS
(120-Page TPB with COLOR)
$19 US
SHIPS FEBRUARY 2007

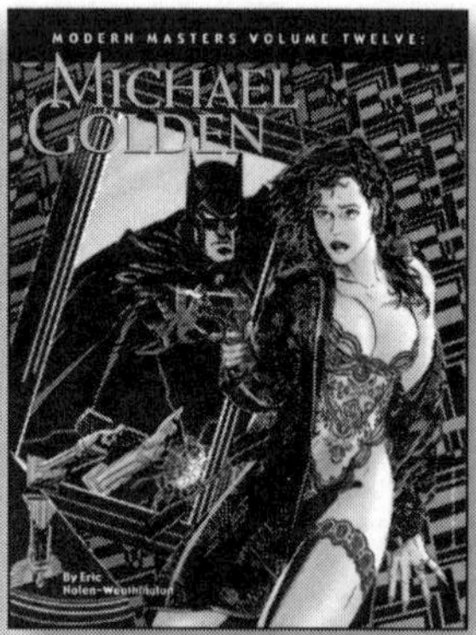
MODERN MASTERS VOLUME TWELVE:
MICHAEL GOLDEN

V.12: MICHAEL GOLDEN
(120-Page TPB with COLOR)
$19 US
SHIPS JUNE 2007

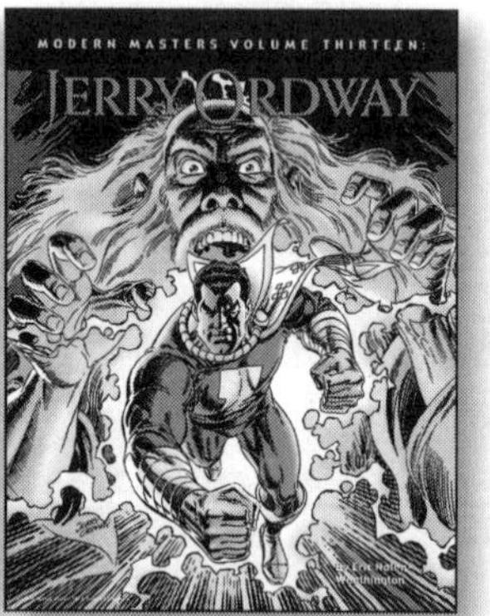
MODERN MASTERS VOLUME THIRTEEN:
JERRY ORDWAY

V.13: JERRY ORDWAY
(120-Page TPB with COLOR)
$19 US
SHIPS AUGUST 2007

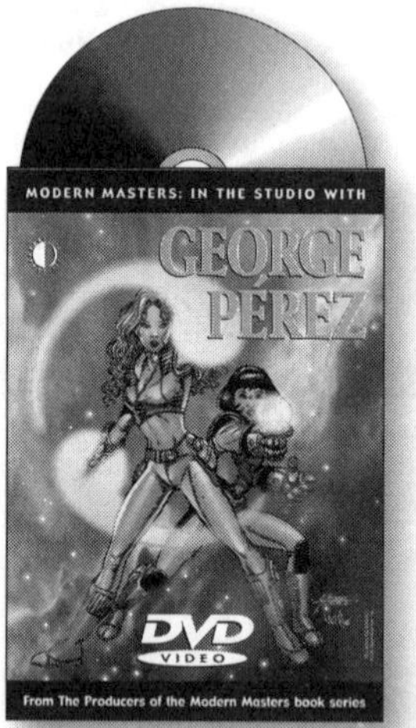
MODERN MASTERS: IN THE STUDIO WITH
GEORGE PÉREZ
DVD VIDEO
From The Producers of the Modern Masters book series

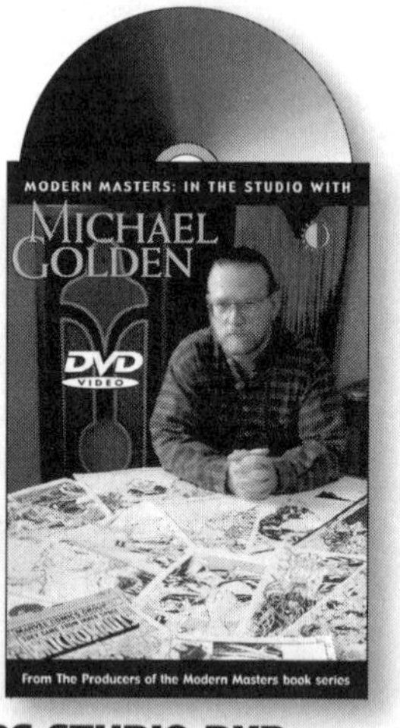
MODERN MASTERS: IN THE STUDIO WITH
MICHAEL GOLDEN
DVD VIDEO
From The Producers of the Modern Masters book series

MODERN MASTERS STUDIO DVDs
GEORGE PÉREZ (NOW SHIPPING)
MICHAEL GOLDEN (SHIPS JULY '07)
(120-minute Std. Format DVDs) **$35 US EACH**

TwoMorrows. Bringing New Life To Comics Fandom.

PayPal VISA MasterCard

TwoMorrows • 10407 Bedfordtown Drive • Raleigh, NC 27614 USA • 919-449-0344 • FAX: 919-449-0327 • E-mail: twomorrow@aol.com • www.twomorrows.com